D0068726

Rethinking Modernization

Anthropological Perspectives

Edited by John J. Poggie, Jr., and
Robert N. Lynch

Greenwood Press
Westport, Connecticut ● London, England

Library of Congress Cataloging in Publication Data
Main entry under title:

Rethinking modernization.

Papers presented at a symposium held at the University of Rhode Island on May 27-29, 1971.
Bibliography: p.
1. Social change—Congresses. 2. Social evolution—Congresses. I. Poggie, John J., ed. II. Lynch, Robert N., ed. III. Rhode Island. University.
GN320.R49   301.24   72-826
ISBN 0-8371-6394-3

Library of Congress Catalog Card Number: 72-826
ISBN: 0-8371-6394-3

First published in 1974

Greenwood Press, a division of Williamhouse-Regency Inc.
51 Riverside Avenue, Westport, Connecticut 06880

Manufactured in the United States of America

Contents

Illustrations

Photographs

Figures

Maps

Acknowledgments

This volume is the outcome of a symposium held at the University of Rhode Island on May 27-29, 1971. The symposium was organized around the theme of modernization in conjunction with Margaret Mead's stay as Visiting Distinguished Professor of Anthropology at the University during the spring semester of 1971. Through the generous financial support of the University's Office of the Vice President for Academic Affairs we were able to invite to the campus the anthropologists whose papers make up this volume. The Vice President's office also provided the financial resources necessary to edit and prepare the book for publication.

Although it is impossible to name all the individuals at the University of Rhode Island who contributed to the overall intellectual and social success of these meetings, we extend to all of them the sincere thanks of ourselves and all the participants. We would be remiss, however, if we did not mention the roles played by Dr. E. James Archer and his successor as Vice President for Academic Affairs, William Ferrante, as well as Dr. Werner Baum, President of the University. These men offered their support in the planning and realization of the meetings and this volume of papers. To our colleagues Ralph W. England, Robert V. Gardner, Leon F. Bouvier and John A. Senulis of the Department of Sociology and Anthropology, who served ably as chairmen of the sessions, we extend our heartiest thanks.

We particularly recall Professor William Rosengren's opening remarks to the symposium underscoring the saliency of the issues we had come together to discuss. His part in the success of the conference went well beyond the expected duties of a departmental chairman, and we especially thank him for his efforts.

The experience of organizing, participating in, and editing the results of this symposium has been both stimulating and rewarding. Our positive experience stems from the fact that we were very fotunate to have attracted such an outstanding group of anthropologists concerned with the topic of modernization. We thoroughly enjoyed working with them during the sessions and appreciate the quality of their papers.

In the editorial task of preparing this volume we received considerable help and encouragement from Pertti and Gretel Pelto as well as from Richard V. Travisano. They read various drafts of the manuscript and offered pertinent suggestions for improving the text. Erika Poggie deserves special mention; she had the important task of typing numerous pages of nearly illegible prose into crisp copy.

John J. Poggie, Jr.
Robert N. Lynch
Kingston, Rhode Island

Rethinking Modernization

1

Introduction

It is quite apparent to even a casual reader of contemporary social science literature that the term "modernization" is used with a variety of different meanings. In his book entitled *Modernization* (1966), the political scientist Myron Weiner points out that the term has a history that goes back to the nineteenth and early twentieth centuries when it was used mainly to refer to ". . . growth of rationality and secularism and to a process by which men broke away from the constraints of tyrannical regimes as well as the constraints of superstition." In contrast to this, Weiner states that the term is often used today ". . . as another word for economic growth or as a more palatable synonym for still another elusive concept, westernization." There is in his handling of the concept the implicit definition of modernization as the process of change from pre-industrial to technologically developed civilizations.

The anthropologist Manning Nash uses the term in his book on change in Burmese village life (Nash, 1965). In *The Golden Road to Modernity* Nash states that since World War II:

> . . . the new nations of Asia and Africa are discovering ways and means of transforming traditional societies into modern ones. The process of social and cultural transformation they undertake has few analogs in past history. Modernization on this scale, and with this speed, has rarely been conceived, and more rarely carried out (1965:1).

Everett Rogers, the communicationist, probably goes the furthest in rigorously defining and using the concept in his book *Modernization Among Peasants* (1969). To him the term is conceptualized as ". . . the process by

3

which individuals change from a traditional way of life to a more complex, technologically advanced, and rapidly changing style of life." Rogers further points out what he considers to be several of the misconceptions about modernization:

1. Modernization is not necessarily synonymous with "Europeanization" or "Westernization." Modernization is a *synthesis* of old and new ways and varies in different environments.

2. Modernization is not necessarily "good." It brings a mix of constructive and destructive effects depending on the situation and on the perspective of the observer.

3. "The process is not unidimensional and therefore cannot be measured by a single criterion or index." Such variables as level of living, aspirations, literacy, education, political participation, cosmopolitaness, and more, are involved in the modernization process (1969: 14-15).

These references from three different disciplines illustrate the multidimensional nature of the concept. The eclectic nature of the concept of "modernization" suggests that a number of different theoretical perspectives might be useful for structuring research on these processes. However, we feel that it is possible to deal with modernization as a multi-processed phenomenon and still conceptualize it as a single domain. We shall do this in this book by considering all of the processes of modernization as broadly representing a single general "stage" of cultural evolution. We shall discuss this stage in a later part of this introduction.

MODERNIZATION AND ANTHROPOLOGY

Up to now the study of modernization has been characteristically associated with political science and economics. Political scientists have studied, among other things, the formation of new nations, while economists have studied growth in the economic domains of new nations and developing ones. Among anthropologists, on the other hand, concern with modernization as a worldwide process has been sporadic. Although anthropologists certainly recognize that change is among the most important and extensive sociocultural processes going on in the world today, there has been some reluctance to deal with the phenomenon in the discipline. Traditionally those anthropologists who have studied change usually approached it through a paradigm which stressed the impact of outside influences on the "equilibrium" of traditional peoples. What has emerged more recently is a more inclusive evolutionary paradigm for conceptualizing both general long term and particular localized adjustments. [We have in mind the work of Sahlins and Service (1960) and the "rediscovery" of Steward (1955) and White (1959).] Yet it is only most recently that anthropologists have utilized their new paradigm to understand the contemporary world (e.g., Service, 1971 and Ribeiro, 1968).

One illustration which dramatizes the need for a more inclusive theoretical perspective on modernization is the difficulty many teaching anthropologists experience in their attempts to integrate traditional ethnohistoric information with current ethnographic materials in such courses as "American Indians," "Peoples of Africa," or "Society and Culture of Latin America." For example, it is becoming increasingly difficult to leave out of one's course presentation the striking changes which Indian groups have undergone during their association with American government and society. The policies of federal administrations in this century—manifestations like the movement to urban centers with concomitant shifts in reservation life—these are areas which demand theoretical coverage just as did the distribution of languages and cultures in an earlier day.

The reluctance on the part of some anthropologists to pursue the study of modernization is seen at all levels. Even at the community level of study, which anthropologists are most accustomed to pursuing, there has been comparatively little focus on modernization. As recently as 1958 in his study of a changing Guatemalan Indian Community, Manning Nash pointed to this tendency of the discipline when he quipped, "I am aware that this study is the sort of enterprise anthropologists do not often undertake" (1958: iii). In a sense, Nash is apologizing for deviating from the norm of doing an ethnographic study of a "timeless" village community. Instead, he chose to emphasize reciprocal adjustments by Indian and Ladino peoples to a new work setting.

One finds this "norm" of anthropological research expressed in many ways in the literature of the 1950s. Looking, for example, at the volume *Anthropology Today* (Tax, 1962) which represents a summary of the discipline twenty-five years ago, we note that there is no mention of the topic of modernization; the term does not even occur in the index. Anthropologists in the early 1950s *were* concerned with applied anthropology, but mainly in terms of how the anthropologist could smooth the way and lessen the "cultural gap" between "the people" and technical assistance personnel.

Since 1958, of course, there have been a growing number of studies by anthropologists dealing with various kinds of change. In the 1961 edition of the *Biennial Review of Anthropology* Vera Rubin (1962) evaluated the literature on the "anthropology of development," and found no extensive evidence that anthropologists had moved beyond the traditional concerns with culture change and applied anthropology. In a very recent evaluation of the accomplishments of the several disciplines involved in development studies, Cyril Belshaw (1972) concludes that anthropology has still not developed a comprehensive framework to deal with modernization as a worldwide process.

Vera Rubin attempted to explain anthropology's position relative to the study of change. She suggested that anthropologists have had a strong ambivalence about the increasing pace and pressures of contemporary change. On the one hand they are concerned with protecting the people they study from undue disruption, while on the other hand they desire to see all peoples benefit from some of the supposed progress of modern technology and social institutions. In her conclusion, Rubin clearly identifies the basis of this ambivalence and notes the ramifications:

> If a single technological change may drastically alter the fabric of a society, should the introduction of the steel ax be discouraged, since it is unlikely that all the possible disruptive chain effects of the innovation can be controlled? Favoring the stone ax, however, is also a form of action, and it becomes increasingly difficult to alter the tide of change and rising expectations: [the anthropologist] . . . may find it increasingly difficult to maintain a state of ambivalence (1962: 158).

Other authors have also pointed out the paradoxical position of many anthropologists on the question of international development. Glynn Cochrane, for example, feels that the discipline has been too academic in its approach to culture change, too willing to scorn applied anthropology as a worthy undertaking, and too parochial in the scope of its studies. He apparently feels that the anti-colonialist, "pro-native" orientation of anthropologists could have been more effective in influencing policies of "economic development" if researchers had been willing to become more actively engaged in the politics of modernization. In his words:

The sociology of the *total* society in emerging countries has been ignored. Anthropologists have hardly ever felt it necessary to take a *professional* interest—as opposed to making value judgments and voicing political opinions—in the expatriate class. Could anyone deny that, as far as colonial territories were concerned, the 'science of man' was simply the science of *some* men? Preferably 'native'?

It is unfortunate that the American Anthropological Association has not adopted a more forward role toward international development policy. This is an odd omission in view of the criticism of colonialist policies offered by individual anthropologists. The omission of anthropology from the international agency scene could have been legitimately protested by the Association. Ironically, the Association itself has also been in the early colonial mold, being content to maintain internal law and order. Other national anthropological societies and associations have done no better (1971: 9).

It is difficult to ignore this claim that anthropologists' perspectives on change are influenced by a strong anti-colonial, anti-imperialistic stance. Many anthropologists view economic and political penetrations by industrial nations into pre-industrial areas as inevitably detrimental to indigenous peoples. Rather than become involved with this action from the scientific or advisory point of view, it would appear that their negative feelings often result in their avoidance of the situation. On the other hand, those who do become professionally involved with planned change and development —applied anthropologists—are often branded as "second-rate" by some of their colleagues (cf. Jorgensen and others, 1971).

There are many contemporary anthropologists who decry the whole process of modernization, bemoaning its negative effects on non-Western societies. For example, in a recent issue of the American Anthropological Association Newsletter, Virginia Abernathy (1971) has echoed the sentiments of Thomas Gladwin (1971) on the destructive consequences of modernization:

Gladwin's objection to the destructiveness of the values and social forms adhering to "modernization" as exported to Third World nations is well founded. A facet of "modernization," which appears particularly damaging, is the illusory promise of plenty, or of inexhaustible supply guaranteeing livelihood to all (Abernathy, 1971: 8).

These feelings appear to arise from a combination of motives. For some anthropologists there is the lingering romanticism concerning the "simpler ways of life" and the greater harmony of man-nature relationships in pre-industrial societies; more frequently, however, anthropologists have been perturbed by the fact that modernization processes have resulted in net losses—of economic independence, adequate nutrition, and social freedom from bureaucratic coercion—for previously semi-autonomous "folk societies." Until very recently, most anthropologists expressed their ambivalence about these processes by avoiding serious theoretical research focused fully on modernization processes.

There are several good reasons for anthropologists to have this particular perceptual and emotional set concerning modernization. One of the reasons for the discipline's stand is in the tradition of ethnographic empiricism. Our discipline is still strongly committed to describing little-known cultures "before they are gone." Considerable prestige accrues to contemporary anthropologists who study "exotic" localized cultures, as witnessed by the recent case of Napoleon Chagnon (1968) and his study of the Yanomanö in Venezuela, or Leopold Pospisil's (1958) study in the early 1950s of the Kapaku Papuans of the Central Highlands of New Guinea. Both of these studies were carried out in tribal societies at the brink of a great transformation, but in areas still part of the "last frontiers."

A second reason underlying the stance on modernization is the general ahistorical orientation in anthropology which results in a "slice-of-life" view of cultures. What the anthropologist often obtains, perhaps in spite of his stated intentions in fieldwork proposals, is an "ethnographic present" description of the culture. Studying the ethnographic present, especially in ideational terms of cognition or "cultural norms," in a population conceptualized as "localized," is not compatible with dealing with the dynamics of modernization and worldwide delocalization.

Third, even when confronted with a field situation in which "outside influences" are changing the communities he is studying, the anthropologist is more often than not reluctant to interact with the "outside agents" of change, as he might lose the rapport he has built up in his face-to-face interactions with the local people. He has a "pro-client" orientation, and a strong tendency to operate as if every group studied is close to being an isolated and autonomous population. As one anthropologist characterizes the discipline in regard to development studies:

> It is, however, still true that most anthropology involves an intimacy of involvement with the culture being studied which is not typical of other disciplines. Anthropologists tend to identify with the people with whom they work. Such identification has some obvious risks, of losing broader perspective, of losing sight of the fact that the anthropologist is still in some sense an outsider, of playing a role as spokesman for the culture. On the other hand . . . it is in the very nature of anthropology that the materials be obtained at the grass-roots level, and that development be viewed primarily from that perspective (Belshaw, 1972:91).

PRECURSORS OF MODERNIZATION STUDIES

It cannot, of course, be denied that some anthropologists have been dealing with cultural change from a theoretical and empirical perspective for quite some time. One can trace a history of growing concern with change from the mid-1930s down to the present day in some of the major, frequently cited works of anthropologists. With hindsight we see these as fitting into a developmental pattern leading to current theories and concepts of modernization, but in their time they were perhaps somewhat on the fringes of the range of variation in our discipline.

The most frequently cited early study of the effects of technological innovation on primitive culture is by far Lauriston Sharp's paper "Steel Axes for Stone-Age Australians" (1955). This paper recounts the effects of the introduction of European short-handled steel axes into the lives of the aboriginal Yir Yoront in northern Australia in the mid-1930s. One effect of this technological change was the lessening of women's and children's dependence on men. The men no longer held a monopoly on this essential tool since an abundant supply of European axes from nearby mission stations and other sources was made available to everyone.

Another important result of the proliferation of steel axes was the weakening of trading partnerships between men of different tribes and a consequent reduction in the importance of annual intertribal trading and ritual gatherings. (It was the increased *availability* and *durability* of steel axes, rather than their superior cutting quality, that had the great social consequences). Finally, Europeans who supplied the steel axes came to dominate relationships with aboriginals, thus creating an overarching commercial and administrative relationship which weakened the pre-contact sex, age, and kinship factors in power relations.

Sharp focused his study on the effects of a single technological element on the equilibrium of a traditional sociocultural system. He did not emphasize the more general, super-community processes by which relatively autonomous local groups are transformed into dependent marginal sectors of the larger Euro-American-dominated social system. Nor did he at the time consider what was happening to the Yir Yoront as part of an irreversible, ongoing worldwide process.

Another well known study illustrates a different and more inclusive handling of modernization. In *The Folk Culture of Yucatan* (1941), Robert Redfield assessed the impact of urban influences on the traditional cultural systems of three communities—a town, a peasant village, and an isolated, relatively autonomous village—that represented points on a continuum from "more urban" to more isolated, autonomous "folk society." Redfield considered how a number of sociocultural characteristics appeared to change with increased proximity to urban influences. He found that:

> . . . the peasant village as compared with the tribal village, the town as compared with the peasant village, or the city as compared with the town is less isolated; is more heterogeneous; is characterized by a more complex division of labor; has a more completely developed money economy; has professional specialists who are more secular and less sacred; has kinship and godparental institutions that are less well organized and less effective in social control; is correspondingly more dependent on impersonally acting institutions of control; is less religious, with respect both to beliefs and practices of Catholic origin as well as to those of Indian origin; exhibits a tendency to regard sickness as resulting from a breach of moral or merely customary rule; allows a greater freedom of action and choice to the individual; and . . . shows a greater emphasis upon black magic as an ascribed cause of sickness (1941:338-9).

Redfield identified these "city-bred" changes as manifestations of three more general processes—cultural disorganization, secularization, and individualization. Thus we see in this treatment of change a multidimensional and regional approach which emphasizes the urban center as an important factor in three general processes of sociocultural change. This handling of change is in contrast to the single trait-equilibrium approach of Sharp, for it takes us out of the single community into a more inclusive regional network. We recognize these types of changes today as part of the worldwide process of "delocalization." Redfield sees the changes that take place along the folk-urban continuum as largely negative in character. Thus, in his view, the well-integrated homogeneous folk way of life gives way to a disorganized, secularized and impersonal urban existence.

Margaret Mead's study of Peri, a Manus community in the Admiralty Islands, is another landmark work in modernization studies. The community had been the locus of very rapid change following the influx of American military forces during World War II. In fact, Mead feels that this case represents:

> . . . the record of a people who have moved faster than any people of whom we have records, a people who have moved in fifty years from [tribal life] to the twentieth century, men who have skipped over thousands of years of history in just the last twenty-five years [1928-1953] (1956:21).

Mead conceptualized the case of Peri in terms of the processes of diffusion and culture contact which were operative when thousands of American servicemen streamed through the islands of Oceania during World War II. Contrary to Redfield's negative assessment of extensive change in the Yucatan case, Mead suggests that change among the Manus people, although extensive and rapid, did not lead to social disorganization. On the contrary, in her words, the Manus experience suggests:

> . . . that rapid change is not only possible, but may actually be very desirable, that instead of advocating slow partial changes, we should advocate that a people who choose to practice a new technology or enter into drastically new kinds of economic relationships will do this more

easily if they live in different houses, wear different clothes, and eat different, or differently cooked, food (1956:372).

Mead's interpretation of the events on Manus is systemic in nature. She organizes her materials with an inclusive perspective. This systemic approach is in contrast to working with only a selected number of sociocultural traits. Her position on the desirability of rapid change, as seen in the above quotation, implies the possibility of worldwide regularities in the consequences of change.

During the 1960s anthropological perspectives turned toward an ecological and evolutionary view of change. John Bennett's *Northern Plainsmen* (1969) illustrates the "new holism" of ecology. This work stresses the adaptation by trial and error of four major social groups (American Indians, small farmers, cattle ranchers, and Hutterite colonies) to the northern plains of North America. Bennett is also concerned with the succession of societal types over the past 100 years in a series of ecological niches in the region.

We can end this brief review by reference to a recent study which follows the same general paradigm but takes on a much more macro-evolutionary focus. Richard N. Adams' study *The Second Sowing* (1967) is concerned with how new social forms emerged, were retained or were eliminated in Latin America over the course of the past four centuries. With Adams' work we are no longer talking about precursors of contemporary modernization theory, but are dealing with recently developed theory. His model is evolutionary, and is concerned with the selective retention of social and cultural forms. This is a Darwinian theoretical position applied to human sociocultural systems. Perhaps the most distinctive feature of Adams' modernization research is his concern with distribution of energy sources and political power, both of which have often been ignored by earlier anthropological work on modernization.

It is paradoxical that we are considering the ecological-evolutionary paradigm as the culmination of a series of theoretical positions developed in the recent history of anthropology. There has, after all, been a strong tradition in the discipline for the theoretical consideration of change in evolutionist terms. The study of cultural evolution on a global basis stems from the nineteenth century evolutionists who reconstructed pan-human cultural stages, although in many cases without the supporting data. Even though the Boasian reaction to nineteenth century evolutionism turned many anthropologists away from the study of evolution, there were others who continued to be concerned with this question. V. Gordon Childe's *What Happened in History* (1954), Leslie White's *The Evolution of Culture* (1959), and Julian Steward's *Theory of Culture Change* (1955) have all presented theoretical treatments of general culture evolution. However, the important distinction between these evolutionary formulations and recent modernization theory was that these formulations were used to explain the past more than to understand the present. Certainly, Sahlins' and Service's (1960) integration of general and specific evolution (cumulative worldwide shifts in energy utilization vs. local adaptations to changing environments) provides a theoretical framework for relating local cases of change with the worldwide historical trend of major stages of cultural evolution. Yet in spite of the great influence they have had on contemporary social science thinking, even Sahlins and Service have been slow to recognize the extensive applicability of their formulation to the contemporary world.

In 1971 Elman Service published *Cultural Evolutionism* in which for the first time an anthropologist responded to critics from outside the discipline with an attempt to apply evolutionary theory to the contemporary world scene. Still, even in this recent book by an outstanding evolutionary theorist, there is no attempt to conceptualize a contemporary stage of cultural evolution. The anthropologist in the present tradition of modernization studies who has developed a worldwide typology of modernization is Darcy Ribeiro (1968), a Brazilian anthropologist. His formulation comes very close to describing a contemporary stage of cultural evolution.

It would appear that anthropologists' ambivalence towards contemporary change has hindered their perception of modernization as the *ongoing* processes of a *new stage* in the general evolution of human culture. They have generally directed their theoretical work toward limited applications of cultural evolutionary theory. And yet, anthropologists are among the most concerned individuals studying the world's sociocultural change.

The time has come for anthropologists to rethink modernization from a more inclusive perspective. Few of us would deny what Vera Rubin (1962) calls the worldwide ". . . tide of change and rising expectations." This global process involves more and more of the world's peoples becoming increasingly delocalized and drawn into the networks of national and international political, economic, and cultural activities in a way never before experienced. As Meadows and her associates have so dramatically documented in

The Limits to Growth (1972), the world we live in is a unitary system and must be understood as such if we are to save it from our own destruction. The contemporary nation-world stage of cultural evolution represents a transformation in sociocultural process. Thus, by the same token, it requires a corresponding transformation of our theoretical perspectives. It is paramount that anthropologists attempt to describe and to understand ongoing sociocultural evolution in the context of the relevant theory of our discipline if we are to reflect the reality that surrounds us and overcome what Kaplan and Manners (1972) call the "crisis in anthropology."

MODERNIZATION AS A PHASE OF THE INDUSTRIAL REVOLUTION

We view the processes of modernization as a continuation of the industrial revolution, which in turn must be looked on as a "stage" in the worldwide progression of evolutionary transformations that mark the course of human culture history. There is a tendency to think of the industrial revolution as primarily a nineteenth and early twentieth century event, but there is good reason to consider it as having several phases which have manifested themselves in different ways in different parts of the world. Hence, the events of the nineteenth and first half of the twentieth centuries may be considered phase I of the industrial revolution—a period of intense but relatively local changes in the means of production and the consequences of such change in England, Europe and North America, as well as the subsequent effects of these changes on the rest of the world (see Table 1). It was during this phase of cultural evolution that Euro-American economic and political controls were spread around the world in the form of colonialism.

The years since World War II have seen a worldwide expansion of industrialization and commercialization. We call this period phase II of the industrial revolution. This phase involves more than just simple "diffusion," with the same things as phase I reoccurring in each newly affected area, for the nations that have already gone through phase I have drastically changed the worldwide environment in which new change is taking place. Some of the most important characteristics of the post-World War II phase of cultural evolution include:

(1) Rapid (geometric) increases in amounts of energy utilized for

economic and political purposes, most of which is controlled by the "super-powers."

(2) Termination of overt *political* colonialism in many areas, but with varying forms of economic control and indirect political control replacing the formerly ubiquitous Euro-American colonial administrations.

(3) Division of power blocs in the world into "capitalist" and "socialist" sectors, resulting in further competition among the big powers in control of marginal economics areas (the DEW line among the Eskimos, United States military presence in Spain, Soviet Russian activities in Cuba, United States involvement in Indochina and Soviet and American involvement in the Middle East).

The first phase of the industrial revolution had profound (and often destructive) consequences for many non-European peoples, e.g., the American Indians. The second phase is even more worldwide and perhaps more diversified in its manifestations, in part because of the varying degree of nationalism as well as religious and ideological proselytizing that now accompanies economic development. Furthermore, there is the spread of a supposedly humanitarian content in the Euro-American development policies, according to which the native peoples around the world are to be brought into full participation in the "benefits" of industrialism and modernization.

There is, we suggest, a third phase of the industrial revolution looming, for which we propose the label "limits of growth phase."

We have listed, in Table 1, some of the salient processes and features of each phase of the revolution as they have affected different parts of the world. We divide the regions of the world into three sectors relative to the industrial revolution: primary (Europe and North America), secondary (zones of early European contact and economic exploitation, such as Latin America and Africa), and marginal (zones of minimal early European contact like the New Guinea Highlands). These zones are mainly defined by geographic distance from primary centers, but in the case of marginal sectors they also involve "functional distance", as with the highland native groups of Middle America, New Guinea, and the Philippines, or with such conquered encapsulated groups as many American Indian tribes.

It is phase II which we are mainly concerned with in this volume. We call the collective processes of this phase *modernization*, and consider it the most

Table 1.
Processes Characteristic of the Industrial Revolution

M O D E R N I Z A T I O N

	Phase I *19th c. to WW II*	Phase II *Post WW II to 1970s*	Phase III *1970s and beyond*

PRIMARY SECTORS	Industrial revolution
	Rapid growth of
	  machine technology
	Laissez-faire
	  capitalism
	Democratization of
	  political process
	Rise of commercialism
	Rationalism and
	  secularization
		World perceived as a
		  single ecosystem- con-
		  straints on technological
		  growth
		Rise of planned
		  economics
		Spread of social
		  welfare programs
		Big power political,
		  economic dominance
		Countercultures
		Population planning
			Worldwide political and
			  economic planning
			Increased cooperation
			  among big powers
			Limits to natural
			  resources
			Limits to economic
			  growth
			Population decline

SECONDARY SECTORS	Colonialism (political
	  & military control)
	Creation of markets
	  for finished goods
	Economic exploita-
	  tion (labor, agri-
	  cultural products,
	  raw materials)
	Missionization
		Intensification of outside
		  economic control
		Nationalism (internal
		  growth in education,
		  health & welfare
		  services)
		Peasant wars of liberation
		Economic development
		  and technical aid
		  schemes
		Political instability
		Urbanization and
		  industrialization
		Rapid rise in population
			Intensified competition
			  for raw materials
			Rise of political alliances
			  (confederations among
			  secondary powers, and
			  satellite formation of
			  primary zones)
			Increased international
			  economic participation
			  and dependency

MARGINAL SECTORS	Exploration
	Some military control
	Some missionary
	  activity
	Minimal trading
		Rapid & extensive
		  contact with outside
		  world
		Centralized political &
		  military control
		Influx of finished goods
		Growing sedantism,
		  creation of preserves
		Wage labor
		Missionization, techni-
		  cal aid programs,
		  health services
		Attempts to preserve
		  native cultural patterns
		Migration
			"Detribalization"
			Deculturation
			Increased involvement
			  in centralized political
			  and economic sphere

recent phase of worldwide general cultural evolution. This phase differs significantly from its precursor in its increasingly accelerated rate of change, which is resulting in the delocalization of all human cultures.

CURRENT ANTHROPOLOGICAL PERSPECTIVES ON MODERNIZATION

This volume brings together some of the views of anthropologists regarding this contemporary stage of general cultural evolution. We have purposely used the term modernization in our title because of our discipline's earlier reluctance to face the reality of modernization (Latin root *modo* = just now). Certainly we recognize that the term is rather vague, that it is polytypical, and is "unattractive" to many anthropologists. However, as a tag for our conceptualization of what is going on in the world today, and what is just now beginning to be a central concern in anthropology, it is very useful.

The ten papers in this volume, focused as they largely are on phase II processes, give an indication of the kinds of concerns and thoughts that twelve anthropologists have regarding modernization. They serve as an index of contemporary anthropological thought in this area of theory and research.

The papers in this volume can be seen as a reflection of a new orientation in anthropology. This new paradigm relies heavily on concepts from ecological theory. We see little of the older static functional or cultural paradigms which characterized the discipline in previous years. The new paradigm is basically diachronic in its assumptions. It concerns interactional processes with feedback mechanisms affecting ecological systems. There is concern also for the adaptational effects of these processes on individuals and groups. We see this orientation as the most powerful paradigm yet to emerge as a central focus in anthropology. The importance of evolutionary theory (general and specific) rests in its capacity to account for a large part of the phenomena anthropologists deal with. Furthermore, the evolutionary paradigm defines not only the relevant problems to be researched but the proper approach to these problems (Kuhn, 1970). In the papers in this volume we see the use of the paradigm at the regional, community, and individual levels of analysis, as well as considerations of the interrelationships between microcosm and macrocosm spheres of activity.

Margaret Mead's assessment in this volume of a number of development schemes emanating from the United States illustrates the kinds of "unexpected" results that accompany any large scale program of technical change. She uses these illustrations of unforeseen consequences to dramatize the shortcomings of the kind of simplistic and unidirectional thinking that characterized most aid programs prior to World War II. Unidirectional thinking may be characterized as a paradigm wherein "A does something (develops, changes, etc.) to B, but without any consideration of feedback (transaction) between B and A." In place of this unidirectional paradigm, Mead suggests through a number of examples that sound development programs require actions based on the transactional effect between social systems. Thus we suggest she is advocating the kind of ecological-historical paradigm we have discussed above.

In the same vein, Richard N. Adams in his paper shows that there are differential consequences for different peoples in the process of worldwide economic growth. While primary industrial nations such as the United States, Britain, Japan, and the U.S.S.R. are using increasing amounts of raw materials from the rest of the world, they are at the same time creating an economic environment with which developing nations must cope. Adams argues that the only way that developing nations can reduce the "gap" between themselves and the primary nations is for the primary nations to slow down their rate of economic growth. Without "deceleration," as he calls it, the developing nations of the world will never be able to change their relative economic and social power position. This illustrates the kind of complex socioeconomic interrelationship that exists in today's world and which cannot be explained by the application of simplistic unidirectional models. According to Adams' thinking, the ecological systems paradigm is called for.

Charles Leslie also considers international systems. He analyzes the historical interrelationship between Eastern medical systems and their ties to the Western traditions of medical science and practice. His findings show that these medical systems are complex constellations of different traditions and practices, ranging from the Ayurvedic herbalists in India to large state-supported medical programs in China. According to Leslie, understanding these complex systems demands an historical and transactional account of their current configuration.

Pelto and Poggie have also employed an ecological paradigm in their consideration of regional models of modernization. Their study of the modernization of two superficially similar community networks in Mexico illustrates how quite different results may occur in networks depending on a complex interplay of factors in the local ecological settings. Thus one network they studied apparently experienced some "spreading of the wealth" as a result of large scale technological inputs, while the other experienced an intensification of existing social and economic inequalities. This is the type of "adaptive radiation" that is to be expected in the ongoing interplay of human communities and their environments.

Frank Cancian's work is concerned with a fundamental assumption underlying economic development theory and practice. He demonstrates that economic behavior is virtually never based on only economic values. Thus he lays to rest the myth of the "economic man," wherein Western man is supposedly highly "rational" in his economic behavior, while men of other traditions are supposedly under the constraints of cultural and "traditional" influences in economic behavior which make them "maladapted" to modernization of the economic sector. Cancian's argument leads us to look for the nature of economic values in the contexts of the social system in which they operate rather than in terms of a polar typology in which Western man is misconceived as an utterly rational cost-accounting marvel.

Robert Lynch's focus is on political behavior in a small Indian community. He views political behavior as a series of adaptive transactions between the local system and an agency of the United States government. According to Lynch, the political behavior that takes place in a Northern Paiute community in Nevada is understandable as an adaptive response to an increasingly complex social environment. In this case, the main focus is on both the Indian's and Bureau of Indian Affairs' adjustments to the introduction of parliamentary procedure in community decisionmaking.

In the Landberg and Weaver paper, on the other hand, there is a consideration of economic behavior of Swahili people in coastal Tanzania as related to plantation and urban influences in this region. Individuals' economic behavior is tempered by social, economic, and cultural realities of life in the coastal villages and urban centers. Individuals' behavior is understandable as adaptive strategies to an increasingly complex socioeconomic environment.

Robbins and Thompson deal with the interrelationships of individual psychological processes to the type of environment created by urbanization in Uganda. They ask the question, "What strategies do individuals adapt when faced with an environment of growing material complexity and alternatives?"

Adaptation to Christian missionaries in the two Eskimo communities Thomas Correll studied involved the interplay of language, religion and social organization. Different policies regarding the use of English and Eskimo as the vehicle for instruction resulted in two quite different adaptive configurations. Norman Chance, in the final paper of this volume, argues that the educational policies now in effect among Alaskan Eskimos are maladaptive for much of contemporary Eskimo life because the values of Eskimos are not presently incorporated into their school experience. According to Chance, a truly adaptive educational policy would allow Eskimos freedom to decide the course of their own educational experience.

Each of these papers has as its theoretical orientation the study of adaptive responses to changing environmental conditions. Explicitly or implicitly they all follow the ecological-evolutionary paradigm. These papers cover only a small part of the complex descriptive-theoretical "map" of modernization. They are intended to provide a sampling across a topical domain, to be elaborated on by individual students of modernization in terms of their own interests and predilections.

2

The opening paper of the symposium was Margaret Mead's assessment of modernization from World War II to the present. Dr. Mead's career as an anthropologist spans nearly a half century and gives her a unique vantage point from which she describes changing thinking concerning social and cultural change. Probably no other living anthropologist has had comparable firsthand experience with modernization, and it is therefore fitting that she has introduced many of the themes taken up in other papers in this volume.

Changing Perspectives on Modernization[1]

MARGARET MEAD

Margaret Mead is Adjunct Professor, Department of Anthropology, Columbia University, and Curator, American Museum of Natural History. Dr. Mead is one of the early graduates of the famed graduate program in anthropology at Columbia University under Franz Boas, and has done extensive field work on culture change and socialization in the Pacific Islands. Among her many publications dealing with modernization are New Lives For Old *(1956) and* Cultural Patterns and Technical Change *(1953).*

In considering modernization I think it would be useful to emphasize what it is that we can learn at this unique period in history. If we do not take advantage of this opportunity we will never again be able to learn about ourselves in the same way. Spread out in front of us and accessible to use at this moment is every stage of technological development. We also have today almost all the varieties of culture contact that have ever existed and all their different forms. These range from individualized culture contact situations such as the single ambassador from a developed country to a less developed country, to a missionary, modernizing government official, or emissary of a particular industry, and to the massive sorts of contact that have gone on since World War II.

The one case of massive culture contact that I studied involved the Manus of the Admiralty Islands in Papua New Guinea. Some 20,000 people with twenty different languages had box seats watching two million Americans go through their small archipelago and were exposed to the whole paraphernalia of a modern technology. They hung from the top of the operating room watching operations; on ships they were up on the bridge with the captain; they were down in the engine room; and they had a type of instantaneous access to complex technology which nobody with a simple level of life has ever had before. In New Guinea the contacts since the war have been even more striking. We have had instances of people coming through three different groups of interpreters—three language mediations—before they could talk to an outpost of the Trust Territory government. Some of these people arrived stark naked, because as yet they had had no means of getting clothes; they had washed the pig fat out of their hair and were perfectly prepared to put on full European dress at once. They knew that the Europeans [Europeans are what we call Australians in New Guinea] do not like pig fat. They also said that they had decided they would like a school and a hospital. They had already built the buildings and asked if the government would please send them the necessary officials tomorrow morning. Crossing boundaries of thousands and thousands of years within two or three days' walk has never happened before because there has never been the complexity of technology that we have reached today, accessible to people at very simple technological levels.

We also have an opportunity to compare these transformations with the effects of sixteenth and seventeenth century European exploration and colonization. I recall, just a few years after World War II, a time when Arthur Raper was talking about some small spot in the Middle East, and he said that nothing had happened there since "the Romans had a Point Four program." As I reviewed the set of papers that have been assembled here, I became acutely aware of the difference in the processes of modernization that have accompanied different levels of technology in different periods in history. We will be organizing our discussions around the concept of modernization. What we actually mean by modernization today is a post World War II phenomenon. We are dealing with an order of diffusion that has never occurred before. One of our tasks here is to sketch in the dimensions of how the phenomenon we know as contemporary modernization, differs from social and cultural change in the past. We now have world-wide information systems, and we must recognize that today's very rapid purposeful diffusion has different results as compared with the effects of earlier diffusion.

When some people talk about modernization they place particular emphasis on how large societies transform small ones, an approach which still expresses a good deal of the climate of pre-World War II opinion. At that time anthropologists and sociologists, on the whole, felt that most of this transformation was alien and imperialistic and negative, that the small societies were being transformed against their will by the great societies. It also represents the present wave of feeling that we find among contemporary students who are again asking the kind of questions that were asked in the 1920s. "What right do we have to go and transform these people who are living this beautiful life?" All these questions are coming up again. For example, we have the question of the right of the Eskimo to live in a technologically archaic fashion requiring an incredibly large land area to nourish each individual, being counterposed against the desire of people who want to put a pipeline through parts of Alaska. The present climate of opinion coincides with a worldwide technological and communication expansion that brings what happens in these small societies into quite a different juxtaposition with national and international affairs. I think if —even in the early 1940s—anybody had suggested the possibility of national decisionmakers having to seriously consider the rights of small societies they would have been considered naive. Yet today, we are considering the right of the Eskimos in Alaska to hunt as they have hunted for thousands of years, a right to be protected from any of the advances of civilization except the ones they happen to want. These rights are being weighed against the claims by the power companies who must fulfill the energy needs of millions of people.

A second example is the discussion in the Southwest about strip mining on Navajo land to feed a power plant producing power by archaic methods that happen to be cheap at the moment. It has been possible to persuade some of the Navajos that the employment the power plant and strip mining have brought into the area is worthwhile because the amount of local pollution is reasonably slight. The power that is being produced is being sent to southern California where the pollution laws would not permit anybody to build a power plant of the same sort. I think these two cases dramatize the new relationships between the environment, our concern for the environment, the growing demand for power, particularly in the modern world, and the ethical questions that are being discussed at the present moment.

ANTHROPOLOGICAL ATTITUDES TOWARD PURPOSEFUL CHANGE IN HISTORICAL PERSPECTIVE

It is useful to go back and look at the history of anthropologists' attitudes towards purposeful cultural change from just before World War II to the present. It was, so we thought, reasonably clear in the 1930s and early 1940s that the thing that anthropologists should do was to protect backward societies or isolated peoples from too rapid change. We thought slow change was better than fast change, that less change was better than more change, that it was a pity to disturb the life of isolated peoples who were reasonably balanced in relationship to the territory they had and the technology they were using. We thought it was a pity that this balance should be altered by the inroads of larger systems, parts of which were incompatible with these small systems.

The American Ethnological Society had its 75th anniversary in the early 1940s; this was before the bomb, before we had explored the world completely, before we had really begun to relate ourselves to outer space. However, we were thinking about the possibility of an international organization to succeed the League of Nations and people were already talking about the possibilities that later led to the formation of the United Nations. It was clear then that this would lead inevitably to some discussion of the fate of the small societies in the world. I read a paper (Mead, 1943) at that meeting in which I proposed that we treat the small island societies in the Pacific as laboratories for the training of international civil servants; that we face straightforwardly the fact that somebody was going to insist on some kind of relationship to all the small islands, including the islanders themselves, who are usually left out of most of these discussions.

There were no inhabitants of small Pacific islands who did not want some of the things from civilization once they had seen them. Any belief that they liked lighting the house by candle nuts and dressing in bark cloth was rubbish. I have never seen a group of people who want to dress in bark cloth once they have had cloth. Bark cloth is a very inferior form of material, except for its value to tourists. I suggested there would be certain things that they would want—for example, some medicine, some means of lighting, and a few other things—and, given the power situation in the world, every square mile of territory in the Pacific would eventually be of interest to some political power. There was no way in which you could put the islands of the Pacific outside the spheres of competitive political influence. This was before we knew about space travel and before we realized that our present Trust Territory in Micronesia is some of the most valuable real estate in the world. There is just a little land above the surface; you look at the ocean and you see just little spots of islands. Yet this is one of the best takeoff places in the world for anyone serious about travelling in outer space. This possibility has enormously transformed the meaning of these little islands from pre-war times, when they were primarily refueling and air bases for possible military operations. Therefore, given the fact that small islands were going to be politically important to somebody, some disposition was going to have to be made of them. This is something that I believe we are still not facing.

It is impossible for any group of people to be living at any level in any way without affecting the rest of the world today. If we decide to let every Eskimo have a large number of square miles in which to hunt with a harpoon, this immediately affects decisions made all over the world; it might even affect international oil concordats and the kind of power plant Consolidated Edison builds in New York. Clearly, the fate of each small primitive people has become inextricably intertwined with what is going on in other places.

What I said in 1942 and 1943, therefore, was that some great power or group of great powers is going to have to nominally preside over these islands. If we turn them into trust territories, for instance, let us turn them into laboratories for training international civil servants. We could require anyone who was going to work in the international field under the proposed new international organization to function as the chief emissary of the outside world on these islands, and do what the people want. If the people wanted to move fast, he could help them move fast; and if they wanted to resist outside influences, he could help them do so. However, he would have to work with them over a period of time and find out what it was like to live in a totally different culture.

From the back of the room an anthropologist, who at that moment was clearly associated with communism, stood up and said that this was an outrage; this was a denial of the full right of the peoples of the Pacific to share in modern technology and in all its results, and he felt that they had a perfect right to modern plumbing! If my critic hadn't mentioned plumbing, I am not sure I would have grasped the whole position, for anybody who has ever been on a Pacific island knows that what they do not need is a bathtub; they have the whole Pacific Ocean to bathe in every day. It was a dramatization (remember this comment came from an anthropologist and a very well educated one) that very graphically illustrated the climate of opinion that was developing in the world regarding the rights and privileges of small societies in relation to technology. People who lived on an island two miles by three lapped by the Pacific Ocean were nevertheless going to have bathtubs!

TECHNOLOGICAL MODERNIZATION IN ONE GENERATION

I saw the writing on the wall clearly enough at that meeting. I went away feeling that we were going to hear technological modernization advocated for every country in the world in one generation. This, I said, was what was going to be the climate of opinion in the postwar period, and indeed it was (Mead, 1953). Consequently I realized we might as well settle down and face it; this was what we were going to be up against. What it amounted to was glorification of modern technology. This is one issue on which the United States and the Soviet Union agreed completely. At that time they both assumed that economic and technological advances were invariably good, unmitigatedly good and that it was romantic to believe anything else. The industrialized nations of the world must make available to everybody else running water, followed by airlines, steel mills and all the rest of it —immediately. The fact that the Soviet Union and the United States were rivals did not change this; it simply meant that people could play one off against the other. We went to underdeveloped countries and told them what to ask for from the Soviet Union, and the Soviet Union sent emissaries telling them what to ask from us. So they asked for a dam from one country and a steel mill from the other.

At this point a lot of people predicted that if it had taken the Soviet Union thirty years to industrialize and it took us one hundred, India could probably manage it in fifteen and China in ten. It is very hard to credit these predictions today, but they were all over the place immediately after World War II. Furthermore, it was claimed that new nations, whether composed of peasant or tribal peoples, would not have to be put through the same agonies that industrialization had meant for the workers in Britain, Western Europe, the United States and the Soviet Union. This would not have to happen because what the developed countries had taken out of the hides of their workers was now in the form of capital which could be nicely transferred to all the other countries, and they could have the benefits without any of the agonies. We were going to export the technological advantages of modernization to all parts of the world.

EVOLUTIONARY STAGES OF MODERNIZATION

There were also a variety of discussions as to whether every country had to go through the same evolutionary stages. We heard a lot about cultural evolution, whereby a developing country might undergo relatively rapid changes that have taken thousands of years in other places and not follow the same sequence of stages. For example, if you go into a country where it is very hard to build roads and even harder to build railroads, you do not build roads and you do not build railroads, you just build airports. And you turn your transport immediately into airplane transport and skip the intermediate stages of railroads, roads for trucks, and all the rest of it.

This type of development depends again on ideology. The Soviet Union firmly believes in its own scheme of evolution, and its own scheme of evolution contains a large amount of mythology, just as ours does. They believe that there was once a lovely primitive form of communism, when things were collective and the sexes were equal (This is being invoked by Women's Liberation today as another piece of mythology). Then the dreadful institutions of private property and patriarchal kinship were invented, and we had the whole growth of this evil capitalist society. In reaction to capitalist society, socialism goes back to more collective goals. In dealing with really primitive people, like some of the Siberian tribes, the Soviets have systematically yanked them out of any collective generosity they had had, and put them into the nastiest form of private property that they could think up so they could get over it and move to a collective system.[2] Now this is the grossest form of ideological evolutionism, the belief that there is an inevitable course of social evolution, and you can only get the right kind of societal collectivity if you first have the wrong kind of capitalism; you could not possibly get there by any other route.

We ourselves do not recognize that we also have an ideology, because it is so technological rather than articulately political. I remember once years ago Kurt Levine saying very worriedly as a German who had come to this country, "Why do Americans have no *Weltschmerz?*" I answered, "Because we have no *Weltanschauung.*" Now today we are overdosed with *Weltanschauung*, and we have a lot of *Weltschmerz*. However, as of the 1940s and early 1950s we did not have any *Weltanschauung* or any *Weltschmerz* either. We just had the Eisenhower era, and the ideology of this period was that technology was good for everybody and the more advanced technology you had, the better. However, we suffered from another form of technological mythology in also believing that tribal and peasant people had better go through the earlier stages that we had gone through. Under this heading, you sell them your old school bus, you send them your outdated sewing machines, and you give them the lowest possible level of your existing technology, so that they can go through the simple stages that we went through. We have sent a tremendous amount of our outmoded technology to other peoples—more consumer technology than production technology—so they can learn and make all the mistakes that we did.

The general assumption was and still is that it would be good for other people to go through the idiotic convention we endured of putting an engine in the front of a car because the horse was there; but the horse was never there for them, so why perpetuate our pieces of nonsense? Why not design something that fits? There has been a general unwillingness in the Western industrialized countries that are "helping" all the rest of the world by exporting their technology to them to realize that the exportation of technology is occurring in a *new* period of history, and a *new* period of technology.

One of the debates that went on in the 1950s was the dispute over the various kinds of modernization strategies that were used primarily by the western nations. One strategy was offering them the old technology, saying, "It will take them a long, long time to learn, and so we had better start them with the simplest possible stuff we can export." This involves our obsolete equipment which we are eager to sell anyway. Of course, this is what we do with our firearms all the time now; we send our out-of-date fighter planes and our out-of-date tanks and our out-of-date guns all over the world fomenting violence and revolution. We do this as a way of getting rid of outmoded technology, so we can have enough money to build another gun of a different type.

At the other extreme are the people who said, "Send them the most advanced technology"—a complete modern steel plant or a modern textile mill. Then somebody would come back and report that the equipment was stacked up somewhere in the city, that nobody has ever used it, and that there was nobody who knew how to use it. Now it is absolutely ridiculous to send this modern technology out where there is nobody to operate it, yet this was the idiotic thing that we were doing.

There emerged yet another related discussion about how one could evoke from all these peoples with different degrees of relationship to the modern world the kinds of behavior that were appropriate to operating modern equipment such as airplanes. We had a fascinating discussion, I should say in about 1952, at a meeting of the Society for Applied Anthropology in Canada, where an Englishman proposed that the way to make nomads from the Middle East into good pilots was to invent a condensed version of the English public school, cold baths and all. He claimed that the English public school (that is the English private school) built the right kind of character for this task. You would take tribesmen from somewhere in the Middle East and send them to three months' condensed English public school and thereby give them the right character to operate airlines. This infuriated the Canadians who did not want anything English; so the discussion did not really deal with the issue but with the Canadian rejection of English moralities (I might add in passing that this is about the level that most anthropological discussions reach; we are not as sophisticated about our own culture as we are about other cultures).

No one looking at things in the 1950s was very much concerned with the human aspect of modernization, but merely with the problem of how modern technology was to be introduced everywhere with the least possible damage. Anthropologists, sociologists, and some educators were concerned with reducing the damage, if any, by having as little dislocation as possible. They pondered such problems as what did you do to prevent terrific conflicts between young and old and to minimize disorganization or juvenile delinquency (Mead, 1963a). However, there was very widespread agreement that technology was good, that substituting new forms of power for old forms of power was good and whether you believed you could skip stages or not, you thought it was absolutely necessary to distribute power there. Certain individuals said that countries that have no coal or oil should be sent atomic reactors; they do not take up very much space and an atomic energy plant can quickly be installed.

There were also the suggestions that we could take people with classical educations and let them read gauges. It was very hard to turn them into good mechanics because of their aristocratic intellectual tradition which forbid the use of one's hands. Thus it was argued that you could take people with a classical Burmese education or an Indian education or a Greek education and turn them into people who could function in an atomic plant even though you could not get them to mend an automobile or a truck. This was another way in which we could short cut stages of development and take advantage at another level of what was already available.

THE GROWING RECOGNITION OF PROBLEMS

By the early 1960s we were beginning to recognize a series of difficulties. We were beginning to analyze the relationships among the developed countries and the underdeveloped countries, and at that point "underdeveloped" became a pejorative term and was changed to the "developing countries." In 1963 the United Nations had a conference on scientific and technological aid to the emerging nations (Mead, 1963b). The general belief still held that technology was completely good and the main problem was discovering the means to export it to the less industrialized countries. Related to this was the concern with raising enough working capital while at the same time arranging for the competing major powers to cooperate in getting them what they needed. At about this time alert people were beginning to say that we were not going to be able to export our modernized technology to everybody in the world, and not everyone would benefit from it. Instead, the gap between the poor countries and the rich countries was going to increase (Theobold, 1962). At that point the dichotomy between the rich and the poor countries was invented, an idea which is spiritually appealing but very inaccurate because the countries of the world are actually on a continuum (Mead, 1967). The idea was given currency that it was the rich versus the poor; the poor countries were going to get poorer and poorer and poorer and the rich were going to get richer and richer and richer. Furthermore, there was not going to be any way to prevent this, because the poor countries were the ones that were producing raw materials.

We must realize that modernization in Africa or New Guinea or parts of South America was thought to depend upon getting people to grow crops that are commercially valuable in the world's markets. So, you have coffee grown in the mountains of New Guinea or you have schemes to have people grow rubber. These schemes involved taking peoples who had lived on subsistence agriculture and giving them a commercially valuable crop. The crop itself had to be sold in the world market and was absolutely dependent on the state of the market. Analysts like Robert Theobold (1962) pointed out that the minute rubber or coffee or cotton or wool was grown in a way that gave a decent wage to the people who grew it, the developed countries would merely produce it synthetically, and would stop buying their cotton, wool, or rubber. Anthropologists who have studied particular small countries are very conscious of what happens if you take a tribe and start growing coffee, for instance, and the bottom falls out of the coffee market. Anybody who has ever worked in the Caribbean has seen this happen over and over again. One little island starts selling something, and if it works, every other Caribbean island starts selling it and the market price falls. Everybody is disappointed and disgruntled and miserable and the impetus toward change, which may have been quite genuine at the start, is depressed and destroyed.

"THE GREEN REVOLUTION"

The economists who had been promotiong large scale industrialization realized that this emphasis had resulted in the depopulation of the countrysides in favor of the cities. They began to comprehend that this incredible increase in urbanization was very, very dangerous and that something ought to be done about agriculture which they had been virtually ignoring in their concentration on industry.

There followed a brief period of great excitement, the Green Revolution, in which everything was going to be solved by miracle rice and miracle wheat. These crops are, without a doubt, miracles of modern technology. In the International Rice Institute in the Philippines they have collected all the forms of rice that have ever been grown anywhere in the world, grown them in experimental seed beds, and analyzed them genetically. From this they can now produce a seed with a given growing time, a given kind of grain, and a given height of stalk that will resist disease and weather. They can prescribe a grain which will be absolutely appropriate to an area and give a tenfold increase in yield; what we had done in agriculture before tended to give only a ten percent improvement. People are going to worry about their own prejudices, their own social organization, their religious beliefs, and their caste behavior rather than a ten percent improved growth; but nobody is going to oppose a tenfold increase. This has a kind of technological massiveness that simply overwhelms all the reservations that many of us have talked about.

In 1968 there were still people in the Philippines who talked mainly about food habits and the fact that people preferred one kind of rice to another. However, the Philippines were importing rice from everywhere in the world at that time because there was a shortage and they were eating *any* kind of rice. The possibility of a tenfold increase in yield here produced a new wave of optimism. Instead of having rural people rushing into the cities and becoming a burden, we were now going to have a kind of agriculture that would support people in the country for several generations while they got *ready* to absorb all the wonderful new technology.

THE ENVIRONMENTAL CRISIS

What followed was the real recognition of what was happening to the environment and the environmental crisis. When this was heralded by Rachel Carson's *Silent Spring* (1962), the technological and scientific establishment did its best to discredit it and to discredit her. Gradually the terrible damage to the environment began to become visible. We began to realize that we were facing a worldwide ecological crisis, that we did not have inexhaustible supplies of the atmosphere, oceans, and rivers. We found that, without recognizing it, we had crossed a line between the old types of technology and the kind of greater food supply and greater amenities and greater possibilities that were the givens in a new era in which we were endangering all the life support systems of the entire planet. Almost overnight the image of technology changed in the minds of a lot of the general public and particularly of students, from being a beneficial thing that was going to bring all peoples into a fuller and better life, into a demon.

We have had, of course, a great many other manifestations of this new kind of "demonology," but it has changed the whole conceptualization of what modernization means. Instead of hailing the Green Revolution we are now recognizing that when we export these beautiful new grains we are exporting with them pesticides and fertilizers and, therefore, exporting pollution. We cannot depend on the Green Revolution after all.

There are additional hazards, although they are somewhat overemphasized. For example, if an entire country plants one kind of seed, a pest could wipe out the whole of that crop. The safety that resides in diversity, in the very diversity provided by small societies, has been analyzed recently in a critique of the attempts to introduce large scale agricultural schemes in East Africa (Campbell, 1971). Each little farmer in this area knew that he had a little bit of land that would work when there was a drought, and another little bit of land that would work when there was too much rain, so that virtually each individual or household had some security against the adversity of climatic disorders. When you introduce large scale monoagriculture, with one seed, you may be exposing entire segments of a country to famine. If we had the whole world to draw on, and if we had a large enough surplus of food and the ships to transport it, we might be able to care for a region that had such a famine. Unfortunately, we do not have this capability, and consequently the new technology is increasing the potential for famine. We have to look everywhere for the significance of such breaks in natural cycles which are the result of the technology that has been developed since World War II. Ideas about the pros or cons of technology, such as these new biochemical industrial developments, have to be tempered by these newly realized consequences.

It was 1965 when Robert Theobold introduced into the discussions of the World Council of Churches considerations about what was going to happen between the rich and the poor countries due to our emphasis on synthetic products. It was 1971 when Barry Commoner, in a speech to the United Nations non-governmental groups preparing for the Stockholm Conference on the Environment, pointed out that we may have to go back to natural products. He argued that the cost of using cotton is far less than the pollution cost of the energy expended in producing synthetic substitutes (Commoner, 1971). We are now going to have to look realistically at two sets of factors: (1) the extent to which the materials themselves are nonbiodegradable, and (2) the energy costs of producing synthetics. Actually the whole shift from the use of wool, cotton, rubber and other natural products to the production of synthetic substitutes on which technological progress of the developed world is presently being postulated may have to be completely reversed.

It took only five years to make this drastic change in understanding what is happening; of course, this view is as one sided in many ways as was the earlier one. Fear about the new kind of seeds, fear of the results of monoagriculture, fear of the destruction of species that are essential in the various life support systems, fear that we will exhaust the atmosphere and contaminate the oceans before we manage to reverse this kind of behavior is now gripping a great many of the planners of the world. Even the smallest groups of primitive people are caught in this. Should the Eskimo go back to his harpoon; and, since we cannot manage New York City, should we glorify the ecological balance that was established by handfuls of Indians without the technological means of destroying the buffalo?

At present one of the things that we are hearing about that is playing a considerable role both in some anthropological discussions and a great deal of student enthusiasm, is that the American Indians were great ecologists. The honest truth is that there were not enough Indians in North America to damage the environment very much. The Indians had a level of technology that did not enable them to kill too many animals. The minute they got guns they went after the buffalo with the same or perhaps greater enthusiasm as other peoples had shown. However, at the time when the American Indians lived in very widely dispersed tribes, they did have a symbolic relationship to the environment which we are going to have to emulate at a more complex level. The Indian who, after he had eaten a fish, put the bones back in the creek and said, "Little brother, go back and be born again so I can eat you again" was symbolically talking about recycling. That is a perfect mythological, religious, poetic statement of recycling in which man recognizes that he is a part of nature and that his life depends upon recognizing that he is part of nature instead of standing apart from it.

THE SIGNIFICANCE OF DIVERSIFICATION

We are developing a feedback into worldwide theories of change of the experience of small groups in a variety of ways. For instance, the recognition that safety lies in diversification is also being currently expressed in consumer movements under the aegis of Ralph Nader and his associates who warn shoppers, "Use the detergent that is least contaminating, but don't all use the same one. We will give you a list of ten detergents that we think are better than the other thirty and will do less damage, but don't everybody in the neighborhood use the same one because if you do you might produce absolutely unknown results!" The recognition that the minute you have something synthetic you have done something so different to the environment and that magnification and amplification endanger the environment gives a completely new value to diversification, to small cultures, to their particular ways of doing things, and to variety in every part of the world.

Variety has now been given a new standing it did not enjoy before. It is an answer to the people who advocated a unified world order, advocating the disappearance of all these idiosyncratic, odd little tribes and parochialisms in favor of uniformity and efficiency. It used to be hard to argue with those people on behalf of diversity. They said standardization would mean people were going to have more to eat, better medical care, longer lives, lower infant mortality, and all that would be good. Today it is not hard at all, and people are turning to diversification as a strength and as a protection. Before people felt you either preserve the beautiful local native culture, and that was charming and romantic and unhealthful, or you had mass education, mass medical care, and a decreased infant death rate. This is no longer the argument, and diversification is now becoming a refuge.

This can be also illustrated with the question of a world language (Mead and Modley, 1968). We now realize that the only way we can save the little languages of the world so that they make their contribution to the world is to have a secondary world language that is not a language of a major power. If it is a major language, it will spread at the expense of the small languages spoken by the politically powerless peoples. If, on the other hand, we had a secondary language that was of no political importance, everybody could learn to speak it without political implications and all the little languages could survive for poetry and lullabies and all the diverse contributions that they make.

Now it is within this kind of setting that we will here be discussing what happens today in particular instances and particular cases of modernization. Our discussions will to a degree transcend these major pitfalls in understanding. For example, we will not be talking in terms of introducing change into a society by living in the village for three months to find out who the local leader is. It took a lot of anthropological fieldwork to find out who the local leader was, especially in Asian countries where he hides behind a lot of fronts. We would send people in and they would study who the local leader was and how to get the local leader to get the local people to build three miles of road.

That was the only way people thought you were going to get roads built, until we began realizing that you can have a machine that knocks down the trees and lays down the cement behind it as it goes, and then you do not need any local leaders at all. Then the sort of effort and the sort of democratic behavior that came out of it in looking for local leaders suddenly became absolutely irrelevant. Consequently we had a period where the daydream of the technological planners was that we were going to bulldoze all roads through the whole of Asia and Africa without worrying about the people at all.

Hence we come into the present period with the realization that we had better pay a great deal of attention to the people and to the local situation, because spreading these standardized techniques all over the world contaminates, pollutes, and endangers the environment.

NOTES

[1]This paper is an edited transcription of Dr. Mead's address at the University of Rhode modernization symposium.

[2]Films of these policies in Siberia were available in the 1920s but these aspects of Soviet policy are still imperfectly documented.

3

While it has been customary for anthropologists to deal primarily with small-scale, relatively egalitarian social systems, Richard N. Adams focuses his essay on power relations among nation states. His view of the effects of modernization is a pessimistic one which stresses the enormous, albeit rarely mentioned, environmental and social costs attendant to this process. Likewise, his recommendations for the amelioration of some of the negative by-products of the modernization process are unconventional.

Harnessing Technological Development

RICHARD N. ADAMS

Richard N. Adams is currently Professor of Anthropology at the University of Texas and received his Ph.D. from Yale University. Professor Adams has done extensive research throughout Latin America concentrating on problems of political and economic change, as reported in such publications as The Second Sowing *(1967) and* Crucifixion By Power *(1970).*

The purpose of this essay is to explore the relationship between two processes having to do with development. One is ecological, whereby natural resources are, through the aegis of human technology, converted into useful products, waste products and entropy; the other is a sociocultural process of change whereby the fact of organizing some people serves at the same time to render other people beyond control. The principal analogous feature is that in both cases, the act of bringing elements under control, i.e., "organizing" them, simultaneously makes inevitable the rendering of some elements out of control, i.e., "structuring" them, or making them part of the structure of the environment within which one operates.

Leading to this inquiry is the fact that during the last twenty years, our understanding of the process of development has undergone a major change. A central feature of this has to do with abandoning the idea that the underdeveloped world was, in some manner, going to duplicate the stages or processes of growth that characterized the leading industrial nations in their period of early expansion. The major contributions here came not from the well-staffed and financed centers of social science in the United States but from Latin America. The burden of these contrary views was that development of the primary industrial nations took place in considerable part through an implicit exploitation of the secondary powers, and that these latter were therefore undergoing a much slower process of development, almost a specific course of underdevelopment.[1] The central notion is that underdevelopment has a dialectic relationship with development; the former is a contributing factor in the cause of the latter. This is obviously contrary to the doctrine accepted generally among the Western primary powers that underdevelopment stemmed from a combination of underinvestment and cultural cussedness.

At the same time, further effects of modernization were making themselves felt on another front. The gradual growth in the past two centuries of increasing extraction of raw materials and their conversion into waste began some years ago to produce what can grossly be called a clogging of the environment—polluted air, dead lakes, and poisoned rivers, even to the point of turning the oceans into garbage and waste heaps and the atmosphere into an assemblage of noxious gases.

It does not require a great deal of imagination to note that there is something parallel in these processes—the production of underdevelopment and the production of waste. Both are products of development. From a broad perspective both involve a dual production of two very different kinds of products, one highly developed and one marginalized. In both cases, technological advancement has coupled the increased concentration of power and wealth with an increased gap between the highly developed and the less developed. It has facilitated increased production of goods for the advanced sector, and required an increase in the production of waste both directly and through the issuing of expendable and rapidly obsolescent goods. It may well be that these processes are really facets of a single complex process. The production of waste and the marginalization of societies are merely the physical and social aspects of the single process of development.

CONTROL AND STRUCTURING IN HUMAN ENVIRONMENTS

The central rationale for closely examining the analogy between the ecological processes of change and deterioration and those of social marginalization and deculturation is that social organization and culture are merely a special human way of adapting to the environment. All usable forms of energy have some kind of organization; a culture is the way human beings do it, and social organization is one of the ways anthropologists describe it. There is further logic in pursuing the comparison. It serves to indicate not only possible common origins of environmental and human processes, but also to suggest that future thought on problems of control over the direction human social development ought to treat these two processes as being intimately interrelated, and not essentially independent.

The argument to be explored, in its simplest form, is that in their process of expansion, human societies not only actively make waste out of portions of the habitat, but also necessarily make waste out of portions of the populations and cultures of the participating societies. It is also the case, of course, that expansion builds new elements within the habitat, that disappearing older cultural forms are replaced with newer forms. This aspect of the affair has received the lion's share of the attention of social scientists and planners. The at least equally important process of systematic social destruction has been little examined. "Out with the old, in with the new!" has been the byword not only of liberal entrepreneurs and commissars but also of many social scientists.

One problem here is that evaluating the new is seldom done in terms of its general adaptive value for the human species, but rather for the survival of a particular individual, group, or society. The new is promoted for the adaptive advantages of some particular social entity. The appearance of new cultural and social forms almost always implies the destruction of existing forms not only in the benefitting group but also in others. These others, therefore, merely lose culture in the process, and do not receive much of the new with which to replace it. This process of deculturation has not been adequately studied.[2]

The focus of the present discussion is on the possible singularity of the processes that we earlier mentioned. A central idea in this discussion is the concept of *control*. I want to define control as *the ability to exercise a technology that converts and/or changes the arrangement of a set of energy forms.* Control is a matter of having the necessary elements at hand to exercise some kind of change in the environment, and one may be said to have power when he has some such control. We should here distinguish between two kinds of changes that may result from control: mechanical change and the specific case of conversion. Conversion refers to a process of physical and/or chemical composition alterations in the materials composing the forms such that the specific elements involved cannot be returned to their original form. Mechanical changes refer to some simple quantum shifting, loss or addenda, with or without replacement, but whereby the original assemblage can be reformed. Mechanical changes do not necessarily imply conversions, but may entail them.

A technology, in turn, refers to some *set of materials, knowledge, and skills that, when exercised, can do some particular kind of work.* For analytical purposes, it may also be useful to include within the definition of technology a social organization sufficient to exercise the materials, knowledge and skills. The problem is that these elements of technology can be treated as formal issues, whereas social organization may be handled either in formal terms or as relational sets. That is, it may be seen as one form within the technology, or it can be seen as the set of relations that enable the technology to operate.

This brings us to the concept of structuring. Human activity at any point in time starts with a given stock of formal environmental elements. The individuals have a particular technology, a social organization, and cognitive and value systems. Cognitive and value orientation leads individuals to see the habitat in particular ways, influencing potential decisions about exercising control over phases or elements of the environment both to be utilized and to be ultimately expended. This utilization may involve the transfer of energy forms from a state of non-use in the habitat to some use in the social system, or from one context within the social system to another. The ideas people have of their environment are necessarily imperfect; and because of this, as well as the nature of any activity, a certain amount of energy is lost to entropy. The activity necessarily produces a new cultural manifestation while displacing an old one, and if the activity involved any change in perceived quantities or qualities of the environmental forms, there will be implied some variation in the social relations involved. In this manner, the culture and social organization, as well as the habitat, are changed.

In the activities just described, the actors have brought elements of the environment under control. Where this is done to inanimate resources it is referred to as a technological process. When it is done to human beings, it is usually called "organizing." However, at the same time that things, animate and inanimate, are being organized (i.e., being brought under control), some things are also being placed beyond control. Energy conversions lose energy to entropy; material products take the form of wastes for which there is no known technology for control; human beings who are brought under organization by this very act lose some portion of autonomy and find that they are now in some manner being controlled. Something new has entered the structure of their environment. For this reason, I use the term "structuring" to refer to this process whereby elements are placed out of or beyond control. The structuring process acts somewhat differently as it has to do with different kinds of things. Energy forms change their composition, social relationships change their qualities, and the delicate value-object identifications that form the substance of culture are permanently lost, just as permanently lost as the iron from a rusty ax, the wood from a burned forest, or the solidarity between patron and client after the latter rebels against the former. At every point in time, man starts with some given culture and environment and immediately proceeds to structure portions of it; that is, he places some of it permanently beyond or out of control.

In the study of culture change, anthropologists have tended to pay special attention to the continuity of formal aspects and to the process of construction or adoption of new cultural forms. Following a functional predisposition, it has often been assumed that the important aspect of change is that which provides man with his stability and continuity; less attention has been paid to the fact that the very effort to retain continuity implicitly carried with it this structuring process, whereby both habitat and social relations were being placed beyond control. Since man's attention (including many scientists) is usually fixed on the continuity or expansion of his system, this other aspect is seldom considered seriously until the habitat or social organization reaches a critical state that threatens the entire system. Famine, plague, pollution, excessive political repression or economic marginalization, and overpopulation are all conditions that perhaps come suddenly to our attention, but they come into being only after a long period of structuring.

Structuring, in short, is a paradoxical process. By virtue of gaining and exercising control over his environment, man also converts and changes elements of that environment into forms that are permanently beyond his control. The reason to focus attention on structuring is that when things are beyond control, they are not necessarily of no further consequence. On the contrary, they insert elements into the environment which can not be handled with the technology at hand; in many instances no technology is possible for control of these things. Among the effects of structuring, then, is the building of an environment less readily tractable to man's current technologies.

STRUCTURING IN CULTURE AND SOCIETY

The notion of structuring is readily understandable in matters directly concerning the habitat. Changing any portion of the habitat necessarily uses up energy, and when the process is one of conversion, then the energy forms themselves are inevitably altered in ways that do not permit a return to their original state. Of particular concern in this paper is structuring in culture and society.

The term "culture" may refer either to a general, abstract set of processes, or a particular set of processes at some place and at some point in time.[3] Here, we want to identify the specific process which can empirically be observed within some space-time context. Since a culture is the specific concatenation of perceptible energy forms, that is, specific behavioral (and therefore presumably also psychological) processes, or meanings, conjoining human beings who stand in some particular social relation with one another, it follows that a culture comes into being when there is such a concatenation of available energy. Since a great deal of what human beings do involves retaining consistency of meaning-with-forms for some particular set of people, specific cultures remain fairly consistent over some period of time. These are the kinds of things we refer to when speaking of "a culture."

However, the perceptible forms of culture are also in some manner energy forms, in some manner independent of the human organism observing them, whereas meaning and behavioral processes are organic, part of the organism doing the observing. The two are discreetly independent and vary independently. In the very repetition of forms it is inevitable that one or more aspects will be modified so that the very acting out of a culture implicitly entails constant variation. To be accurate, we should hold that a culture never repeats itself, in the same sense that one never steps twice in the same river. However, for the same reason that we call a river "a river," and not "those rivers," so we think of this succession of similar cultures as "a culture." To do so, however, is explicitly metaphorical, treating a set of forms known to be different *as if* they were equivalents. Moreover, we then take that sequence of "alikenesses" and treat them as a continuity or a tradition, thereby assigning to the whole temporal set a concreteness that really exists only in our minds.

Treating the form-meaning-relationships complex in terms of some particular consistence has been useful (for anthropologists, at least) in keeping track of the continuity of culture since, of the three elements, only that of form is discreetly perceptible. Meanings are hidden within the nervous system. Social relations, depending upon your preference, are the association of certain meanings, or are abstractions projected by the social scientists, based on observable interactions or presumed connections. This means that cultural continuities have often been seen in terms of the continuity of forms, not of the complex set of elements as it is defined here. While this has been obviously useful for historical studies, since it provides temporal linkages, it also has obscured the fact that meanings and social relations change over periods of time.

If we ask how it is that some particular continuity of the form-meaning-relationship complex (i.e., a culture) can be retained, we find that it is most often through the retention of a set of social relational characteristics. For example, superordination and subordination are associated respectively with the forms of monarch and subject. When we follow through history, we find that the superordination type of relationship undergoes a whole series of formal and meaning changes (thereby providing the historian with one of his major subjects of argument and discord).

I have gone some length into the nature of culture because in the following we will not be treating culture merely as a sequence of forms, but rather in terms of the form-meaning-relationship (FMR) complex. Most specifically, however, because meanings (the psychological and behavioral elements) are (1) constantly changing, (2) pose methodological problems (that need not be discussed here), and (3) are projected through the more general description of social relations, we will deal operationally from time to time with form-relationship combinations, or form-meaning combinations, assuming that either case will serve our purposes equally well.

CULTURE CHANGE AND DIFFERENTIAL CONTROL

"Culture change" refers to a number of things. Since no two specific acts of culture can ever be quite the same, culture is always changing in a very real sense. On the other hand, since culture is usually seen to reside also in the continuity of some form-meaning-relational set, change can also refer to a change in the relative continuity among the components of the set. It is the fact of change of the first variety which makes change of the second variety both possible and inevitable. For this discussion we can think of the first as "cultural variation" in the same sense that genetic variation occurs through the impossibility of perfect reduplication in case after case. For the second, we can distinguish the total disappearance of a FMR complex as "deculturation." Since no two societies can have the same social relational sets, "acculturation" can refer to the adoption of forms or a form-meaning set in some new social relational context.[4]

The maintenance of continuity of forms in a meaning-relational association is, in itself, a structuring process. Forms, however, follow their own entropic course, whereas the association of meaning and relationship is ephemeral. Of the two, the only one we will treat here is the relational.

In its simplest form, when man takes elements of the environment, both nonhuman and human, and controls them so as to bring them into some particularly meaningful conjunction, he has "organized" them. When man organizes, he exercises control. "Social organization" is the organization of men plus whatever other elements of the habitat may be relevant for the organization. The formation of a nation, a family, a voluntary association, an *ad hoc* committee, a brief conversation over a drink at a bar with a stranger, or a mob storming the palace, are all organizations, for longer or shorter periods. All are events within which man is exercising his control. However, at the same time that he organizes he also simultaneously is placing some things beyond the control of certain other individuals. The conversation at the bar over a drink precludes the husband being at home with his wife. Any specific relationship established will eliminate a range of possible others. When two people become acquainted, there are some things that are no longer within their power, besides such matter-of-fact things as it being impossible for them to meet as strangers later. So it is that all organizational activities both include and exclude; they place certain other activities beyond the possible control of both the individuals involved as well as others who are without control, merely by being excluded from the activity.

Besides the inclusive and exclusive aspects of organization, there is another set of dimensions which are of particular importance in structuring. There are the dual distinctions between (1) equality or inequality; and if inequality, (2) between superordination or subordination.

All systems in which there is any basis for power differentiation (and this includes all sociocultural systems) pose the question of how this differentiation is to be resolved when there is a conflict. Either the power will be distributed more or less equally or not; if not, some party or actor must be superordinated over others. This means differential control. All complex societies have ordered differentiation.

Once differentiation takes place, the problem of the superordinate actor is to stay on top; one way of doing this is by *exploiting* subordinates, systematically withdrawing power from them. This has the dual advantage of (1) keeping the superordinate strong, and (2) keeping the subordinate weak.

A particular form of exploitation involves the added differentiation of inclusion-exclusion. When the superordinate so controls the subordinate that he can effectively deny him access to controls within the system, then he has *marginalized* him—i.e., excluded him from participation in certain controls of the system. Power in complex societies necessarily involves exploitation and may also involve marginalization. I would propose that marginalization is to be found in *all* expanding complex systems. It occurs because a superordinate cannot *both* maximize its own controls *and* maintain equal distribution of control mechanisms through the system.

Exploitation and marginalization are implicit structuring processes in developing societies. Subordinates systematically lose control, and find the environment regularly more beyond and outside of their control, i.e., more highly structured. Among the specific ways subordinates find themselves increasingly with less control, we may mention four: (1) an increase in the number of people, both absolutely and per organization; (2) an increase in the number of power domains; (3) an increase in the number of levels of integration; and (4) an increase in the number of brokerage roles between levels.

The first of these refers to the fact that every social relational system can handle some minimum and maximum of people; none is infinitely expandable, and obviously each has some minimum number of people necessary for its operation. If the number of people exceeds either the maximum or minimum, the system must adjust; it may do this by excluding the superfluous or by recruiting the missing number. It can also reorganize through new segmentation, thereby duplicating its own form, but also adding devices to interrelate the new social entities. It can also reorganize internally along entirely new dimensions which allow for handling greater numbers.

The point is, obviously, that when excessive numbers of people are either added or lost, there must be a reorganization, and whatever it is, the old organization is forever lost, and the new one introduces some new set of constraints on individuals.

A second variety of structuring that occurs with increased input is the multiplication of power domains. This may be merely the replication of existing domains or the kind of change that follows from increasing the amount of control per capita. As more elements in the environment come under control, this control gravitates towards some central point; concomitant to power concentration is the expansion of the contingent domains. As the amount of power in a relational system changes, the relative amount exercised by any subordinate member is reduced; i.e., relatively less control is held by any individual subordinate member. Note carefully the use of the term "relatively." If the total power in the system is increasing, then total available control is obviously increasing. In comparing the states of such a system over a period of time, subordinate individuals may have more absolute control at a later point than at an earlier; the point is, however, that the superiors will have both relatively and absolutely more.

Closely related to domain expansion is the third kind of social structuring, the increase in the number of levels. A paradigm of this process is as follows: As technology increases the capacity to control the habitat, more of the environment is brought under control. The increasing control, by definition, brings more power into the hands of those who effectively make decisions in the society. As the power per capita increases, the society reorganizes internally such that there is a differential concentration of the power in relatively few hands. This concentration leads to the differentiation of the more powerful from the less, and thereby the emergence of new and higher levels of articulation (or integration). New concentrations of control at higher levels necessarily subordinate individuals and groups operating at lower levels. In this way, the higher levels come to form part of a new environment for the lower level actors. Thus the constrictions change and the environment is restructured for *both* higher and lower level actors. The former now control more of the environment, whereas the latter have been subjected to a new series of controls.

It might be argued that this is a one-sided view, and that increasing technological ability in complex societies provides extraordinary benefits for everyone. Subordinate sectors also have the advantages of hydro-electricity, diesel fuel, large police forces, huge armies, giant libraries, computerized information finding, and so forth. However, the choices allowed to subordinate sectors to determine the scope of their participation in these marvels is severely restricted, and is determined at higher centers of control. What they are allowed is decided for them; they have less control themselves.

As the number of domains and levels increase, so does the problem of articulation between them. One kind of structuring that occurs has been called "brokerage," and refers to the establishment of individuals or groups that articulate actors in different domains and levels. Brokers operate horizontally in some cases, between individuals or domains with roughly equivalent power, but of greater importance are those who operate between levels. Lawyers, labor contractors, foremen, key bureaucrats, secretaries, extension agents, and so on, all play roles which serve to articulate the interests of two different parties, and gain something for themselves by thus serving. The success of brokers requires that people become dependent upon them, thereby changing the environment.

In general, then, structuring social organization follows a complex but not obscure pattern. As domains multiply and complicate, as levels increase in number, as power tends increasingly to concentrate at the top, as brokers multiply between the various parts, the individual anywhere in the system becomes increasingly dependent on mediators, on pieces of the environment which in turn may depend successively on other pieces. As complexity evolves, dependence and lack of control by the individual also evolve; but this evolution is uneven and differentiated, and some individuals have greater success at manipulating the system than others. Whole segments may become categorically segregated because in its complexity it is easier for people to deal with stereotypes and chunks. Some of these chunks progressively lose not only their relative control, but progressively receive less of the increased benefit of the system and, in fact, receive *absolutely* less as time goes on. This whole process leads to marginalization.

There is some value, then, to seeing the whole of human society not as something distinct from and opposed to the habitat, but as simply part of the habitat. After all, the distinction between the natural and the cultural, or the natural and the artificial, is one which exists only within our nervous systems; it exists nowhere in the external world. If we can speak of structuring the habitat, we not only can but should also speak of structuring the social organization and the culture. As development and modernization progress, the entire environment of man becomes more highly structured, more beyond the control of the individual, and more inaccessible and forever lost.

It might be mentioned that Lévi-Strauss' distinction between authentic and unauthentic culture now takes on additional meaning. Unauthentic culture, consisting as it does of those phases of culture found in social relations where there is no concrete, direct contact, obviously proliferates with the increasing complexity and expansion of a society in development. Moreover, the distinction between organization and structure can now be applied directly to culture itself, for in unauthentic relations, it is not possible for the members of a relation to unilaterally reconstruct the nature of the relation and the form-meaning complex. Individuals may cease to participate in it, but it will continue to exist in spite of them. The structuring of social relations in development necessarily also structures the culture. The major exception to Lévi-Strauss' thesis that must be taken in this connection is his lament that this is solely a product of having complex cultures. It is obvious that such structuring existed in primitive societies as well. To voluntarily change language and many other customs also is quite beyond the possibilities of individuals in essentially egalitarian political relations. They are as much the slave of structure as are we; the difference is that they have less man-made structure to contend with.

MARGINALITY AND WASTE

Before continuing with the relation of development to structuring, I want to compare marginalized populations and waste. This will permit us to better examine whether the structuring of the environment and of social relations are analogous or related processes.

Waste is the process and product of human technology that is left over—a residue not of immediate use, to be distinguished from the intended product. We produce wastes at all levels of technology, from the extraction of the raw materials to the industrial processing and ultimate domestic consumption. At all points, residues are cast off into the habitat. These include hard materials, liquid and gaseous products.

Waste is not totally lost to man. When it is not of a readily decomposable variety, it occupies a place in the habitat, creating part of the new structure. In addition, much of it might be reprocessed by a further technology for use in some kind of product, either similar to or distinct from the earlier one, and from which presumably will come further wastes. It is important to note here, however, that the reconversion of wastes requires some additional technological and engineering activities, not merely the same ones used previously.

We have described marginality as the process whereby some human beings have their major controls over operation in a particular system taken from them, so that their remaining autonomy of action does not apparently conflict with the dominant system. For example, there are cases of peasants with no lands who are totally dependent on landholders for their welfare, and whom the landholder then keeps as a labor supply for his private use; these are cases of urban labor kept in a state of periodic unemployment (Marx's "reserve army") or constant underemployment such that they never fully articulate their own controls in the system. Marginal peoples are obviously most often found in the lower or lowest economic strata of a society. However, they are not limited to these strata; they may emerge wherever there is an effective monopoly or oligopoly of control over the survival of a population; or where in some manner the major controls have been taken from the individuals involved.

The obvious similarity between waste and marginal populations has been frequently noted in history. Marginal peoples have often been referred to by those in power as "human garbage" or "human trash." Aside from the folk usage, however, there are important analogies. I would suggest (without being prepared at this point to demonstrate it) that they in fact do share the following features:

(1) The rate of production of these "waste products" varies directly with both the rate of expansion and the technological level of the system. As a system expands through either the extension of present technology or the introduction of new technology, the waste and the production of marginal people also increase.

(2) Some waste and some marginals "decompose" rapidly and effectively reintegrate into the environment. Organic wastes particularly may do this. Among low sector marginal populations the morbidity and mortality are almost always higher than is normal for the society, and they thus literally die off more readily and return to the environment.

(3) Some waste and marginals may be reintegrated into the system, but to do so means that a new technology must be brought into play. A marginal population that does not undertake some new adaptive stance will forever remain marginal. Since they are marginal, because they have no adequate controls, they can leave that situation only by achieving some new set of controls. They may regain controls once lost, or adopt some new ones formerly not available to them.

If one reflects on the situation of Blacks, Chicanos, and Indians in the United States, he observes that they have all suffered severe deculturation as a consequence of their economic and political positions, but in recent years have been creating new organizations, not mere continuations of earlier organizations. The older organization of these marginals usually included a bifurcated set of cultures, one used by the marginals within their own population and seldom known outside because there were no social relationships on which these cultural elements could ride, and a second culture which was their "contact" culture, the culture of their articulation with the dominant groups. This usually strongly reflected the marginals' position—manifesting subdued behavior, non-aggression, tolerance of a high degree of social discrimination, and acceptance of occupation role stereotypes. The "Uncle Tom" syndrome, the classic Chicano "vendido," and the nonagressive reputation of the Puerto Ricans,[6] all reflect particular contact culture of a marginal group, as do the wail of "Sí, patrón" of the

Guatemalan Indian laborer, and the famous stony silence of a group of Andean Indians.

These populations originally underwent systematic deculturation, with some acculturation depending upon the specific politico-economic capabilities of the particular individuals or groups. The Blacks, of course, underwent the severest deculturation of all as slaves. Chicanos have, in fact, retained considerable Mexican quality, but are deculturated to the degree that they have limited access to Mexican sources and cannot afford Anglo substitutes. Surviving American Indians have principally been deculturated and, like Chicanos, vary in their economic possibilities of acculturation.

A new posture is symbolized in "Black Power," "Brown Power," and "Red Power," and manifest in new aggressive organizations. It is not surprising that it is a new generation that takes the lead. The older men may agree and applaud, but it is among the young that learning the new organization, the new "technology," is fastest and easiest. Unfortunately, the successful readaptation of a marginal population requires more than learning to organize aggressively. Organization will make the presence of these groups more apparent, but besides the power implicit in organization, they need the power base of resources. An important feature of the Black Muslims is that they also own property. The Mafia, no matter what else it may do, collectively controls a great deal of real estate. Labor unions have accumulated investments and property so as to become important powers quite independent of their membership.

There is one absolutely crucial difference between marginals and waste: the former are alive and human, and can take positive action in their revindication,[7] whereas the latter can only be reemployed at the hands of some other party. Waste may be reemployed, either by simply being picked up and used for some new purpose, or through a new technology that might be devised whereby a whole class or type of waste may be converted into some usable form (e.g., such as water purification plants, recycling of bottles and cans, use of scrap metal for industrial production, etc.).

Marginal populations have the same two alternatives available to them. In those systems where mobility is possible individuals may escape separately. They may also act collectively, in which case they exercise (what may be for them) a new technology and new controls, and escape the marginal status. Their success depends not merely on their desire and right in some legal sense, but on their ability to make their rights hold in the real world.

Waste and marginals are sufficiently alike both in genesis and process that the analogy is worth more than passing notice. Just as waste requires the application of new technology if it is to be brought back into the system, so marginal populations need new technology if they are to find a more powerful place in the system. Waste and marginals, if neither undergo reprocessing nor disintegration, will remain waste and marginals.

A real test of whether waste and marginality are basically products of a single structuring process, or are merely interesting parallels, might be made by the careful comparison of both in a developing system. Is their emergence roughly proportional in growth? Do they equally represent some characteristic feature of growth? For the present I must leave these unanswered, and proceed on an "as if" basis, i.e., as if they were either one, or sufficiently similar to be so treated. Technology consists of skills and knowledge as well as tools. Presumably the holder of the skill and knowledge is as likely to be outdated as is the tool itself; both can be marginalized by more "advanced" or efficient technology.

THE STRUCTURE OF DEVELOPMENT

We approach the central point of our argument. I have tried to show that in the development of human society, there is a basic similarity, possibly an identity, of the process of habitat and social exploitation and loss of energy, and of the process of complicating society and culture and building up a social and natural environment that is increasingly composed of uncontrollable elements. Thus, the pollution of the ocean is as intractable as the Department of Defense; it proves as hard to get rid of plastic bags as it is to rid oneself of salesmen or bureaucrats. Governments, when they attempt the latter, usually resort to the same process for both, i.e., trash dumps and old peoples' homes (or trash homes and old peoples' dumps).

What has happened is that the process of development itself has become structured. That is, within the community of nations of the world, the problem of development is not merely one of economic well-being, but one of political survival. Nations failing to develop economically find their political inferiority increasing; they find that they *must* develop, whether they wish to or not. I have referred to this process as "structural escalation."[8] Nations are caught up in a structural process, i.e., a process beyond their control, in which they find themselves having to develop, and to take steps to increase their controls. Like it or not, a special value has been placed on increasing input into the society, on extending their controls, on incorporating more of the habitat, on enlarging their organization.

If it is so that the amount of structure in a system increases with the development of that system, then it follows that the more highly developed sectors will be more highly structured; through achieving greater controls, they have also created new structure both for themselves and for other less developed members of the world community.

Let us differentiate between three distinct but interdependent patterns of development (only the first two of which are usually considered to be modernization): primary, secondary, and marginal development.[9] Primary development sets up the hinterland basis for secondary development, and marginal development occurs as a concomitant of both. Both primary and secondary development generate marginal sectors. While these sectors usually have clearcut geographical dimensions, they are not necessarily congruent with national boundaries or with the rural-urban dichotomy.

Primary development refers to that leading industrial sector which finds its principal home and expanding base in the major industrial countries of the northern hemisphere. However, it has outposts elsewhere, and through the emergence of the transnational corporations, it may involve multiple nationalities. "Underdeveloped nations" are characterized by that combination of borrowing and readaptation that we have called secondary development. While secondary development usually characterizes only the underdeveloped nations, even those with relatively high industrialization, marginal development is to be found in both primary and secondary areas. Appalachia, the Carolina coast, Andean highlands, and southern Italy are rural, and the ghettos and slums are urban manifestations. Marginality applies to the condition in which certain populations (in both primary and secondary nations) find themselves relegated to the least remunerative activities, to manual labor and semiskilled work, dependent upon interest quite beyond their control.

MARGINALIZATION: BY-PRODUCT OF DEVELOPMENT

Marxist theorists hold that marginality is entirely a product of the process of capitalism; I see it as a by product of the power concentrations of *all* complex societies. Most Latin American theorists, I believe, hold to the first view. It is true that most developed capitalist economies can rarely keep the entire labor force in full employment, and the least skilled and those socially least able to fend for themselves are consigned to unemployment or underemployment. In secondary areas this entire condition is badly exacerbated by the introduction of capital intensive technologies. The other side of the picture is that any developing complex society will, through progressive concentrations of power at higher levels, necessarily produce greater subordination, and this inherently makes the employment picture dependent on the power interests of those who control the societies. The most apparent overt difference between socialist and capitalist countries, in this respect, seems to be that in socialist countries marginality tends to be manifest more in economic underemployment and exclusion from political participation, rather than in the unemployment and underparticipation in politics that characterizes capitalist countries.

Marginalized peoples are those furthest removed from the centers of power and decisionmaking within any national society. It is possible to distinguish varieties of the marginalizing process, from that of an almost purely economic variety most commonly found in the poorest agrarian hinterlands of secondary capitalistic development, to an almost purely political variety, more characteristic of advanced socialist nations. Underemployment, however, is a product of technological advancement, and no matter what its overt form, it cannot help but make itself felt in advanced socialist and capitalist nations alike. Nations differ in the specific devices that have been invented to provide the necessary level of economic subsistence for such populations, but in general capitalist nations tend to manifest unemployment coupled wth welfare and charity systems, whereas socialist nations, as mentioned earlier, tend to rely on more widespread underemployment.

Marginal populations are often ethnically distinct, as are the Blacks and Chicanos in the United States, the Indians in Middle America and the Andes, the Chaqueños, Bolivians and Chileans in Argentina, the Lapps in Norway, the south European laborers in northern Europe, Blacks and Colored peoples in South Africa, and so forth. However, ethnicity is merely a differentiating marker, and not a fundamental functional component of technological and economic inferiority, or of geographical ghettoization.

The process of development brings in its train the emergence of a number of distinctive population components. Within the primary areas are the skilled laboring populations and the middle class. In the secondary areas there has emerged a vast tertiary sector, composed of employed and underemployed, involved in all sorts of middle and lower economic level activities dependent upon the drippings from the expanding industrial and agrarian sectors. The stable middle class that nineteenth century liberal planners envisaged for Argentina, Mexico, and the other areas of rampant economic liberalism seldom appeared in the form desired. The middle sector that emerged was neither stable nor very middle class. Instead, it was poor, and insofar as access to the better leavings was possible, it formed the underpinnings of the upper sector. The growing tertiary sector of Latin America is history's answer to the effort to duplicate industrial middle classes of the primary nations.

The recognition that the process of modernization includes delaying the development of secondary areas and producing marginal sectors is an important addition to our understanding during the past thirty years. In this regard it is important to clarify the broader role of the primary nations. Not only have human populations been seriously subordinated, but the habitat itself is reacting with violence. The combined threats of overpopulation and environmental destruction have become so apparent that even Catholic countries are quietly exploring solutions for the first, and both primary and secondary areas are suffering the byproducts of industrial success. Although still far from satisfactory solution, the real ecological problems that surround us are so overwhelmingly obvious that politicians as well as journalists, scholars, and just plain people are looking to save the habitat.

Both the worst conditions and the greatest concern are manifest in primary areas and their immediate hinterlands; but the carnage of industrial and technological expansion is also in evidence in secondary areas, where it receives considerably less attention. If we explore the reasons behind the secondary area's apparent lethargy in attacking these problems, we find that it is not an absolute disinterest in problems of pollution, but rather a more overbearing interest in expansion and development. If the primary nations suffer pollution, at least they have higher standards of living to show for it. Secondary areas might be more willing to overlook the disadvantages of this facet of modernization if they, too, had access to the advantages.[10] So the response, in its most cynical form, is to put off concern until development is achieved. In matters of population control, there are still segments of the upper sectors in Latin America which insist on seeing population increase as a crucial index of national expansion and growth—and so it would be for their labor force interests.

The same reasoning that is behind this lack of interest on the part of secondary areas is also grossly manifest in primary areas. The best excuse the United States government has been able to give for not taking more expensive precautions for preserving the habitat and for improving the circumstances of its own marginal populations is that our national security is threatened by the guerrillas of Southeast Asia. Our own expansive interests, because they are deemed necessary to our survival, take precedence over the problems of marginal populations and the habitats of the world.

As in other matters, the marginal populations suffer the most. One of the less explored facets of this problem is the unidentified number of dead from contact with new lethal insecticides and herbicides. Miners of West Virginia and elsewhere in the world still enjoy one of the lowest life expectancies in the so-called civilized world. Incredibly high DDT counts have been reported in mothers' milk of rural Guatemalan women unprotected from the heavy doses of insecticides and herbicides used by cotton farmers. [11]

The reason to discuss these different kinds of development is not to reiterate their obvious differences but to indicate that they are all products of the same process, the increased extraction of energy from the environment, and the increased structuring of the society and habitat resulting therefrom. Marginalization and secondary development are not some kind of developmental lag, but are intrinsic parts of the developmental process when a few nations develop technologically at a rate far in advance of others. What some people have seen as the "dislocation resulting from modernization" is an intrinsic part of modernization. Primary development is clearly the most destructive of all, and it is therefore the advanced nations and the advanced sectors of secondary areas that generate the greatest problems of pollution and waste in the habitat and force the greatest cultural and social changes in the society. It is the colonial world that has, naturally, seen the most extensive amount of deculturation. What is less realized outside the areas where this has occurred is that the process of development, beginning with the industrial revolution and its spread through nineteenth century liberalism, through colonial and quasi-colonial processes, brought sufficient derived power into the non-European areas of the world for this particular phase of cultural destruction to be inevitable and intense.

This deculturation calls for considerably more than sentimentality; it is attendant on development not only in the traditional areas, but occurs with equal violence in primary areas. There is a cardinal difference, however. Culture change in primary areas usually occurs with a replacement by new elements, new forms, new sets of meanings and often new social relations. When it occurs in secondary areas, as often as not it is simply deculturation, a restriction of social relations; and where replacements occur, they may be leftovers from the primary areas. New cultural forms in secondary areas have greater problems of acceptance, and when one turns to marginal populations, it is sheer deculturation, with little or no cultural replacement and few new cultural forms developing from local sources of technological and economic growth. Obviously, since these populations do not have access to the productive resources of the primary areas, their cultural regrowth has to depend upon residues of their earlier culture and the limited possibilities that a damaged environment permits. Inventions occur regularly in any society, and they occur just as much in marginalized populations as in primary or secondary. Were cultural growth sheerly a matter of intellect and imagination, these populations might well outstrip the technologically advantaged, if for no other reason than that is the major material with which they have to work. Yet insofar as cultural growth is measured in terms of the development of external forms through which the society increases control over the environment, then the marginalized necessarily are, in fact, kept in a subordinate position, a position generally characterized by relative social fragmentation and deculturation.

Whatever answers there may be to the challenge, a continuing expansion of technological control in primary areas must by its very nature bring further structuring in its train. The more successful a society is in its expansion and control over other societies and over the habitat, the greater is the structuring of the habitat, and the greater is the lack of control of any single operating unit within the domains of power thus created. It is clearly the primary areas that are most directly involved in this. It is no adverse reflection on the intellectual qualities of Argentine and Egyptian scientists and engineers to observe that their satellites are not yet circling the earth; it

merely reflects where they stand in terms of the overall picture of development.

OPTIONS FOR THE PRIMARY NATIONS

The idea that primary areas are in any sense retreating from overt dominance is illusory when one looks at the power structure of the world.
Whatever the Third World may be politically, it clearly remains technologically dependent on the primary powers. It is somewhat ironic, then, when
we look to the kinds of solutions that have been tentatively suggested for the
solution to underdevelopment. Western politicians and economists have
now gone through a large kit bag of efforts, none of which has proved very
successful. Economists have recently begun proposing that innovations in
labor-intensive technology for underdeveloped areas may be a solution,
indeed an impending necessity for secondary and marginal sections. This is a
step in the right direction, but one might go further and ask whether the
same kind of thinking might not be applied to primary areas. At this point,
most primary area thinking has revolved around ways to increase consumption and recreational activities, to reduce the number of days being worked.
These are steps in the right direction, but so long as production increases, so
must waste. May we not need a system which reduces production of goods
and activities that are environmentally costly and socially restrictive? If we
merely increase recreational areas, along with expanding population and
recreational time, we will merely exacerbate the problems of the habitat.

At the same time in the real world of Western economic expansion, the
giant transnational conglomerates have come into view. Partisans of these
enterprises argue that they can achieve international peace since they carry
technical knowledge to other parts of the world and mix the bureaucrats and
laborers of many nations; indeed, it has even been suggested that they might
replace governments, since they will be shortly wealthier than most nations
on earth. [12]

Both views are illusory. These international behemoths still have a clearcut national allegiance, and a dominant technological base. If they are asked,
"Whose side are you on?" they can readily answer. The expansion of industry
and commerce through such organizations is part of the expansion of the
primary nations, individually and collectively. The difference between them-

and their predecessors is that they have given up hook-and-line fishing for the greater yield offered by net fishing—or if seen from another view, they have taken to fish poisoning.

Societies which have achieved a level of primary development, for whatever reason (and while unquestionably important, how this occurs is a question that takes us somewhat afield of the present discussion),[13] have developed a set of values and behaviors that promote the expansion of the society. Increased praying, or spinning a prayer wheel, it can be argued, leads to no significant expansion of the society. However, the production of Krupp armor piercing shells, Coca Cola, Fiat diesel locomotives, or Ely Lilly drugs is a different story, for not only are natural resources being exploited and expended but the products are transforming the environment. Furthermore, the production of these elements contributes to the expansion of their producing society so long as consumers can be found. Such consumers are first found in the home ground; but these soon prove not to be enough, for it is hard to argue that every home should have two or three diesel locomotives. So the secondary development areas are important areas of expansion for the primary nations.[14]

Socialist analysts argue that the process is unique to the capitalist world, and that it is not so in socialist countries. More extremist partisans hold that only total isolation from the capitalist world could bring about the development of currently underdeveloped areas. It is certainly true that the process of growth by capitalism is one way that these developmental differences occur, but the mere conversion to another political system does not resolve the harder ecological-sociological relationships of environmental control. Building dams and steel plants, obtaining arms, ammunition, drugs, and medical processes are as much a part of Chinese and Russian national expansion as they are in capitalistic nations. The increase of production per capita and smog levels are equally products of both political systems. In addition, underdeveloped nations continue to need foreign capital and techniques at critical points in their own growth, and the primary nations have to date been the major providers of these elements.

The problem simply is not one that will be eliminated by changing the political system, although political action surely has a role to play if anything is to be done. The question, however, is to what degree the human world has structured itself into an untenable position, built itself an environment that is increasingly impossible to handle, and created a series of disparate ways of life that depend upon the continued escalation of competitive control over the environment.

THE CONTROL OF STRUCTURING: REDUCTION OF PRIMARY DEVELOPMENT

We are confronted with an apparent dilemma. The more our technology improves so that we control more of the environment, the more we succeed in complicating and enlarging the uncontrollable portion of the environment. The more we exploit the habitat, the more it becomes unexploitable; the more we organize society, the more resistent it becomes to our abilities to organize it. The more the primary industrial nations advance their technology, the less chance there is for the secondary nations to achieve some kind of parity with the primary nations. The more primary and secondary development, the more it seems that populations become marginalized. Two processes which have heretofore been regarded as separate, one ecological and the other socioeconomic, are here being looked at as if they were in fact one. To summarize how we see this, we can characterize it now in terms of a single process, the harnessing of technological development.

When a society has an improving technology, more of the habitat is extracted and converted into product, waste, and entropy. Energy is channeled (i.e., expended and converted) into products which permit both the biological expansion of the population and the use of a constantly increasing amount of energy per capita. To *use* this constantly increasing amount of energy, the society invents ways to allocate it, and among the major ways to expend this energy is to use technological processes that are increasingly energy-costly (i.e., have a high energy cost for a small increase or improvement of a product), and to expend greater amounts of time in nonproductive activities. Thus it is that not only *can* bureaucracies grow into large "do-nothing" monsters, but in so doing they are operating functionally since they are energy-costly and nonproductive. The process of building big, clumsy, inefficient social organizations is just as good a way as any of getting rid of the incredible amount of energy that has been brought under control, and it can be argued that it may well be better than war.

Great energy build-ups occur as societies develop, and as more energy gets into a system its control becomes ever more important. The process is obscured, however, because energy takes many forms—indeed, *all* forms —and no society has ever attempted or wanted to evaluate its activities and cultural life in terms of energy. Nevertheless, the importance of energy control becomes clear when we see that in expanding societies, *some* individuals in fact do get control over the crucial energy forms, and *these* individuals are those who are most important in determining what happens in the society.

Moreover, the process used by individuals who act as the collecting points of energy concentration is, in principle, the same for those dealing with inanimate matter (e.g., making atomic piles) as those dealing with social relations (e.g., running the economic growth of the United States petroleum industry). In both cases, concentration of energy requires the expenditure of a great deal of energy. The process of unleashing the energy harnessed in the nucleus of an atom requires not only complex economic, political and social controls, but the unleashing itself releases to entropy a huge quantity of energy. Similarly, the building up of Standard Oil was done through the marginalizing of countless small producers, and the construction of the oil industry today, certainly one of the most powerful in the United States, involves keeping essentially oligarchic controls over the entire petroleum business. Consumers, retail dealers, laborers, technicians, and executives are all marginalized, as is the United States government itself to some degree. Generations of people have been employed and unemployed in terms of the welfare of an enterprise, and few devices have been established whereby they, or even the owners of shares, could really control the companies. Even the owners can be marginalized. The great social structure built around United States industrial growth has been extraordinarily energy-costly; it had to be. Such growth could not have been achieved apart from such energy cost.

Turning back to development in the world at large, there seem to be these inescapable conclusions: (1) technologies are being developed principally for the forward advance of the primary nations; (2) this advance of the primary nations slows the developmental process of secondary nations; and (3) the pattern of development in both primary and secondary nations is to increase energy-costs, i.e., increase conversion to waste, marginality, and entropy in order to hasten the process of development.

One obvious response to the problem expressed in this form could be to seek some form of development that is less wasteful and marginalizing. Two kinds of alternatives offer themselves: (1) to devise new developmental processes of technology and society that concentrate on renewable energy resources and on the reharnessing of waste and marginal products; and (2) to reduce the rate of the developmental effort so that absolutely less of the total environment (habitat and society) is reduced to waste and marginality. The first of these has been the most common response to date, and any discussion of it would require entering into the fast growing and technically complex literature on ecology and natural resources. The second, however, has been less openly discussed, and has been broached mainly in individual cases, such as the termination of the SST and in the attempts to eliminate work on biological warfare. There may be little to be gained in a discussion of the reduction in developmental efforts among secondarily developed nations, since their goal is quite the contrary. When one reviews the tragic levels of living that are still in evidence throughout much of the world, it is obvious that wherever development may be reduced, it should not be in those secondary areas.

The remaining alternative is to reduce the destructive and marginalizing effects of primary development. Emphasis in primary countries needs to be placed on the development of technologies that do not necessarily lead to their continuing primacy, but rather to a more rational survival technology for both the habitat and the human population. Since it is the primary technologies that are doing the major damage, it becomes not merely a question of finding technologies designed to avoid waste and marginality, but to materially reduce the rampant operation of the primary technologies.

After all, a core problem of the underdeveloped or traditional areas lies in the fact that the primary nations have thus far found themselves incapable of controlling their own developmental processes. Their development has been a major contributor to the fouling of the habitat, to the unleashing of the full dimensions of human reproduction, to the widening of the technological gap, and to carrying the horrors of professional killing to a new high. I cannot, offhand, think of one really major developmental problem shared by underdeveloped nations which is not in part traceable to the accelerating development of the primary nations. If they are a major source of the problem then it is among them that solutions must be sought. To frame the problems of modernization in terms of dealing *only* with the dependent portions of the equation is naive. To the degree that the problems of secondary and marginal areas are generated by the primary sectors, their solutions must also be sought in the primary areas.

Development in advanced nations is apparently suffering from structural escalation, an escalation that is beyond control of most if not all actors. Increased environmental and social control has been given top priority within the systems, and the culture reflects this by threatening extinction if the society fails to expand. The answer would seem to lie in restraining this escalation of competitive development. There is little possibility of reducing the technological gap between primary and secondary areas in the foreseeable future so long as the present growth competition continues; on the contrary, it seems destined to continue to expand. While economists address themselves to this in economic terms, its significance in social and cultural terms is clear; continuing marginalization and problems of secondary development on the one hand, and the continuing destruction of the habitat on the other.

It seems inevitable that part of the solution must lie in decelerating the growth of primary powers, their constant expansion, their voracious consumption of raw materials, and their gigantic production of consumption goods for an unready world. Deceleration of the growth of the primary areas would both reduce their demands on the secondary areas and their structuring of the environment. There are obviously a mass of problems and questions implicit in this alternative, not the least of which is whether it is pragmatically possible. There are not many well documented cases in human history of societies which, while apparently still in expansion, undertook the intentional and planned deceleration of their own growth. A few possible cases (without respect to quality of documentation) that come to mind include the restriction of population growth through advancing the age of men marrying in Ireland following the great famine of the nineteenth century, and the institution of female infanticide by some Australian aboriginal groups due possibly to the loss through ecological inadequacy. In both these instances (both of which concern specifically population expansion) the restrictions were probably imposed only after disaster struck. Is it possible for human societies to undertake to restrict their own growth *before* disaster overtakes them? Certainly if catastrophe alone were enough, then the famines and plagues that have periodically appeared in India would long since have led to some kind of local control devices; if they have, there is little evidence to show that they have worked.

Moreover, the problem here is not merely a question of population control but of control of technological and economic expansion and the related habitat exploitation processes. Insofar as I know, the only cases of reduction of economic growth have occurred through the fairly simple but harsh process of losing out in some competition, either economic, political (i.e., human competitors) or ecological (i.e., nonhuman competitors). Since restriction in growth means reducing the expansion of controls over the environment, one obvious outcome would be that other expanding systems would take advantage of the restrictions to better their own situation.

The fact that the state of the world today is more threatening to the welfare of humanity than has been the case earlier is probably quite irrelevant in this context. Humanity is in no sense a single organization, and all evidence makes it clear that decisions are made in terms of ideologies of particular groups (sometimes national, sometimes not) and not in terms of the survival of the world or humanity as a whole. Nor is this unreasonable; most peoples of the world face more immediate threats than the demise of the world population, and if their ideologies are to have survival value, they have to be apt in terms of more immediate problems.

The suggestion is, then, that controls need to be exercised over the process of structuring if we are to have a world in which life is to be made better for all mankind, and not merely the primary area populations and the lucky or clever niche holders in secondary areas. It is also proposed that the process of growth, expansion, and structuring by the primary areas is itself structural, i.e., is itself uncontrollable. Does this mean that there is no possibility of achieving some control over this process? The answer to this is that it depends upon the nature of the structuring.

Remember that "structure" in this formulation refers to those aspects of the total environment which are beyond man's control. Theoretically we can sort out those things "beyond control" into those which *might* be brought under control, given an appropriate technology; and those things which theoretically can never be brought under control. The progress of science has been, of course, to bring more and more things under control; it has also made us more aware of the difficulty and even the impossibility of bringing certain others under control.

We may be able to recover marginals and waste, if we can achieve the social and cultural devices necessary. However, we will never be able to convert the smoke, gases and ash that were once a house back into that house; nor will we be able to reconstruct the intricate form-meaning social relational complexes that once composed an aboriginal culture. We know the differences between the extreme cases of structure and organization, but for most problems we will not know ahead of time whether technologies can be devised. The notion of structuring, however, reminds us that *if* we do devise a technology for some kind of organization, we will thereby necessarily also be adding in some fashion to structure.

Returning to the principal question at hand, is it possible to devise technologies, means of organizing man and his habitats, so as to stay the process of structural escalation, to slow down the development of primary powers, to thereby release greater development of secondary areas and, finally, to reintegrate marginal populations so that they have some real autonomy of self-development?

I confess that at present my impression is that such a series of eventualities could only take place under very severe and stressful circumstances. Man has not been known for his self-effacement or humbleness, or readiness to give up one ideology for another. Human societies change, but insofar as they follow any plan it is a plan representing some limited set of interests.

However, if we were to achieve such a difficult goal, what would we then have? Referring back to points already made, we would:

(1) Reduce efforts to develop technologies that will serve only the advance of primary nations, and concentrate scientific and engineering efforts on problems of development of secondary areas, and on problems in the huge realm of structures—i.e. biology, medicine, pollution, birth and mortality control, urban planning and design; in short, all those areas that are currently regarded as of secondary importance in comparison with the expansion and maintenance of defense and war-making establishments. To reduce the growth curve of primary nations does not mean to reduce scientific and technological development. It does mean to drastically re-orient its activities, and to see to a major reinforcement for the scientific establishments of secondary areas.

(2) There should be clarification of the ways in which economic and technological growth in secondary areas are related to growth in primary areas. To date insufficient attention has been given to the actual mechanisms at work. Study of the varying forms of dependency is important, as political interests have led many things to be included under what is at present a very crude category.

(3) The reduction and virtual elmination of waste and marginality would have to be seen as a major goal. The whole assumption that development requires increasing energy-costly activities would have to be discarded.

Technology and planning would be directed toward low energy cost activities, toward dependence on renewable resources and gradual move away from rampant exploitation of non-renewable resources.

Is it possible to begin to take steps in these directions? Again, it is possible, even though terribly unlikely. If primary areas could devise ways to decelerate their growth, the structuring process would be slowed. However, if dependency exists between primary and secondary nations, then such a decision would be workable *only if* it were made jointly by both areas. Were the primary nations to cut back severely on their structuring processes, only to have the secondary nations accelerate theirs in a sheerly competitive way, then the gains of control by one set of parties would be quickly neutralized or negated by the other. The dialectic that exists within the primary-secondary relationship is still far from well understood, but if we argue that to deal with the secondary areas alone will not bring about adequate development, it is equally obvious that the control of primary areas alone will not achieve a desirable reduction in the rate of structuring.

It should be clear by now that the discussion has taken a utopian turn. We speak of things which *might* provide serious solutions *if* there were any way of reaching them. There is no evidence that nations are going to forego their "manifest destinies;" that the superpowers will give up their expansive manias, or their ideological rationales; that underdeveloped nations, if given the chance, would not try to achieve the same expansive careers as their more industrialized predecessors. There is, unfortunately, absolutely no evidence so far that human societies can consider the condition of humanity as a whole above their own national interests, nor even hold in check their own national expansion short of overwhelming evidence of impending catastrophe.

On the other hand, it is not clear that these things are entirely beyond possibilities of control; and so long as there is some possibility of harnessing development for the good of mankind, so long as there remains a possibility of controlling control, then we must continue to worry about the problem. As it stands now, development has apparently moved out of control; it is producing good and evil indiscriminately.

NOTES

[1]This development is associated principally with the names of Oswaldo Sunkel, Anibal Quijano, Fernando Cardoso, and a number of other Latin Americans, as well as Andre Gunder Frank.

[2]This fact has received attention in recent years from former colonial areas where systematic attempts have been made to recover older culture forms, a patently frustrating exercise and an impossible one if done with any thought given to imbuing them with their former meanings. The concerns with Black history, Chicano history, and the revisionism now current in American Indian history all reflect the motive of recovering and reinstalling some of the virtues of the older cultures. Parallel efforts followed the Mexican Revolution, the Cuban Revolution and presumably will continue to occur at any time that a society undertakes to reject its condition of dependence and seek autonomous action.

[3]The discussion of culture in this section is not intended to break any new ground, but merely place emphasis on some aspects of the phenomenon that will be used later in the essay.

[4]Other varieties of change are distinguishable, but are not necessary in the context of the present discussion.

[5]*Authentic* culture is a set of forms and meanings that exist within some "concrete relations between individuals." *Unauthentic* forms are those which link individuals at a distance and through abstract intermediaries, such as through administrative or political arrangements. ("Valemos nos mais que os selvagens," an interview with Claude Lévi-Strauss published in *Mito e linguagen social* edited by Roberto Cardoso de Oliveira, et al., Rio de Janeiro, Tempo Brasileiro, 1970, p. 144. The translation is mine.)

[6]Frank Bonilla, "Beyond Survival: Porque seguiremos siendo Puertoriqueños," ms., 1971. A perusal of criticisms made by Bonilla on reading the first draft of this paper led me to add this section on marginality and waste. Whether or not it deals adequately with the problems he raised, I am indebted to him for requiring me to think further on the matter.

[7]The term "revindication" occurs through the Latin American literature on dependency and marginality; it refers to gaining some set of conditions that permit a given population an adequate set of controls and participation. Its usage is symbolic in that it implies regaining a human condition that exists in the most primitive of human societies.

[8]*Crucifixion By Power: Essays in the National Social Structure of Guatemala, 1944-1966* (Austin: University of Texas Press, 1970), pp. 89-94.

[9]The primary-secondary distinction is elaborated upon in my *The Second Sowing:*

Power and Secondary Development in Latin America (San Francisco, 1967). Marginality is
being specifically defined here for the present argument.

[10]This is, of course, an exaggeration; in fact, there are planners and politicians in
underdeveloped areas who are very active in these problems. Unfortunately, they are
in a weak minority as yet when in competition with developmental or private
interests.

[11]Personal communication, Tagli Farvar.

[12]The literature on this topic is growing rapidly; the comments made here are in
particular response to a review by Robert Heilbroner, "The Multinational Corporation and the Nation-State," *New York Review of Books* (Vol. XVI, No. 2, Feb. 11,
1971: pp. 20-26).

[13]See reference, footnote 9.

[14]Proponents of the filter-down theory of economic development would presumably hold that even the marginal populations will eventually benefit by primary area
expansion.

4

When one thinks of "modernization" it is often in terms of something new acquired from the West. More often than not, the new items thought about are material in nature—a new steel mill, a dam, a road, or new high-yield seeds. Charles Leslie draws our attention to another aspect of modernization—the crucial role played by systems of ideas, as exemplified by the historical changes in Asian medical systems. He also points to a conscious process of the selective retention of ancient and contemporary aspects of medical knowledge that may be a general feature of modernization around the world.

The Modernization of Asian Medical Systems

CHARLES LESLIE

Charles M. Leslie is a professor in the Department of Anthropology at New York University and received his Ph.D. from the University of Chicago. Professor Leslie has done field work in Mexico and India, and is currently interested in medical anthropology and modernization. His major publications include Now We Are Civilized *(1960), an account of change in a Mexican Indian city,* Anthropology of Folk Religion *(1960), and a forthcoming volume,* Toward the Comparative Study of Asian Medical Systems.

Modernization is a long-term and self-conscious historical movement. Being modern, or wanting to become modern, means defining one's self in opposition to some aspects of received tradition. Yet modernity has developed its own traditions. Artists and scientists build upon the modernity of their forebears, and generations of men and women have transmitted more or less modern cultures to their children. Rather than assuming that tradition and modernity are categorical opposites, as those who study modernization processes sometimes do, we should try to understand the traditional dimensions of modernization.

Whether one traces the origins of modernity from the Italian Renaissance, the Reformation, or the transformations of the eighteenth and nineteenth centuries, modernizing movements have never been totally antitraditional. On the contrary, such movements in Western society and throughout the world have characteristically looked forward by looking backward. They have encouraged an experimental attitude toward social and cultural change, in opposition to a rigid holding-on to established forms, in part by searching the past for more authentic traditions. Modernizing movements in Western society have looked back to Greek and Roman antiquity, and alternately, in the Gothic Revival and some forms of socialism, to the Middle Ages. Or, to take another example, anthropology is a modernizing form of social thought that has looked to a past in which men lived in a hypothetical state of nature, to the "living antiquity" of contemporary folk societies, and to the archaeological remains of preliterate and early civilizations. Evolutionary conceptions of human nature and of cultural history, which form the core of anthropology, have established for modern people a traditional conception of themselves as living in a progressive, changing world.

In sum, my first point is that modernity is not traditionless, and although it favors social and cultural change, it is selectively rather than categorically opposed to institutions and modes of thought handed down from the past.

I emphasize the ideological aspect of modernizing movements, but modern ideologies are functionally and causally related to historical changes in social organization and technology. As my subject is Asian medicine, I will summarize these changes by contrasting traditional and modern civilizations. Modern society shares urban settlement patterns, stratified class systems, complex occupational structures and differentiated religious and state and market institutions with the traditional civilizations. However, in modern society production comes to be dominantly industrial rather than craft organized, the scale of social institutions shifts to mass society structures rather than rural-urban regional structures, and proletariat and middle-class institutions displace peasant and artisan institutions. In the context of these changes, the ratio of achieved to ascribed statuses shifts in favor of achievement, and this shift changes and increases the role of knowledge in human affairs.

I have reached my second point, which is that we attribute great importance to the character and social role of knowledge in modern society. In particular, we believe that scientific knowledge and institutions played a necessary causal role in the modernization of Western society. Galileo, Kepler, Newton, and Harvey are men whose ideas were prime forces in the transformations of world view and technology essential to modernity, and yet, in the study of non-Western societies, there has been relatively little concern with the corresponding role of knowledge and ideas in the modernization process.

Western social scientists interested in modernization processes in Asian countries have neglected indigenous scientific traditions, apparently assuming that the only scientific knowledge and institutions relevant to modernity are Western. This Western-science ethnocentricism is consistent with the tendency to assume that modernity is categorically antitraditional, and that *we* are modern while *they* are traditional. It is reinforced by the conviction that no traditional civilization could have created knowledge with the culturally transforming qualities of modern science other than one based upon the achievements of ancient Greece. This conviction is often expressed by Western scholars. For example, Erwin Schrodinger, a Nobel Laureate in physics who wrote on the evolution of the scientific world view, had this to say, quoting John Burnett's *Early Greek Philosophy*:

> It is an adequate description of science to say that it is "thinking about the world in the Greek way." That is why science has never existed except among peoples who came under the influence of Greece (1956:102).

Western-science ethnocentricism is widespread among philosophers and historians of science, and it is even found among historians who argue that the revival of Greek culture in the Renaissance retarded the growth of science, delaying the scientific revolution until the seventeenth century.

Schrodinger's argument in this case is that the Greeks created traditions which were necessarily antecedent to the evolution of modern science, the development of which required the overcoming of Greek tradition.

I want to make a final preliminary observation. In studying nineteenth and twentieth century Hindu medical institutions, I was impressed by the mixture of stethoscopes and astrology, modern knowledge and appeals to the authority of ancient texts; however, I have found similar patterns in the history of Western science. The Swiss medical philosopher Paracelsus (1490-1514) was an early and militant leader in the development of modern medicine. Although he rejected the works of the second century Greek physician and philosopher Galen by appealing to the superior authority of Hippocrates, he was nonetheless a strong believer in astrology. Vesalius, a Flemish anatomist (1514-1564), criticized the teaching of anatomy in his day, but he believed that his own work was in the tradition of Galen. The work of William Harvey (1578-1657) on the circulaton of the blood was in historical perspective a refutation of Galenic physiology, but Harvey considered himself to be working in the tradition of Galen and quoted the Greek physician to support his arguments. In fact, despite criticisms of it, humoral medicine continued to be taught in Western medical schools until the germ theory of disease, genetics, and chemotherapy developed in the late nineteenth and twentieth centuries.

Scientific knowledge is thought to evolve in a cumulative manner that distinguishes its history from that of religion, art, and politics. For this reason, the contemporary revival of early Hindu and Arabic medicine seems retrogressive to many practitioners of modern medicine in South Asia and to Western doctors who have worked there. These doctors should realize that medical revivalism is not solely a recent phenomenon, or limited to Asia. For example, in sixteenth century Italy new translations of Hippocratic and Galenic writings encouraged progressive changes in the medical curriculum and in methods of instruction. Professor C. D. O'Malley writes:

> Hence it was, under the influence of the revival and recovery of Greek medicine and especially of Hippocratic medicine, that clinical, bedside teaching gained a new importance and a definite place in the curriculum . . . The introduction of clinical teaching within the medical school so that the students as a group accompanied their teacher to the bedsides of the ill, both to observe their physician-teacher's methods

and to practice those methods under his observation and direction, was a phenomenon of the sixteenth century and a product of the Italian medical schools. (1970:95)

Thus, I will argue in this paper that we may better understand modernization processes in Asian countries by studying them as they are manifested in the domain of scientific institutions; and we may learn about the modernization of our own traditions by the comparative study of Asian science. Medical institutions are particularly accessible to this kind of study because they are well documented. Furthermore, because Asian medicine is widely practiced, it can be studied directly and in detail. Such study should be a corrective to Western-science ethnocentricism, and it may have practical value for people who want to improve the delivery of medical services to Asian communities.

THE GREAT TRADITIONS OF SCIENTIFIC MEDICINE

Three scientific medical systems evolved during antiquity and in the Old World and are still practiced in learned and folk tradition forms. These are the Greek, Ayurvedic, and Chinese medical systems. In the nineteenth and twentieth centuries the practitioners of these medical systems have been greatly influenced by the evolution of modern medical knowledge and professional institutions. Most Asian countries provide for the registration of practitioners of both Asian and modern medicine, and in many places schools, research institutes, pharmaceutical companies, and associations of practitioners cultivate Asian medical traditions. My own research has been in India and will provide the primary case material for this essay, but I must first describe the three systems of antiquity.

Greek medicine developed around the Mediterranean Basin, receiving its most complete formulation in the work of Galen during the second century A.D. This tradition was continued in Christian and Islamic societies during the Middle Ages, and was carried to South and Southeast Asia with the spread of Islam. The classical texts of Greek science and medicine were translated into Arabic, and medical learning flourished between the eighth and fourteenth centuries. The system was called Unani, or Greek Medicine, and is still practiced in Pakistan, India, Ceylon, and other countries under that name.

In South Asia and in China two other great medical traditions developed and diffused to distant societies. The South Asian system was called Ayurveda, which means "knowledge of life" or "longevity," and though Arabic physicians were certainly familiar with its leading texts, it may have been taken to the Mediterranean area at an earlier period. Plato, for example, may have been influenced by Ayurvedic concepts (Filliozat, 1964). More certainly, the spread of Buddhism to China was accompanied by exchanges of Ayurvedic and Chinese medical knowledge. Yet Chinese medicine was distinct from the Ayurvedic and Mediterranean medical systems and was in turn carried to Korea, Japan, and Southeast Asia with other Chinese influences.[1]

Despite contact between their nuclear areas during their formulation, the Mediterranean, South Asian, and Chinese medical systems achieved their classic great tradition form under conditions of relative isolation, and they each developed distinctive theories and practices. One can, however, point to generic characteristics that they have in common: (1) they became professional branches of learning based upon secular scientific theories in the millennium between the fifth century B.C. and the fifth century A.D.; (2) professionalization was achieved by standardizing learned practice through appeal to the authority of texts (the Hippocratic Corpus, Galen, the Saṁhitā of Charaka and Susruta, and the *Nei Ching*); (3) these texts elaborated medical theory and practice beyond the knowledge or skills of laymen and folk practitioners; (4) this training validated claims to special social status; and (5) these claims were in turn supported by codes of medical ethics.

All the civilizations with *great tradition* medical systems developed a range of practitioners from learned professional physicians to individuals who had limited or no formal training and who practiced a simplified version of the great tradition medicine. Other healers coexisted with these practitioners, their arts falling into special categories such as bone setters, surgeons, midwives, and shamans. However, the complex and redundant relationships between learned and humble practitioners, and between those who were generalists or specialists, full or part-time, vocational or avocational, naturalist or supernaturalist curers, is clarified by professionalization in the great tradition that defined the relative statuses of legitimate practitioners and distinguished them from quacks. Professionalization in the Chinese medical system is quite extensive, for they developed an elaborate bureaucratic system for instruction and examinations to qualify physicians, along with what Joseph Needham writes "can only be described as a national medical service" (Needham and LuGwei-djen, 1969). Yet state patronage was also given to learned medicine in South Asia and the West. Indian Buddhism, in particular, encouraged the organization of hospitals, and, in the home region of each system, armies required regulated medical services.

Besides resemblances in the social organization of medical services, the three great tradition medical systems arose from common physiological and cosmological roots. One example of their generic linkage was their reliance on humoral theories: four humors in the Mediterranean tradition (yellow bile, black bile, phlegm, and blood); three humors in the South Asian tradition (Kapha, Pitta, and Vayu); and six humors in Chinese medicine (the chhi, which were held in the sway of Yang and Yin). The humors were alignments of opposing qualities: hot-cold, wet-dry, heavy-light, male-female, dark-bright, strong-weak, active-sluggish, and so on. The equilibrium of these qualities maintained health, and their disequilibrium caused illness, whatever the number of humors. Equilibrium was regulated by an individual's temperament in dynamic relationship to age, sex, climate, season, food consumption, and other activities. Diagnoses required skill in observing and correlating physical symptoms and environment. Therapy utilized complex medications, physical manipulations, and modification of the patient's diet and surroundings.

Finally, the Asian and Mediterranean medical systems conceived human anatomy and physiology to be intimately bound to other physical systems. Sherrington's description of the world view of Jean Fernel, a physician in sixteenth century Paris, would also apply to Chinese or Hindu physicians:

> The macrocosm fulfilling its fast circuits and epicycles of meticulous precision, its rising and its settings, its movements within movements, was an immense body fashioned after the likeness of man's body (Sherrington, 1955:61).

This conception united medical theory and knowledge with astronomy, astrology, mathematics, and natural philosophy.

As forms of adaptation, these medical systems rationalized the relation of men to their environment by postulating an equilibrium of basic elements in nature. The arrangement and balance of elements in the human body and in human societies were microcosmic versions of the larger universe. Preventive medicine and curing were an effort to maintain or to restore equilibrium. Professional curers were educated in the complex and abstract scientific theories of their tradition. This special knowledge, and the skills associated with it, gave them authority as curers, and they were distinguished from laymen by symbols of medical authority and by ethical codes appropriate to their occupation.

THE ADAPTIVE SIGNIFICANCE OF SCIENTIFIC MEDICAL TRADITIONS

Many critics argue that, aside from the placebo effect that might issue from resorting to authoritative curers, the therapeutic practices based upon Arabic, Chinese, and Ayurvedic medical theories had little effect toward improving the biological adaptation of the populations in which they were practiced. Practices like the use of Chaulmoogra oil for leprosy were advantageous, but others were disadvantageous, so that the emergence of scientific medical traditions of the kind we are describing would not, according to some, have increased the Darwinian fitness of the populations in which they developed. These critics would maintain that only the changes in scientific knowledge and in the organization of the medical profession in the nineteenth and twentieth centuries have brought people into new relationships with their environment which, for the first time in medical history, have significantly increased the Darwinian fitness of populations.

The fact that the germ theory of disease, modern surgical technique, chemotherapy, and social medicine have enormous biological consequences for mankind should not obscure the possible adaptive value of traditional medicine. Yet assessing the effects the Arabic, Chinese, and Ayurvedic medical systems may have had on the Darwinian fitness of the populations in which they were practiced is a difficult task and requires that we distinguish, in the first place, between medical theories and actual practices. Many contemporary practitioners of the great tradition claim that the theories set forth in the classic texts are still valid. Whether or not the theories continue to have scientific value, the directions in the texts for making clinical observations, recording particular diseases, and their extensive *materia medica* may have given traditional physicians some measure of effectiveness they would not otherwise have had. Certainly, to the extent that they influenced behavior, the recommendations in the classic texts for maintaining health would have encouraged personal cleanliness, a modest and balanced diet, an orderly environment, and some rational responses to epidemics. We also need to inquire what the proportion of learned to folk practitioners was in different periods and the degree to which an effective practice developed in the great tradition medicine was adopted by folk practitioners.

To measure the adaptive significance of traditional medical systems, one would also have to take into account the evolution of disease. A few organisms detrimental to man, such as tetanus, gangrene, rabies, plague, and typhus have natural habitats in soil, wild animals, and insects which indicate that human populations may have suffered from them before the domestication of plants and animals and the growth of densely populated, sedentary communities. However, "man is the only known host for most of his pathogenic organisms," and since few can survive outside the human body for more than a day or two and "fewer can actually multiply in the inanimate substances commonly present in the human environment," they must be transmitted from person to person, usually through close contact between donor and recipient.[2]

Many disease organisms could only evolve in large human populations with high birth rates, since they live for short periods in their hosts, cause high mortality, and leave their survivors immune to further infection. The diseases for which man is the only host and that were absent from America before European contact, probably evolved during the rise of Old World civilizations: measles, smallpox, chickenpox, influenza, mumps, whooping cough, pulmonary tuberculosis, and leprosy, are representatives of this group. These diseases had a devastating effect on American Indian populations.

The point is that through the centuries the populations in which the Arabic, Ayurvedic, and Chinese medical systems were practiced evolved resistence to many illnesses, and the mechanisms of natural selection through which this occurred were probably largely independent of the efficacy of these medical systems. The disease organisms also evolved in relation to their host populations, so that their histories must be considered. Leprosy disappeared from Europe, but without any apparent connection with changes in medical knowledge or practices relevant to it, and the incidence of tuberculosis declined in the nineteenth and early twentieth centuries in a manner that could not be attributed to the mecical systems of the time (Dubos, 1965).

Another claim is that Chinese and Indian medicine contain therapies which are either unknown to modern science or not understood and used in Western medicine. Acupuncture, the Chinese practice of inserting needles of varying lengths and thickness at specific points on the surface of the body, is known to achieve impressive results. As I write this essay, The *New York Times* is publishing accounts of acupuncture used to anesthetize patients for major surgical operations. Two American biologists who observed such operations in Peking are also reported to have "become convinced that Western pharmacology had much to learn from traditional Chinese medicine" (Topping and Topping, 1971). Rauwolfia is used in India and is an example of a drug introduced to modern medicine from the Ayurvedic system; it is safe to assert there are others like it as yet uninvestigated.

On the other hand, at a symposium on medicine and culture in which these issues were discussed, Dr. Francisco Guerra said that contrary to the Chinese government's claim "that the local pharmacopoeias are worthwhile; they are trash" (1969:252). After many years of research, Dr. Guerra concluded that:

> The contents of the indigenous pharmacopoeias are of little real use. The only valuable thing in connection with them is the ritual . . . [Furthermore] the consensus of professional pharmacologists . . . is that native pharmacopoeias are negligible from the pharmacological point of view (1969:238 and 305).

Another participant in the symposium responded to the idea that modern therapies were known to ancient Indian physicians by saying:

> It really isn't enough to show that foxglove was used before digitalis . . . one surely has to focus on the fact that there is very little margin of births over deaths until the 18th century and it seems to me that it is impossible to show at a larger level that any of this treatment did anything at all (McKeown, 1969:254).

Clearly, the efficacy and adaptive value of the traditional scientific medical

systems for Old World populations is a problem for historical research and
not an issue to be resolved by the claim that their long duration proves their
worth, or by the counter claim that effective medical knowledge is an
invention of modern science.

THE COMPARATIVE STUDY OF MODERNIZING
MEDICAL SYSTEMS

We turn now from the debate concerning the biological efficacy of
traditional Asian medical systems to the relationships between the professional practice of modern and traditional medicine in Japan, China, and
India. Modern medicine evolved from new research in anatomy, physiology,
and other sciences, and from the professional associations that emerged in
seventeenth and eighteenth century Europe. However, a medical system
based upon a standardized medical curriculum, systems of registration and
state regulation, a structure of paramedical workers subordinate to
physician-surgeons, and a high degree of technological skill evolved in the
nineteenth and twentieth centuries. It is this system that is most relevant
when one asks about the impact of Western ideas on traditional societies.

The comparison of Japan, China, and India is instructive, in part because
the state policies effecting modernization have been quite different in each
country. Furthermore, the symbolic role of traditional medicine in the
national society varies. The role of the state is greatest in China, where the
government sponsors a national medical system that integrates Chinese and
modern medicine, and least in Japan, where the state supported system is
thoroughly modern and traditional medicine is limited to private practitioners. The Indian case stands between the Chinese and Japanese extremes;
Indian governmental support goes primarily to modern medicine, but
traditional medical institutions also receive state recognition and aid. From a
symbolic perspective, traditional medicine is being modernized in China as
part of the regular medical system, whereas in Japan it forms an irregular
practice. The symbolic role of indigenous medicine in Indian national
culture is ambivalent—it is widely used by all classes of people and felt to be
a central part of the cultural heritage, yet the knowledge and ethnics of its
practitioners are said to have declined from those of former times. In some
respects an irregular medical practice and in other respects part of the regular
medical system, the modernization of Ayurvedic and Arabic medicine in

India brings them into an ambiguous paramedical relationship to modern scientific medicine.

JAPAN: SELF-WILLED MODERNIZATION

The Japanese Imperial Court adopted the learned tradition of Chinese medicine in the seventh century. A physician was brought from Korea in 602 A.D. to instruct a group of thirty-four students, and twelve students were sent to China for medical study in 608 A.D.[3] The Portuguese and Spanish introduced some knowledge of Western medicine during the sixteenth century but were expelled in 1638, when the Tokugawa regime closed Japan to European contact except through a single Dutch trade mission at Nagasaki. For the next two centuries a series of talented physicians attached to the Dutch mission taught Western medical science to a few Japanese scholars. In 1774 the first European book translated by Japanese scholars and published in Japan was an anatomy text. The translation of other medical texts followed, and the *Ranpo-igaku*, or the school of Dutch medicine, was established in learned circles before the period of national isolation ended with Perry's arrival in Japan in 1853.

Two competitive schools of Chinese medicine developed in Japan during this period. The school of Goseiha, or "latter day medicine," was so named because its practitioners subscribed to a Neo-Confucian philosophy that dated from the Northern Sung dynasty (960 to 1126 A.D.). Their goal was to interpret all pharmacological and other therapeutic techniques according to the Yang and Yin principles and other traditional categories of Chinese metaphysics. The school of Kohoha, or "classicism in medicine," set out to reform medical learning by opposing the Goseiha school, advocating return to the empirical, clinical spirit of the classic, *Shang han lun*, and its author, Chang Chung-ching.·

A leader of this reform movement in Chinese medicine, Yamawaki Toyo, published sketches in 1759 of his observations at the dismemberment of a criminal which indicated the fanciful nature of the anatomical theories expounded by members of the Goseiha school. Yamawaki's work persuaded the most influential physician of the classical revival in Chinese medicine that the *Shang han lun* had been corrupted by later authors, and led them to criticize portions of that text because "Chang Chung-ching could not have written such silly things" (Otsuka, in Leslie forthcoming). The translators who published the first textbook on European anatomy in Japan had also observed a dissection, and in the preface to their work acknowledged that "Yamawaki showed what was the true method of inquiry" (Bowers, 1970:398). One of their students is credited with establishing the "Dutch school" of medicine (Ranpo) in the late eighteenth century, and in 1793 a member of this school published a text on internal medicine to which a leading physician of the classical revival in Chinese medicine contributed a preface.

The point of this history is that a revival movement in traditional Chinese medicine in eighteenth and early nineteenth century Japan facilitated the introduction of new scientific knowledge, along with changing attitudes toward the ways that such knowledge should be validated. However, both schools of Chinese medical learning became competitive with Ranpo medicine as the nineteenth century progressed. Jennerian vaccination was introduced in 1824 by advocates of Ranpo medicine, and in the following generation Chinese medical learning declined in prestige relative to the new system.

After the Meiji Restoration in 1868 the government used the German medical system as a model for Japan. An examination system begun in 1875 was extended to the whole country in 1879. Although no physician was licensed to practice after 1883 who could not qualify in modern medicine, the study of Chinese medicine continued on a much reduced scale, and a few physicians used medications from the Chinese pharmacopoeia. Moxibustion and acupuncture were treated as separate, limited specialties to be licensed by local governments. These techniques never lost favor with the public, and in 1971 there were approximately 40,000 active practitioners.

Chinese medicine gained new popularity in Japan after the Second World War, and a Society for Oriental Medicine was founded which by 1971 claimed over one thousand members. Dr. Yasuo Otsuka[4] attributes this resurgence to the concern of laymen and physicians with the adverse side effects of synthetic drugs, compared to Chinese herbal medications; to the increasing specialization of modern medicine, to the detriment of the holistic, clinical perspective, which is preserved, on the other hand, in Chinese medical practice; and to the willingness of physicians who use Chinese medicine to listen to their patients' complaints.

In short, the medical system of Japan evolved in the nineteenth and twentieth centuries along with the international development of modern science and professional institutions. In this system, moxibustion and acupuncture are practiced as limited paramedical specialties, and Chinese herbal medicine is practiced by client-oriented physicians who must first qualify in medicine based upon modern science. Their practice is in this sense an "irregular" form of medicine. This relationship between Chinese and modern medicine evolved through processes of complementarity as well as opposition between traditional and new medical knowledge, with the agents of reform and innovation in the eighteenth century utilizing a rhetoric of traditional medical revivalism.

CHINA: REVOLUTIONARY MODERNIZATION

In contrast to the Japanese, learned Chinese physicians had greater access to Western knowledge during the seventeenth and eighteenth centuries but were less responsive to it. According to the historian Ralph Croizier, Chinese medical scholars "were almost totally indifferent" to translations by Jesuit scientists in Peking of the new European research on anatomy and physiology:

> Even the bestowal of royal favor after a judicious application of the newly discovered cihchona bark to cure a fever in the K'ang Hsi Emperor, failed to change this. With the weakening of the Jesuits' position in Peking, Western medical influence disappeared almost without a ripple . . . Chinese medicine . . . took little interest in things radically new and foreign until faced with Western *force majeure* in the nineteenth century (Croizier, 1968:34).

The scientific traditions of the Old World civilizations are compared by Joseph Needham to rivers that flow into a sea where their ethnic qualities disappear in "the universality of modern science." He argues that science and technology in China generally showed a higher level of achievement than in Europe from the first to the sixteenth centuries, but from Galileo's time Western science overtook that of the Chinese, "leading in due course to the exponential rise of modern science in the nineteenth and twentieth centuries" (Needham, 1970:397).

Needham calls the period in which a form of Western science surpasses the achievement level of its Chinese counterpart a "transcurrent point," and calls the time at which forms of Western and Chinese science merge in the ecumenical sciences of the modern era a "fusion point." He maintains that the transcurrent points were earlier and the intervals between them and the points of fusion were shorter in the physical sciences than in the biological sciences.

Since by a historical coincidence the rise of modern science in Europe was closely accompanied by the activities of the Jesuit mission in China, there was relatively little delay in the juxtaposition of the two great traditions . . . On the physical side, the mathematics, astronomy and physics of the West and East united very quickly after they first came together. By 1644 . . . there was no longer any perceptible difference between the mathematics, astronomy and physics of China and Europe (Needham, 1970:397).

The transcurrent point for these sciences occurred in the opening decade of the seventeenth century and fusion occurred within a generation. However, the transcurrent point in medicine was later and lasted over a longer span of time, while the fusion of Chinese and Western medicine into "a unitary modern medical science" has yet to occur. Needham reports that by the end of the eighteenth century European knowledge of anatomy and surgery surpassed that of the Chinese, and that throughout the nineteenth century the sciences basic to medicine were more advanced in Europe than those in China. He catalogues nineteenth century progress in areas such as pharmaceutical chemistry, bacteriology, immunology, antiseptic surgery and anaesthesia, and he might also have credited the West with progressive changes during the eighteenth and nineteenth centuries in the social organization of medical education, research and practice. He doubts, however, whether the transcurrent point was "much earlier than 1900, perhaps 1850 or 1870," on the grounds that the new knowledge did not greatly affect the patient's welfare: "if we judge strictly clinically, the patient may not have been much better off in Europe than in China before the beginning of the twentieth century (Needham, 1970:407).

I doubt that there are adequate medical records to use clinical efficacy as a measure for comparing the achievements of Chinese and Western physicians in the eighteenth and nineteenth centuries. The important fact is that Chinese medical scholars, unlike those of Japan and India, showed little interest in modern science until the late nineteenth century, and that the Chinese government made no significant effort to develop the institutional structures of a modern medical system until the second decade of the twentieth century.

Medical missionaries began to found hospitals and clinics as early as 1835 but did not have access to the whole country until 1860, and even by the beginning of the twentieth century there were only a few hundred Chinese physicians trained in Western medicine. In the 1920s the best medical schools were all missionary organized, and their policy was to train physicians as thoroughly as they could according to standards in Europe and America, rather than try to meet the need for large numbers of practitioners by giving shorter courses of study. The government had been slow and indecisive to develop medical policy, but in 1915 it adopted the Western curriculum as the official means to qualify for practice. In that year, too, the Peking Union Medical College received a grant from the Rockefeller Foundation with which it developed into the research and educational institution that set standards for the rest of the country. During the 1920s the Union Medical Colleges in Peking and other cities reduced the dominance of missionary schools. However, there were less than three thousand modern doctors in all of China in 1927, and when the Communists gained power in 1949 there were approximately fifteen thousand doctors for a population of five hundred million people. Their education was still indebted directly or indirectly to the work of Christian missionaries (Croizier, 1968).

Chinese intellectuals began to recognize the need for a modern health system in the 1890s. They attributed Japan's increasing power to the scientific and technical innovations the Japanese were adopting from the West, and used the social Darwinian arguments of the period to advocate medical reform. Their idea was to create a superior new system by combining the best of Chinese and Western medicine. In 1903 a joint course in both systems was inaugurated at Peking Imperial University, and in 1910 a council in Shanghai began publishing a periodical entitled *Chinese and Western Medicine*.

After the First World War, iconoclast reformers attacked Chinese medicine along with other aspects of the traditional culture as obsolete and superstitious remnants of feudal society. In this context, advocacy of a synthesis of Chinese and Western medicine, which had been a "progressive" position, now became a "conservative" one.

One tactic of the new cultural conservatives was to claim that the five elements did not refer literally to earth, fire, water, metal, and wood, but were symbolic devices similar to those used for theory building in modern science. Furthermore, they claimed that the yin-yang theory referred to positive and negative electrical charges, and that the meridians of acupuncture anticipated Harvey's conception of the circulation of blood. Another tactic was to propose a division of labor based on different putative virtues of Chinese and Western medicine. Thus Chinese medicine was held to complement the Western mechanistic treatment of parts by maintaining an organic view of the whole person. Chinese therapy was said to be best for internal medicine, while Western therapy was best for external medicine. Furthermore, these conservatives argued that Chinese medicine should be given state support because it was cheaper, more available to the masses, and better understood by them than Western medicine.

In the 1920s and 1930s professional societies, journals, colleges, and hospitals were founded to revive Chinese medicine in competition with the growing influence of Western medical practice. Physicians trained in Western medicine had organized a professional association in 1915, and for the next thirty years pressed without success to gain exclusive state recognition, along with state regulated standards of education and practice. The Ministry of the Interior issued regulations in 1922 which recognized Chinese medicine as a legitimate practice parallel to Western medicine, but seven years later the new Ministry of Health announced a policy to abolish Chinese medicine. Local associations of Chinese medical practitioners successfully opposed the policy, however, and in the process organized their own national association. By 1930 fifteen colleges of Chinese medicine had been founded with curricula that included some modern medicine. After considerable debate, the government began licensing physicians of Chinese medicine in 1933, and two years later a Kuomintang Party resolution advocated that they be given equal status with Western trained physicians. Despite these events, Croizier summarizes the period as one in which:

Western medicine controlled the government's health machinery and served a small proportion of the urban population; Chinese medicine, generally unchanged by contact with modern science, remained the common source of medical relief for the overwhelming majority of the people (Croizier, 1968:144).

The Kuomintang and its predecessor's policies vacillated between supporting advocates of Chinese and Western medicine, and were ineffectual in any case.

The Communists, who assumed power in 1949, have evolved a health policy that gives Chinese medicine an honored place in a well-ordered system of government medical services. This seems paradoxical to observers who recall that before 1949 Communist writers had criticized Chinese medicine as a feudal heritage, or who note the Marxist commitment to science and who believe that the only scientific medicine is the "Western" system. Good scientific (pragmatic) reasons existed for the Communist decision to utilize Chinese medicine in the state health system. If there were only ten to fifteen thousand doctors trained in modern medicine in 1949, there were close to five hundred thousand practitioners of Chinese medicine. Moreover, while the doctors with Western training required an expensive infrastructure of pharmaceutical plants, laboratories, hospitals, and colleges, the practitioners of Chinese medicine could utilize existing resources and an apprentice system to give patients herbal remedies or other forms of therapy to which they were accustomed.

The Communist policy of utilizing Chinese medicine seemed initially to be a pragmatic expedient, but within a few years its ideological significance became obvious. In 1954 the modern medical profession began to be accused of bourgeois prejudice toward Chinese medicine. It was argued that because Chinese medicine was a natural science it had been relatively independent of the past social structure, and that the learned "Confucian doctor" had disdained medical practice. It was thus argued that the accumulated empirical knowledge and wisdom of Chinese medical practice was a creation of the people. The duty of physicians trained in Western medicine was to drop their bourgeois concepts, and work with traditional physicians to create a new medical system. Criticism of medical specialists was part of a larger Red vs. Expert campaign to prevent the technical intelligentsia from disputing the power of Party leaders. Thought reform was used to extort abysmal public confessions from leading medical educators of their errors in criticizing the anatomical concepts of acupuncture or other theories and practices of Chinese medicine.

The symbolic role of Chinese medicine goes beyond its practical use in meeting the demand for medical care or as an instrument of power politics. According to Ralph Croizier, the superiority of Western science and technology and the need to import it on a large scale threatened the Chinese with loss of cultural identity. Medicine became a symbol of Chinese identity for the modernizing conservatives of the pre-Communist period, Croizier reasons, and in Communist ideology it continues to serve this psychological need. He adds that because the old society has been "smashed" by the revolutions of modern times, the Communists can use traditional medicine to symbolize the genius and continuity of Chinese culture without risk of reviving other objectionable institutions which were associated in the past with medical learning and practice.

The campaign to revive Chinese medicine was accelerated by the Great Leap Forward, which began in 1958, and again, beginning in 1966, by the Cultural Revolution and the advent of the "barefoot doctor." Twenty-one colleges for Chinese medicine existed by 1966 with approximately one hundred thousand students, and an additional sixty thousand students were registered for training in an apprentice system. Courses in Chinese medicine and hospital beds for its clinical teaching were incorporated in the modern medical colleges, and Chinese and Western medicine were practiced side by side throughout the system of health services.

Even so, Ralph Croizier argued that compared to medical systems in other countries which have attempted to combine traditional and modern elements, the Communists have failed to create a new system that combines Chinese with modern medicine. The Communist revivalists, like their conservative counterparts in the 1920s and 1930s, want to synthesize the theories of Chinese and modern medicine, but Croizier claimed that the differences in their metaphysical premises make a synthesis logically impossible. Except for occasional articles on traditional Chinese therapies, medical journals resemble the medical literature from other countries. Croizier also observed that foreign specialists who visit Chinese medical institutions find themselves in the familiar clinical and laboratory settings of modern medicine.

Croizier concluded that the revival of Chinese medicine had not greatly affected medical modernization. Although he maintained that modernization may have been facilitated by associating new health practices with the familiar forms of traditional medicine, he estimated that between 1949 and 1966 the proportion of traditional practitioners to physicians trained in modern medicine was reduced from ninety-five percent to about fifty percent. He further estimated that during this period not over ten or fifteen percent of the medical budget went to traditional medicine. Thus, in his view, the revival of traditional medicine was less significant as a force in the development of the Chinese medical system than as an expression of "the central pressures and compulsions in modern Chinese intellectual life" (Croizier, 1968:237).

I have used the term "symbolic traditionalization" in writing about Ayurvedic and Unani medicine in South Asia to describe the association of familiar, long-established ideas and practices with structurally new institutions (Leslie, 1969:46-55). In the present essay I am arguing that symbolic traditionalization is a characteristically modernizing process. This differs from Ralph Croizier's interpretation of the symbolic role of traditional medicine in modern China. He emphasized the *symptomatic* aspect of medical revivalism in expressing anxiety about cultural identity. I would emphasize the *causal* aspect of medical revivalism in facilitating structural changes in the medical system and in the overall pattern of Chinese culture.

It is presumptuous to argue with Croizier's profoundly researched and thoughtful study, and I do so only by comparing the Chinese case with the historical pattern described at the beginning of this essay. Undoubtedly, Chinese intellectuals did express anxiety about the loss of cultural identity as China imported Western science and technology. However, from the Renaissance to the present day, wave after wave of revival styles have characterized Western society. Although the West has imported massively from the rest of the world, Western revivalism since the Renaissance has not transpired because Europeans felt that these importations threatened their cultural identity. Europeans felt that there were certain positive "pragmatic" values in past forms in the contemporary context.

Rather than assuming that the symbolic role of revivals is only a consequence of the tensions created by change, we should ask the more general question, where has the modernization of traditional society occurred *without* symbolic traditionalization? Since I can think of no example, I believe that revivalism is not merely a symptom of the psychological tensions created by modernization; it is an ideology that helps create what Marxists call a "mode of consciousness," a way of perceiving and thinking and feeling about the world and one's relationship to it that moves people to actions that profoundly change their circumstances.

The paradox of revivalism is that it creates the new by resuscitating the old. It is, in Sorel's phrase, a retrospective mythology, but one very different from those of traditional cultures, for they assume continuity with the past, while the myth of revivalism posits an historical discontinuity. People seek to restore that which they believe has been lost or has become degraded. A revivalist ideology contrasts the glory of what a people once were with what they have become. By simultaneously evoking pride in past achievements, discontent with present circumstances, and hope for the future, it inculcates the historical self-consciousness through which men deliberately choose their destiny.

However, no ideology guarantees the virtues it inculcates. Democratic ideology has been used to tyrannize, Christianity to enslave, socialism to exploit. Here lie the interesting problems. Since the metaphysical premises of Chinese and Western medicine make it impossible to achieve the goal of a theoretical synthesis, Croizier seems to me to have underestimated the utility of the ideology in changing the medical system. However, he also implied that the goal was a source of spuriousness. To abandon it in practice would be to assimilate assorted useful items from traditional medicine into a fundamentally modern Western medical system, and at the same time to maintain the goal in theory would be to use it for purely expressive purposes to symbolize a progressively spurious identity—symbolically Chinese, in fact modern and Western. Whether or not this is a correct evaluation of the Chinese situation, the revivalist ideology may be spuriously employed. I will describe the modernization of Ayurvedic and Arabic medicine in India to show the paradoxes and ambiguities of this process.

INDIA: THE AMBIGUITIES OF MODERNIZATION

Muslim rule brought Middle Eastern physicians to India when medical learning still flourished in Islam. From the thirteenth century on Muslim physicians compiled anthologies of translations from Ayurvedic texts, and adopted drugs and other therapies from Ayurvedic practice. In the sixteenth century Hakim Yoosufi, a physician in the courts of Babar and Humayun, is said to have synthesized "Arabian, Persian and Ayurvedic thought and produced a composite and integrated medical system" (Hameed, No date: 17). Scholars like Hakim Yoosufi probably had counterparts among Ayurvedic physicians. Certainly, Hindus became Unani physicians without converting to Islam, and Muslims became Ayurvedic physicians. Muslim rulers acted as patrons of famous Ayurvedic scholars, and Hindu aristocrats patronized Unani physicians. Many overlook or deny these facts because of religious animosity, but a leading historian of ancient and medieval India has commented, "The practitioners of the two systems seem to have collaborated because each had much to learn from the other, and, whatever the *'ulama* and the *brahmans* might say, we have no record of animosity between Hindu and Muslim in the field of medicine" (Basham, forthcoming).

By the nineteenth and twentieth centuries the traditional beliefs and practices of Ayurvedic physicians were radically different from the classic texts, and were deeply influenced by the Galenic (Unani) traditions in Islamic medicine. Ayurvedic practitioners, for example, often classified and interpreted illnesses in a manner that resembled Unani practice, having added a fourth "humor" (blood) to the three humors of the classic texts.[5] Moreover, although sphygmology, or pulse lore, is absent from the Ayurvedic classics, it was well developed in Unani medicine and eventually became the symbol of an Ayurvedic physician's skill. The reputation of sphygmology was such that by the nineteenth and twentieth centuries it had become more a technique of divination than a rational diagnostic method. Great physicians were said to perceive every circumstance that caused a patient's illness and to foretell the exact course it would take by examining the pulse. Furthermore, Ayurvedic practitioners had adopted mercury, opium, and other items from the Unani pharmacopia, and traditional medical lore was profoundly influenced by alchemy, a science prominent in Islam but not in the classic Ayurvedic texts.

The ironic aspect of this situation is that these syncretic medical traditions are the ones that nineteenth and twentieth century Ayurvedic revivalists have known and believed in, yet the revivalist ideology has claimed that the introduction of Unani medicine to India caused Ayurveda to decline. The ideology also asserts that the development of modern medical institutions in India caused the further deterioration of Ayurvedic knowledge and practice. This creates another ambiguity, for the revivalists have professionalized Ayurveda by adopting institutional forms, concepts and medications from modern medical science. These changes continue a long tradition of medical syncretism, and rather than declining, the Indian medical system has advanced through adopting new knowledge and institutional arrangements. Yet the logic of a revivalist ideology *requires* a theory of decline to justify self-conscious efforts to direct the path of history toward a new life.

Before analyzing the role of revivalism in modernizing the Indian medical system, I must clarify the character of that system.

In the United States and other industrial countries laymen and specialists assume that a single medical system exists with comprehensive jurisdiction in all matters of health—a hierarchy of paramedical specialists dominated by physicians, standard curricula for training health specialists, standard therapeutic techniques, and ways of generating new skills and knowledge. Contrary to this assumption, the medical system is in fact a pluralistic network of different kinds of physicians, dentists, clinical psychologists, chiropractors, health food experts, yoga teachers, spirit curers, druggists, Chinese herbalists, and so on. The health concepts of a Puerto Rican worker in New York City, the curers he consults and therapies he receives will differ from those of the Chinese laundryman or the Jewish merchant. They in turn will differ from the middle class believers in Christian Science or logical positivism. While the institutions of modern scientific medicine are extensive, well organized and powerful, so that the concept of a single, standardized hierarchical medical system is closer to reality in the United States than in India, we need a pluralistic model to study the medical systems in either country, or we need to consider the concept of a single medical system as a heuristic device to formulate questions about the ways that real systems diverge from it. In either case we should not assume, as laymen and physicians in the United States usually do, that the ideal of a uniform medical system controlled by physicians is intrinsically superior to other forms and should be the goal of all societies. The pluralistic structure of the Indian medical system might best develop toward goals that would enhance the advantages of pluralism while correcting its disadvantages.

I have mentioned Ayurvedic, Unani, and modern scientific medicine, and have said that they overlap and merge, giving rise to syncretic practices. I call the syncretic traditions of Ayurvedic and Unani medicine *traditional culture medicine* to distinguish them from the medicine of the classic texts. The physicians who cultivated learned versions of traditional culture medicine identified themselves as either Ayurvedic or Unani practitioners and were familiar with some classic texts, but their understanding of them was shaped by later syncretic commentaries and oral traditions. Thomas Wise, a surgeon in the Bengal Medical Service who published a comprehensive description of Ayurvedic theories and practices in 1845, wrote:

After some enquiry I find there are not more than four or five persons in this part of India who are acquainted with the Hindu Shastras . . . A very few practitioners may still be found in the neighborhood of cities . . . in whose families the ancient treatises of their forefathers are studied, and transmitted from generation to generation. I have had the happiness of knowing such a family of hereditary physicians, rich, independent, and much respected . . . (They would not sell or let their manuscripts be copied) from a belief that all the good to be derived from their possession, which God had bestowed on the individual and his family, would vanish on the work being sold, or even the precepts communicated to unauthorized individuals (Wise, 1845:V).

Learned practitioners of traditional culture medicine still exist, but from the beginning of the nineteenth century syncretism with modern medical knowledge and institutions has largely transformed these traditions into *professionalized Ayurvedic and Unani medicine*. Its practitioners are trained in colleges, join professional associations, prescribe commercially manufactured drugs, serve governmental health agencies, work in hospitals, write articles for medical journals, and do other modern professional things that the learned physicians Thomas Wise knew did not do.

Different degrees of syncretism with modern medicine exist, but the dynamics of professionalization cause those who oppose syncretism, as well as those who advocate it, to adopt ideas and practices from the modern medical profession. For example, the ideologists of Suddha (pure) Ayurveda have advocated restoring theory and practice to that of the classic texts by eliminating accretions from other systems. Yet they have acted in the same way as their opponents, they have lobbied to influence governmental health policies, written tracts comparing the discoveries of modern science to passages in the ancient texts, joined associations, and organized schools. Of course, none of these things is in the classic texts. As American and English social scientists favor progress, they sometimes err in the study of modernizing processes by assuming that "conservative" ideologists block modernization. In revivalist movements ideological "conservatives" may be as powerful modernizing forces as "progressives."

I have distinguished five aspects or kinds of medicine that are important for the argument of this essay. I will enumerate them, adding others to the list with the purpose of placing these five in the fuller context of the pluralistic Indian medical system. These are: (1) the Ayurvedic medicine of the Sanskrit classic texts; (2) Unani medicine of the classic Arabic texts; (3) the syncretic medicine of traditional culture which evolved among learned practitioners from the thirteenth to the nineteenth centuries; (4) professionalized Ayurvedic and Unani medicine, which has continued the syncretism of the past, transforming learned traditional culture medicine by assimilating modern knowledge and institutions; and (5) modern scientific medicine. Modern medicine is often called *allopathy* in South Asian countries to distinguish it from indigenous medicine and homeopathy.

Another kind of traditional culture medicine is (6) *folk medicine*, which encompasses midwives, bone setters, supernatural curers, and other specialists, most of them part-time practitioners. The concepts and practices in folk medicine draw upon the humoral theories, cosmological speculations, and magical practices in learned medicine and religion, but systematic studies of the relationships between learned and folk medicine have not been made. The term "indigenous medicine" is used in India to refer to the folk and learned dimensions of traditional culture medicine, together with the classic texts.

(7) *Popular culture medicine* emerges with the institutions of mass society—industrial production of medicines, advertising, and the school system. It continues the syncretism of traditional culture medicine, transforming and displacing it with an amalgam of concepts and practices. It combines the humoral concepts of hot and cold foods with concepts of vitamins, traditional physiological concepts with the germ theory of disease, and popular astrology and religion with faith in modern science and technology. It utilizes patent medicines and drugs from modern chemotherapy, along with industrially prepared Ayurvedic, Unani, and homeopathic medications. Laymen practice popular culture medicine on themselves and their kinsmen, but many practitioners are full-time specialists. For example, professionalized Ayurvedic and Unani physicians, and modern doctors in private practice, may in large part practice popular culture medicine.[6]

(8) *Homeopathic medicine* is a special form of popular culture medicine so widely used in India it must be listed here. It originated in Germany in the nineteenth century, and was based on the concept of creating resistance to an illness by administering small doses of it. Homeopathy is a variant of modern medicine grounded in biological vitalism, but in India its practice assimilates elements from Ayurvedic and Unani traditions to form a distinctive

popular culture medicine. Many self-instructed part-time practitioners are active, but schools also exist, as do clinics, hospitals, associations of practitioners, and other institutions of professional practice; some of these institutions are funded by state governments. Physicians and paramedical specialists trained in modern medicine, and professionalized Ayurvedic and Unani physicians may themselves use homeopathic medicines and occasionally recommend them to others.

My intention is to list categories for constructing a model of pluralistic South Asian medical systems. I do not intend to itemize all varieties of curers and medical belief in India, or in a single region or city. Additional kinds of practice could be related to the model in a more extended study than the present essay. For example, *Siddha* as a Tamil language variant of Ayurveda practiced in South India and Ceylon, and *Tibbi* is a variant of Unani medicine that combines the Galenic tradition with supernatural curing based upon sayings attributed to the Prophet. In addition, *naturopathy* is a recognized therapeutic system among educated urban Indians. Its more successful practitioners establish sanatoria where patients are given special diets, baths, massages, and courses of exercise, but, like homeopathy, this is a variant of popular culture medicine.[7] Siddha, Tibbi, and naturopathy we set aside, along with other practices we do not need to name for the purpose at hand.

The last category we need to list in order to construct our model is (9) *learned magico-religious curing.* All classes of people in India resort frequently to magical and religious therapy, and practitioners range from illiterate villagers to sophisticated urban pandits. Supernatural curing blends with other practices at the levels of folk and popular culture, but at higher levels of learning the ideas and roles associated with supernatural curing command a prestige that sets them apart.

This raises an interesting problem for historical sociology. The classic medical texts are not entirely secular and without magic in the manner of modern science, but the traditional culture medicine was saturated with magical and religious elements. A problem for historians will be to identify the processes through which the relatively secular and rational medicine of the texts was transformed into the magico-religious forms of traditional culture medicine. I am suggesting a long-term trend of *sacrilization* in learned Ayurvedic and Unani medicine (in the Table 1 model, the transitions that would occur in moving from the G to the D region). Furthermore, I believe that professionalization processes have tended to reverse this historical pattern in the nineteenth and twentieth centuries by *resecularizing* Ayurvedic and Unani medical learning (in the Table 1 model, the transitions that would occur in moving from the D to the B region). Although these changes have involved ambiguities, my argument is that a revivalist ideology has facilitated this historical reversal and other modernizing trends caused by efforts to enhance the professional status of Ayurvedic and Unani physicians.

The main tenets of this revivalist ideology evolved early in the nineteenth century in the conflict between Orientalists and Anglicists. The Anglicists wanted the ruling East India Company to establish an English language school system with the practical purpose of training Indian men for jobs in British enterprises and with the ideal of reforming Indian society by educating a class of men and women in the liberal arts and scientific thought. The Orientalists were cultural pluralists who advocated that reforms be undertaken by utilizing indigenous institutions rather than by the wholesale introduction of an English educational system. They admired Indian civilization, arguing that it had fallen on evil days but could be reformed by selectively encouraging practices that still expressed the enlightened spirit of antiquity and by translating Western science into Indian languages. For example, a member of the Orientalist faction surveyed traditional education in Bengal in the 1830s, and one of his recommendations was that medical textbooks be written in the Bengali, Hindi, and Sanskrit languages to combine modern science and local practices, "European theory and Indian experience" (Adams, 1941:436-437). Free copies of these books would be distributed to learned Ayurvedic and Unani physicians and public examinations based on their content would be periodically announced by the government. Special awards would be given to students who did well on the examinations and to their teachers.

Although the British Orientalists were sympathetic to Indian culture and learned its languages, they criticized the lethargy, ignorance, and superstition which they thought abounded in Indian society, and they constantly spoke of the need to revive and invigorate the culture. They were men of the Enlightenment and enemies of ignorance and superstition in Western society who thought that Western civilization had only recently emerged from "the dark ages." It was natural for them to think in a revivalist idiom, for their ideology transposed the myth of man's decline from the Garden of Eden into secular history by inventing the concept of decline from the religious tolerance, scientific accomplishment, artistic creativity and democracy of

Table 1.

Model of a pluralistic South Asian medical system showing regions of typical practice, degrees of affinity among practices, and hypothetical distributions of full-time and part-time practitioners

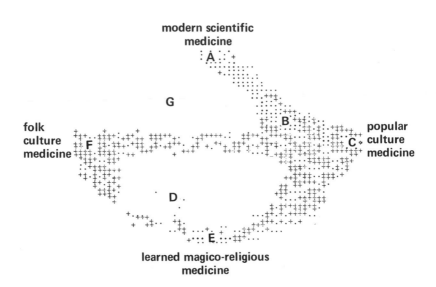

Regions of typical practice:

A = physicians trained in colleges and schools of modern scientific medicine

B = professionalized Ayurvedic and Unani physicians

C = homeopathic physicians

D = learned traditional culture Ayurvedic and Unani physicians

E = pandits and other religious specialists with reputations for unusual healing powers

F = folk practitioners

G = classic Ayurvedic and Unani text descriptions of medical education and practice

:::: = full-time practitioners, one for each dot

╫╫╫ = part-time practitioners, ten for each cross

Greek and Roman antiquity. For India they imagined a past culture as reasonable, tolerant, natural, simple, and refined as the Mediterranean world was supposed to have been, and they sought out Hindu scholars who confirmed this conception. Together they formulated a theory of decline in medicine and in other cultural domains.

The theory for the decline of Ayurveda compared the rational spirit and comprehensiveness of the early texts with contemporary medical practices to the disadvantage of both learned and folk levels of traditional culture medicine. Decline was attributed to the Buddhist doctrine of *ahimsa* (nonviolence), which was said to have caused dissection to be abandoned, with the subsequent deterioration of surgery and anatomical knowledge. In fact, the classic text on surgery was composed in the Buddhist period. Decline was also attributed to Muslim conquest and support of a rival medical system, followed by British conquest and patronage of yet another rival system. In addition, it was attributed to the Hindu customs of overvaluing authority as a method of validation, and of treating knowledge as a secret. Finally, it was supposed to have followed from using inferior drugs as substitutes for rare and valuable ones, so that the ancient medicinals lost their effectiveness and quack physicians attempted to compensate by progressively resorting to magical charms and spells. Thus, traditional culture medicine was described as being in an abject state. Overgrown with superstition, only a few elements remained from antiquity as ruins that testified to a glorious past.

The theory of decline from a golden age of medical learning provided the ideological ground for professionalizing reforms. Printing presses had been introduced, and though learned practitioners often considered the texts too sacred to be made public, relatively inexpensive editions of the medical classics began to be published. Ayurvedic physicians sent their sons to the modern medical schools which were first established in Calcutta, Bombay, and Madras in mid-nineteenth century and later in other cities of British administration.

A class of physicians had emerged during the first half of the century who had some knowledge of "English medicine." In 1839 an Indian observer in Bombay asserted that only four or five Ayurvedic physicians in that city knew Sanskrit well enough to read the medical classics, but that some hereditary physicians "call themselves 'English Doctors' . . . and administer English medicines . . . (though) they are not at all educated and know nothing of the European Medical Science."[8] By the closing decades of the nineteenth century this class included kinsmen in joint practice who were trained in either Western or indigenous medicine and individuals who were trained in both. Some of these physicians were entrepreneurs who hoped to revive Ayurveda and improve their own careers by starting companies to manufacture traditional medicines for commercial distribution, by founding schools which would adapt Ayurvedic learning to the bureaucratic structure of modern education, and by sponsoring charitable dispensaries.

The next step in professionalization was to organize regional associations of practitioners. India is more diverse linguistically than Europe, but by the first decade of the present century an association of professionalized Ayurvedic physicians was founded that bridged linguistic regions with a program urging government recognition and aid for research on indigenous drugs and for Ayurvedic schools, hospitals, and dispensaries. Though Gandhi and Nehru were cool to medical revivalism, it gained support from other leaders of the Independence Movement, and, linked with this powerful force, continued to inspire a proliferating literature, the founding of colleges, and sporadically successful attempts in various states to gain governmental support.

My impression is that Ayurvedic physicians took the lead in the professionalization of learned traditional culture medicine, but Unani practitioners were also active. Late nineteenth century revivalism inspired the publication of vernacular translations of Unani texts and the founding of colleges. In response to the ecumenical ideology of the Independence Movement, schools were established in the 1920s and 1930s in which students could study either Unani or Ayurvedic medicine. A nationally prominent school in Madras offered programs in Unani medicine, Ayurveda, and Siddha, the Tamil language medical tradition. Schools of this kind incorporated modern knowledge in their curricula, offering basic science courses and clinical instruction in modern diagnostic techniques and therapies. The more successful ones had teaching hospitals, rudimentary laboratories, dissection halls, anatomical charts and other modern teaching aids. Still, most of these efforts were privately financed. Where state aid was given to these institutions and to Ayurvedic or Unani dispensaries, it was a minor part of the total expenditure for health purposes.

When India became an independent nation just after the Second World War, it had approximately fifty hospitals and fifty-seven colleges of Ayurvedic or Unani medicine. The Ministries of Health in several states had

Boards of Indigenous Medicine responsible for running government dispensaries, registering practitioners, and regulating school curricula. Companies with regional and in some cases national and international markets manufactured Ayurvedic and Unani medicines which they advertised and distributed in a modern manner. National associations of practitioners sponsored conferences, published journals, and lobbied for legal privileges equivalent to those of physicians trained in modern scientific medicine.

Thus, encouraged and justified by the idea of reviving the heritage of indigenous medical science, Ayurvedic and Unani physicians had modernized the learned practice of traditional medicine. They were middle class urban entrepreneurs and members of Brahmin or other high castes. By professionalizing indigenous medicine as the profession of modern scientific medicine had evolved in India, they shaped careers for themselves, transformed the learned practice of traditional culture medicine into a modern blend of popular culture and scientific medicine, and created within the pluralistic Indian medical system a dual structure of professional medical institutions.

A major difference existed between the revivalist ideology of the professionalizing Ayurvedic physicians and the thought of the British Orientalists who first inspired them. The cultural models which were used to reform Western civilization were thoroughly demythologized. The Englishmen who admired ancient Greece did not believe in its gods, and while they thought that the new science of the seventeenth and eighteenth centuries revived the spirit of Greek civilization, they did not believe that it was a literal resuscitation of ancient knowledge. In their view modern science made Greek science obsolete. They were very self-conscious about this perspective because it had been an issue of considerable consequence in the modernization of European culture. Humanistic revivalism initiated the traditions of modernity in the Renaissance by using the authority of a classical ideal to oppose scholasticism, but the scientific revolution of the following centuries, while continuing to pay homage to classic ideals, had challenged the literal authority of the classical model. The British Orientalists were heirs to this dialectical progression.

In contrast, the professionalizing Ayurvedic physicians believed in the Hindu gods of the ancient texts and in the traditional culture medicine which their activities transformed. The main concepts in the classic texts —that related equilibrium systems exist in the human body and the universe, and that these systems are composed of five elements *(panchbhuta)*, seven body substances *(dhatu)*, and three humors *(tridosa)*—were also part of the traditional medicine in which they believed, so that their goal was to resuscitate ancient medical science. Since they believed literally in the authority of the classic texts, and at the same time were impressed by the accomplishments of modern science, they set out to demonstrate that the institutions and scientific theories of modern medicine were anticipated in the ancient texts.

These and other arguments justified radical changes in the organization and content of traditional education and practice. However, the point I wish to make is that every argument involved its advocates in ambiguities. To maintain, for example, that Ayurveda had declined because British colonialism introduced an alien system, Ayurvedic professionals had contrasted the image of a large medical college to the simple household of an Ayurvedic physician. The wisdom and healing skills of an Ayurvedic doctor were said to exceed by far those of ostentatious doctors with elaborately equipped clinics, and neither his practice nor his profound teaching to devout students required the bureaucratic organization of impersonal hospitals, laboratories, and dissection halls. Yet as Ayurvedic schools were founded and their facilities improved, they appeared to become inferior versions of modern medical colleges. Rather than resuscitate the creative power of Ayurvedic learning and its prestige relative to modern scientific medicine, these schools seemed to attract students who had failed to gain admission to other institutions. The reasons were clear enough: even the few graduates who became successful private practitioners would not enjoy the legal privileges of modern doctors, and in the state health services physicians trained in these schools were considered to be qualified only for positions with low pay and limited responsibility.

In fact, Ayurvedic and Unani medicine have evolved in an ambiguous paraprofessional relationship to modern scientific medicine. When the social history of modern medicine in India comes to be written, it will show that the demand for medical services from the nineteenth century to the present time has far exceeded the capacity of modern medical institutions, so that they have developed in reciprocal relationship to the modernization of Ayurvedic and Unani medicine. Without acknowledging that they have done so, modern medical institutions have depended upon the professionalization of indigenous medicine to meet a substantial portion of the expanding need for professional care. At the same time, the ideology of the modern medical profession has opposed the claims of Ayurvedic and Unani institutions to greater state recognition and support. The paramedical subordination of these institutions to the modern medical profession has been maintained, but the relationship itself has been an unwanted one. Similarly, the professionalizing Ayurvedic and Unani physicians have been unhappy with the relationship and have sought to deny it by seeking autonomy as an independent profession.

The important point is that the modernization of Asian medicine in India has not been a one way process in which Ayurvedic and Unani physicians have borrowed ideas and institutional forms from so-called Western medicine. Modern scientific medical institutions have themselves developed in a distinctive manner because they have assumed that Ayurvedic and Unani institutions were there doing medical jobs Indian society wanted and needed to have done.

Ambiguities remain in the social and cultural role of professionalized Ayurvedic and Unani medicine, but there are signs that they are becoming less acute. The revivalist ideology has done its work for the time being and no longer commands the loyalties it aroused a generation or two ago. The Government of India passed a law in 1970 establishing in the Ministry of Health a Central Council of Indian Medicine to register physicians, regulate education and practice, and cultivate research. The concepts of Ayurvedic and Unani medicine are a respected part of the common Indian culture. The President of India is known to resort to Ayurvedic and Unani therapies, as do other distinguished citizens. If a wizard of modernization decided that "traditional medicine" was an impediment to progress and abolished tomorrow the whole infrastructure of professionalized Ayurvedic and Unani practice, he would create a medical catastrophe.

CONCLUSION

The argument of this essay has been a long one, but the moral is brief. To go forward the modern world has had to look backward. What it has seen there is the image of a good society; it has used this image as an ideal model to criticize present circumstances and to strive to take destiny in its own hands.

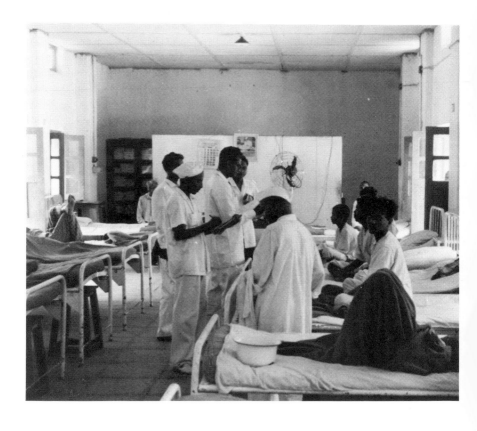

Physicians on Rounds in Hospital, Ayurvedic Research
Institute, Jamnagar, Gujarat

Photo by Charles Leslie

Classroom Instruction, Ayurveda College, Poona, Maharashtra

Photo by Charles Leslie

Preparation of Medicine in Herb Store Room, College of
Indigenous Medicine, Ceylon

Photo by Charles Leslie

Patient, Nurse, and Ayurvedic Physician, Ayurvedic
Hospital, Calcutta, West Bengal

Photo by Charles Leslie

This struggle has a common pattern, but in the contexts of different times and places it has worked out in different ways.

In Japan a revival movement was used to reform medical learning in the eighteenth century, while the country maintained almost complete social isolation, but responded to new scientific knowledge from the West. This prepared the way for an autonomous decision by the ruling elite to adopt modern scientific medicine for the legally sanctioned medical system. The resurgent revival of Chinese medicine in recent years lacks much of the symbolic value of revivalism in contemporary China or India, but it does symbolically criticize the legal monopoly of the modern medical profession, and the technocratic orientation which neglects the pastoral functions of medical care. It stands, therefore, for the humanization of medical practice.

In China, after formerly being a middle class movement, medical revivalism has been directed toward revolutionary ends. In both its early and present phase it inculcates cultural pride in opposition to the humiliation of Western imperialism, but as a revolutionary revival it is being used for drastic changes in the social order. It symbolizes the new egalitarian culture based on folk and popular culture traditions. It is used to humble the pride of "experts," those professionals who claim autonomy from social criticism in their work. Moreover, it symbolizes the pastoral functions of medicine which make it a "calling" to serve humanity rather than a self-serving career. Revivalism is a fundamental ingredient in a radical program of modernization which at the same time facilitates the maximum use of resources in the traditional medical system to create a comprehensive system of health care.

In India the medical revival resembles the bourgeois movement in China but has a longer and more complex history. By the time of independence it had built a much larger infrastructure of professional institutions, but since it was never made the instrument of a strong centralized policy—or caught the fancy of the Independence Movement—it has worked out its internal contradictions in a pluralistic, modernizing context. In doing so it has created a dual system of professionalized medicine in which the Ayurvedic and Unani practitioners and their institutions are in an ambiguous "quasi-paraprofessional" relationship to modern scientific medicine.

In all three societies revivalism has been a powerful instrument for transforming the medical system; and in all three systems medical knowledge and practice are symbols of the power science has to decide the fate of individual sufferers and to define a way of life.

NOTES

[1] Needham maintains that the overall influence of Indian medicine through the spread of Buddhism to China was minor, and with respect to Greek and Arabic medicine, he writes, "It is really hard to find in it (Chinese medicine) any Western influences" (1970:18-19).

[2] Ronald Hare, "The antiquity of diseases caused by bacteria and viruses, a review of the problem from a bacteriologist's point of view," in D. Brothwell and A. T. Sandison, eds., *Diseases in Antiquity* (Springfield, Illinois: Charles C. Thomas, 1967), pp. 115-31. Also see T. Aidan Cockburn, "Infectious diseases in ancient populations," in *Current Anthropology* (Vol. 12, No. 1, February, 1971): pp. 45-62. When I wrote this section I had not read two new essays directly concerned with the adaptive significance of Chinese Ayurvedic and Unani medicine: F. L. Dunn, "Traditional Asian medicine and cosmopolitan medicine as adaptive systems," and Ivan Polunin, "The ecology and evolution of disease in the Chinese, Hindu and Arab worlds," in *Toward the Comparative Study of Asian Medical Systems*, Charles Leslie, ed. (Berkeley: University of California Press, forthcoming). Fred Dunn emphasizes the importance of differential access to medical care in estimating the efficacy of these systems. Certainly, the learned practice of these systems was primarily accessible to the elite classes, and historical records only tell us about the learned traditions.

[3] John Z. Bowers, "The History of Medical Education in Japan: The Rise of Western Medical Education," in C. D. O'Malley, *The History of Medical Education*. UCLA Forum in Medical Sciences, No. 12 (Berkeley: University of California Press, 1970), pp. 391-416. My summary of Japanese medical history is based on this article, John Z. Bowers, *Medical Education in Japan* (New York: Harper & Row, 1965), and upon Yasuo Otsuka, "The Chinese Traditional Medicine in Japan," in *Toward the Comparative Study of Asian Medical Systems*, Charles Leslie, ed. (Berkeley: University of California Press, forthcoming).

[4] Dr. Otsuka kindly gave me the data from the annual statistics issued by the Japanese Ministry of Health for 1969. (See table on page 108.)

[5] The three humors (*tridosa*) of Ayurveda are often translated as wind (*vayu*), bile (*pitta*) and phlegm (*kapha*). In classic theory, blood (*rakta*) was a body element (*dhatu*), not a humor (*dosa*).

[6] Physicians do not practice just what they were taught in medical school, or what is in medical textbooks. They adapt their practice to the values and concepts of reality of their own social class and to the modes of interaction their patients expect, or will at least accept. Thus, allopathy is not simply "Western" medicine transplanted in India. Cultural variations in the institutions of modern scientific medicine occur in relationship to variations in popular culture medicine as one moves from India to Japan, Russia, or the United States. These variations have been almost totally neglected by medical sociologists and anthropologists.

⁷During the Independence Movement, Congress politicians and Ayurvedic physicians tried to persuade Mahatma Gandhi to endorse Ayurvedic and Unani medicine, but Gandhi had no taste for these systems, or for modern scientific medicine; instead, he experimented with nature cures which employed special diets and mud baths.

⁸From my notes, made at the Bombay Record Office archives in 1963.

Health Specialist	Number	Rate per 100,000 population
Physicians*	113,630	112
Practitioners of acupuncture and/or moxibustion	65,790	64
Traditional orthopedicians	7,492	7
Practitioners for massage and similiar techniques	61,605	60

*Of both modern and Chinese medicine, since practitioners of Chinese medicine must qualify as modern doctors.

5

The rethinking of modernization involves not only questions of theory and conceptualization as raised by Mead, Adams, Leslie and others, but also requires a critical look at methodological questions. In the Pelto and Poggie paper we see the development of an argument for the usefulness of regional approaches to the understanding of modernization. As is the case with Adams' focus on nation-states, this regional perspective represents a broadening of the more usual focus in anthropological fieldwork. By utilizing information collected in two regions in central Mexico, these researchers demonstrate that the regional approach is essential for some questions concerning modernization.

Models of Modernization: A Regional Focus

PERTTI J. PELTO AND JOHN J. POGGIE, JR.

Pertti J. Pelto received his Ph.D. from the University of California, Berkeley, and is currently Professor of Anthropology, University of Connecticut. Dr. Pelto has done research on cultural change among Finnish Lapps, Indians and whites in northern Minnesota, and Indian and Mestizo peasants in Central Mexico. Among his recent publications are The Snowmobile Revolution *(1973) and* Technology and Social Change *(with H. Russell Bernard) (1972).*

John J. Poggie, Jr., is Associate Professor and Chairman of the Department of Sociology and Anthropology, University of Rhode Island. He received his Ph.D. from the University of Minnesota. Professor Poggie has done field work on social and cultural change in central Mexico, Puerto Rico and among fishermen in southern New England. He has written on such topics as a new city in rural Mexico and folklore among fishermen in New England. His recent book, Between Two Cultures *(1973), chronicles the forces of change acting on an American-Mexican.*

Researchers dealing with the subject of modernization have often pointed out that certain core features of industrialization, commercialization, urbanization, and related developments take relatively similar forms in different parts of the world. There is a feeling—in both lay circles and among researchers—that the "big picture" displays major commonalities throughout the world. In this paper we do not intend to deny that modernization involves many worldwide similarities of both processes and products. On the other hand, we argue that to focus mainly on the broad general tendencies may not be the most productive and economical way to build systematic and useful theories of modernization. We will first very briefly review some main lines of research and thinking on problems of modernization, and will then discuss ways in which studies organized in terms of geographical regions offer possibilities for both theoretical and practical advances in the study of sociocultural change processes.

Much of the literature on modernization has focused attention on the conditions and situations that produce supposedly "modern" psychological or cognitive characteristics in individuals. For example, researchers have looked for the factors that produce "modern attitudes," "progressive thinking", or "achievement orientation" among peasant and tribal peoples who are confronted with alternatives to their traditional ways of living. Inkeles and associates (Inkeles, 1969; Smith and Inkeles, 1966) have been developing a new pan-human measure of modernity. Their definition of modernity includes the following kinds of items: openness to new experience, both with people and with new ways of doing things; the assertion of increasing independence from authority of traditional figures; belief in the efficacy of science and medicine, and a general abandonment of passivity and fatalism as responses to social and economic difficulties; ambition for oneself and one's children to achieve high occupational and educational goals; emphasis on timeliness and planning in advance; strong interest and activity in civic and community affairs and local politics; and finally, keeping up with the news, and preferences for international and national news over purely local interests. Thus they are asking in their research "How far is there an empirically identifiable modern man, and what are his outstanding characteristics?" (Inkeles, 1969:210). Working with data from Pakistan, Nigeria, Chile, Argentina, India, and Israel, Inkeles and his associates have found that there is in fact very considerable cross-cultural uniformity in the kinds of influences that bring about "modernization" among individuals. They say that "One must be struck by the exceptional stability with which variables such as education, factory experience, and urbanism maintain the absolute and relative strength of their impact on individual modernization despite the great variation in the culture of the men undergoing the experience and in the levels of development characterizing the countries in which they live" (Inkeles, 1969:225).

Everett Rogers has studied modernization among peasants in India, Kenya, Colombia, Brazil, and Turkey. Using factor analytic techniques in his analysis of the Colombian data, he concludes that ". . . modernization is multi-dimensional, composed of at least three distinct dimensions: external communications; orientation to change; and innovative leadership orientation." He emphasizes that a major factor in modernization is ". . . a capacity to communicate by way of urban contact and the mass media, combined with the associated ability of individuals to absorb mass communication messages" (Rogers, 1969:340).

Allen Peshkin and Ronald Cohen (1967) have attempted to define major "values of modernization." They find that ". . . there is no simple relationship between the holding of modern values and action consonant with these values." Rather, ". . . all modernizing values are capable of selection by elements in the environment. By designing research such that age, sex, rural or urban residence, years of western schooling, socioeconomic background, tribe, religion, and several independent variables can be related to the modernizing values described here, hopefully the factors in the society which tend to select modernizing values will be so indicated that the society's value system may evolve toward a wider acceptance of these values" (1967:19). According to Peshkin and Cohen ". . . the 'good life' everywhere seems to be more and more characterized by optimal output, dissemination and utilization of information, ideas, material goods, wealth, and energy resources (including manpower) . . ." (1967:20).

In his book, *The Passing of Traditional Society*, Daniel Lerner (1964) argues that the psychological characteristic of empathy is a key to understanding the modernization process among traditional peoples. Lerner states that ". . . we are interested in empathy as the inner mechanism which enables newly mobile persons to operate efficiently in a changing world. Empathy, to simplify the matter, is the capacity to see oneself in the other fellow's situation" (1964:49-50). Lerner's major hypothesis is that ". . . high empathetic capacity is the predominant personal style only in modern society, which is distinctively industrial, urban, literate and participant" (1964:50).

Joseph A. Kahl has examined ". . . some social concomitants of industrialization and urbanization" (Kahl, 1959). Unlike the preceding studies, all of which concentrate attention on the characteristics of individuals, Kahl focuses on more general social changes such as population growth, population shifts from rural to urban settings, increased division of labor, changes from localism to nationalism in people's orientations, growth of formal education systems, development of new systems of social stratification, expectations of increasing standard of living, changes in family structure, and greater organic solidarity of society. Like most researchers, Kahl focuses most of his attention on modernization as it applies to cities. Thus he notes, "I have been stressing in this paper what seem to me to be the processes of change which tend to create a universal way of life in modern, industrial cities" (1959:71).

Economists and political scientists have perhaps been more concerned with elements that may be important in promoting modernization, especially in terms of industrialization and the development of "modern" political systems. Thus, economists have studied factors such as accumulation of capital, development of cash economies, and formulation of national fiscal policies that may be used to promote development (cf. Rostow, 1960; Polanyi, 1944; Gerschenkorn, 1962; Hagen, 1962; and others).

Political scientists have developed propositions concerning decision-making structures, courts, and modes of representative government as they relate to shifts from traditional peasant social systems to modern nation-states. Lucien Pye (1966), for example, has emphasized the crucial role of institutional frameworks that transform tribal and provincial identifications into more nation-oriented behavior (cf. Weiner, 1966; Galanter, 1966; also many others).

The studies cited thus far point to certain very general trends and conditions of modernization and industrialization throughout the world. At the macrocosm end of the continuum there are the theories and descriptions dealing with national economies and sociopolitical systems. At the micro-level of analysis, on the other hand, the personalities, attitudes, and other characteristics of individuals are studied as both factors in, and results of, the modernization process.

Field oriented anthropologists, on the other hand, have frequently oriented their research interests toward the study of traditional communities and have examined the effects of modernization on small local groups. Thus Redfield and his associates, in studying culture change in the Yucatan region of Mexico, examined the ways in which civilization, ". . . its satisfactions and discontents, comes to a Mayan village" (Redfield, 1950). Similarly, Charles Leslie has studied the world view of the Zapotec Indians of Mitla, Oaxaca (*Now We Are Civilized*, 1960), a community previously studied by Elsie Clews Parsons (1936). Leslie introduces the main focus of the research, saying ". . . throughout the study we describe the world view of townspeople as it has evolved under the pressure of social change. By analyzing the nature of the community during the past twenty years, and by reasoning from our knowledge of the region as a whole, we outline changes in the life of the community which have resulted in large part from an expansion of commerce in Oaxaca" (Leslie, 1960:xi).

George Foster has devoted a great deal of time and energy to examination of modernization in the Mexican town of Tzintzuntzan (Foster, 1967). In this research Foster has the very great advantage of a long time span, for his first-hand data from this community cover nearly three decades. His initial field work took place from 1944 to 1946 and the data from this research provided a base line for later comparisons as he restudied the community, especially in the years between 1959-1966. Although his research has centered for the most part on this one community, Foster nonetheless generalizes about an attitudinal characteristic he believes to be very prevalent among peasants throughout the world—the "image of limited good." This cognitive feature, he feels, promotes conservatism and traditionalism among peasant peoples.

There are scores of other studies by anthropologists that are concerned with modernization of individual communities or small traditional popula-tions. The great variety of these research efforts is illustrated by such books as the Andersons' *Vanishing Village*, a study of a Danish maritime community in the modern world (1964); Manning Nash's *Machine Age Maya: The Industrialization of a Guatemalan Community* (1958); Margaret Mead's *New Lives For Old: Cultural Transformation of the Manus, 1928-1953* (1956); *Eskimo Townsmen* by John and Irma Honigmann (1965); and Miles Richardson's *San Pedro, Colombia: Small Town In A Developing Society* (1970). This list could, of course, be extended many times over.

The community study approach used in anthropological studies produces rich and detailed descriptions of how rapid social and cultural changes have transformed the lives of individuals and local groups. On the other hand, such studies often depict local developments without sufficient attention to the ways in which the local community is articulated to the larger regional and national socioeconomic and political systems. Moreover, anthropologists frequently have placed heaviest emphasis on the unusual and different—the exceptional cases of modernization, good and bad. Thus it is not clear how these studies can be built up into a more generalized theoretical framework.

Even in those cases in which two or three communities in a region are systematically compared in terms of social and cultural changes, the cases are frequently selected because of some particularly striking contrast, without reference to what may be going on in the rest of the region. These anthropological studies have also frequently lacked data about the processes whereby wide-ranging commercial, political, and economic processes reach the local community area. The larger picture of modernization impinging upon the particular communities is often not examined.

The unrepresentativeness of individual community studies has sometimes been noted by anthropologists. Foster, for example, recently commented that "I am acquainted with Friedrich's accounts of revolution and violence in the Michoacan village he studied, and have often marveled at how different two communities with the same basic culture and historical backgrounds can be" (Foster, 1970:313). Thus, presumably, the generalizations that Foster has derived from his study of Tzintzuntzan (also in Michoacan) are not necessarily transferable to other communities in adjacent regions. In a comparative study of two Jamaican fishing villages, Davenport (1956) found that these ecologically similar communities are very different in their social and cultural patterning of resource utilization. He discovered striking differences in organization of fishing crews, modes of recruitment to crews, and quite dissimilar personality characteristics (also, cf. Aronoff, 1967). Toshinao Yoneyana has compared two farm villages in Japan, pointing out important differences in their processes of modernization. They are, in fact, in two different regions, but he points out that ". . . differences that have always existed between Kaminosho and Kurikoma are partly the results of adaptations to somewhat dissimilar environments and partly due to unequal territorial access to the influence of cities" (1967:330). Walter Goldschmidt and associates (1965) have examined comparisons and contrasts between herdsmen and farmers in East Africa. They found that differences between herdsmen and farmers are quite important even when the two groups share the same linguistic and cultural identification. These differences, related to environmental variations, appear to be quite significant even when quite close together in geographic location. The description of three different ecological adaptations in fairly close proximity described by Fredrik Barth (1956) also illustrates the importance of microenvironmental variations within regions.

These examples have been cited in order to point out that the details of what actually happens to small communities undergoing modernization are likely to manifest significant differences because of *intraregional variability*. Some communities have been described as adapting swiftly and "painlessly" to modernization; others are described as suffering progressive deterioration and decay of "cultural integration;" still other cases involve strong resistance to the pressures of change and modernization. Clearly, any strategy of research that is to make full sense of these kinds of variations needs to include systematic study of more than just one or two or three communities within their regional settings.

REGIONS AS "NATURAL" UNITS

The problem as we see it is to develop a level of analysis that: (a) takes note of different microecological contexts; (b) allows for study of the range of local situational variation that we know exists (e.g., household composition, socioeconomic means); (c) allows for the analysis of the systematic relationships of communities to one another; and (d) includes the analysis of relationships to wider sociocultural systems. Geographers have demonstrated that any single community has multiple ties to both smaller and larger communities in patterned constellations of settlements. Studies utilizing "central place theory," developed by Walter Cristaller (1933), have demonstrated this interrelatedness of communities in regional settings. One can argue, therefore, that the *natural* unit of analysis should be a *system* of communities.

It is true that if one focuses on a single modernizing community within a region he will see change going on. However, those single community processes may be unrepresentative of the range of significant adaptations that people are making in different parts of the system. Systems of communities are often isomorphic with natural geographic features such as coastal strips, intermontane basins, islands, valleys, and plateaus. Sometimes regional systems can be defined by the political boundaries, but often it is more useful to conceptualize them in terms of a combination of political and physiographic features.

There are a number of studies in the anthropological literature that are based on a regional instead of single community focus. The East African Ecological Project, cited above, is an example in which the researchers examined a series of variations in cultural patterning and related characteristics within a general area rather than concentrating on a single culture or a single community. This approach permitted them to locate and describe variations in cultural, social, and psychological patterning that reflect ecological differences within the region. The Harvard anthropological researchers, who have invested considerable effort in the region of Zinacantan and neighboring *municipios* in Chiapas, have collected data from a number of different communities, but their work to date does not appear to reflect a systematic interrelating of these data at the regional level (Vogt, 1969).

The Northern Plains Ecological Project of John Bennett and his associates is a good example of an explicitly region-oriented study. These researchers have studied the differential ecological adaptations of farmers, ranchers, Hutterian Brethern, and Cree Indians within the environmental constraints and possibilities of southern Saskatchewan. Several of their major publications involve data from more than one community, and their studies examine interrelationships among the different occupants and their respective ecological niches within the region. The study is particularly interesting, as the adaptations of the several groups are quite different and the differences cannot be accounted for simply in terms of variations in ecological situations. The Hutterian communities and their ecological adaptations, including their responses to modernization, differ from their neighbors in ways that reflect ideological and religious variations rather than simply pragmatic and economic factors (Bennett, 1968; 1969).

Charles Erasmus (1961, 1967) has studied modernization among the Mayo and Yaqui Indians in northwest Mexico, an area in which large scale irrigation projects, crop changes, and other technological developments have been introduced. Erasmus looks at developments in the area from the point of view of both the more rural Indian populations and the Mestizo populations in the towns and small cities of the area. His study involves comparisons among these populations, instead of focusing on just one or two communities. Louis Faron's (1967) study of "A History of Agricultural Production and Local Organization in the Chancay Valley, Peru" also focuses on a regional system rather than a single community.

In the late 1950s, Frank and Ruth Young carried out research in the Los Llanos region in South Hidalgo, Mexico, in connection with the introduction of a new industrial complex into a previously agricultural intermontane valley (Young, 1964, Young and Young, 1960a, 1960b, 1962a, 1962b, 1966, 1967). In this study, the Youngs identified a network of twenty-four communities within the Los Llanos region. In a much more systematic fashion than many of the other studies cited, the researchers focused on the types of interrelationships among the communities within the research area. The twenty-four communities in the study vary in size from small clusters of households with less than 100 persons to larger towns with several thousand inhabitants. This same region, the area around Ciudad Industrial, has been the focus of a more recent study which will be examined in more detail later in this paper.

As already suggested, these regional studies, whether focused on modernization or on other kinds of social and cultural processes, make possible systematic study of the range of variation within particular political-geographical "zones" rather than depending on single communities as "type cases." These regional studies make it possible to treat individual communities as parts of "larger systems," and they also afford improved frameworks for study of relationships to national and international systems of economic and political networks. At the same time, the regional focus of research can permit application and testing of general cross-national modernization theories in relation to the specifics of individual environments and sociocultural systems.

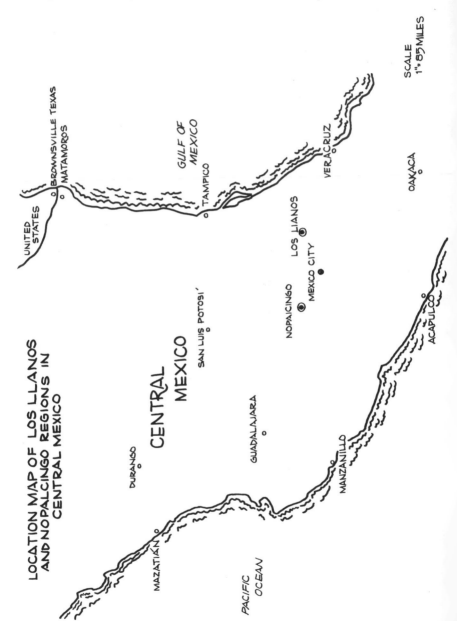

LOCATION MAP OF LOS LLANOS AND NOPALCINGO REGIONS IN CENTRAL MEXICO

TWO REGIONAL PROJECTS: LOS LLANOS AND NOPALCINGO

It will be useful at this point to take up two regional research examples in order to examine some of their characteristics more fully and note some of the possibilities for developing macroregional models from this kind of research. The first of the projects discussed here, that of Los Llanos, is actually a continuation of the Youngs' study of Ciudad Industrial and environs. The region that had been studied by Frank and Ruth Young in 1958 was restudied in 1966-1969 (and continuing) by a team of anthropologists from the University of Minnesota (Poggie, 1968; Miller and Pelto, 1968; Poggie and Miller, 1969; Mundale, 1970; Miller, 1973).

In this follow-up study in the 1960s we had the advantage of the solid baseline of quantified data obtained by the Youngs in their earlier research. The fact that the Youngs had organized their research in terms of an intervillage network enhanced the usefulness of these baseline data. From the earlier descriptions of the intervillage network (updated by pilot research in 1966), we selected communities for intensive study that represented the range of variation within the network. The communities selected for intensive research included those which the Youngs had studied intensively in the past. The general purpose of our project was to examine the impact of the new industrial city on the traditional agricultural communities within the region. We expected that differences in the relationships of the villages to the industrial city would reflect geographical proximity, previous economic conditions in the communities, and other specialized ecological features of the communities within the region.

Our research design in the Los Llanos project included several types of data collection. Initially the region was visited by one of our Minnesota group, accompanied by a Mexican psychologist, for purposes of a pilot study and reconnaissance. During this initial phase, communities were selected for intensive research, their general characteristics described, and demographic data were collected. After the completion of the pilot study phase, an ethnographer (Poggie) moved into the region and took up residence in the industrial city. From this base he collected structured data in all thirty of the villages and hamlets located in the Los Llanos region. His strategy was to work with key informants in each of the thirty-odd communities, obtaining information about institutional development and the types of contacts that each community had with other communities in the region. He also familiarized himself with other special characteristics of the region.

During this key informant stage of the project groundwork was laid for survey interviews in samples of households in the communities selected for intensive research. A later phase of research involved collection of psychological data from subsamples within the survey research sample. Data were collected using a modified version of the TAT (Thematic Aperception Test) as well as a Spanish language version of the MMPI (Minnesota Multiphasic Personality Inventory) adapted for use in Mexico. Throughout all phases of the research project, participant observation and key informant data were obtained to add depth and context to the more quantified materials. In addition to these major aspects of the research, other specialized types of data were collected in order to gain understanding of commercial elaboration, the school system, and social stratification within the area.

In the several phases of the project, our research design has included systematic comparisons between factory workers, farmers, and commercial operators. These comparisons are structured in terms of intracommunity differences—that is, the workers, farmers and entrepreneurs are all co-residents in the sample communities. We felt that comparisons between workers in Ciudad Industrial with farmers in the traditional villages would not be nearly as theoretically significant and informative as comparisons involving persons who live together in the surrounding communities. In the course of systematic farmer-worker comparisons, we found that there were also differences among inhabitants of different villages beyond the variation that appeared to result from occupational roles.

In several phases of the Ciudad Industrial research project, data collection and processing has involved cooperation between our research group and social scientists in Mexico. The survey research operation that involved intensive interviewing in approximately 500 households was carried out by the Instituto Mexicano de Estudios Sociales under contract to the Minnesota project. Details of the interview schedule were worked out in conferences between ourselves and the IMES staff.

Similar arrangements of international collaboration were worked out in connection with the psychological data. The MMPI and TAT responses were collected by psychology students at the National University in Mexico City under the direction of Professor Rafael Nuñez.

An input-output analysis of agriculture in one of the communities was carried out by a Mexican graduate student in agricultural economics directed by his major professor at the National School of Agriculture in Chapingo. Thus the structure of research in this project involved complex collaborative arrangements among several different disciplines staffed by individuals from the United States and Mexico.

In the early phase of the research we assumed a considerable homogeneity among the inhabitants of the different villages of the region. Our theoretical interests were focused on the contrasts between farmers and workers in their attitudes and behavior with regard to modernization. As preliminary analysis progressed, however, it became apparent to us that there was considerable differentiation among communities in terms of the impact of the new city on community life. For example, we found that general contact with the industrial city was a good predictor of a community's development. We also found from our participant observation that each community tended to have (to varying degrees) a unique configuration of behavioral styles depending in part on the number of factory workers who resided in the town, the political status of the community, its size, and other factors.

On the other hand, results from analysis of the social survey data showed that in spite of the fact that there were significant differences between farmers and workers on many dimensions related to modernization (e.g., values, attitudes, material style of life, aspirations, etc.), there was no indication that a large "cultural gap" in life styles had developed between farmers and workers. We could not regard these two groups as having developed into distinct occupational "cultures."

We found that the communities within the region were becoming increasingly differentiated from one another in terms of their emphasis on such features as periodic markets, residential areas for workers, medical facilities, fiestas, recreation and diversion, wage employment possibilities, and communications facilities. The importance of this growing differentiation is underscored by the fact that the communities are linked to one another by a dense network of bus, train, and automobile transportation.

The two factors of intercommunity specialization and tight transportation network lead us to conceptualize the entire region as a "dispersed city." Like many cities, the Los Llanos region has its factory complex (Ciudad Industrial), its "downtown" commercial area (Xalpan), workers' "residential suburbs" (Benito Juarez and Estacion), and more traditional "old town" area with fiestas and other activities (Cerro Grande). The differences between the

Los Llanos region and a typical North American or European city are visible in the open spaces of maguey plantings and the barley and corn fields that separate the different parts of the "city." It is also of interest that there is no pall of industrial and automobile exhaust haze over the valley, although the growth of industrial and commercial activity certainly runs the risk of damage to the ecological balances of the area.

From our participant observation in the communities surrounding Ciudad Industrial we learned that the workers in these communities had no great urge to actually live in the industrial center. In fact, just the opposite was true; negative valuation of Ciudad Industrial as a place to live was quite common among our informants. They spoke of restrictions on activities in the industrial center which reflected general policies of the administration. The policymakers were intending to maintain Ciudad Industrial as a special kind of place. The number of houses, the numbers and types of commercial firms, the sale of liquor, and the building of other types of manufacturing plants were all tightly controlled by the administration. These restrictions discouraged workers from seeking residence in the industrial center; they found their traditional villages and towns more congenial. Thus we found that very few workers from the local communities sever their ties with fellow villagers and townsmen when they obtain employment in the factories. We have argued (cf. Poggie, 1972; Miller, 1973) that this co-residence of farmers, workers and others in the Los Llanos region is one of the chief factors in the lack of sharp differentiation between factory workers and other occupational groups.

The patterns of modernization that are developing in the Los Llanos region could not have been explored effectively if we had concentrated our efforts on just one or two selected communities. Moreover, focusing research on the industrial city itself would not have provided satisfactory materials about the influence of the factories on the surrounding populace. Lessons learned, at times accidentally, in the Ciudad Industrial research led us to a more consciously regional approach in our next research effort.[1]

The valley of Nopalcingo is about two and a half hours by automobile northwest of Mexico City. Hence, its position in relation to the metropolitan area is not very different from that of the Los Llanos region just described. Both of these locations are in the central highland area of Mexico; both are relatively dry areas of considerable elevation; the maguey plant and pulque drinking are features of the economic and social systems of both areas; and both were dominated by large haciendas in pre-revolutionary days.

Furthermore, the Mexican governmental policies of modernization extend to both regions. The commercial system of modern Mexico, marked by the growing network of automobile, bus, and truck traffic, and rapid dissemination of store goods such as clothing, plastic shoes, plastic kitchenwares, and other features, is reaching out into both these areas. Increasing numbers of television antennas are visible in the Nopalcingo area as they are in the Los Llanos valley region. The pace of change is rapid in both populations.

Nonetheless, there are important differences in specific features of the ecological situations of the two regions. Compared to the Los Llanos area, Nopalcingo is a relatively more isolated pocket, with only one paved road leading into the valley area. Instead of a dozen or so haciendas sharing socioeconomic power in pre-revolutionary days, Nopalcingo was dominated by one very large hacienda located in the middle of the valley at Espiritu Santos. The valley floor of Nopalcingo has much more water available for crop-growing than does the Los Llanos area, and it is therefore possible to have a relatively productive system of irrigated agriculture. Indeed, in earlier days this valley system produced a great deal more wheat, corn, and other crops than the Los Llanos region. This important environmental difference reflects the fact that the Rio Lerma flows directly through the Nopalcingo Valley. During summer growing months the problem for the Nopalcingo peasants is often the flooding of the river, rather than lack of water.

Because of these environmental features, the Nopalcingo Valley area has been a target for governmental projects in river control, irrigation systems, and general improvement in agricultural productivity, including changes of cropping patterns. A large investment has been made by national and state governments and other agencies in technological modification of the valley, and most of this has gone into hydraulic features, amounting to an investment of eighty to ninety million pesos. Thus the technological modernization of the valley system, influenced by local environmental conditions, takes a quite different form than that described for the Los Llanos region, in which modern factory technology has been the major input.

Nopalcingo Valley is a rather small region; the distance from the southeast entrance to the farthest corner (in the northwest) is about forty miles. At places the valley is only eight or ten miles wide. A total population of approximately 50,000 people live in the Nopalcingo region. Approximately half of the population is of Indian cultural identity, divided between Mazahua and Otomi-speaking peoples. The Mazahua Indians are clustered around the southernmost part of the valley system, most of them along the Rio Lerma canyon just outside the entrance to the Nopalcingo Valley. The Otomi people are on the north side of the valley. Several of these communities are overwhelmingly Indian in composition, but other villages are of mixed Indian-Mestizo population structure. The larger communities such as the head town of Nopalcingo are largely Mestizo, but with some neighboring barrios inhabited by Otomi and Mazahua people.

The agricultural lands of the valley floor are divided among thirty-seven ejido communities. These communities were the recipients of the lands that were divided amongst peasant populations when the haciendas were expropriated in the early 1930s.

Travel among the villages of the valley is made difficult during the rainy season by the fact that roads are not surfaced, and they are often subject to flooding. Heavy rains quickly turn the roads into impassible quagmires.

Bus service links most of the towns in the valley system to one another and to points outside the valley. However, during the rainy season the buses frequently do not succeed in ploughing through the mud from one town to the next, and the travellers must wait for drier weather. For example, the cluster of population that includes a large Otomi community and a sizeable mestizo population in the northernmost part of the valley system has much better road contact with areas to the north (outside the valley system) than they have with communities within the valley itself. Similarly, the towns in the northwestern corner of the valley system are linked by road to the next valley system toward the west rather than to the town of Nopalcingo. Thus, although these communities have important ties *within* the valley, they are also tied into networks of communities lying outside the system. Telephone service is available only in the town of Nopalcingo (nineteen telephones in 1970). Compared to communications and travel in the Los Llanos area, the flow of people and information in Nopalcingo is rather slow and irregular.

During the seasons of the year when agricultural work is not pressing, many of the people (especially males) in the Nopalcingo Valley travel to the cities or to other areas to seek part-time wage work. Nowadays many of the people, both household heads and young single men, go to Mexico City for temporary work in construction and other unskilled labor, and in earlier times a number of the people in the valley have been braceros in the harvest fields of Texas, New Mexico, Arizona, and California.

Research in the Nopalcingo Valley has been carried out sporadically by various Mexican researchers and others in connection with the development programs now going on in the valley region. For example, a team of researchers from Ibero-Americana University studied the pottery industry and other aspects of life in the town of Santiago (Mazahua Indian community) and a Master's thesis has been completed by a Mexican researcher on life in the town of El Nopal, which is a barrio hamlet adjacent to Nopalcingo. This same Mazahua community was also the subject of a recently published monograph (Iwanska, 1971). In the summer of 1967, the Instituto Mexicano de Estudios Sociales (IMES) of Mexico City carried out survey research in the valley on contract with Plan Lerma (the United Nations-Mexican development agency). The data from 1967 provide a kind of baseline and a fund of information which was used by researchers from the University of Connecticut in a pilot study in the summer of 1970 and subsequent years.

During the summer of 1970, researchers carried out participant observation and informal interviewing in a number of communities of the region. Some of the field workers lived in the old hacienda now occupied by the Plan Lerma staff. This made possible intensive study of the developers and their interactions with local leaders. Another team of field workers studied details of the pottery industry in Santiago. Preliminary survey data were collected from three communities, focusing on material style of life, dietary intakes and perceptions of food use, modern occupations, and geographical locations.

The relationships among the communities of the region had been delineated in a preliminary way by the IMES researchers in 1967 and some additional confirmation of this patterning was obtained during the summer of 1970.

Data on people's perceptions of "healthy foods," characteristics of occupations, and salient characteristics of different communities were obtained by means of a modified semantic differential technique. Respondents were asked to rank a series of items on seven-point scales. For example, in the matter of healthfulness of food, each food item was to be ranked on the scale from 2 (very unhealthy) to 7 (very healthy). Similarly, each occupation, such as truck driver, doctor, teacher, pottery maker, seller in the market place, and merchant, was ranked from 1 to 7 on a series of qualities such as "clean-dirty," "religious-unreligious," "much money—little money," and "good for my sons—not good for my sons". In the same manner, a series of communities including small villages, the town of Nopalcingo, the town of Atlacomulco outside the system, and the cities of Toluca and Mexico City, were to be rated 1 to 7 on qualities similar to those used for the occupations. Researchers found that, with some careful explanation, both Indian and Mestizo respondents were able to make these ratings and appeared to understand the meanings of the questions.

In preliminary analysis of these data, we have found that both Indians and Mestizos rate the cities higher than the towns and villages in all kinds of "good" qualities. At the same time the supposedly desirable qualities, including "religious," were assigned to the higher occupational categories. Thus the people of the region, both Indians and Mestizos, rated occupations and communities *of the outside world* as more desirable than their own occupations of pottery and farming. Pottery-making was especially low in all of these ratings, whether rated by Indian pottery-makers themselves or by their Mestizo neighbors.

Another part of the analysis of these data has indicated that "material style of life" as a measure of economic well-being appears to be a powerful predictor of acceptance of new innovations as well as of adequacy of diets.

These data from research in the Nopalcingo area indicate that the people of the area in general aspire to the things of modern life—to "higher" occupational categories, more income producing activities, and the material and other benefits that such economic activities could bring. At the same time they rate the things and qualities of urban centers as more desirable than the conditions in their native villages.

The behavior of the people appears to support these data from their responses to questions. That is, numbers of them seem willing to travel to distant areas to look for work in attempts to accumulate cash with which to realize some of the new things of modern life. There also is strong evidence of rapidly rising expectations with regard to education, particularly in the increased enrollments in the local grade schools.

COMPARISON OF LOS LLANOS AND NOPALCINGO REGIONAL SYSTEMS

From the research that has been carried on in the Los Llanos and Nopalcingo regions we are able to note that there are indeed important similarities in the trends of modernization in these two valley regions of highland Mexico. There is a particularly striking rise in aspirations (in education, occupations, material things) among people in both areas. This is in marked contrast to the relatively static expectational levels of Mexican peasants who have not received modernizing inputs. Other striking similarities in the trends of modernization in the two areas include a rising material standard of living as seen in modern household furnishings (television sets, radios, sewing machines, blenders and the like), as well as larger items such as automobiles, trucks, and mechanized agricultural equipment. Furthermore, in these regions we note an intensification of communication links with regions outside the valley systems. This includes an increase in media materials—magazines, newspapers, radio and television.

The general similarities in our two modernizing regions of highland Mexico are in keeping with the findings of Inkeles, Kahl, Rogers, and others discussed above. That is, these and other trends reflect worldwide patterns of modernization stimulated by inputs from outside the local scene. In these two regions of Mexico, as appears to be the case in many parts of the developing world, there seems to be an ever-increasing link-up with areas of the urban sectors of national systems. Consumer goods, a cash economy, and the behavioral complexes that accompany these economic changes are becoming more and more part of the social life of the hinterlands.

In spite of the general similarities in modernization processes, our researchers have been struck by the important *differences* between the Los Llanos and Nopalcingo situations. A striking difference already noted is the types of technologies introduced into the two areas. In the Los Llanos instance, modernization takes the form of quasi-urban industrialization, while in the Nopalcingo case agricultural development based on river irrigation is the focus. In the Nopalcingo case this modernization program is based on what is essentially an intensification of the traditional agricultural economy of the region, whereas modernization in Los Llanos involves a sharp departure from the past agrarian economy. The agricultural base of Los Llanos can be shunted into obscurity, overshadowed by the completely new incomes and occupations of factory production. The contrast between factories and intensified farming also involves significantly different implications for population size. Modernization of agricultural techniques in Nopalcingo is likely to lead to sharp population decline, whereas the reverse has been the trend in the Los Llanos case.

An important difference in the diffusion of modernization throughout the

Carrying Out Peasant Work in Los Llanos

valley systems is immediately visible. Los Llanos is a region with increasingly high traffic density, with high levels of communication from the factory center outward to the villages, as well as within the intervillage network. An intensified network of bus lines links the communities of the Los Llanos region, in addition to which the number of private vehicles makes the traffic patterns of the region almost comparable to metropolitan lifeways. This is one of the factors which led our researchers to refer to the Los Llanos region as a "dispersed city."

In Nopalcingo, on the other hand, modernization influences introduced by Plan Lerma and governmental change agents appear to travel at a much slower rate. Apparently there is something about agricultural modernization that involves much lesser intensities of communication within the local system. There is not a steady daily traffic back and forth from the center of cultural change in the valley system, and the rate of introduction of new information from outside the system appears to be much slower in the Nopalcingo case than in Los Llanos.

In fact, the most striking thing about the Los Llanos regional case is the high level of new information input. At the beginning of the modernization process in the 1950s there was a large input of new persons—new factory workers—into the area. A very large number of new structures had to be erected, and the manifestation of a whole new way of life—middle class living—was physically introduced into the Los Llanos scene. In addition it should be noted that the factories of Ciudad Industrial do not simply endlessly crank out the same old products in the same old ways. Rather, a number of different products have been introduced—new types of automobiles, city buses, and others which call for retooling activities. New types of social organization in the form of labor unions and a wide variety of other changes have added new information processing features into the industrial complex. Informational inputs that are visible in the form of telephone services, newspapers, magazines, and other printed materials are much more evident in Los Llanos than in Nopalcingo.

We suggest that a major difference between the two regions is in the structure and especially the speed of the communication of information related to modernization. We also suggest that there are features in agricultural modernization and perhaps other related types of rural changes that involve relatively moderate changes in communication patterns compared to

Industrial Production in Los Llanos
Photo by John Poggie

Vista of Irrigated Corn in Nopalcingo

Photo by William Kelly

Indian Woman Preparing Tortillas in Nopalcingo
Photo by William Kelly

the quantum leap in informational processing that occurs when large factories are introduced into a region.

It may not be unrelated that these differences in communications structures have different implications for the vested interests within the regions. In some significant ways the traditional elites (especially the commercial operators) of the Los Llanos region have not been able to monopolize and control the patterning of new resources and wealth of the area. The new patterns are so different that local merchants and other power holders find themselves to a certain extent bypassed in the restructuring of commercial transactions and power allocation.

In Nopalcingo, on the other hand, where there is a slower pace of change and with inputs of modernization focused into certain main modes of communication, the local commercial operators and political leaders have been able to manipulate changes to their own advantage. The basic sources of income and the basic nature of what is produced have not changed, and no large influx of outsiders has altered the patterning of power relationships.

The peasant who is indebted to local merchants must sell his crops at harvest time at less than parity prices and cannot bypass these timeworn economic channels by seeking factory employment or other alternatives within the valley system. His alternative is to leave the valley completely through migration to city jobs or other wage work in distant places. Furthermore, the patterns of interrelationships among the communities of the region do not appear to have been altered by modernization as they have been in the intervillage network of Los Llanos. Therefore, the persons holding political power in these communities can still operate within their same well-defined channels of influence, now buttressed by the increasing affluence of a modernizing economy. The large input of new economic resources into the valley region brought about by the development of the irrigation system and other related policies of the development planners do produce some changes of patterning, but basically these do not short-circuit the already entrenched systems of political and economic privilege.

The implications of this part of our comparison include the possibility that in the Los Llanos region there is a restructuring of the social stratification of inequalities with the rise of a new middle class (composed of workers and other persons directly benefiting from the new economic order), and this new class of persons has some chance of undermining a portion of the established elite stratum of the region. Changes in the distribution of economic, political, and social privileges are likely (Mundale, 1970, Simon, 1968). On the other hand, in the Nopalcingo situation our data indicate that the effects of modernization will tend to increase the economic and political power of the established elites of the region. The overall rise of "gross national product" and general affluence of the region may work to the relative *disadvantage* of the most poverty-striken portion of the population, the Indians.

From the research data we have available thus far, we can therefore predict that continuing modernization in the Los Llanos region will result in a new and different structure of social stratification, while the processes of modernization in the Nopalcingo region will result in an intensification of the present stratified distribution of political and economic power. It seems particularly likely that the disadvantaged position of the Indian populations and other lower socioeconomic groups of Nopalcingo will not be improved. On the contrary, it seems likely that they will experience a *relative* deterioration of their socioeconomic situation during this process of modernization. More research will be necessary in both cases in order to monitor the continuing effects of these processes.

"UNIVERSAL" AND "SPECIFIC" (REGIONAL) MODERNIZATION

It should be clear by now that our suggestions about universal processes of modernization and specific regional variations in sociocultural change can be regarded as somewhat analogous to the differences between general and specific evolution noted in biological research. Understanding of the general processes of biological evolution has been furthered by two basic types of studies: (a) study in detail of the *mechanisms* of evolution—genetics, biochemistry, the structure and processes of the DNA molecule and cell replication mechanisms, etc.; and (b) detailed studies of *individual* evolutionary lines in their adaptation to particular types of environments (e.g., the evolution and ecological adaptations of horses, baboons, wolves, etc.). These latter studies have added greatly to our understanding of the processes of "specific evolution". Anthropologists such as Sahlins and Service (1960), in addressing themselves to processes of cultural evolution, have also made use of a distinction between general and specific evolution. As several authors have pointed out, general evolution ("general modernization" in the case we are talking about here), proceeds without regard to specifics of environment and local ecology. Specific evolution, on the other hand, involves the details of individual adaptations—both the successes and the failures—that are the fates of local populations.

When we fully realize the implications of these two perspectives we may come to the conclusion that for a great many people, including governmental planners, local leaders, revolutionary agitators, and people in general—the more important focus of attention is often on the specifics of *their particular situations* rather than on the broad generalities of the evolutionary process. Thus, when we come down to the pragmatics of action and social processes as they touch the lives of people, their adaptive decisions must be made with reference to specific environmental contexts, with particular constellations of relationships to urban centers and national states. They are less concerned with broad generalizations about factors in industrialization and rates of modernization than they are with exploiting their unique stores of natural resources and with their particular relations to urban and national informational sources. They are also concerned with the problems of dealing with their own special constellation of power elites and economic vested interests.

We are not arguing that the general principles or uniformities of modernization are irrelevant or immaterial. We are, however, asserting that very important practical as well as theoretical aspects of the modernization process are ignored if all our attention is on cross-national, cross-cultural and cross-continental similarities. In the two cases we have described briefly in this paper, the overall *general* processes of modernization look much the same. However, the outcomes—the end products in the form of transformed social systems—will be different for the two regions.

This impact of local environmental context and situation-specific events is strikingly clear in another rapidly developing region not far from the Nopalcingo area. The Valle de Bravo region, like that of Nopalcingo, is a river valley with new hydraulic developments. In this case, however, the building of a dam for hydroelectric purposes resulted in the inundation of local crop lands, leading to the creation of a scenic artificial lake. When wealthy families from Mexico City (including an ex-president) built weekend homes at this lake, a new boom period in tourism and "weekendismo" was inaugurated. The ways of life of the local townsmen and the Mazahua Indians in nearby villages were rapidly transformed into service-oriented occupations and the new tourist-oriented commercialization. Thus far it appears that the expansion of the local economy has been more of benefit to outsiders (and the wealthy city people) than it has been for local Indian and Mestizo inhabitants. This case of regional development involving combination of new hydroelectric installations and resort tourism has patterns of impact that are very different from those of Los Llanos and Nopalcingo (Paredes, n.d.).

In more general terms, it may be suggested that certain areas of central Mexico will experience general decline and deterioration as modernization proceeds. Other areas will very likely see increased affluence and general socioeconomic advances through the operation of the same general processes of modernization. The same unevenness of modernization and development is visible in various parts and regions of developed nations like the United States. The importance of specific studies (that is, regional studies) is of immediate practical consequence, as we have suggested above, but it is also of theoretical importance. In the final section of this paper we will present some general guidelines and research suggestions for maximizing the usefulness of regional studies in modernization.

THE REGIONAL FOCUS—THEORETICAL ADVANTAGES

As indicated earlier in this paper, we feel that modernization studies that concentrate on single communities are often too narrow in focus to uncover some of the important processes at work in modernization. On the other hand, cross-cultural or cross-national studies that point out pan-human or pan-societal universals are too abstract to be useful in explaining the processes whereby individuals and societies transform themselves in the face of specific types of modernizing influences.

From the experiences gained using regional research designs in the Los Llanos and Nopalcingo projects, we suggest that this strategy of research offers a number of features that are particularly advantageous for the study of processes of modernization. Unlike the one community focus of earlier anthropological studies, the multicommunity nature of this style of research permits investigators to examine systematic interrelationships among the different sizes of towns and villages of a developing region. In almost all cases it will be necessary to select a small number of communities for intensive field study, but these can be chosen in terms of their representativeness (in terms of size, resources, ethnicity, geographic location, etc.) within the regional network.

Although *any* community or region selected for research is to a greater or lesser extent an arbitrarily selected segment from a larger ecological system, a regional network of communities can, for purposes of analysis, be treated as a system with quantifiable input-output exchanges involving the local physical environment, as well as microcosm-macrocosm transactions involving the local population with wider national and international power systems.

The transactions of a region with the wider world include the flow of goods and services; transmission of information through mass media, governmental agencies and other means; and the movement of persons through inward and outward migration. All of these system changes are in principle definable and quantifiable. At the same time, the *quality* of these transactions with the wider world is often as important as the quantity of the relationships.

An anthropological research design that has a regional focus usually must deal with a pluralistic cultural scene. Even in cases where there is a seeming uniformity of cultural patterning within an area, it is probably most useful to conceptualize the research units as "populations" rather than "cultures." *Intra*regional and *intra*community variability of behavioral patterns is often of great importance for careful study of sociocultural change processes affecting local populations. An analysis of such processes of change is often best pursued with research strategies that assume heterogeneity rather than uniformity of peoples' actions and responses (cf. Graves, 1971, Wood and Graves, 1971, Robbins, et al., 1969).

We envision the regional approach to be particularly useful in theory-building within broader ecological "zones" such as "The Central Highlands of Mexico," "West Africa," "The New Guinea Highlands," "The Northern Plains" and other geographical units with common historical backgrounds, similarity of relationships to national and international power centers, and general equivalence of physical environments.

ELEMENTS OF THE REGIONAL RESEARCH STRATEGY

A regional research focus generally requires team research with a multidisciplinary membership. In order to examine patterns of modernization and adaptation in a specific region, it is essential to have information about local biological resources, climate, water resources, and other data for which economists, agronomists, engineers, geographers, and other specialists need to be involved.

It should be clear that the focus on a region for intensive study permits the research team to have a certain amount of elbow room and flexibility that is not possible within single communities as research foci. The sizes of regional research areas vary considerably, of course, but usually there will be a number of settlements from which representative communities for intensive research can be selected. Such selection should be based on intraregional differences and cultural styles—e.g., Indian and Mestizo community differences—as well as differences in community size, articulation to regional centers, and differentials in exposure to modernization influences.

It seems clear that some quantified baseline data are essential in order to examine the processes of adaptation and modernization within a specific population and to compare communities within the region. Some sort of survey interview data (usually in the form of extensive data from a series of households) need to be gathered in such a way that numerical comparisons can be made among different communities. These numerical data would, however, be very difficult to interpret without the help of extensive "contextual" qualitative data.

The patterning of developments in several different communities within a region needs to be examined in systematic terms. There may be important differences between one community and another which are best understood in light of the larger developmental process to which they articulate. Differences in the modernization processes from one community to another are often best understood in terms of their differences in details of microenvironmental context—that is, the different contingencies that impinge on the populations of these communities, rather than as simply "cultural differences." This is not to deny that cultural differences of some sort may be important in explaining aspects of differential modernization. However, "cultural" explanations of differences from one community to another often mask or obscure the ways in which two different populations are actually in different positions with regard to economic resources, political power, and other practical contingencies. For example, the differences between Indian and Mestizo populations in rates of acceptance of modernization and new economic inputs in the Nopalcingo Valley might be thought of as cultural differences between the two groups, but this explanation does not take into account the fact that the Indian populations on the whole have much less direct access to political power and economic advantage. It may be that the populations are about equal in their intentions to take advantage of new resources and new processes of modernization, but they have unequal means for doing so.

Very often the activities of governmental programs and other agencies of modernization are conceived in terms of regional projects. In fact, both the Los Llanos and Nopalcingo research projects correspond in a general way to the areal scope of planned programs. The congruence between the "cognitive maps" of the agents of modernization and the researchers can be an important factor in enhancing both the theoretical and applied usefulness of the research. (It may be noted in passing that a regional scope in anthropological research also is likely to improve our articulation with archaeological investigations which provide us with significant background concerning earlier cultural developments in our regions.)

While the regional focus for research that we are suggesting here is aimed at developing descriptions of particular individual situations of modernization, a first step toward greater generalization using this method might consist of the construction of types or "models" of regional development. Thus we may find from detailed study of several different regions (for example, in the Mesoamerican area) that there are a small number of basic "varieties" of ecological contexts, each with strong tendencies toward developing particular sets of responses to the inputs of modernization.

Still using Central Mexico as our example, we suggest the following potential regional models:

a) Rural industrialization (e.g., Los Llanos region)
b) Tourist and weekendismo area (e.g., Valle de Bravo)
c) Agricultural intensification (e.g., Nopalcingo)
d) Rural marginal backwaters (areas noticeably lacking in new development inputs from governmental or other sources)
e) Plantation extractive regions
f) Other special types

Careful, controlled comparisons among the several different types of regions within a general ecological zone such as the central Mexican highlands can make it possible for us to sort out similarities of process that crosscut local environmental differences. The patterns of migration from rural regions to urban centers may be a good example of this type of process. On the other hand, certain striking developments in particular regions may turn out to be very special localized phenomena. Since we are looking at these processes in terms of adaptations within a general evolutionary framework, some very unusual developments in certain types of regions may turn out to be of great evolutionary significance *even though the processes appear at this time to be quite localized and "particularistic."*

In arguing for a regional approach to the study of modernization, we feel that this strategy offers a workable compromise between the overly particularized descriptions of individual communities and the highly generalized grand theories of modernization. The regional focus keeps us in touch with empirical realities in a manner that permits us to see systems of social response as they operate in particular contexts. At the same time, regional scenes of modernization are "big enough" that the more generalized processes of modernization can also be seen in operation. Thus we are arguing for a particular kind of middle-range theory and research strategy which can have applicability to a potentially wide range of situations but is grounded in specific empirical studies.

NOTES

[1] There are some situations where the anthropological field worker finds himself unable, because of time and money limitations, to carry out a full regional study of the type we are suggesting here as an ideal model. In these circumstances we would nonetheless suggest that field workers conduct a series of structured interviews among different communities of the region being studied. This "spot checking" in a region can enable the researcher to determine the extent to which his research community fits in with and is representative of the broader system.

6

Much of the discussion of economic development involves the assumption of polar types of economic systems—the traditional and the modern. These polar types are perceived as differing not only in technological sophistication but also in terms of the way the economy is influenced by cultural traditions. Frank Cancian argues in his paper that people in all economic systems, whatever the level of productivity and complexity, behave "economically" in terms of the cultural context in which they live. Thus Cancian rejects the notion of the entirely rational (i.e., not culturally influenced) economic man, and calls for a reassessment of cross-cultural comparisons in economic modernization.

Economic Man and
Economic Development

FRANK CANCIAN

Frank A. Cancian is currently Professor of Anthropology at Stanford University and received his Ph.D. from Harvard University. He has done field work in rural Italy and in southern Mexico among Mayan Indians, and specializes in economic anthropology. His publications include Economics and Prestige in a Mayan Community *(1965) and* Change and Uncertainty in a Peasant Economy *(1972).*

Students of economic development have sought to conceptualize and explain the very real behavioral differences between traditional and modern people in a number of ways. Though once popular, the idea that modern men are rational in their economic behavior and peasants are irrational has passed out of use in the scientific community. Recent literature on agricultural development seems to be framed in terms of a contrast between economic and noneconomic influences on economic behavior. Those who see peasants as substantially different from modern people explain the difference by saying that noneconomic factors have a greater influence on peasant economic behavior. Those who wish to minimize the difference assert that peasants are as greatly influenced by economic factors as modern people. Neither approach places much emphasis on the influence of noneconomic (that is, cultural) factors on the economic behavior of modern people.

I believe that once the cultural context of modern economic behavior is recognized, the essentially value-dominated nature of comparisons between traditional and modern economic systems becomes strikingly apparent. Once we recognize how thoroughly cultural factors influence modern economic behavior, we are left unable to make simple scientific comparisons across cultures. In this situation intracultural comparisons of various kinds may produce valuable scientific results that aid economic development, but intercultural comparisons and decisions about the allocation of economic aid must be firmly and explicitly grounded on ethical principles.

In this paper I want to elaborate these points and comment on why the rather standard anthropological position I take is not commonly accepted in modern societies. I will review some positions on the "economic man" issue, and then try to show that comparisons of economic and noneconomic influences on economic behavior pose a bogus question. Although the structure of my argument may evoke images of straw men, I hope that the initial review of current statements will convince the reader that my adversary is alive and well. In fact, he flourishes among students of agricultural development.

THE ISSUE: ARE PEASANTS ECONOMIC MEN?

Are peasants economic men? Wharton's summary of a major conference on *Subsistence Agriculture and Economic Development* provides an excellent starting point for a look at current positions:

Throughout the meeting a fundamental issue repeatedly raised concerned the dominance of economic versus noneconomic forces upon the economic behavior of subsistence farmers. For some participants the general conditions of subsistence agriculture automatically delimit an area where, on net balance, the noneconomic frequently outweighs the purely economic, leading to behavior that goes against the postulated behavior of economics. For others, the economic forces dominate the noneconomic, and the observed behavior patterns are considered quite consistent with the postulates of economics (1969:456).

The problem leads to a controversy about the usefulness of economic theory for the study of subsistence agriculture. Wharton formulates three positions from the arguments of the many economists and other social scientists attending the conference. The extremes around an intermediate position are:

> . . . those who accept the noneconomic dominance of economic behavior and therefore argue for a total recasting of economic theory to handle the economics of subsistence agriculture . . . (and) . . . those who maintain that . . . subsistence and peasant farmers are highly rational and economic in their behavior, surmounting all such negative forces whenever the economic gains and returns outweigh the losses and costs. According to this view, leisure, work, thrift, and wealth with an eye to the marginal calculus are significant and are identical with, or not too dissimilar from, that which can be observed in modern societies (1969:457-458).

Behrman, in his study of *Supply Response in Underdeveloped Agriculture*, has also found a tripartite division useful for characterization of positions on a less general version of the fundamental issue:

> The various *a priori* hypotheses about the supply responsiveness of underdeveloped agriculture to price changes may be divided into three major categories: 1) The hypothesis that farmers in underdeveloped agriculture respond quickly, normally, and efficiently to relative price changes. 2) The hypothesis that the marketed production of subsistence farmers is inversely related to price. 3) The hypothesis that

institutional constraints are so limiting that any price response is insignificant (1968:3).

T. W. Schultz (1964) and W. O. Jones (1960) were the early spokesmen on the side of those who believe that economic theory is applicable to traditional economies (the formalist position). In his now classic book, *Transforming Traditional Agriculture*, Schultz is dedicated to the hypothesis that, "There are comparatively few significant inefficiencies in the allocation of the factors of production in traditional agriculture" (1964:37). Yotopoulos (1967) and Behrman (1968) have supported Schultz's general position in the context of detailed empirical studies of Greek (Yotopoulos) and Thai (Behrman) agriculture.

The classic exponent of the side that believes that economic theory is not appropriate for characterizing subsistence agriculture (the substantivist position) is J. H. Boeke. In his *Economics and Economic Policy of Dual Societies* he writes:

> Anyone expecting Western reactions will meet with frequent surprises. When the price of coconuts is high, the chances are that less of the commodities will be offered for sale; when wages are raised, the manager of the estate risks that less work will be done. . . . This inverse elasticity of supply should be noted as one of the essential differences between Western and Eastern economies (1953:40).

Finally, here are two statements from the most recent edition of Samuelson's text, *Economics*:

> In impoverished India, cows are sacred animals and, numbering millions, are allowed to walk through the streets foraging for food. While a naive economist might regard these herds as a prime source of protein supplements to an already inadequate diet, the more profound scholar will take the psychology of custom into account when analyzing Indian economic development (1970:5). . . . the Kwakiutl Indians consider it desirable not to accumulate wealth but to give it away in the *potlatch*—a roisterous celebration. This deviation from acquisitive behavior will not surprise anthropologists; their studies show that what is correct behavior in one culture is often the greatest crime in another (1970:16).

In sum, economists recognize a real difference between noneconomic or institutional factors and economic ones, and there is a real difference between those who see the noneconomic or institutional factors as dominant among subsistence agriculturists and those who do not.

THE PROBLEM: THERE ARE NO ECONOMIC MEN

Students of agricultural development differ on the relative importance they give to economic and noneconomic factors in the economic life of subsistence agriculturalists or peasants. Yet they are virtually uniform in their implicit assertion that the comparison of economic and noneconomic factors is a valid one. I will argue that it is not.

Economic man always operates within a cultural framework that is logically prior to his existence as economic man, and the cultural framework defines the values in terms of which he economizes. This is a platitude to anthropologists and economists alike. It is a simple restatement of the idea that the "given" institutional framework of the economic system may vary. However, it can be transformed into the conclusion that there are no economic men; i.e., there are no men whose economic activities are free of culture. If this is so, then perhaps the differences between men who respond to "economic" incentives and those who apparently do not is a difference in the degree to which observers have succeeded in specifying the institutional framework.

This following discussion elaborates and defends these assertions in three ways. First, I will suggest how the argument applies to the characterization of Zinacanteco economic life. Then I will discuss our own customs briefly, and finally I will try to characterize the logical structure of the economic man model more fully.

●*Zinacanteco Economic Life*

Zinacantecos are Maya Indian corn farmers who live in the highlands of Chiapas, Mexico and farm in the lowlands with traditional slash and burn techniques. They hire workers to help them at various points in the agricultural cycle and sell the excess over family food needs at various outlets in the area.

In a recent study of economic change in the community I viewed Zinacantecos as economic men (Cancian, 1972). Within this framework it is possible to show, for example, that farmers who hire many workers give larger gifts at recruitment (hiring) and more luxury items in addition to food and wages during the work period. At the same time small farmers may get the few workers they need less expensively by using particularistic ties within the community. It is also possible to show, on the one hand, that farmers who produce and sell large amounts tend to endure the bureaucracy and complication of selling to government agencies that pay relatively high prices. Farmers who sell small amounts, on the other hand, usually take the lower prices offered by private buyers who come directly to their fields at harvest time. In sum, Zinacanteco practices may be seen as attempts to economize time and money within the many constraints of their situation.

Another view of their hiring and marketing behaviors leads to a different conclusion. With reference to recruitment of workers, one might say: "despite the fact that they must often sell their previous year's crop at inferior prices in order to pay workers for weeding the new fields in June, Zinacanteco employers usually drink, often to the point of drunkenness, with each worker when they recruit him in San Cristobal (the market city). And when they return from the lowlands they provide a feast including so much drink that workers typically find it advisable to sleep at the employer's house and return to their families the next day." Or with reference to the marketing of corn in the highlands, one might say: "Though the fare to San Cristobal is high, farmers often take only small amounts of corn to the market at one time. This practice permits them to enjoy a number of days in the city." Clearly these customs and a number of others that could be described in similar terms represent situations in which Zinacanteco economic behavior is less than maximally efficient. In describing these "inefficiencies," I have shifted my emphasis to the institutional constraints, the customs, within which Zinacantecos work. However, all economies have such an institutional setting.

●Relativism and Cross-cultural Comparison

Though extreme to an anthropologist sensitive to the ultimate similarities of values across cultures, Samuelson's (1970:16) statement that ". . . what is correct behavior in one culture is often the greatest crime in another" expresses the essence of relativism. I want to emphasize the aspect of relativism summed up in the statement: "We have customs too." Although everybody knows this, it appears to be forgotten from time to time in the study of subsistence agriculturalists. Implicit, and occasionally explicit, in the application of the economic man model to subsistence agriculturalists is the comparison with modern economic systems in which the concept of economic man is presumed to describe a substantial part of economic behavior. Given our customs and the logical nature of the model, this comparison is a silly one.

Our customs do not hinder our efficiency. This is not because we have peculiarly distinct customs, but because we define efficiency in the context of our customs. If we consider our productive output as contrasted with our customs, it is easy to see how our production can be vastly increased by simple alteration of custom. An obvious example is the day of rest or weekend; think of the savings in capital investment in plant and equipment and churches that could be effected if we spread work and worship evenly over the days of the week. The reduction in capital tied up in plants would probably not reach the twenty-nine percent implied by adding two days each week to the five already worked, nor would the cost of churches be reduced by the eighty-six percent implied by eliminating six out of seven of them. However, there is no doubt that the savings and the consequent increases in production through alternative uses of the capital would be substantial. It is of course ridiculous to suggest that we completely abandon the social advantages of a common day of rest, but it is equally ridiculous to see ourselves as constantly maximizing economic goals.

In the first instance, then, there is no difference between our customs and those of others. The fact that we have managed to specify institutional constraints on our economic system so that we appear to maximize economic goals in "economic" activities is not a difference between our society and other societies. It is, though, a difference between the degree of experience we have in specifying the institutional constraints peculiar to each society.

Many analysts of modern industrial society properly emphasize the degree to which economic activities are differentiated from other aspects of life in such societies. In addition, they properly emphasize the contrast with other societies in which economic life is not so differentiated from other aspects of life. It is our ideal, within very important limits, to divorce our productive activity from many other aspects of our lives. However, this real difference between industrial men and subsistence agriculturalists does not mean that the former lead completely differentiated economic lives and the latter wholly undifferentiated economic lives. The difference is a matter of degree.

Though some interpretations of the theory of pure capitalism suggest that the differentiation might be complete in modern societies, clearly this is not the case. Like our tendency to behave according to the economic man model, our differentiation of economic life from other aspects of life is compromised by custom. We believe that workers should be hired for their ability to work and not because their cousin happens to be the foreman, and that college students should register on IBM cards because it reduces the cost of training them for productive lives. On the other hand, a foreman who fired a worker for a costly mistake might have the sympathy of others under normal circumstances but would be inviting costly disrespect if the error was made the week after the worker's son committed suicide. Likewise, the university that organizes registration so that many students stand in line overnight in order to turn in cards they have previously filled out will be subject to pressure, not because the students will catch colds or because they have something more productive to do, but because the waiting is clearly not worth the savings that might be effected.

In sum, we too have customs, and our customs quite appropriately come before our total devotion to an abstract ideal represented by economic man. While it is important to compare customs across societies, the question implied by comparison of degree of cultural versus "economic" influence on economic decisions across societies as wholes involves very serious logical problems.

●The Logical Structure of the Hypothesis of Economic Maximization

My principal assertion is that economic man always lives in a cultural context, and that economic and noneconomic (traditional or institutional) forces for change form an incomparable pair of features of any society. In elaborating this argument in its abstract or logical form it may be helpful to begin with a distinction between the economizing or maximizing framework for viewing human behavior and the hypothesis of economic maximization. The former is a general framework in which human behavior is viewed as the outcome of decisions arrived at by maximization of whatever goals need be attributed to the actor in order to make his behavior appear as maximization. The latter, which embodies the economic man model in actual research, is an empirically testable hypothesis which asserts that in many situations involving economic life men will allocate their efforts so as to maximize economic return. While the former is a useful general strategy for the study of an entire culture, the latter is always tested within a cultural context.

Many sociologists and anthropologists would claim that they make independent measures of values and then use them to formulate a contingent hypothesis including economic and noneconomic factors in decision making while the economists include only economic factors. I think they often tend to use the economizing or maximizing notions as a general framework which is not meant to be contingent in any way. That is, they use the general framework or orientation as a way of ordering their observations. In these terms, a successful study is one in which all values, attitudes, motives, and other impetuses to behavior are specified so that the actor appears to be maximizing (see Cancian, 1966; Burling, 1962). By contrast, the economist who limits his goals to the maximization of economic returns has the option of stating an empirically testable hypothesis. He may ask if, given the following conditions, the behavior under study produces maximization of economic returns; and he may genuinely determine his answer to the question on the basis of empirical data.

However, in the controversy about the relative dominance of economic and noneconomic forces upon the economic behavior of subsistence farmers, the economist is no better off with his hypothesis of economic maximization than are other social scientists who use the general maximization orientation. This is because economic and noneconomic (or better "institutional") forces are not parallel elements in the operationalization of the theory represented by the hypothesis of economic maximization. No matter how the hypothesis of economic maximization is stated, it is always tested within a huge *ceteris paribus* assumption about the institution setting. Even in the most purely "economic" situations there are always a number of (often implicit) institutional constraints. Thus, whenever the hypothesis of economic maximization does not accurately describe human behavior the economist may stick to the institutional constraints and assert the lack of economic maximization given his picture of the constraints. Or, he may change his picture of institutional constraints so that they cover the behavior which does not represent economic maximization. In this sense, the hypothesis of economic maximization is like any other hypothesis; failure to confirm it is never final.[2]

I conclude that since economic factors are always dependent on the prior

definition of noneconomic factors, it is impossible to make the statement
that noneconomic factors are more or less important than economic factors.
This means that comparative research that asserts the dominance of economic
factors in one place and noneconomic factors in another is meaningless.[3]

INTERNAL COMPARISON AND INTERNAL DIFFERENTIATION

If institutional constraints (i.e., noneconomic factors) can be taken as
constant and invariable, then the problem of their logical priority is circum-
vented and comparative research is possible. Here I wish to describe two
types of research that meet this condition and are potentially useful to the
policymaker who hopes to aid the economic development of a society or
group. Both internal comparison and internal differentiation research focus
on comparative rates of change within a group and avoid comparisons across
groups.

The internal comparison approach seeks to answer directly the interesting
question about what kind of program will be most effective for a particular
group. This approach is developed and well illustrated for economists by
Matthew Edel in a paper entitled "Innovative supply: A weak point in
economic development theory" (1970).[4] He says:

> The study of innovated supply has also tended to ignore a more
> important contribution to development policy implicit in the
> dichotomy of motivations it keeps rediscovering. It is not that any
> group of people is either all-responsive to the market or not responsive
> at all to anything but direct promotion of mental or social change.
> Rather, in most cases, either market stimuli or direct promotion may
> do something to increase effort in new lines of production. The most
> economical mix of policies to achieve a given production of a new
> product may include a combination of both *subsidies* to price (to induce
> more output in proportion to the elasticity of response) and direct
> *promotion* (through business motivation courses, community develop-
> ment programs, advertisement of the attraction of urban life or other
> means) (1970:18).

In discussing his own comparative study of the effectiveness of promotion
and subsidy in the Columbian Acción Comunal program, Edel makes the

point that is fundamental to the internal comparison approach, that knowledge of the comparative effectiveness of different programs (subsidy and promotion in his case) can be used to determine the most effective mix to use in fostering development within the society studied.[5]

The internal differentiation approach is based on the identification of segments of the population most apt to innovate and thereby get change moving. Rather than differentiating programs as Edel does, it differentiates individuals. Research in rural sociology is often of this type, as is my theory relating position in the Zinacantan stratification system to willingness to take risks on new farming practices (Cancian, 1972, Chapter 8). This approach does not ask whether the group in question responds quickly or slowly in comparison with other groups which might receive the same allocation of resources from those who control them. Instead, like internal comparison, it identifies the most effective way to introduce economic change once the decision to commit resources to a particular society or group has been made.

CROSS-CULTURAL COMPARISON, POLICY AND THE ETHICS OF AIDING DEVELOPMENT

Cross-cultural comparisons of economic responsiveness were criticized above because the institutional constraints that must be set in order to make them are not constant and unvarying across cultures. Thus, the outcomes of the comparisons vary with the setting of the constraints. The further conclusion that such comparisons cannot be made is untenable from a practical point of view, for in the course of human affairs men must and will make comparisons and evaluations.

Here I want to briefly explore the policy implications of the argument I have made about the logical structure of research on economic responsiveness. My argument leads to ultimate despair only if we seek in research some objective, scientific, and impersonal means of making comparisons and evaluations. If we are willing to see and accept the setting of institutional constraints as a fundamentally human and nonscientific act we have no research problem. This is so because the logic of research described above permits comparisons after the institutional constraints are set. We are only required to remove the cloak of scientific respectability from the process of setting constraints.

Once this is done, the policymaker is restricted to a more limited set of questions for research. If we frame his questions in terms of economic aid between nations, he may query in two ways. First, given a commitment of so much aid to a nation which has particular goals, how can aid be used most effectively? This is the question of internal comparison discussed immediately above.[6] Or, he may ask, with these resources and given this program, where will aid produce the greatest material return to the dollar?[7] However, he may not ask the general question, who are economic men and who are tradition-bound men? Nor may he justify his allocation of resources on the basis of an answer to this question.

Since the first two questions seem sufficient to sustain the efforts among nations to promote economic development, the limitation placed on the third question may seem trivial and irrelevant to practice. I do not think this is so. It might be trivial if we lived in a world or a nation that carefully moderated the value it placed on economic achievement, but we clearly do not live in such a world or nation. As long as men value economic men, the spurious attribution or denial of that quality to other men will make an important difference and must be done in a guarded manner that denies it ultimate significance.

MODERN MEN'S THOUGHTS ABOUT TRADITIONAL ECONOMIC SYSTEMS

The value modern men place on economic man is part of the broader orientation of our time. This broader orientation includes the scientific, technological and objectivistic approaches to human problems. These approaches are currently under attack by spokesmen of the "counterculture." Here I want to briefly explore the relation between my view that the economic man issue is a bogus one and what Theodore Roszak (1969, Chapter 7) has lableed "the myth of objective consciousness," and wish to speculate about the aspects of our culture that blind us to the limits of the economic man model. Since my characterization of the model is old hat in economics and anthropology, the continued misuse of the model in the study of traditional economic systems is particularly puzzling.

Roszak successfully identifies both our drive to subject all life to the objectivity that has contributed so greatly to our technical success and material well-being and the distancing and stratifying effect that this effort inevitably has on human relations. He points out that, "The ideal of the objective consciousness is that there should be as little as possible In-Here and, conversely, as much as possible Out-There. For only what is Out-There can be studied and known" (1969:220). He also relates this tendency to what he calls "invidious hierarchy":

> As soon as two human beings relate in detachment as observer to observed, as soon as the observer claims to be aware of nothing more than the behavioral surface of the observed, an invidious hierarchy is established which reduces the observed to lower status. Of necessity he falls into the same category with all the stupid things of the world that fill the Out-There (1969:222).

The struggle to be objective about human values so that the benefits of technical success can be brought to those who are members of traditional economic systems has led to a philosophically unsupportable effort to construct values out of science, and to a parallel blindness of the scientist to the basic values that support his own activity. It is commonly and correctly observed that the skills that enable men to go to the moon cannot solve the simplest moral dilemma, but it is still hard to believe that this is so, for our technical accomplishments are truly awesome. Without a doubt, the open envy of those who do not share in the benefits of our technological accomplishments does not help us to place them in proper perspective.

If there is any social scientific generalization that will help explain our blindness, it is probably the proposition that those who stand at the top of a stratification hierarchy find it hard to see real conflicts whose resolution might threaten their position. As the envied, it is in our interest to see the problems as part of the Out-There, as part of the objective, observable, manipulatable world that can be modified by simple attention to the objective science that has brought us to where we are. Even as we are able to assert the full humanity of those lower in the hierarchy of abundance, we are bound by our position to see the difference in nonhuman, technological terms, for technology serves our interests as the explanation of human differences, while the submission of the technical to the dominance of human values does not.

Thus, we are driven to the objective approach to human problems both because technology has benefited us and because humanity threatens us. We often fail to see that our economic system is embedded in custom and values, and we even objectify frankly ethical social changes in our society. Programs which will bring new dignity to women and the poor are supported by the argument that they will increase productivity and that present conditons waste resources—and the dignity itself is eventually allocated on the basis of productivity. For better or worse we revert to our material well-being when in doubt, and this leads us again to an objective stance and evaluation in terms of technological competence, by which time we have lost sight of the human concern that first impelled us down the road.

The idea that we are relatively free of noneconomic motives in our own economic life is the quintessence of this blindness. It permits us to categorize others in terms of the degree to which they, unlike us, are influenced by such motives. In this way, the economic man issue which has been discussed in this paper embodies the aspects of modern culture that Roszak has so aptly characterized. The counter culture argument that humanness is of greater worth than objectivity is used to reject these aspects of objective and technological modern culture. Furthermore, in a parallel fashion, my assertion that cross-cultural comparisons are meaningless unless preceded by a clear ethical position, rejects the sterile objectivism inherent in the economic man question as it is currently asked.

A firm commitment to our own humanity and that of others means that we must accept the onerous responsibility of our power and the ethical responsibility to control our self-interest. This is a call for noblesse oblige only to those who see power as its own justification, and it is a call for revolution only to those who imagine power to be a transitory phenomenon. To others, hopefully the majority, it is a plea to recognize that values come before power and technological competence. Whatever we do to each other, it will at least be more honest if we recognize the limits of science and objectivity. If we can inform and guide our science by ethical principles, we will have exercised our unique privilege as humans—the privilege to assert that, for our own purposes, we are more important than the world around us.

NOTES

[1]This paper was presented at "The Impact of Western Ideas on Traditional Societies: a Symposium on Modernization," University of Rhode Island, May 29,

1971. It was prepared at the Center for Advanced Study in the Behavioral Sciences, Stanford, California, during the tenure of an NIMH Special fellowship. I am grateful to these institutions and to Francesca Cancian and George Collier, who commented on earlier drafts. The core of the paper comes from Appendix D. of Cancian (1972) and is used with the permission of the Stanford University Press.

[2] The finding that the hypothesis of economic maximization does not apply to a given situation has important practical consequences within the framework of normative economics. These are situations where the economist's client sets the constraints and is presumably prepared to live with the consequences—where the economic man framework and the hypothesis of economic maximization are used to test allocative efficiency given available resources and other constraints. Within the framework of positive or descriptive economics, where the goal is simply a description of behavior and not optimal allocation given known constraints, the tables are turned and defining the constraints becomes the crucial empirical question. Although the efficient-allocation problem of normative economics and the institutional-definition problem of descriptive economics do not offer commensurable elements, it is clear that in many situations changes in constraints provide massive power over outcomes when compared with changes in allocative efficiency like those sought by the economist. Concrete examples of this balance between institutional constraints and allocative problems were presented above.

[3] Some of the participants in the modernization conference interpreted the arguments made above as a radical relativist position that denies the meaningfulness of all comparative (cross-cultural) research. It is not; as will become clear below, I am objecting to the illusion that some dimensions of comparison have objective priority over others and to the blatantly ethnocentric definitions used in comparisons of economic and noneconomic influences on economic behavior. Given the self-consciousness about the assumptions involved in definitions of dimensions of comparison, it seems to me that comparative research is no less possible than any other kind of research (see note[6]).

[4] Edel is interested in the treatment in development theory of businessmen and factory workers as well as peasants, and he finds parallel arguments for each.

[5] Another part of Edel's argument in his stress on the importance of learning in the process of change. "Interactions of promotion and subsidy are made more complex by the learning that can take place from participating in new activity. Both individual familiarity with an activity, or the observation of the success of others at it, can improve the willingness of people to undertake it, or their effectiveness in it" (1970:18). And, ". . . the debate between 'traditionalism' and 'elasticity' theories has ignored learning effects as well as intermediate degrees of elasticity . . ." (1970:23).

[6] In cross-cultural comparisons we are setting uniform constraints across known and recognized diversity, while above we assumed that uniform constraints were

appropriate to the entire domain within which the comparison was made. However, if cross-cultural comparison involves the potentially arbitrary setting of institutional constraints across cultures, then any comparison faces similar dangers across subcultures, social and economic ranks, and, ultimately in the infinite regress, across individuals. Only societal consensus and humane assertion can rid us of this problem.

[7]Of course, the setting of goals, including ones such as achieving maximum total material production or Pareto optimality, must be recognized as valuemaking acts devoid of objective rationales.

7

The domain of political modernization on the local level is a difficult one to analyze because of the numerous types of pressures which motivate individuals at any one time. Robert Lynch has been able to analyze political change in a Northern Paiute Indian community by observing day to day events and the decisionmaking activities of a tribal council over the course of several years. Lynch's analysis shows that the outcome of political modernization is understandable only if we consider the give and take between local and outside forces that impinge on the local level political process. Along with Margaret Mead, Lynch rejects the unilinear model of modernization and advocates a more open adaptational framework for looking at political change.

Political Modernization in a Native American Community[1]

ROBERT N. LYNCH

Robert N. Lynch is Assistant Professor of Anthropology in the Department of Sociology and Anthropology at the University of Rhode Island. He received his Ph.D.

from the University of Minnesota. Professor Lynch has done field research in rural northern Minnesota and among American Indians in the Great Basin of the United States. This paper reports on one aspect of politics and social change in a reservation community, and reflects his primary interest in political anthropology.

It is certainly no exaggeration to say that the most frequently discussed topic on American Indian reservations these days is change, whether it involves more of some existing facility such as housing or education, or the introduction of something dramatically new, such as a new industry or form of government. Just as there are many points of view on what changes should be seriously considered by members of the Indian community and the staffs of various federal government agencies charged with "developing" reservations, so there are differences in the evaluation of the success of the numerous plans and procedures introduced to Indian groups. My aim in this paper is to describe a series of events surrounding the introduction by the Bureau of Indian Affairs (BIA) of a new form of community government—a tribal council presumably modelled after the familiar Anglo-American village council with its elected officials, open "town meeting," and rules of parlimentary procedure. In addition, I wish to discuss the way in which I arrived at a formulation of this process of political change, or "modernization."

During the course of a year's research on the Brownsville[2] Northern Paiute reservation in the Great Basin there were numerous occasions when it was clear that the Indian people were being evaluated by various members of the local Indian agency. The BIA had introduced a new form of local government and was anxious to measure its effectiveness in the areas of policymaking and social control. Support for my interpretation of the actions of the government people came in the form of frequent suggestions by the Indian agent, who would advise those present at a council meeting on the "correct" manner of making a motion, or would answer questions concerning some interpretation of the group's new constitution. Both the Indian agent and, on occasion, the agency superintendent were accustomed to comparing the manner in which the Indian people utilized the new political complex with the way in which the local political system outside the reservation operated.

Quite often the Paiute did not "measure up" to the agent's expectations. When there should have been a vote on an issue in the meeting, there would be none. If there was an important matter to be discussed with the public, attendance would be spotty. When a vote was taken the losing side refused to recognize that they had lost and simply ignored the decision. This did not happen during every tribal council meeting, but it did occur often enough to compel the agent to frequently remind those present of their "errors." Finally, it was not simply the variance in procedure which troubled the agent, but the lack of sufficient agreement among the Indian people, without which he could not carry out the Bureau's, or the Indians', wishes.

What this indicates is that the agent was looking at political change among these Northern Paiute as a unilineal and a unidirectional process. His attempt to compare the performance of the Indians during their tribal council meetings with similar council meetings outside the reservation was based on the assumption that the two political institutions (town council and tribal council) would eventually match, given the existence of common elements.

When, after a few council meetings, the Indian people were not "measuring up" to the agent's model of small town government, it was no surprise that the direction in which he looked for the discrepancy was toward the Indians. If one is asking the question, as the agent was, "What is the reason these Indians cannot seem to handle their political affairs, even after we have provided them with the means?", then the answer will inevitably point to a shortcoming on the part of the Indian community.

It was at this point that I became troubled, since this same form of comparison between donor and client has often resulted in the client group being labeled "backward" or "underdeveloped." This view does not take into account the uniqueness of the social and cultural environment into which the new "trait" is being incorporated. Neither does it recognize the essentially creative process of adaptation by which the people in the client community restructure their social relations in the face of newness of any kind. There is a good deal of literature in the areas of "development" and "modernization" which exemplifies this unidirectional model for the course of change, and I want to examine some of it next. After that I shall argue for an alternative evolutionary model by which to conceptualize cultural change, one which leaves open the direction taken and the outcome achieved by the recipient group. Then I shall describe the sequence of events on the reservation, beginning with the traditional background of the Brownsville Northern Paiute and ending with the recent developments during the late 1960s.

Finally, I shall offer some comments on the ability of an evolutionary perspective to better handle the processes involved in political change and the course of events I observed among the Paiute.

THE MODERNIZATION PROCESS: ALTERNATIVE MODELS

While there are varying definitions of modernization in the social science literature, the following comments by Eisenstadt (1966:1) seem to represent a consensus:

Historically, modernization is the process of change towards those types of social, economic, and political systems that have developed in western Europe and North America from the seventeenth century to the nineteenth and have then spread to other European countries and in the nineteenth and twentieth centuries to the South American, Asian, and African continents.

This formulation of the course of modernization suggests a unilineal progression of forms from "traditional" to "modern." This progression has often been conceptualized as consisting of stages or phases (Eisenstadt, 1966; Coleman, 1968; Hah & Schneider, 1968). While arguing that every case of political modernization need not *necessarily* entail passage through similar stages, Coleman (1968:398) nonetheless lists five characteristics most often associated with the concept of a modern polity and the process of modernization: (1) progressive structural differentiation, (2) an ethos of equality, (3) an increase in the functional capacity of political institutions, (4) a fundamentally Western democratic model as basic to political modernity, and (5) the nation-state as the essential, if not "natural" framework of political modernization. In addition to these elements, the emphasis placed on political elites as the key decisionmakers in a modernizing nation should be considered a sixth characteristic of many of the studies of political development (Coleman, 1968:400; Hah & Schneider, 1968:145-146).

If one is operating at the level of nation-states and comparing the development of political systems in countries affected by Western ideas, then it is certainly permissable to rate each nation against a standard, such as the United States or a European country. In this case it may be productive to ask under what circumstances and in what manner (that is, through what stages of development) "traditional" political systems are transformed into "modern" ones (Weiner, 1965:107). In making this kind of comparison between the recipient and the donor systems the degree of similarity is usually gauged in terms of economic output over a certain period, or the extent to which "new nations" behave politically similar to those in the West. One simply stipulates the standard against which the recipient is being measured (modernity), determines a baseline from which the client begins its development (the traditional), and keeps track of the inputs to the developing state, all the while measuring the effects of the new elements on the client. After a period of time the comparison is made and the client is rated "developed," "developing," "underdeveloped," or perhaps "backward." At this point the donor will make further policy decisions based in part on the rate of change of the client system.

The model of modernization sketched above is derived, implicitly or explicitly, from a nineteenth century theory of cultural evolution defined by the anthropologist E. B. Tylor as the study of ". . . the general development through which culture as a whole has passed 'stage by stage'; [and] on the other hand the particular 'evolution of culture along its many lines' " (Sahlins & Service, 1960:4). This dual nature of the evolutionary process has often gone unrecognized, or the two forms have become confused by many writers. Anthropologists who accept the application of Darwinian theory to the evolution of cultural as well as biological forms and processes distinguish between "specific evolution" (the adaptive process) and "general evolution" (a grand movement of forms in a certain direction) (Sahlins & Service, 1960:6-7). Consequently, one can conceive of the general evolutionary movement of human societies toward greater amounts of energy utilization, from groups of hunters to wage earners in an industrial society. Yet at the same time there may exist a host of particular subsistence strategies which human groups have adopted to fit their distinctive environmental settings, ranging all the way from industrial wage labor to hunting, fishing, herding, and peasant farming. These are the many solutions to the fundamental problem of maintenance that take the form they do because of a number of cultural, historical, and environmental (natural and social) parameters.

While the stress in the general evolutionary movement of human cultures from simple to more complex is on the *course* of such evolution, the emphasis in specific evolution is on the *processes* which account for this change. Darwin's main theoretical contribution, which he himself recognized, was the concept of natural selection. As Donald Campbell (1965:22) notes with reference to the natural world:

> By this process [natural selection], concepts of planned shaping and teleological emergence became unnecessary. Instead, blind and haphazard variations, when differentially propagated due to the exigencies of different environments, could account not only for drift and divergent speciation, but also for the exquisitely purpose-like fit of organic form to environmental opportunity, and for progressive advance in adaptedness and complexity.

This model of the selective retention and transmission of biological forms provides the basis for the analogous model for the selective propagation of cultural forms.[3] Both models, according to Campbell (1965:27), may be seen as instances of a more general model of adaptability which includes three essential elements:

(1) *The occurrence of variations:* haphazard, random, blind, or planned (mutations in organic evolution, exploratory responses in learning, and innovation and borrowing of cultural elements).

(2) *Consistent selection criteria:* selective elmination, propagation and retention of certain types of variations (differential survival of certain mutants in organic evolution, differential reinforcement of certain responses in learning, and the differential access to, or acceptance of, cultural elements or social forms).

(3) *A mechanism of transmission:* preservation, duplication, or propagation of the positively selected variants (the rigid duplication process of the chromosome-gene system in plants and animals, memory in learning, socialization and enculturation of human infants).

Looked at in light of the above model of evolution, both the process of trial and error in the adaptation of a human group to the problems its natural and social environment presents and the adaptation achieved by an animal species to its habitat are analogous instances of the same specific evolutionary process. Adaptation is a creative process which depends on variation and the selective retention of elements, be they organic or cultural, and is seen as the major (if not the only) nonrandom orienting factor in the process of evolution (Simpson, 1949:159). There is always selective pressure on the group to incorporate certain elements in its attempt to survive; if changes occur in either the number and variety of elements available or in the environment, we can expect some change in the resulting forms. Similarly, if there are instances in which no change has occurred for some time then our assumption is that environmental pressures have stabilized, since change "for its own sake" cannot be handled by this model.

Elman Service (1971:10) has this to say regarding the processes of adaptive selection in the process of cultural evolution:

> Cultural changes are normally constrained by problems of adaptation. Inventions and discoveries, borrowings, unconscious "accidents," political plans, changes from whatever source, provide the cultural variations for potential evolutionary selection. But their eventual fate in the process of selection depends on the adaptive problem and context. They have to fit, to be selected for, as instruments within a complex environment.

Note that Service views the "raw material" for cultural change in relation to the selection pressures on the group, concluding that adaptation is problem-oriented and not some grand design imposed from without. In applying this perspective to communities which are receiving inputs of new cultural and structural elements, we would not *necessarily* expect them to duplicate the course of change taken by the donor system or even to closely resemble other modernizing communities.

Even if a number of communities (or nations for that matter) have received the same modernizing elements, the course each takes depends as much on the community's cultural-historical past and on the environmental problems to which its members are adapting. If either or both of these elements —community and total environment—differ between donor and client or among clients, then it would be more reasonable to expect *differences* in their courses of change. The changing community or society *may* take the same series of steps followed by its donor society, even starting from a different point (evolutionary convergence), but there is a good chance that it will not. In either case the question of the course of modernization is an empirical one; to assume similarity on the basis of the nature of the input alone is completely unjustified. The problem of predicting the course of modernization which a client community will take is indeed a very complicated matter.

If we view all Indian reservations as a single type of community, marginal to and dependent on the larger society and not simply as communities similar to their non-Indian neighbors, then an even more complicated picture emerges. Not only do they differ from the larger society in cultural tradition, but their development and present position has evolved in a very different environment from that of the bulk of American communities. To expect these dependent communities to necessarily resemble their dominant neighbors is to neglect the principles of adaptive response embodied in the selective retention and transmission processes of specific cultural evolution. Realistically, we should expect reservation communities to diversify in the face of modernizing pressures. Multiple solutions to similar problems have been the rule in organic evolution, and the analogous process of "adaptive radiation" applies to the cultural realm as well. The paleontologist George Gaylord Simpson (1949:53) explains how this specific evolutionary process operates to expand the potentialities arising within a single basic structural type:

> Adaptive radiation is, descriptively, this often extreme diversification of a group as it evolves in all the different directions permitted by its own potentialities and by the environments it encounters.

In sum, a picture emerges of the modernization process which is quite different from the one which stresses uniformity of direction of the client due to uniformity of inputs from the donor. Adoption of an evolutionary perspective which stresses the adaptive responses of groups to the pressures of their total environment precludes our expecting clients to invariably parallel the course of change taken by their donors. On the contrary, the selective retention of cultural elements during the adaptive process ensures that a measure of diversity and originality results from the encounter between dependent communities and their more powerful neighbors.[4]

All this relates to my concern for the developmental model of political change to which the Indian agent subscribed. The specific evolutionary perspective, involving as it does a concern for the adaptive solutions hit upon by a modernizing community, has led me to ask a quite different question. Instead of "What (further) measures need to be taken to make this Indian community over into the image of its White neighbors?", I would ask, "What adaptive responses did the community make, given the nature of the community itself and the inputs that changed the total environment of the reservation?"

THE SETTING: ENVIRONMENT, CULTURE AND HISTORY

Of the 125 residents of the Brownsille reservation, over 90 percent are Northern Paiutes, one of the Intermontane Shoshonean groups who inhabit the Great Basin of the desert West.[5] Julian Steward (1938:xii) distinguishes two broad cultural sub-areas within the basin-plateau region: an eastern one which in the nineteenth century contained mounted bison-hunting bands of Ute, Bannock, and Northern Shoshoni; and a western region comprising the pedestrian Northern and Southern Paiute and Western Shoshoni, who were collectors of wild plants and hunters of small game. It was only with the mid-nineteenth century silver boom in western Nevada and the gold strikes in California that the ancestors of the present Northern Paiutes secured their first horses and began in earnest their adaptation to the dominant Europeans in their midst.

The environmental setting which the Northern Paiute traditionally exploited consists mainly of a series of large valleys covered with sagebrush and greasewood and lying between parallel chains of mountain ranges running in a north-south direction. The valleys are between 4,000 and 6,000 feet in elevation and receive between five to twenty inches of rainfall annually. This semi-arid steppe region is known as the Great Basin, and includes all of Nevada, eastern California, southeastern Oregon, and western Utah. The area is characterized by interior drainage; that is, its rivers and streams do not run to the sea but terminate in salt flats or lakes within the basins. Areas away from the streams support a limited amount and variety of vegetation. Small animals such as rabbits and squirrels provided the bulk of the people's animal protein, but occasionally deer and antelope were taken in the piñon and juniper zone between 6,000 and 9,000 feet. Rabbits and deer were hunted communally, but the major portion of the diet for these foragers consisted of plant foods collected by the women.

The Northern Paiute and other Western Shoshonean groups spent most of the year travelling about in search of plant foods and were reduced to a single household or two most of the time. The precariousness of the food quest and the individual nature of the women's gathering activity made it difficult for large groups of people to remain together for very long. Yet there were times when families did come together for a time, during the communal rabbit, antelope, or mud hen drives and the annual pine nut harvest and winter encampment. At these times the amount of food available allowed such a population concentration. The communal rabbit drives and antelope hunts were usually directed by men who had proven their worth countless times before. These "rabbit bosses" had extensive authority during these drives, but they gave it up once the activities were done and the game divided. They were not allowed to bequeath their position of leadership to anyone else. There thus emerges a picture of aboriginal Northern Paiute life, with small scattered family clusters as the main social form during most of the year. There were only occasional and shortlived periods of communal subsistence activities directed by ad hoc leaders.

With the coming of Europeans into the Great Basin valleys, the Northern Paiute and other Indian groups were forced to the edge of starvation as cattle ate their grasses and their piñon trees were cut for firewood. Many families attached themselves to ranches or to the rapidly growing mining towns, where the men worked as cowboys and miners while the women secured work as domestics. Throughout most of the Great Basin, reservations were formed which provided a residential focus for Shoshonean groups in the vicinity, thus precluding the need to move Indian groups any great distance from their traditional territories. Such was the case with the small (twenty acre) reservation set aside for the Northern Paiute adjacent to the town of Brownsville (see Map 1) just after the turn of the present century. Paiute had been living near the town and on the surrounding ranches in the valley, and with the new reservation and Indian school they were drawn to their present location at the outskirts of the town.

The 1920s and 1930s were a time of transition for the Brownsville Paiute on their new reservation. Wage work continued on the ranches in the valley and in the homes of the Whites in town. The Indian children attended the agency's day school on the reservation and the population stabilized around the present (1971) figure of 125 persons, comprising twenty-eight households. We may look upon this period of settling down, both near the town and on the reservation, as a kind of extension of the communal phase of the traditional Shoshonean yearly round. Instead of occasional rabbit drives, pine nut dances in the fall, and the succeeding winter encampment in the hills, the people of Brownsville were now "camping" together throughout the entire year. Related families built their houses in clusters, just as they had formerly traveled together in search of wild plants or animals, and day-to-day activities were centered at the level of these family clusters or "bunches" as they are called by the Paiute today.

When there was need for a spokesman to represent the Indians in town, there was no single man to step forward as a "chief" to plead their case; but men known for their reputation in directing communal hunts and ceremonies emerged, representing one or another of the bunches. Decisions affecting a sizeable portion of the community's residents were reached by a process of discussion and consensus. If no consensus was reached there was no *public* policy enacted; instead there was just agreement among the members of particular bunches. Thus the early reservation form of sociopolitical organization resembled the pre-reservation situation; authority was centered in the individual household composed of related members or at the level of a cluster of these households when camped together, and not at some "band" or "tribal" level.

Although the reservation is a distinct community within the larger American social system, the political field has always included members of the Indian agency, the local office of the BIA. Social control of Indians on the reservation and in the town frequently involved special agents of the Bureau, and supplemented the traditional Indian methods of self-help, ridicule, and gossip. Indians also acted as political middlemen in dealings between the reservation and the town or agency. Just as these men tended to be chosen by the same criteria as communal hunt bosses in the old days, so the freedom to follow or disregard their advice remained. One could simply move away in former times and enlist the services of another hunt boss. Likewise, in early reservation times people could simply ignore any particular spokesman and support one of their own. Differences of opinion among the community members on the reservation were translated into disagreements over public policy, and competing individuals and their supporters crystallized into political factions. These modern factional groupings are based on the clusters of kinsmen known as bunches, which nowadays generally include some nonrelatives as well. This was the political situation, then, when in the middle of the 1930s the BIA introduced the idea of an elected tribal council to handle the public affairs of the reservation.

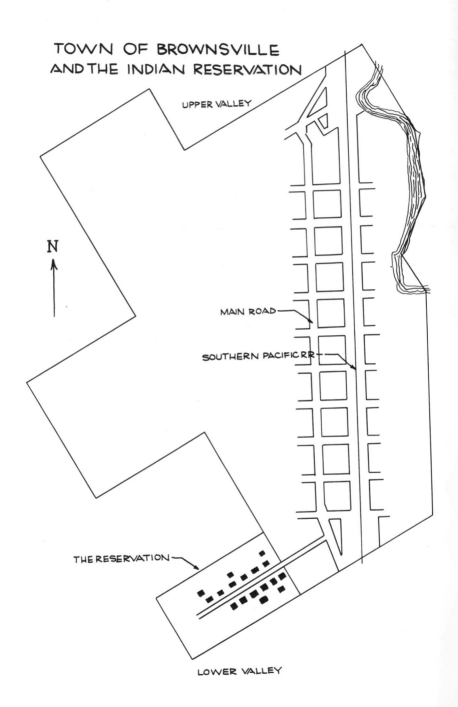

TOWN OF BROWNSVILLE
AND THE INDIAN RESERVATION

UPPER VALLEY

N

MAIN ROAD

SOUTHERN PACIFIC RR

THE RESERVATION

LOWER VALLEY

DIRECTED CHANGE AND THE COMMUNITY'S RESPONSE

The Indian Reorganization Act (IRA) of 1934 provided for self-government by the residents of many American Indian communities.[6] Through its regional agencies, the BIA began the task of introducing an assemblage of political elements which has generally included the following items:

—a tribal council whose members are elected by popular vote, usually through secret ballot;

—regular public meetings conducted according to Anglo-American parlimentary procedure;

—the use of majority rule through voting to decide council issues;

—a tribal constitution and bylaws detailing, among other things, the procedures and rules concerning the above elements; and finally,

—Indian agency personnel employed in the role of advisors.

The IRA did not provide formal channels to link tribal councils to local, county, or state governments, and linkage to the federal government was channeled through the Bureau of Indian Affairs.

The Indian community at Brownsville did not have a tribal council in operation until 1940 but had already formed a committee in 1937 to draw up a suitable constitution under the 1934 act. In the 1937 committee and in the first tribal council a representative from the local Indian agency acted as coordinator. In addition, a number of persons from outside the community have been involved in reservation political affairs over the years. They may be divided into three broad categories:

(1) There was a resident Indian agent on the reservation from 1910 until the mid-1930s, and a resident teacher taught at the day school from 1910 until 1935, when Indian children entered the town's public school.

(2) The agency has employed a variety of nonresident "community workers" who have periodically assisted the community in matters of health care, education, welfare benefits, and legal assistance from the 1930s until the present.

(3) Since World War II the number of agency employees trained to administer and deliver services such as federally supported job training, mutual help housing for low income families, and anti-poverty programs such as Operation Mainstream has increased. These Bureau personnel have been joined by representatives of the state's Intertribal Council, an Indian

Signs of Our Times Community Bulletin Board (1968)

Photo by Robert Lynch

group interested in various community development programs and funded from federal government sources. Each of the persons performing the services mentioned above has assisted the Brownsville Paiute in formulating and implementing its public policy, even though they were most often sent to the reservation for other reasons. The bulk of the transactions involving the reservation and outsiders has been channeled through these people, whose position as political middlemen has intimately involved them with both parties.[7] The Paiute have found this method of conducting business to be compatible with their traditional authority structure, which generally involved a few respected individuals in the periodic role of advisors and resource persons.

As a consequence, one of the Indian community's responses to constant agency involvement in its political affairs has been the ready acceptance of outsiders as advisors and resource personnel. Members of the tribal council or its public feel free to request favors and seek support for various endeavors from these outsiders. A common practice is to elect someone from the Indian agency—the superintendent or one of the numerous government specialists—to various committees. These outsiders then carry on duties which range from such things as securing nominations for an upcoming tribal council election to updating the tribal roll in connection with the Northern Paiute claims case against the federal government. Ready access to men from the Indian agency is assured, since one or more is routinely present at the monthly council meeting. Their presence also allows the agency to monitor community activities and gauge the effectiveness of its efforts in the community.

The Paiute's use of outsiders to secure resources does not stop with the Indian agency but extends to members of the state's Intertribal Council and to the town of Brownsville. Four of the five members of the board directing the construction of mutual help housing on the reservation are prominent members of the Brownsville business community. In addition, during the renovation of the community hall in 1968, frequent visits by members of the Intertribal Council, which was managing the construction, provided an opportunity for numerous requests by the Brownsville tribal council, especially during periods when funds were low or materials did not arrive on time.

Another aspect of the Indians' employment of middlemen as go-betweens and spokesmen has been the emergence of particular local Indians who have played this vital role. From the founding of the Brownsville reservation onward there have been certain Indians, both men and women, who have acted as middlemen for the community in its dealings with outsiders. While in the past their authority may have stemmed from their achievements as a hunt boss or dance director, more recently recognition has been accorded individuals who have served on the tribal council or on one of the committees which have operated since the 1930s.

One way by which the agency has managed to keep itself involved in reservation life has been through its differential support of these Indian middlemen. Since the 1950s, men from the agency have consistently supported a particular man's efforts in the community, and he in turn has provided them with a vital link to the Indians. If it were not for this particular Indian, there would be many more complaints by Indians that people from the Bureau simply drive around the reservation in their official cars without ever stopping to visit. Without someone on the reservation with whom the agency could communicate by letter or telephone, the gulf that separates the two systems would be difficult to bridge. This man has been chairman of the tribal council longer than anyone else since the founding of the reservation, and his performance has in turn been enhanced by his ability to get agency support for his endeavors. So regular a channel has this association become that when another person was recently elected chairman of the council, the agency continued to write and to telephone its established contact in the community, much to the latter's annoyance. Of course, the Indians have played this same game with nearly equal success. They greatly admired a former tribal operations officer and did all they could to cooperate with him, a cooperation agency personnel do not always get.

While many of the day-to-day dealings with Indians on the reservation have involved a certain few Bureau employees in the role of advisors and friends, quite persistent attempts have been made by the agency to change the operation of the tribal council. This is the institution which is seen as most important in carrying out the mission of the federal government, which is to change the decision-making procedure to one which will enable the small community to effectively govern itself, particularly if its relationship to the Bureau should eventually be terminated.

THE TRIBAL COUNCIL: ARENA FOR CHANGE

While the development of the tribal council must be viewed as a direct result of agency efforts, there was relatively little agency reliance on the council for the first twenty years of its existence. The twenty acres of reservation contain no wealth which needs managing, save for the house sites of the people. The collaboration between agency and council began in 1939 and was initiated by the agency, but this limited cooperation did not result in a substantial increase in the council's activities.

Since 1945, however, the degree of agency involvement in reservation affairs has resulted in a growth in the activity of the council. There has been a transformation of the leadership in the community from an ad hoc basis to an institutionalized council. People on the reservation in turn are now concerned with who fills the offices of the council, primarily as a result of the council's role in securing and administering grants and training programs and its formal dealings with outsiders.

An example of this heightened concern is seen in an episode surrounding the 1961 election. When a group on the reservation challenged the legitimacy of that year's tribal council election due to alleged low voter turnout, the government was brought into the picture to act as referee. The people's insistence resulted in the arranging of another election, and the incumbent chairman was returned to office.

After a number of years of slowly increasing activity, the tribal council began to come to life in the early 1960s, and for the first time the Indian people were articulating their demands directly to their chairman, who in turn sought advice from the Indian agency. When the tribal council met with the Brownsville town council and the U.S. Public Health Service to determine the procedures for tying the reservation into the town's sewer system, the three groups met on an equal footing; no one from the Indian agency was present. Again, when a woman from the reservation attempted to bring up a personal grievance with the town council during this same meeting, the mayor looked for guidance to the tribal council chairman. The tribal chairman, in turn, made it clear that the Indian community was interested in sewers at this time, not in settling personal matters. (Through this maneuver, the tribal council chairman was also gaining the non-Indian recognition he would subsequently need to deal effectively with matters pending on the reservation.) As it turned out, his decision to separate private from public issues during the town council's meetings was supported by the Indians when they subsequently voted to restrict private matters to informal meetings with tribal councilmen.

The chairman of the tribal council when these events took place was Roger Wilson, a quiet, middle-aged man and the one Indian referred to by outsiders as the "chief" at Brownsville. Roger has held office since the mid-1950s, a total of about fifteen years, and probably comes as near as any individual can to being a reasonable choice to represent the diverse elements at Brownsville. When I first went to the reservation in 1964 there were many who said that Roger simply did not accomplish much of anything and that the tribal council seldom even met (Roger himself told me he had given up trying to get apathetic people to come to meetings). Yet over the years Roger and his supporters have garnered the majority's votes in one election after another, an indication that for all his alleged shortcomings he is the only one who can make much out of reservation politics.

The Wilson family on the reservation is not a large one, consisting of Roger, his wife and children, Roger's widowed mother, her two sisters and their husbands, and his divorced sister and her children. Yet what they lack in numbers they seem to compensate for in ties to others on the reservation, in the nearby town, and at the agency. In fact, the Wilsons have been criticized by some on the reservation as being too oriented to the Whites in town, a charge which is coupled with the accusation that the Wilsons, who are not full-bloods, think they are "too good" for the rest of the Indians. Yet it is difficult to see how Roger could have been so successful if he had not gone beyond his own kinsmen for support. It is his name which is first mentioned when inquiries are made in town about the Indian community and its leadership; the agency people keep his telephone number handy and call him often, and copies of his letters may be found in the agency's files. He and his family have been praised by outsiders as diligent and hard-working, "the kind of people one can talk to and be certain of results." In fact, the agency continued to deal with Roger even after he had resigned from the council for a year, bypassing the new chairman and his council.

The scope of Roger's influence may be appreciated by noting that he is the sole Indian involved with sports programs such as Little League in the town, and the only one from the reservation to hold a position in town, having been appointed to the local Selective Service Board. He has a steady job as a heavy equipment operator at a nearby mine, his wife works as a part-time domestic at a motel, and his oldest boy is in college. He has patterned his lifestyle after that of the White majority in the areas of work, education, public service, and his home life; yet he has the ability to appeal to the more traditional elements on the reservation as well, since he is often critical of agency policy and in favor of maintaining some of the patterns of Indian life which concern the making of public policy in the council. He fills the classic role of the middleman, with a foot in each camp, and he takes the risks attendant with such a position.

From 1964 to 1966 Roger and the tribal council worked diligently to plan a number of community projects, among them the new sewer system, the blacktopping of the reservation's main road, and the securing of local law enforcement for the Indian community. Unfortunately, these plans did not immediately materialize. When the tribal council elections were held in 1967, Roger did not run for reelection. At that time he was greatly discouraged by the lack of support given him by the bulk of the Indian community, and sensitive to some of the negative feelings being voiced about his effectiveness. A new slate of officers, representing the "opposition" grouping in the community, was elected to office. Within a short while the new council, composed entirely of women related to each other through uterine links, had introduced a new style of politics. Whereas the previous council headed by Roger had generally assumed a low-key position on community matters, the women from the larger Moore family grouping who made up the opposition thrust themselves into prominence immediately by inserting a series of reservation informational items into the local newspaper. There was a very real effort on the part of the Moore women to publicize the aims and activities of the tribal council to the general public, an effort prompted no doubt by the lack of exposure they had hitherto received as residents of the reservation. It was certainly a wise move, for most of the townspeople had generally associated the Wilson family, and Roger in particular, with the local Indians.

The Moore women differed from Roger and his relatives in a number of ways in addition to their demeanor during council meetings (which was forthright, even aggressive at times) and their lack of a widespread base of support outside the reservation. They make up about one half of the reservation's total population, and are heavily represented by women who were born in Brownsville and whose husbands married into the community from other reservations. This condition, which has made their men "outsiders" in the community, has also thrust the women into leadership roles in a way very different from their counterparts among the Wilsons and the rest of the reservation. Women among the Northern Paiute generally do not get involved in public meetings, and they certainly do not openly challenge the incumbent council and members of the agency, as some of the Moores had.

Two of the Moores elected in 1967 remained in office for the entire year, until Roger was elected again in 1968. The vice-chairman took over the running of council affairs amid some changes of personnel due to resignations. Betty Moore was in her mid-thirties, divorced, and the mother of three children. She has worked steadily at a laundry in town, maintains a house, and managed to get deeply involved in local politics to a degree few would have expected.

Her companion on the council—the two women were inseparable during their administration—was her middle-aged aunt (her mother's sister) Ada Johnson. Like most of the Moore women in Brownsville over the past half century, Ada had married a man from one of the large reservations a few hours' drive away. The family had recently moved a large farm house in from one of the ranches in the valley, and Ada and her husband had just finished planting a front lawn when she was elected secretary of the tribal council. She had worked in town in the past, but her husband's job on one of the large ranches in the valley appears to provide adequate support for the couple and their three boys, all of whom live at home, one with his wife and baby.

Of the two women, it is Ada who commands the most respect from people on the reservation and at the agency. She is demanding and insistent in her dealings with others, and her cool manner and sharp tongue have forced people to avoid her at times or allow her to have her way when confrontation is unavoidable. I have heard agency men praise her hard work on the council while at the same time remarking about her overpowering manner. She and her niece Betty were a formidable pair at the monthly council meetings. They wasted few opportunities to corner an agency man visiting the community about some matter, and they began immediately to write letters to the agency and to the state's Intertribal Council requesting help for the Brownsville reservation. Both women had been very critical of Roger's administration, and the two families have led a strained existence on the reservation, each taking every available opportunity to point out to me the shortcomings of the other.

Moore Women and Author at Informal Get-Together
(1968)

Photo by Robert Lynch

Although the Wilson council had done a lot of the planning for a variety of community projects, these were not completed while Roger was in office. During its term in office, however, the Moore council supervised the installation of the new sewer lines and the paving of the roads. In addition, they organized a major clean-up effort to rid the reservation of its junk cars and cooperated with the state's Intertribal Council (ITC) to paint every house in the community. The ITC secured a grant from a private foundation to repair the decaying community hall, while at the same time it and the new council established a job training program with funds from the Office of Economic Opportunity. Finally, the tribal council mustered support for the Save The Children Federation program and organized a committee to handle its activities.

Despite all these accomplishments, the Moore council failed to enlist widespread public support for its endeavors. Nor did the Indian agency, which had worked so closely with the council on the new programs, appear to wholeheartedly endorse the women's style of operation. In fact, even though the increased tempo of activities involving outside agencies working with the tribal council began to bear fruit in the community, the Indian people grew to actively oppose the women on the council.

This seemingly paradoxical opposition to a council that was getting things done was due in large measure to the body's unorthodox methods of operation. When the council chairman Betty and her secretary Ada attempted during a meeting to make policy decisions without first allowing the issue to be fully discussed and brought to a vote, an open split developed within the group in power, with over half of them (the Moores) siding with the former chairman Roger Wilson and his followers. The agency's representative was present, and he advised Betty to follow normal parliamentary procedure, which she reluctantly agreed to do. He also seemed to be against the incumbents, which had the effect of convincing others in the audience of the inappropriateness of the council's actions. As if on cue, the attendance dropped at council meetings during the remaining months of 1967, with people explaining their absence with the remark that the women on the new council "fight too much." In subsequent sessions personal grievances were raised (in direct violation of an earlier council resolution against such topics), and when the council secretary Ada and a woman from the audience got into a fist fight during a meeting it seemed that support for the Moore regime had slipped to its lowest point.

Work on a Community Clean-up Project (1968)
Photo by Robert Lynch

Renovating the Community Hall—Center of Tribal
Council Activity (1968)

Photo by Robert Lynch

Perhaps the influence of the Indian agency in reservation politics was never so dramatic as it became after the group's constitution arrived from Washington in April 1968. The Indian agent announced during a council meeting that the document (which had been nearly two years in the making) would now allow the Indian community to make the necessary changes in its political process so that the tribal council would become an even more effective instrument for securing outside aid. The agent explained that the community would have to hold an election under the new charter—the first "legitimate" tribal council election in the reservation's history—and that the formation and operation of the new council would follow the new rules. At this time an election committee was chosen to receive nominations, and in the weeks that followed a number of names appeared on the list fixed to the community hall's bulletin board. Roger Wilson was persuaded by the agency men to seek the chairman's job and reluctantly agreed. In fact, many people were particularly concerned that the women be voted out of office and that a slate of men, who were generally much less outspoken in public gatherings, be installed.

The tribal council election was held in May 1968 and Roger and his supporters were returned to office, a feat which required that nearly half of his support come from the rival Moore grouping. Both the agency and the Indian people were relieved that Roger was in and Betty and Ada were out of the council. Roger's victory was a particularly pleasing turn of events for the agent, who all along had supported Wilson and his policies. Of course, much of the agency's success in implementing directives from the Bureau has been a direct result of the high degree of cooperation given them by Roger and his supporters. At the same time, the people on the reservation had begun to realize that some of the benefits which had come about during the tenure of the Moore women had really been initiated during Roger's previous administration. Furthermore, even though many of his most vocal critics had accused Roger of doing little for the community, their uneasiness during the short but eventful regime of his opponents had convinced them that the gains made under the Moores were not worth the distress many of them suffered during public council meetings.

Nevertheless, the attempt by the Indian agency to persuade the tribal council to approximate the procedures regularly associated with a New England town meeting did not diminish with Roger's return to power. There has generally been a regular process of "coaching" carried on during council meetings by the Indian agent and one or two other outsiders. At times the Indians would disregard the agent's suggestions, as when he advised them to appoint an executive committee in addition to the tribal council with the purpose of involving as many people as possible in the political process. Those present at the meeting simply listened quietly to this request, but no one made any move to implement the idea then or during the remainder of 1968. It was simply relegated to the background where suggestions or requests end up when there is little apparent support for them. The same treatment was given to the news from a visiting community coordinator that a special meeting was being held in a nearby city to discuss problems of Indian health. The session was sponsored by the state's all-Indian organization and was open to the public. He suggested to the council that it appoint a delegate or two to attend in the name of the reservation and to report their findings to the community at a future council meeting. Betty Moore asked if there were any volunteers to attend the meeting, and when no one answered, she concluded that the council would "look into the matter." There is generally a feeling on the part of the Brownsville Paiute that someone will attend these meetings and report to the community. If no one does, the Indians know that the agency generally lets them know the outcome of such conferences anyway. This kind of "casual" approach to certain issues which the agency often feels will directly benefit the Indians is frustrating to the agent as well as to some of the Indians. In this case one of the Moore men eventually did go to the conference—he regularly went to the city to visit a girlfriend—but we heard nothing further about it during the following council meetings.

Often, however, the Indians do rely on the agent to mediate differences of opinion which come up in council meetings, and he is always eager to give his opinion or to render a judgment. Once during a particularly heated exchange between Betty Moore as council chairman and Roger Wilson as spectator, the agent stepped in to support Roger's position, even to the point of telling Betty that she had to allow Roger's point because it was correct parliamentary procedure. She reluctantly agreed, although it was evident at the time that she felt the agent's actions were "unfair." In one sense she was right, for the agent was usually very close to Roger and his family, communicating with him far more than with anyone else in Brownsville. Yet in another sense the agent's support for Roger's position simply followed his and the agency's attempt to instruct the Indians in the correct use of parlimentary procedure during their meetings, and in this case his support fell behind Roger's motion to have a vote—a move which Betty had tried to block by ignoring Roger's motion and attempting to push on with other business.

Despite repeated attempts by well-meaning outsiders to speed up the decisionmaking process during council meetings, Roger and the council steadfastly refused to "short-circuit" the usual procedure of open discussion until virtual consensus was reached. Perhaps the most explicit illustration of such an attempt to alter procedure came when a member of the state's all-Indian organization tried to convince Roger and the council that they had the power to make decisions on their own without first securing the will of those present. Citing the new constitution recently returned to the reservation as the legal basis for his argument, the man, himself an Indian, said that it might make matters flow more smoothly if the council simply made many of its decisions first and then announced them to the people. After all, he maintained, the new constitution delegated such powers to the council which was elected by the people to act in their behalf; it was not necessary to go to the public on every item of business. Yet the members of the council, each of whom had just raised his hand in a show of support for the issue on the floor, categorically refused to accept this rendering of the council's powers. Too often during the tenure of Betty Moore and her Aunt Ada they had witnessed this same kind of "railroading" of items through the council without any prior attempt to gain the public's acceptance. The resulting conflict had convinced most of the people present that it was better to explain carefully and in sufficient detail just what was planned, for often it was misunderstood and if passed under these conditions would not command the people's allegiance.

The recourse to majority voting to settle differences of opinion which arise during discussions is another procedure introduced by the Indian agency, and one which has had spotty success. Presently there is a very real reluctance to resort to voting during council meetings; it has not been wholly integrated into the rhythm of deliberations thus far. In 1968, in eight tribal council meetings (four under each administration), I only observed the use of voting in ten out of forty-seven distinct issues decided. Of these ten instances, just three cases involved following the normal procedure of making a motion and seconding it, discussion of the motion on the floor, and the eventual call for a vote. The remaining seven instances consisted of motions being made and then being treated as if they themselves were an affirmative vote, and of votes being called for without a motion having first been made. These seven cases of "broken balloting" were usually resorted to after it appeared that enough discussion had gone on to insure a high degree of consensus among those people present.

Using a motion to break a deadlock and secure an immediate vote is a maneuver used only twice during the 1968 council meetings, and both times it was Roger who initiated the move. The third instance of making a motion before proceeding to a vote was the work of Roger's long-time secretary and supporter, herself a Moore. These three cases were brought to a vote to reach a decision after often heated debate. The first instance involved Betty and Ada's attempt to close off a dirt road which ran by Roger's house in the belief that it would avoid automobile accidents at the entrance to the reservation. Roger (who was not in office at the time) and his supporters fought the attempt; aided by the agent's counsel given during the proceedings, Roger made a motion that a vote be taken to see if the entire community supported the Moore women's suggestion. The vote was overwhelming against closing the road.

The second time a vote was called to break a deadlock was when Ada of the tribal council accused me of prying into others' business because I was engaged in taking a census at the request of Roger's vice-chairman. I explained during the meeting that the purpose was the compilation of an up-to-date tribal roll, a necessity for the Northern Paiute claims case then in the courts. Ada and the vice-chairman argued the merits of my doing the research, and after a number of others had spoken on the issue, Roger made a motion that the people vote on whether or not I should continue the census. The vote was nearly unanimous in favor of my continuing the work.

The third motion and vote involved Ada in a heated argument with some other Moore women about the latter's claims on some prizes Ada and her family had won during a celebration in town. Amid the misunderstanding and commotion, one of the Moore women made a motion to the effect that in the future members of the tribe not get involved with outside activities unless certain understandings were first agreed upon during a council meeting. Again the vote went in favor of the position which had been argued by the maker of the motion. In these three instances, then, a deadlock was eventually broken when one of the parties felt he or she had enough support to take a vote, and in two out of three cases that someone was Roger Wilson.

These three occasions when majority rule settled what had become a stalemate were really the only times in which the complete procedure of voting was used in the tribal council in 1968. The other seven instances in which some form of "voting" was used did not involve breaking a deadlock, for in all cases the suggestion to "vote on it" came after agreement had been reached. The alternative manifestation of unanimity was simply for someone to make a motion that such-and-such be adopted; the agreeing nods from the audience were enough to insure closure. In the rest of the forty-seven cases in which the tribal council made decisions, however, the majority (nearly 80 percent) were settled through the attainment of consensus, without the request for a motion or a vote being made. There was enough discussion prior to, during, and after the council meeting to insure that most people would support a particular point of view, or at least would not actively oppose it during the meeting.

It appears that efforts by the agency and other outsiders to change basic decisionmaking procedures in the tribal council at Brownsville have initially met with limited success. The agent has had to accept the fact of certain Indian beliefs regarding the setting and implementing of the community's goals. On the other hand, the Indians seem less reluctant to abide by the advice and counsel given them by the agent; in fact they frequently seek the aid of the agent in matters which involve political and judicial procedure. It is not a simple situation in which one party gives and the other receives, nor is it one in which neither accepts anything the other offers. Rather, it is a case in which both parties are interested in making gains without giving up too much of what they consider important. The Indians want the programs and other sources of funds which the agency and other outside organizations can provide, and they will try to accommodate the conditions which are imposed on these resources. The agency must have the cooperation of the Indian community if its programs and personnel are to be used to their planned capacity, and its people have had to make a series of compromises in order to achieve these goals.

DISCUSSION AND CONCLUSIONS

My initial concern in this paper has been to examine a way of conceptualizing political change which was unidirectional and based on a model of a single "modern" society, the United States. Although this picture of political development was the one which the Indian Bureau's field agents subscribed to, we have seen that it is also the one which is found in much of the literature of the social sciences (excluding anthropology), and is called "modernization theory." The "theory" is much more accurately labeled "ideology," since the vision of nation-states eventually approximating the Western democratic industrialized model is a modern normative version of nineteenth century and earlier notions of progress. Yet "modernization theory" persists in the social sciences, government, industry, and among the general public in the United States and in the West in general. The reasons for its appeal and tenaciousness are not difficult to find, as this passage from a recent review of the concept of modernization demonstrates:

> It provided the modernization theorist with a cognitive map consisting of familiar, stable categories derived from his immediate experience as a citizen of a 'modern' society, according to which data derived from 'relatively non-modernized' societies could be gathered, sorted, and interpreted. Moreover, this map not only provided a set of categories for ordering the present of these societies, but by depicting modernization as an inexorable process of change in the direction of 'modernity' it provided a glimpse of their future as well, a glimpse made all the more comforting to the West by the assurance it gave that these societies would follow along its own familiar path to modernity (Tipps, 1973:207).

This is the model that the Indian agent adhered to, and it is the vision which has guided much of this country's assistance programs overseas. Yet we know that nations and communities faced with new outside influences do not always follow along the familiar path to "modernity" taken by this country, for various reasons. It is because this unidirectional model of modernization fails to account satisfactorily for the richness of response and the often rather dissimilar paths chosen by "target" nations or communities that I have argued for an alternative model of modernization, one which allows for creativity in the process of adaptation.

The use of an evolutionary perspective provides the necessary mechanisms (sources of variations, selection and transmission of variants) to aid our conceptualization of the entire process of social and cultural change. There are a number of things the evolutionary model prompts us to consider in our research on modernization, and I shall discuss them briefly by way of a summary.

First, the unit of analysis—in this case .the Indian community at Brownsville—must be regarded as being both a source of variations which may eventually become retained and as an active part in the adaptation process itself. Too often the community is looked upon simply as the recipient of the new "trait," with no thought to the possibility of its generating its own sources of variation or otherwise creating new configurations through selective retention and local interpretation of particular elements. For example, the vital role of political middleman among the Brownsville Northern Paiute is a continuation of the existing role of hunt and dance boss. Public decisionmaking procedures involving a good deal of discussion among adults appear to have been very basic to the pre-European Shoshonean way of life and have formed an integral part of the current tribal council operation on the reservation. It is too easy for outsiders to see "nothing there" worth adding to, and development agents tend to have the "urban renewal" perspective when approaching communities, which generally means they think they must "start from scratch," leveling any existing structures before introducing their own.

Second, the key concepts of variation and selective retention focus our inquiry on both the sources of variation and the nature of the elements involved. In the first case, the federal government's Bureau of Indian Affairs is primarily charged with introducing a series of dramatic changes to reservations, leading eventually to self-governing, economically viable entities, some of which may become part of the surrounding state and county structure through eventual termination. In addition, we are reminded that any human community has a somewhat unique cultural and historical past which must be considered if introductions are to be successfully adopted. In both instances it is vital that recognition be given to the picture each party involved in the interaction carries of what it eventually expects will occur. With the Indian agency holding up a model of town meeting governance as the only means to achieve community development and often refusing to allow much deviation from it on the part of the Indian community, there exists a potential snag in the process of change.

The concept of selective retention of variations in social change directs us to expect an often "incomplete" acceptance of new elements, with the attendant condition that those "traits" which are accepted may be altered to fit into the existing social and cultural conditions of the community. When the Paiute at Brownsville were assigned various persons from the Indian agency to aid them in adjusting to reservation life, the one thing which the

Indian people expanded upon with a fervor that at times created considerable trouble was their tendency to use these outsiders as go-betweens of various kinds. They were asked to provide references for local Indians traveling and working beyond the town of Brownsville; they became a ready source of small loans and other favors, and a link to those higher up in the agency who could provide still further resources; finally, these Bureau people and many prominent people in town became spokesmen for the Indians' legal rights and mediators in their quarrels with family and relatives. This last task as agents of social control on the reservation has lately fallen more often on the shoulders of the local sheriff's office and the chief of police, although in the early years of this century there were special agents of the Indian Bureau appointed for the job.

When the Indian agency set itself up as the "gatekeeper" between the reservation and the federal government and the larger society, and the community had become dependent on this single channel for most of its outside resources, an interesting process began to take place. Beginning in the middle years of the 1960s, the Indian communities in the Great Basin and elsewhere began to organize statewide agencies to aid in reservation development and to insure the protection of individual civil rights. In addition, the contacts with local and state government agencies were expanded until, in the latter part of the 1960s, Brownsville had opened up a number of alternatives to the Indian agency and BIA. These pathways included federal government agencies such as Community Action Programs, VISTA, and National Youth Corps; private foundations which were financing construction and job training on the reservation; the state's Intertribal Council, which provided funds for community development projects of various kinds; and private agencies such as Save The Children Federation, which enabled some of the children and their families to afford school clothes and trips they otherwise would not have had. All of these developments are based on the premise that the more channels open to an enclave community such as Brownsville, the greater the chance that resources heretofore held solely by the Indian Bureau will be available, and often greater in variety and number. The Indian people at Brownsville had learned how to manipulate a system imposed upon them by the very same agency which now has to compete for its "fair share" of development projects!

Third, the concept of adaptation involves us in attempting to conceptualize the impact of a variation on the community in terms of the response made, while at the same time it reminds us that this series of trial and error moves is taking place within the normal give and take of dealings between the federal government and the Indian community. There is no longer any excuse to conceive of directed social change as something in which one party simply "does something" to another. Both the Indian agency and the Indian community have been involved in a continuing series of reciprocal transactions, in which first one and then the other party assumed the upper hand. As a result of this ongoing relationship spanning a rather intensive period of about six years (1966-1972), both the agency and the community have produced a record of their mutual attempts at political change which looks something like this:

For their part, *the Indians have generally accepted*:

(1) the fact that outside resources are obtainable in greater abundance by some cooperative effort within the community and with outside agencies;

(2) the real possibility that they can outflank the Indian agency by appealing to other "competing" social agencies for desired resources;

(3) the reality that, while they may be able to bargain with the Indian agency for certain things, they just as certainly can lose out on programs if they are not careful (as happened with a loan program for housing repairs for the elderly, which was lost through lack of adherence to BIA directives);

(4) the discovery that outsiders now accept their tribal council as the legitimate governing body for the community, something which has served to make them very responsive to appeals by the council for support.

In like manner, *the Indian agency has accepted*:

(1) the existence of the above conditions which pertain to their dealings with the Brownsville Indian community, realizing that the federal government's day-to-day operations on the reservation can be flexible, as long as their mission appears to be succeeding;

(2) the often annoying procedures by which most public policy decisions continue to be made in the tribal council meetings, which resemble to varying degrees the government's idea of an efficient town council;

(3) the existence of a network of communication and cooperation which extends beyond the tribal council members to the various subgroups on the reservation whose members will often not respond to blanket requests by the agency or their councilmen, but must instead be convinced individually of the worth of a particular proposal or program;

(4) a number of (to its agents) cultural or customary "quirks" in general

existence among the Brownsville Paiute, such as their casualness regarding time in general and appointments in particular; a pattern of council meetings best described as "organized confusion;" and the general reluctance on the part of the losers in a political battle to accept the loss and continue to work for their own ends—they generally withdraw from the political arena, avoiding council meetings and members of the opposition for varying lengths of time, behavior which greatly hampers the council's effectiveness.

At the same time that it is possible to sketch the elements in their mutual relationship which both the Indians and the agency people recognize and accept as part of the rules of their political game, there are certain points on which neither party has so far compromised.

The Indians will not assume the degree of autonomy in their political affairs which the agency's tribal operations officer expects them to manage. While he has attempted to persuade the tribal council to make many of its own decisions regarding the conduct of certain members of the reservation, the council has often refused to appear to be telling anyone what he or she can or cannot do. To avoid this distasteful confrontation they have relied on the agency people or other outsiders, and this outside reliance of course is really just a part of their colonial heritage, one which we could say they have adopted with dogged thoroughness. At the same time, however, other members of the agency staff who are older and more senior in the Indian Service have rewarded just this kind of submissive behavior. Thus the tribal council is caught in the midst of a changing policy among its most intimate outlet to the outside, and although the avowed mission of the Bureau is to make Indian communities self-sufficient, their agents do not always act in such a manner as to reach that goal. At the same time, the Indian community has already found that certain strategies involving a mix of autonomy and submission have paid off handsomely, and appear determined to persist in this kind of attitude as long as there is a payoff.

The agency still sees the behavior of some of the Indians in the council meetings as terribly wasteful of time and energy. In addition, the rough-and-tumble style of some of the meetings is viewed as a sign that the Indians do not really want to "progress." If they did, the agents argue, they would follow our directions and they would get what they and we want—more capital, better living conditions, and a chance to transform their community into something they could all be proud of.

The agents' most persistent criticism of community affairs is that they are so *disorganized*. It is this "political instability" which worries the agency, and some of the Indians too. And yet, as I hope has been made clear here, Indian-government relations have been marked at times by quite productive encounters. The notion that communities undergoing or experiencing some kind of planned change must "do whatever they are told" by those directing the program is a position which may or may not be the most productive one in the long run. For whatever else may be the desire of the federal government in its attempt to change communities such as Brownsville, the only enduring object would appear to be that the people adopt the program and incorporate it into their daily lives. The precise manner in which this is done and the exact shape these activities will ultimately assume should be an empirical question and not a set of normative standards adopted because a similar program worked in this manner in such-and-such a community.

The fourth and final point which an evolutionary perspective suggests is that of an open-ended course along which the community will proceed, and the sobering thought that "more" is not necessarily "better" (or more adaptive). Our focus is directed to the circumstances under which the community is attempting to adjust to the new inputs and to the nature of the responses themselves. The notion that modernization is "a unilinear process of progressive change toward a model of modernity patterned after a rather utopian image of Western society" (Tipps, 1973:216) must be replaced with one which views the interaction of agency and Indians as a potentially creative one in which it is possible for hitherto unknown forms to emerge and perform adequately to attain particular goals.

The Indian community at Brownsville is in the midst of change, and it is not at all clear just what shape the political system will assume in the next few years. Although the tribal council has adopted a number of elements deemed "necessary" by the Bureau for community development, it has rejected some and incorporated others in a changed form. On the other hand, the agency itself has adjusted its demands in realistic terms to the successes and failures (as it defines them) of its own program. It should not surprise us; it seems it could hardly be otherwise. Yet for a number of reasons this idea of mutual adaptation is a difficult one to sell to those who conceive of modernization as a single pathway to prosperity. At least part of the problem has been the paucity of empirical cases at the local level which show the intricacies of the give-and-take of outside agents of change and communities slated for developmental change. The remainder has been the adherence to a conception of modernization which is value-laden and not terribly empirically sound or theoretically productive. As one writer has assessed the use of the concept of modernization:

> In the end, however, the most important referents of the concept are normative, not empirical. Stripped of its scientific pretensions, the concept of modernization becomes little more than a classificatory device distinguishing processes of social change deemed 'progressive' from those which are not (Tipps, 1973:222).

My hope is that this kind of normative statement will be replaced by a formulation which seeks to appreciate the diversity of changing communities whose members may desire some measure of improvement in their lives. It may still be possible to achieve many of the goals generally associated with modernization in communities such as Brownsville, and in ways as yet not deemed "modern."

NOTES

[1] This is a revised and expanded version of a paper read at the symposium "Modernization and the Environment: The Impact of Western Ideas on Traditional Societies," held at the University of Rhode Island, Kingston, May 27-29, 1971. My thanks go to the members of the symposium for their very pertinent comments on the paper, and to John Poggie, Stanley Aschenbrenner, J. Anthony Paredes, and Pertti and Gretel Pelto for their critical suggestions for improving the paper.

Field research among the Brownsville Northern Paiute during 1968 was supported by a grant from the National Science Foundation (GS-1650), and a summer trip in 1971 by a grant-in-aid from the University of Rhode Island.

[2] The name of the community, as well as those of the individuals mentioned in the paper, have been changed to preserve the privacy of the people among whom my wife and I have lived and worked periodically since 1964.

[3] For an excellent critique of the analogous use of organic evolutionary theory to understand social evolution, see Utz (1973).

[4] Adopting this evolutionary model of cultural change poses certain problems for change agents and their clients. Without a pretty firm notion of what the community "should look like" as a result of a newly introduced program, it is difficult to visualize development people staying at their tasks for very long. Although it is outside the

scope of this paper, I would only comment that perhaps such an open-ended scheme as the one offered here would only be a practical guide to action if change agents and other decisionmakers realized that their plans had to remain flexible, contingent on the outcome of earlier attempts. They then could make day-to-day decisions based on what had occurred in the community as a result of their inputs, not on the basis of what it would take to produce a replica of community X at their present site. Their aim would be to produce a viable way of life, perhaps in many ways divergent from the "model" community which they may have envisioned when they first made their plans for development, but nonetheless a community which could solve its problems and work out its own future. Yet I remain skeptical that such a policy of "assisted" versus "directed" change will be adopted by donor nations or agencies in the near future; they often have too much at stake politically and economically to allow their clients to work out their own futures.

[5]This summary of traditional Basin Shoshonean life was compiled from a number of a standard sources, the most recent and comprehensive being that of Steward (1970), which includes an excellent bibliography.

[6]Although most Indian tribes in the United States accepted the provisions of the Wheeler-Howard Act (Indian Reorganization Act) of 1934, there were some who rejected it. The Navajo feared a reduction in their livestock, a course of action planned by the federal government to upgrade reservation rangelands (Fonaroff, 1962). Residents on both the Klamath and Umatilla reservations in Oregon also rejected the act, contending that it was an attempt to impose Communism upon the Indian (Stern, 1966:260).

[7]For a fuller treatment of the complex relationship between Indian agency personnel and the Indians of Brownsville see "The Role of the B.I.A. on the reservation: Patron or client?" (Lynch, 1973).

8

Westerners are familiar with an ideological position which stresses individual competition and the necessity for achievement. The Muslim Swahili people of Coastal East Africa display a pattern of entrepreneurial activity that is in part familiar to Westerners yet tempered by an ideology which stresses brotherhood and economic equality. By looking at both the economic behavior and the cultural values of the people in a small modernizing community, Landberg and Weaver disclose the pragmatic nature of a supposedly "traditional and conservative" peasantry. Along with Cancian, Landberg and Weaver show how easy it is to misjudge the response of people exposed to the influences of modernization.

Maendeleo: Economic Modernization in a Coastal Community of Northeastern Tanzania

LEIF C. W. LANDBERG AND PAMELA L. WEAVER

Leif C. W. Landberg is currently teaching anthropology at Fordham University, Lincoln Center. He did his graduate work at the University of Arizona and the University of California, Davis. Professor Landberg's research in Coastal East

Africa emphasized the economic aspects of fishing and small-holder farming among the Swahili people.

Pamela L. Weaver is currently Assistant Professor in the Department of Anthropology, New York University. She received her graduate education at Harvard University and the University of California, Davis. Professor Weaver's field research among Swahili-speaking people in coastal Tanzania focused on local-level politics and the role of ritual in community life.

As a case study in economic modernization, we will discuss the adaptations to a cash economy made by members of Kigombe village, a rural coastal community in Tanga Region, Tanzania, East Africa (Map 1).[1] We will examine both the external constraints on local economic activity and, given these constraints, the strategies utilized by indigeneous innovators and entrepreneurs in their efforts at bringing about change in the village. We will be particularly concerned with the use of certain ideological values by members of the community in legitimating economic and social change.

The inhabitants of Kigombe derive their primary income from fishing, supplemented by subsistence farming and some cash cropping. Their village is advantageously located on the main road to the city of Tanga, the main urban center in Tanga Region and an important coastal port, and, at the same time, is situated next to a large plantation. This plantation, or "estate" as it is called in East Africa, virtually surrounds Kigombe (Map 2). On it is grown sisal (*Agave sisalana*), a plant from whose processed leaves hard fiber is extracted for industrial uses in making rope, gunny sacks, and stuffing for furniture and packages. Although the larger economy of this part of Tanzania is dominated by plantation agriculture, Kigombe nonetheless appears to be little affected by the nearby estate's presence as the village's inhabitants provide the estate with little labor.

The reluctance of most of the village's men to enter directly into the labor force of the industrially organized estate, combined with their apparent preference for the more traditional production activities of the village, might suggest that the village's inhabitants are basically conservative and generally resistant to economic change. This impression, however, is hardly an accurate one. The inhabitants of Kigombe are well aware of the Government of Tanzania's policies for development and are anxious to assimilate new technologies and ideas. Furthermore, they have not completely ignored employment opportunities on the estate or in other sectors of the regional

LOCATION OF KIGOMBE VILLAGE IN RELATION TO TANGA DISTRICT AND TANGA REGION

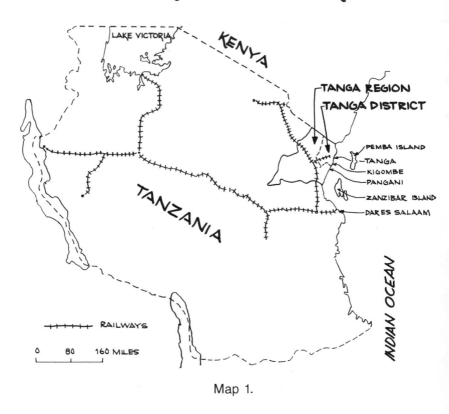

Map 1.

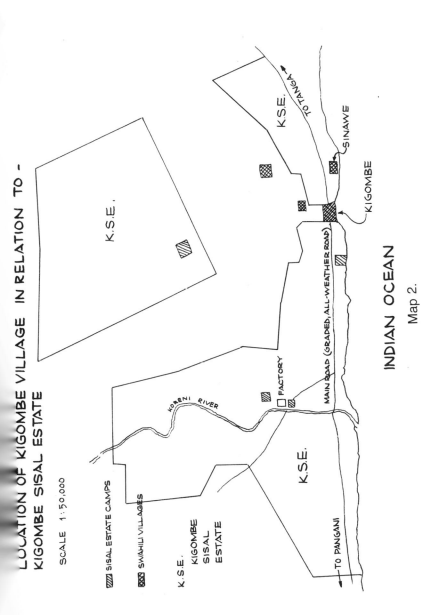

LOCATION OF KIGOMBE VILLAGE IN RELATION TO - KIGOMBE SISAL ESTATE

SCALE 1:50,000

🟦 SISAL ESTATE CAMPS

🔳 SWAHILI VILLAGES

K.S.E. KIGOMBE SISAL ESTATE

K.S.E.

K.S.E.

K.S.E.

KORENI RIVER

FACTORY

MAIN ROAD (GRADED, ALL-WEATHER ROAD)

TO PANGANI

TO TANGA

SINAWE

KIGOMBE

INDIAN OCEAN

Map 2.

SOURCE: Amboni Estates-Limited. Mr. H. P. Ammann, General Manager, Tanga, Tanzania

economy. However, over the years certain external political, economic, and social constraints have contributed to the predominant emphasis of Kigombe adults on rural economic activities. These constraints, derived from the colonial legacy of a dual economy,[2] can be clearly seen in this rural coastal area with its dichotomy between a developed industrial-export sector dominated by the sisal estates and an indigenous underdeveloped sector represented by smallholder fishing and farming.

While most of Kigombe's inhabitants have remained primary producers in the rural sector, at the same time they have attempted economic innovations within the limits of their capital resources. In this regard, appeals to traditionalism have presented an important means for mobilizing individual and community support for these innovative attempts. The local innovators have used aspects of a pervasive ideology of brotherhood (*udugu*) and unity (*umoja*) and other traditional symbols to facilitate and justify change and to rationalize what in Swahili is called *maendeleo*, progress.

At first glance, the reaffirmation of traditional symbols and values creates an illusory paradox; the more that things change within the village, the more its inhabitants seem to remain the same. However, on closer examination such a seeming paradox confuses the rhetoric with the reality of change within the community. As Joseph Gusfield (1967) has suggested, to contrast tradition with modernity in some ways is to pose a false sociological dichotomy. Within this frame of reference, tradition—such as selected symbols of the past—surrounds present actions with a legitimating principle. Tradition, then, is used by innovators as a reflection of ideology to justify future-oriented programs of action.

In bringing about change, the persons and groups who have promoted economic innovations in the village have acted as entrepreneurs.[3] While pursuing their innovative goals with profits in mind, they have coordinated a number of interpersonal relationships and managed other resources, bearing both economic and social risks. As elsewhere in the Third World, the main economic function provided by these indigenous entrepreneurs for the capital-poor smallholder sector of the economy is that of adapting "customary, established means to novel ends" (Geertz, 1967:393). Restraints imposed by the wider economy have limited the environments in which they can most effectively use their assets and have encouraged them to orient much of their entrepreneurial activities toward the development of their own community. As a substantial portion of their assets (capital, labor and skills, and the social obligations which can be enlisted) derive from the community, these entrepreneurs must be responsive to local sentiments and values. The pervasive values of brotherhood and unity represent an ideal for the moral state of the community. Furthermore, these values provide rules for normative action and guidelines for strategies that entrepreneurs and others in the community manipulate in achieving their own ends.

In examining the nature of economic change and the ways in which modernization is rationalized in Kigombe, we will first present a brief introduction to the village. Then we will describe the community's social and occupational structure and the effects of external constraints on the local economy. Following this, we will discuss the various strategies that Kigombe's entrepreneurs have used in capitalizing the small-scale local commercial fisheries. Finally, we will show how the community's dominant ideology both constrains entrepreneurial acitivity, and, at the same time, legitimizes economic changes in the village.

THE COMMUNITY AND ITS ENVIRONS

Kigombe Village, which numbers approximately 1,000 inhabitants, is situated along the shores of the Indian Ocean and between the lands of a large and successful sisal estate. The village and the estate, which takes its name from Kigombe, lie along the main road between Pangani, a town which flourished during the Arab period of Tanzania's history, and Tanga, a city which became prominent under German colonial rule as a railhead and port for sisal and has become the region's commercial center (Map 3). Currently, the city of Tanga is the administrative headquarters for Tanga District and Tanga Region, the larger governmental units in which Kigombe Village is included.

Tanzania is a socialist one-party state and has parallel government and party structures at most levels of the country's administrative divisions (Derksen, 1969). Locally, Kigombe Village is both the administrative center for its government ward of Tanga District and the head of the local branch of TANU (Tanganyika African National Union), the country's official and only political party. Organizationally, both of these units, the Kigombe Ward and the Kigombe Branch, are representative of the smallest effective local-level units of administration for government and party.

As the administrative center of Kigombe Ward, Kigombe Village con-

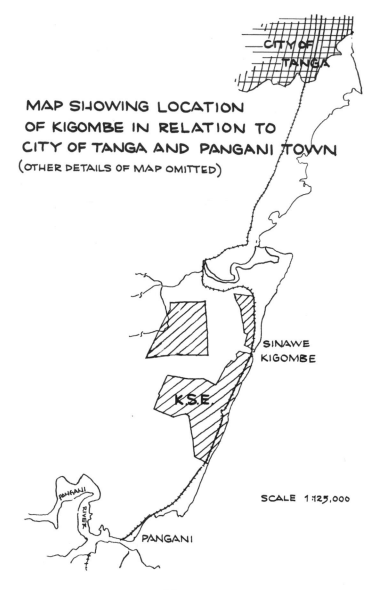

MAP SHOWING LOCATION
OF KIGOMBE IN RELATION TO
CITY OF TANGA AND PANGANI TOWN
(OTHER DETAILS OF MAP OMITTED)

CITY OF
TANGA

SINAWE
KIGOMBE

K.S.E

SCALE 1:125,000

PANGANI
RIVER
PANGANI

Map 3.

SOURCE: Commissioner for Surveys and Mapping, Ministry
of Lands, Housing and Urban Development, United Republic
of Tanzania, Dar es Salaam, Tanzania

tains several governmental facilities. These include a primary court, an extended primary school (standards I-VII), a medical dispensary, a veterinary center, and a Tanga District Council produce market. Kigombe also has a wholesale fish market that, for purposes of taxation, is under the aegis of the Tanga District Council. The market was built and is still operated by the local fishermen's cooperative, the Kigombe Fishermen's Association. In addition to these facilities, the local TANU office is located in the village, where all meetings of the Kigombe Branch are held.

The administrative and political units that take their names from Kigombe embrace more than just Kigombe itself. Included in these are older coastal villages, closely related historically and culturally to Kigombe, as well as newer, less traditional villages near the sisal estate composed predominantly of African migrants from upcountry parts of Tanzania and other areas of East Africa. While many administrative matters are handled locally by government and party officials in these communities where problems arise, Kigombe Village, by virtue of its size and the concentration of governmental facilities in it, is prominent in most important matters concerning the local Ward and Branch. Outside of the sisal estate, which has a social field of its own, Kigombe Village is the main focus for social, economic, and political activities in the area.

In addition to contacts with the inhabitants of the sisal estate camps, provided by various local Ward and Branch meetings, the inhabitants of the older coastal villages are linked together with those of the newer sisal estate camps in an interdependent network of socioeconomic relationships. These contacts are mainly through casual labor performed by upcountry migrants for residents of the older coastal villages and through commercial transactions between upcountry migrants and petty shopkeepers and artisans who serve both the sisal estate camps and the older communities of the area. Communication between these groups of persons is greatly facilitated by the fact that most of the upcountry migrants speak some Swahili, the indigenous language spoken in the older coastal towns. This language skill is often acquired by the migrants in their home areas, as Swahili is the official administrative language of Tanzania and the language of instruction used in the government's primary schools.

THE CULTURAL AND SOCIAL BACKGROUND

Although Kigombe Village is part of larger governmental and political units, for most of its residents the basic social unit is the village itself. As a highly kin-related and almost entirely Muslim village, it also forms the basic moral community for its members. Excluding civil servants stationed in Kigombe and transient agricultural workers, most of the village's residents are Sunni Muslims who follow the Shafi'i rite and speak Swahili as their first or only language. While anyone in the village can claim an ethnic or "tribal" label, traced patrilineally in the older Swahili-speaking communities of the area, such identification has little cultural meaning except for recently arrived upcountry migrants. Particularly for those individuals born on the coast, the self-labels of "Swahili" or People of the Coast (*Watu wa Mwambao*) as referring to persons of a Muslim, Swahili-speaking, coastal culture are more significant in terms of ethnic identity.[4]

While the tribal labels of most of the people in Kigombe no longer serve to distinguish distinctive cultural differences, these ethnic labels historically reflect the fact that the East African coast has been an area of high population mobility, with its villages continually assimilating Swahili from other parts of the coast as well as non-Swahili migrants from upcountry (Gulliver, 1956). Instead of "tribal" ethnicity, commonalities of religion as reflected in worship, culture and a distinctive life style, residence, and ties of kinship and marriage define community membership in this highly mobile social environment. Thus, in Kigombe, as in other Swahili villages of the area, an explicit distinction is made between those who are "citizens" (*wenyeji*, "owners") of the village, and those who are guests or strangers (*wageni*) in it. For one not born in the village, or of parents from outside the village, the main requirements for full assimilation into the community involve at least a nominal profession of Islam, the acquisition of the cultural trappings and life style of the coast, and intermarriage with women of the community. Children of such a union acquire citizenship status and rights in the village through their mothers.

Given the social diversity of Swahili villages and the geographical mobility between them, an ideology of brotherhood (*udugu*) and unity (*umoja*) accommodates people of varying citizenship status—kinsmen, affines, and resident *wageni*—in the daily social life of the community with regard to what they have in common, their religion. As an extension of the premise of the equality of all believers under Islam, this ideology metaphorically relates all individuals to each other as kin, emphasizing cooperation and neighborliness, and functions as the basis of a fellowship of Islam, stressing consensus and unity in the village. Within this ideological framework of brotherhood and equality the exercise of personal authority is heavily constrained.

This constraint, coupled with the always available option for disgruntled people in the community to move elsewhere—to the sisal estates, to the cities, or, through cognatic ties, to other coastal villages—tends to minimize formal, overt authority in the village.[5] Apart from the new government local-level political offices, the roles of which are still being defined within the Swahili traditional context, the few positions with formal authority are those associated with religious offices. These offices, the *mwalimu*, the local religious leader of the community, and the *kadhi*, a judge of Islamic law, are achieved positions. They are secured by individuals who demonstrate their piety over the years by attention to Islamic ritual obligations such as prayer and to the acquisition of knowledge (*elimu*) of Islam by the diligent study of the Koran. Through these activities they obtain respect (*heshima*). A corollary of respect, which is reflected in an informal age grading system within the village, is that control of various sorts of knowledge, and hence also of wisdom and moral authority, ideally increase with age. In addition to the *mwalimu* and *kadhi* there are other older pious members of the community who achieve respect in a similar way. They do so by regular attendance at mosque and deep involvement in the village's social and religious life. It is exactly those men who attend mosque regularly and who have demonstrated their permanent commitment to the village as citizens (*wenyeji*) who form the core of village leaders. They, along with the *mwalimu* and the *kadhi*, are informally recognized by the community's members as elders of the village (*wazee wa mji*).

Leadership and authority in Kigombe are intimately related to the concept of respect. In a community of "brothers," such as Kigombe, the goal is to keep conflict in the village at a minimum, or at least out of the public eye. Disputes usually are dealt with only by those groups most immediately concerned, with an emphasis on settlement of differences through consensus. As a rule, the groups most commonly involved in village disputes and their settlement are particular households or, if need be, larger groups of kin allied with individual disputants. If a dispute cannot be resolved, a religious leader or another elder of the village may be called in as a mediator. In these situations elders can only exercise influence through the moral force that surrounds the respect they have earned by their conduct in village affairs. Characteristically, elders try to settle disputes by appeals to brotherhood and unity within the village. At one level, as mediators, they are appealing to the good will of the disputants to exercise restraint in the interests of the community, but at another they are attempting to obtain submission to the moral authority implicit in the respect they are accorded by other members of the community. Thus, by creating a situation in which the disputants must defer to the wishes of the elders in order to show good manners or respect, disputants run the risk of jeopardizing their own respect if they do not accede to the appeals of the moral guardians of the community.

If entrepreneurs in Kigombe are to be successful, they must be responsive to this moral frame of reference in their conduct toward other persons of the community. The appropriateness of entrepreneurial response stems partly from the ideology that members of the community impose on each other, but that ideology in turn is defined in relation to a larger social and economic reality outside of the community itself. A veiled message for potential entrepreneurs lies within the village's ideological framework of brotherhood and unity which says in effect that enterprise must be sociable if it is to be successful. Indeed, while members of the community would not necessarily express it in these terms, the ideology of brotherliness within the village can be seen as a charter for social taxation on entrepreneurial activities and as insurance against unreasonable profit taking. This does not mean that enterprise by individuals in the community is discouraged; on the contrary, the economic success of entrepreneurs in accumulating capital is acceptable and even applauded within Swahili communities, provided that the entrepreneurs act the role of good citizens.

The community's members define the style, if not the ostensible social goals, for local entrepreneurs within the context of the ideology of brotherhood and unity. Successful entrepreneurs in Kigombe are representative of what Robert Paine (1963:51-55) calls free-holder entrepreneurs. In Paine's terms, free-holder entrepreneurs, as opposed to free-enterprise entrepreneurs, are accountable to the community. In taking profits they avoid offending neighborly values and cooperate with other citizens in raising the productivity of the community. Free-enterprise entrepreneurs, on the other hand, also pursue profit but disregard local values. The latter type of entrepreneur would stand little chance of success within the current social order of a village like Kigombe. However in order to understand the great value placed on a free-hold style of entrepreneurship by citizens of Kigombe, and to appreciate its sustaining external forces, attention must be directed toward an examination of the place of the Swahili in the regional economy, both within its historical and its contemporary settings. With this in mind, we will begin by first examining the nature of Kigombe's occupational structure and its local economy, and then consider the place of Kigombe within the wider economy of the region.

THE LOCAL ECONOMY

The importance of primary production in the local economy is quite clear when the occupational structure of the village is examined. Data presented in Table 1, which are drawn from a social survey conducted by us during the course of our fieldwork, indicate the primary occupations for approximately two-thirds of the men in Kigombe. While not all of the men of the villages were interviewed, enough were included in the survey to give an adequate impression of the relative proportions of different occupational categories.

In the survey (see Table 1) those who are occupied as primary producers represent 69 percent of the total sample; of these, 51 percent are principally occupied as fishermen and 17 percent as farmers. Another 23 percent of the working men in the community are employed providing goods and services (mercantile and vending, other services, religious and medical). Added to this occupational profile are 5 percent of the men who are unemployed or retired and 3 percent who live locally but find salaried employment outside of the village.

Taken by themselves, however, primary occupations give a very incomplete picture of the nature of work in Kigombe. Except for the relatively wealthy few, the men in the village find it necessary to supplement their incomes with various kinds of secondary employment. In discussing subsidiary sources of income, it is especially important to stress that almost every able-bodied man in Kigombe farms. Taking all categories of primary occupations in the sample together, over 90 percent of the persons interviewed cultivate food crops either on their own farm plots or on one which their close relatives own. Kigombe smallholders also cultivate cash crops. These crops, coconuts and cashew nuts, are the main sources of agricultural income for persons who farm as a primary occupation and the second most important source of cash income for those who pursue other occupations.

The importance of fishing as a primary source of daily cash income for the majority of village men may be appreciated by examining some of the

Table 1.
Primary Occupation of Men Interviewed in Kigombe*

Occupation	Number
Fishermen	95
Farmers only	32
subtotal	127

Other:

Within the village:

Mercantile and Vending (17)

Bicycle travelling salesman, novelties & jewelry	1
Coffee vendor	1
Fish salesmen	3
Small cafe or tea shop (*Hoteli*) owner	4
Small cafe or tea shop employee	3
Small general store owner	4
Small general store employee	1

Services (22)

Baker (salaried by a proprietor of a local general store)	1
Carpenter	3
Coconut knapper	1
Handyman, house & fence building, repairs	2
Laundryman	2
Mason	4
Double outrigger canoe specialist, construction and repairs	1
Tailor	5
Tinsmith	1
Truck driver, owner	1
Water carrier	1

Occupation	Number
Religious and Medical (4)	
Koranic school teacher	1
Folk medical practitioner	3
subtotal	43

Unemployed (9)

"Retired"	9

Outside the village:

Kigombe Sisal Estate (4)

Field/Office	2
Servant	1
Truck driver	1

Tanga Municipal Government (1)

Sanitation	1

National Government (1)

Village Executive Officer, Tongoni	1
Grand Total	185

*Data in Table 1 also include our census material from Sinawe, a small neighborhood settlement of Kigombe. We have chosen to include data from Sinawe, as this settlement, although maintaining a separate identity, is closely linked to Kigombe by kinship and religious ties. Sinawe also has the character of a neighborhood in that it is dependent on Kigombe for such services as small shops and eating places or tea shops.

problems associated with obtaining income from the cultivation of coconut palms. Coconut palm cultivation has been long established in the Swahili scheme of agriculture. Moreover, coconuts have a special appeal as a cash crop in that they can be harvested three to four times annually, thus yielding regular and profitable returns throughout the year. Coconut palms also represent excellent investments as old age security since mature trees will continue to produce crops well beyond a man's lifetime. Yet despite the attractiveness that owning coconut palms holds for smallholders on the coast, few Swahili farmers in the Kigombe area are able to possess substantial holdings of coconut palms through their own labor and plantings until their middle age.

Coconut palms, because they take about seven years to begin bearing harvestable crops, represent a long-term commitment of time and labor. However, in addition to the necessity of patience until an income can be realized from the trees, this type of investment also involves high cultivation risks in the early stages of maturation. Like most tree crops planted by smallholders on the Tanga coast, there is usually a high mortality rate among seedlings, some succumbing to insect pests and others to being eaten by domestic cattle and wild pigs.

Most people in Kigombe do not begin working their own farm plots until they reach about the age of twenty. Given the long maturation period of the palms, farmers do not begin to realize a return from their efforts until they are well into their thirties. A relatively small number of people, however, may realize a profit before this age from trees they have purchased or inherited.[6]

In contrast to coconuts, cashew nuts have begun to assume importance as a cash crop only within the last two decades. With the encouragement of the government, there have been significant increases in cashew tree plantings in coastal areas such as Kigombe since the mid-1960s. Cashew nuts now command a higher grower's wholesale price than coconuts and, unlike coconuts, have an export market. Declining world prices, as well as the relatively poor quality of East African copra, have limited the market for locally produced coconuts in East Africa (International Bank for Reconstruction and Development, 1961:371). The bulk of coconuts produced in Kigombe is sold either in the village for use in cooking or in Tanga as copra for the manufacture of cooking oil and soap. Cashew nuts have yet to prove their viability as a cash crop over a period of years like coconuts, but since cashew nuts bring higher wholesale prices than coconuts, most small holders in Kigombe now have young plantings of cashew trees. The sensitivity of Kigombe farmers to wholesale prices and external market demands is indicated by the fact that some farmers in the area who are now starting farm plots choose to plant cashew trees before beginning to cultivate coconut palms. One of the main problems in cultivating coconut palms and cashew trees, especially during the seedling stages, is the erratic nature of rainfall on the East African coast, and, ironically, the one crop of the area which is not affected by variations in the rate of rainfall is sisal.

KIGOMBE AND THE SISAL ESTATE

Although the Swahili generally avoid working on the sisal estates, there are four persons from Kigombe who do work on the nearby estate (Table 1). Ethnically, these persons are all Swahili who were born in Kigombe. Together with four other Kigombe people who work and live on the sisal estate, they represent nearly the total number of persons born in the village who are employed in the local sisal industry.[7] These eight workers represent scarcely more than 1 percent of the total 680 Africans employed on the estate.[8]

While their number is small on the sisal estate, there is a pattern to the types of employment that they hold within its occupational structure. All of the jobs held by these Kigombe men involve higher paying skilled or semiskilled employment (e.g., welder, messenger, production clerk, vehicle driver, storekeeper, and cutting headman). This employment pattern is explainable when seen in the historical context of labor problems associated with the development of the sisal industry.

Sisal was introduced into the Tanzanian coastlands by German colonialists in 1892 after a disappointing period of several years during which experimentation with other cash crops in the area had failed. The plants took well to the soil and climate of the East African coast, and after a period of building up adequate planting stock and marketable reserves, sisal came to dominate the economy of German East Africa by the eve of World War I. Earlier, when the sisal industry was developing, local and metropolitan colonial politics effectively barred African smallholder participation in the growing of sisal in preference for its cultivation on estates controlled and operated by highly capitalized European corporations (Mascarenhas, 1970:60-66). Enormous areas of Tanga Region were alienated for these estates. Most of the land put under sisal cultivation was unoccupied, as the coast was an area of relatively low population density with a pre-European settlement pattern of compact settlements separated from each other by wide stretches of bushland. The larger Swahili settlements thus remained intact, although some, like Kigombe, became sandwiched in between estate lands (Map 2).

These estates with their vast carpetlike rows of plantings very quickly altered the face of the landscape and brought with them demands for labor that the local coastal population could scarcely meet. In fact, much to the consternation of the sisal growers, most Swahili men aggravated the labor problems of the industry by avoiding work on the estates. They did this for at least three reasons. First, since few Swahili villages had been displaced, or their inhabitants dispossessed of crop lands, the sisal growers did not have a readily available supply of labor in the form of a newly created landless proletariat (Winter and Beidelman, 1967: 102). Second, for complex reasons having to do with tensions arising from the divergence of interests between the European settlers and the German colonial administration, the residents of Swahili villages were shielded from conscription and compulsory labor on the estates (Mascarenhas, 1970:73; Iliffe, 1969:54-56, 64-68). Third, compared to the economic alternatives that were available to the Swahili at the time, the conditions for employment for Africans on the estates, either in the form of the limited social amenities or the poor wages that were offered to them, left much to be desired. This was especially true for unskilled jobs involving heavy labor, such as leaf cutting in the fields, where the demand for labor was greatest. An indication of the general low regard Africans held for this kind of employment is the fact that throughout the history of the estates, the lower paid unskilled jobs involving heavy labor overwhelmingly have been filled by migrants from the poorer upcountry parts of Tanzania and adjacent territories which lacked viable export cash crops for smallholders (Winter and Beidelman, 1967:112-115). When profitable cash crops were developed in the upcountry areas of Tanzania which once had had large numbers of immigrants working on the coastal sisal estates, the tide of migration dropped substantially (Mascarenhas, 1970: 73-74, 176-177).

THE REGIONAL ECONOMY AND ITS CONSTRAINTS

Rather than work on the estates, the Swahili, who had been long accustomed to a commercial economy, generally found other more pleasant and just as profitable ways of making a livelihood in the new economic order. A majority of adult working males in the rural Swahili villages continued to gain their livelihoods as primary producers, with heavy emphasis in the shoreline villages on commercial fisheries. Certainly, in spite of whatever adverse effects sisal might have had on local smallholder agriculture, the beginning of the estates clearly was a boon to the Swahili fishing industry. The estates with their salaried labor forces provided a ready market for fish, and as bus transportation improved, markets for fresh fish from rural villages rapidly developed in the expanding urban area of Tanga.

As an alternative to being primary producers, some Swahili men from rural areas pursued unskilled and semiskilled occupations in the city of Tanga.[9] These workers tended to maintain ties with their home villages while living in the city. A powerful incentive to keep up contact with home villages was the meager wage rate for Africans in urban areas, which were quite low relative to the high cost of living in the city. Many urban Swahili households with members who were originally from outlying villages, such as Kigombe, supplemented low cash incomes and expanded their narrowed subsistence base in the city with food from kinsmen in nearby rural areas. These supplies often represented food that, in a sense, was grown by the urban dwellers themselves. Then, as today, a substantial number of rural Swahili living in the city maintained farming plots in their home villages where they had traditional rights in land. These farm plots usually were maintained by remittances to relatives in the villages, who either performed the field labor themselves or hired casual laborers (often upcountry migrants) to do the cultivation, with the produce being consumed or sold through a variety of arrangements made between the managers and absentee owners. On many of these farm plots their urban-based Swahili owners invested heavily in plantings of coconut palms as a contingency against periods of unemployment in the city and as security for old age.

In addition to the provision of money for the management of these farm plots, members of urban Swahili households also were able to reciprocate for those services by providing domiciles for their rural kinsmen who came to the city in search of work. These kinsmen frequently would be young unmarried males: the pattern of youths migrating to the city, which still continues, usually involves young men in their late teens or early twenties. At that period in their lives young men in rural Swahili villages are considered old enough to begin striking out on their own and seeking full-time employment. A substantial number of youths in the villages, probably a majority, never effectively leave the rural sector of the economy later in their adult lives. However, until these youths marry, their bachelorhood represents a time of occupational experimentation. While many of the youths in the villages begin employment in the rural sector of the economy at a relatively early age, this work is often interlarded with other kinds of job experiences found in urban areas or in the company towns of the sisal estates. In seeking these opportunities, young men from Swahili villages in the Tanga Region and those from other parts of the Tanzanian coast leave their natal villages for extended periods of time (see also Caplan, 1968:35-36).

This leave or traveling (*kutembea*) has not taken on any formal pattern within Swahili villages of the Tanga Region, and it is generally seen by most Swahili adults as simply being the time for young men to sow their wild oats. However, an important side effect of this travel is that job skills are brought back to rural villages. In Kigombe, for example, all of those Swahili born in the village who are currently working full-time as carpenters, masons, and tailors (Table 1) apprenticed for their trades on sisal estates or in urban areas such as Tanga, Dar es Salaam, the nation's capital, and even as far away as Mwanza, a town several hundred miles away on the shores of Lake Victoria.

During the colonial period, as now, not all of those who sought work in urban areas necessarily returned to their home villages after their youthful travels. Many of those who were successful in finding secure employment in the city became permanent urban residents. Nevertheless, most of these persons continued to maintain close ties with their home villages. While a variety of social and religious reasons can be cited to explain why urban-based Swahili maintained their ties with rural areas, certain economic facts about life in the colonial city made the maintenance of those contacts practical.

Until relatively late in the colonial period social services in the city were at a minimum, and old age security for African urban residents rested either with kinsmen or in profitable investments for the future. As we have described the situation, the two often were difficult to disentangle. Most kinsmen, however, were likely to be living in rural areas, and unless an urban-based Swahili was able to sustain an income at the end of his working career through some type of investment he was likely to eventually return to his home village because of the high cost of living in the city.

In these circumstances, Swahili urban residents were not frustrated if they had acquired a taste for city life, as returning to a rural coastal village like

Kigombe hardly meant being cut off entirely from an urban area and its pleasures. In fact, such villages may have offered some advantages over dwelling in the city. First, it was cheaper to construct a house there than in the city, and rents were reduced or eliminated. Second, if a person maintained a farm plot, subsistence costs were significantly reduced and some income, albeit a lesser amount, could still be obtained from the harvesting of cash crops. Finally, the regular bus service from the coastal villages to Tanga allowed almost anyone in the rural areas to go to the city when he wanted to market and shop, seek out entertainment, or obtain services. In short, most of the coastal Swahili villages in the Tanga District (Map 1) stood in a suburbanlike relationship to the city of Tanga.

In the colonial situation the probabilities of obtaining substantial long-term investments in the city were quite low for most urban-based Swahili. About the best that Swahili or other Africans could hope for was to obtain rental properties or engage in small-scale shopkeeping.[10] The expansion of African enterprises into larger-scale commercial operations was discouraged by a combination of economic factors, the effects of which are still being felt in Tanzania's post-Independence period (see *The Economist* . . . 1966). On the one hand, the general scarcity of capital in the underdeveloped colonial economy had a dampening effect on all indigenous commercial activity, and had the tendency of limiting African participation in commercial activities involving large amounts of capital. On the other hand, the lack of adequate capital, which limited the type, range, and scale of African commercial activity, was further compounded by the historical fact that most large-scale retailing in the economy had been pre-empted by Indian businessmen who formed a small but economically significant part of the country's population.

In recent history, and probably in earlier periods, Indian merchants have played a vital role in the economy of East Africa. In the days of the Zanzibar sultanate, before the beginning of European rule, Indian merchants were prominent as financiers in outfitting and underwriting caravans into the interior of the East African mainland and in developing the clove economy of the islands of Zanzibar and Pemba. The leading export and import firms of the sultanate were those of Indian merchants, and largely through this commerce they came to dominate the sultanate's wholesale and distributive trade. When the mainland of what is now Tanzania passed into German hands, the colonial government encouraged Indians to emigrate in the hope of using their commercial expertise and their labor and skills in developing the economy.

Throughout German East Africa, as in neighboring Uganda and Kenya, Indian traders were in the forefront of extending the money economy into rural areas by following the expansion of the roads and railways into the interior and by managing small shops in outlying trading centers. Indian businessmen soon became the middlemen between the larger European firms and African farmers and consumers (Mangat, 1969:93; Iliffe, 1969:93-98). In rural areas, Indian merchants became the main outlets for produce by virtue of their strategic locations, controlling the marketing of minor crops in the country (Ghai, 1965:103). Furthermore, as in earlier times, the Indian business community, with family and commercial connections overseas, possessed a competitive advantage in the importation of consumer goods and controlled most wholesale trade and the bulk of the retail trade, leaving African businessmen a relatively minor redistributive role in the economy.

Though the role of the Indians in the economy was vital, their numbers in the countryside were few. When German East Africa passed into the hands of the British after World War I, the number of Indian immigrants to the newly named Tanganyika Territory increased. However, because of British colonial legislation prohibiting the purchase of African land for agricultural use by Indians and restricting Indian residence to designated trading centers, the majority of Indians became urban dwellers (Winter and Beidelman, 1967:95; Ghai, 1965:100-101). While these restrictive policies were designed to protect the African rural population, they had the effect of channeling Indian occupational pursuits along lines that further rigidified the social and economic stratification of Indian over African.

On the coast, smallholder cash cropping and fishing became the preserve of Africans, as Indians, with the exception of a small number of those wealthy enough to purchase German-owned sisal estates as ex-enemy property after World War I, were excluded from the rural agricultural sector of the economy as primary producers. Thus confined to towns, Indians entered those fields of economic activity that were open to them in an urban environment. Occupationally, they tended to concentrate in trade, industries, the professions, and skilled and artisanal employment. Other Indians with adequate education turned to employment in the civil service, filling lower, middle-grade posts not reserved for Europeans.

While the number of educated Africans in the colonial period was relatively small compared to that of the Indian population, reflecting the latter's general economic advantage, African opportunities for skilled employment were correspondingly more limited. For even though the colonial government in later years provided educated Africans with some employment in civil service, its administrative policies implementing indirect rule and the unwritten law of the "colour bar" in colonial British East African territories fostered racial exclusiveness, ethnic communalism, and narrow political loyalties and left educated Africans with little opportunity for skilled employment in the Indian-dominated private sector of the economy.

Since Independence, the layer-cake racial and ethnic division of labor characteristic of the dual colonial economy and its highly pluralist society has begun to break down as both Africans and Indians have realized greater equality of opportunity in many sectors of the economy. Tanzania's socialist policies of national development promise a radical transformation of the inherited colonial order. Thus far in the relatively short span of time since Independence, however, the most dramatic changes in the employment structure for Africans have mainly benefited the educated. These policies have produced opportunities for middle-level management positions in the various expatriate private firms operating in Tanzania and jobs at all levels of civil service. Educated Swahili, like other educated Tanzanians, have benefited from these changes, but the great majority of Swahili of the Tanga region continue to triangulate during their working careers between various alternatives similar to those which were presented to them in the colonial period by the urban, estate, and rural sectors of the regional economy.

Having examined the external constraints imposed on the Swahili rural economy, we now turn to an analysis of the kinds of strategies utilized by the inhabitants of Kigombe in order to modernize their community. As these development efforts have been made through various types of entrepreneurial activities, we will first discuss the general nature of entrepreneurship in Kigombe and then examine its role in capitalizing what is perhaps the most important part of the village's economy, the local fishing industry.

FREE-HOLDER ENTREPRENEURS IN KIGOMBE

Within the constraints imposed by the wider economy, local free-holder entrepreneurs in villages like Kigombe have been instrumental in attempts at modernization. External limitations on the amount of capital and human resources that could be mobilized outside their home villages have encouraged local entrepreneurs to become free-holders by orienting a large part of their entrepreneurial activities toward the rural sector of the regional economy and their own communities. Some of Kigombe's most successful entrepreneurs have expanded their investments outside the rural area and moved to the city of Tanga to manage urban investments. Even these individuals, however, are encouraged by these outside economic restraints to maintain and expand their investments in the village as insurance, and to remain intimately involved in the village's social and religious life.

In the village, the comportment of these and other free-holder entrepreneurs in the conduct of their enterprises is best understood with reference to the ideology of brotherhood and unity that pervades the rhetoric and much of the formal conduct and manners of the community's members. The manifest symbols of being a good citizen in the village are those embodied in being a good Muslim, one who is pious and reaffirms the social and religious values of the community by involvement in mosque affairs, and who, within limits, helps other villagers with his own personal resources. In the process of the fulfillment of this role, entrepreneurs and others in the community achieve respect. As the achievement and maintenance of respect by an individual is a transactional process between himself and other members of the community, an entrepreneur, by adhering to traditional social and moral rules of conduct in achieving respect, legitimates both his good intentions towards the community and his own entrepreneurial activities and profit-taking.

A successful entrepreneur's respect, as well as his economic success, gives him influence in the village but it does not give him unrestrained power. In this regard it is perhaps significant that the most successful of the village's older entrepreneurs are important members of one of the few formally organized groups within Kigombe, the committee for planning the village's annual celebration of the Prophet Mohammed's birthday (*Maulidi*). It is from service on this committee that these men and others in the community may obtain the prestige and respect prerequisite to becoming acknowledged as elders of the village (*wazee wa mji*). All of the persons generally recognized as elders are devout in their attendance at mosque, and all in some way control knowledge or skills (*elimu*) that are valuable to the community. The primary meaning of *elimu*, as learned knowledge, refers to an understanding of the written literature that is of importance in clarifying and codifying the proper religious, ethical, and legal duties and conduct of Muslims. However, the meaning of *elimu* is also extended to include other types of knowledge that are of importance to the community, such as secular education received in government primary schools or commercial expertise acquired by the village's successful businessmen.

It is because of such expertise, in addition to whatever religious knowledge they might control, that the most successful entrepreneurs of Kigombe are included among the village's elders. Like the capital invested in their own business enterprises, the influence that these older entrepreneurs achieve as elders of the village must be managed judiciously if they are to profit from their prestige. The leadership role of elder, for example, can only be exercised consensually. Since the authority of these entrepreneurs as elders comes from the respect that they can command, those of them who would try too baldly to subvert the collective interests of the community to their own ends risk damaging their reputations and personal influence in the community. Thus, while older free-holder entrepreneurs achieve respect and influence in the activities of the *Maulidi* committee by being brought to the heart of the village's decisionmaking council, they also are constrained as elders to adhere to the community's social and moral norms in other spheres of village life.

These constraints preclude types of business activities or degrees of profit-taking that disregard local values. Yet in striving to maintain a public image that archetypically reflects community values, a free-holder entrepreneur nonetheless can use the respect he acquires to his own entrepreneurial advantage. By operating within the role of a model citizen, for example, he is able to protect himself against illegitimate or unreasonable claims on his capital resources through the respect that he commands in the community.[11] Within the context of this stratagem, persons born in the village, in other words those who are full "citizens," have the greatest comparative advantage in becoming successful local entrepreneurs by utilizing their extensive kin ties. In an economy with a low per capita income, such as the one in Tanga Region, customers for budding rural commercial enterprises constitute a valuable and scarce resource. Thus kinsmen, if handled with good business sense, can be an asset rather than a burden on individual entrepreneurial activities. By prudent management of social accounts on the part of both the entrepreneur as patron, and his kinsmen and friends as clients, the enterprises of citizen entrepreneurs in Kigombe often succeed where those of outsiders fail.

For example, in the competition for customers, a citizen entrepreneur in running a general store (*duka*) is able to reduce risk substantially by extending credit primarily to those kinsmen and friends he knows and trusts. The extension of credit—to individuals in small amounts—encourages but does not bind them to trade at his store rather than at those of his competitors. His kinsmen, on the one hand, in protecting a valuable source of credit, generally exercise restraint in the demands that they make on the entrepreneur. The entrepreneur, on the other hand, makes it difficult for disgruntled claimants on his resources to mobilize support against him by observing familial obligations to a wide range of kin and by performing public duties in other spheres of the village's social and religious life. As the extension of credit is a necessary strategem and a social obligation for any shopkeeper, outsider entrepreneurs in this line of business are obliged to follow the example set by the citizen entrepreneur. However, because of their narrower network of friends, and perhaps with few or no kinsmen in the village, outsider entrepreneurs tend to take higher risks by extending credit to both residents of Kigombe and migrant workers from the nearby sisal estate. Since their customers who are citizens of Kigombe are not socially or morally obligated to them as kinsmen, and since the migrant workers are not subject to the same set of social and moral constraints as those of Kigombe residents, outsider shopkeepers are regularly in the local government primary court trying to collect debts.[12]

ENTREPRENEURS AND THE LOCAL FISHING FLEET

Entrepreneurs in Kigombe soften the potential crippling effects of bad debts and poor investments to an extent by not putting all of their eggs in one basket. They characteristically spread risk by making multidirectional investments with the intention that their profits from one enterprise will feed in a circular process into the others. The kind of investment from which an individual will embark on his entrepreneurial cycle varies. In addition to shopkeeping, which usually requires a relatively large amount of capital and rarely represents a first venture, other common forms of investments include operating tea shops or small cafes, expanding holdings in cash crops, building up small herds of cattle, and when the opportunity arises experimenting with new types of investments such as smallholder sisal-growing recently encouraged by the Tanzanian Government.[13] All of these invest-

A Small General Store Near Kigombe Village

Photo by Leif Landberg and Pamela Weaver

ments provide a modest amount of employment for the residents in the village. More importantly, however, investments by entrepreneurs in the local fishing fleet have increased the size of the fleet and have modernized its gear. These entrepreneurial activities have contributed significantly to an increase in local employment and to the prosperity of Kigombe.

The local fleet consists entirely of lateen-rigged double outrigger canoes (*ngalawa*). Depending on their size, these canoes are capable of carrying from one to four men. Most of the canoes in the fleet are independently operated by their owners, while the remainder are owned by non-fishermen. In either case, returns on investments are obtained through a share system in general use which divides the daily profits of individual canoe catches in fixed proportions between the crew members, the owner of the gear, and the vessel owner. An equipment share is taken regularly by the vessel owner for canoe maintenance costs. Most types of gear in use, such as handlines and homemade wicker traps, are not considered expensive enough to deserve shares for maintenance costs. However, for the most modern type of gear in use, nylon gill nets, equipment shares are taken by their owners proportionately equal to those which are taken by vessel owners for canoe maintenance costs. Both of these kinds of equipment shares, which are rather modest ones, represent vessel and gear owner's shares and are deducted from a canoe's daily profits before the remaining money is split among the crew members. If a canoe owner is an independent operator, he receives a crew member's share as skipper of his crew in addition to the canoe's equipment share. The same rule would also apply for an owner of a nylon gill net working as a crew member on a canoe using his net.

The use of canoes with nylon nets may seem like a peculiar combination of old and new technology, but this juxtaposition results from the absence of large capital investments from outside of the community and underlines the fact that the fleet is as modern as it can be within limits imposed by the domestic availability of new technology. The fishermen and free-holder entrepreneurs investing in the fishing fleet are by no means wedded to a traditional technology. In addition to the current use of nylon nets in the fleet, their relatively unsuccessful experimentation with mechanized forms of European fishing technology also illustrates this point.

An outboard engine, purchased by the Kigombe Fishermen's Association, was tried out on several of the village's canoes as an auxiliary source of power and quickly became esteemed by the fishermen for the maneuverability it

Double-outrigger Fishing Canoe
Photo by Leif Landberg and Pamela Weaver

gave a canoe in periods of calm and for the extra speed and added factor of safety it provided in bad weather. Yet in spite of its appeal, the outboard engine remained an experimental technological object. Its operating costs, especially the price of fuel, are prohibitively high for most of the fishermen. These costs are further compounded by maintenance problems due to an inadequate supply of imported spare parts. Various fishermen in the village also experimented with an outboard-powered European-type skiff of about the same length as the local canoes, but it too was rejected. Unlike the local type of canoe, whose relatively deep, heavy hull allows fishermen to work their gear standing up and whose outriggers stabilize against severe rocking action, the skiff proved unsteady for efficiently working gear because of its lightness, broad beam, and shallow hull. In both cases the new technology was rejected for rational reasons, either because of its high operating costs or because it was technologically inferior and poorly adapted to the local mode of fishing.

The local canoes also are superior to the European-type skiff in other ways. They have very shallow draughts and, with their outriggers and large lateen sails, are extremely swift sailing craft. Moreover, their solid hull construction allows them to be sailed and worked without damage in the shallowest of water over the coral barrier reefs that form the main fishing grounds of the area. However, while these canoes are well adapted to local fishing conditions, the introduction of nylon nets has led to increasing dissatisfaction with them.

Nylon nets were introduced into the region in the mid-1950s and rapidly replaced the cotton nets then in use. The older type of cotton net rotted very easily, required frequent repair, and had a life expectancy of little more than a year. By contrast, the more resistant nylon nets of the same design rotted less quickly, required less frequent repair, and had a life expectancy of from three to five years. As relatively greater quantities of first class food fish such as sharks and tuna-like species can be caught with gill nets than can be obtained with other types of gear, and as more earnings per net could be obtained from the longer-lived nylon nets, the increase in per capita income that accrued to their users very shortly led to rising expectations among the fishermen. Owners of nylon nets and crew members of canoes using these nets reaped larger profits and substantial benefits from the new gear. Today this is manifested in their higher standard of living, as seen most visibly in generally better standards of housing and ownership of highly valued consumer goods such as kerosene pressure lamps and bicycles.

Almost every fisherman in the village soon wanted nylon nets because of their obvious economic benefits. Thus, the majority of handline fishermen wanted to fish with nylon nets and increase their earnings, while those already fishing with nylon nets wanted to acquire more of them and further increase their income. However, the design of the canoes ultimately created a bottleneck in implementing these goals. Their hulls are very narrow, scarcely two feet in width. The longest of canoe hulls rarely exceeds thirty feet, thus limiting the space for storing large nylon nets; the largest of these canoes is capable of carrying only three nets at a time.

In theory it would be possible to work more than three nets per vessel by making more than one trip a day, but the lack of refrigeration facilities at the beach market and current methods of retail distribution make this impractical. The fresh fish landed at the Kigombe wholesale fish market is distributed unrefrigerated to consumers by small-scale bicycle salesmen. Their commercial operations are not highly capitalized and the volume that each can handle daily is small, usually not exceeding one large wicker basket full of fish. Although fish can be sold smoked or salted, fresh fish brings the highest price and salesmen smoke and salt fish only as a last resort to preserve unsold or spoiling fish. As most of the salesmen distribute fish to their home villages, which are some distance from Kigombe, and as it is customary for them to deliver to their customers in the late afternoon, a good part of their day is spent bicycling to and from the market. As a consequence, daily sales at the fish market last only from 10:00 A.M. to 2:00 P.M., limiting fishing to the morning hours. Many of the nylon net fishermen are dissatisfied with this arrangement and would like to increase their production by hauling and setting their nets twice a day, once in the evening hours and once in the daylight hours. This is not yet possible, however, because the village lacks cold storage facilities. Gill-netted fish, which set longer in the water after being caught than those taken by handlines, are in a more advanced state of decay when landed. Thus, without refrigeration, an evening's catch of netted fish would spoil before being sold the next day.

An alternative strategy for increasing production with the existing marketing arrangements would be to use larger vessels and set more or larger nets in the same period of fishing hours. Unfortunately, other indigenous types of fishing craft larger than the local type of canoe are in several ways unsatisfac-

New and Old Types of Building Construction in Kigombe
Village
Photo by Leif Landberg and Pamela Weaver

Fish Salesman Loading at Kigombe Wholesale Market
Photo by Leif Landberg and Pamela Weaver

tory as substitutes. European-type fishing boats, which the fishermen are aware of but have not yet utilized, are for the moment an unrealistic alternative in terms of their availability and cost. In the current situation, then, the entrepreneurs and fishermen of Kigombe, with no alternative to the technology in use, can only increase the productivity of the fleet by replicating the most modern existing unit of production, a canoe with nylon nets.

THE KIGOMBE FISHERMEN'S ASSOCIATION

Thus far in talking about the capitalization of Kigombe's fleet we have discussed only the contributions made by individual entrepreneurs in the village. However, while their contributions have been significant, they have not been the only source for the development of the local fleet. The fishermen themselves, as a group, have undertaken entrepreneurial activities for further capitalization. This was done by the formation of a local fishermen's cooperative, the Kigombe Fishermen's Association (KFA). Its formation originally was encouraged by the national government's Division of Fisheries as part of a general drive in the early 1960s to establish local cooperatives in the coastal fishing villages of Tanzania. Kigombe's cooperative, which was registered in 1963, is notable among those in Tanga Region in that it is one of the few that has survived. We do not know the reasons for the failure of the other cooperatives, but some apparent reasons for the success of Kigombe's can be cited.

Probably the foremost external reason for its sustained viability has been the nearness of Kigombe to modern transportation facilities. This, in combination with other factors, has enhanced the village's attractiveness to fish salesmen as a wholesale landing site. Unlike other coastal fishing villages of the region, it has the good fortune of direct access to the main route leading to the city of Tanga, along which several buses pass daily and regularly on their way to the city. While being linked to city markets by bus transportation, Kigombe's rural marketing hinterland is a relatively good one, including the nearby sisal estate which employs a substantial labor force. In relation to other villages of the coast this latter fact has become of great importance since 1964, when the region suffered a general recession with the drastic drop of world sisal prices. In this depressed economic situation, Kigombe Sisal Estate was able to retain a relatively large labor force through better management and avoided closing entirely, as happened with some estates. With connections to both city and rural markets, Kigombe gains further advantage over other fishing villages south of the city of Tanga by being the closest of these villages to the most productive reefs of the area.

However, in addition to exogenous economic and geographic factors such as these, there must be personal incentives for fishermen to support a cooperative if it is to succeed. A primary incentive for supporting the cooperative, probably uppermost in the minds of the Kigombe fishermen at the time of its formation, was their desire to obtain better wholesale prices for their fish. Before the cooperative came into existence a system of marketing was in operation whereby several fishermen sold their catches regularly to a single fish salesman. In turn, this salesman acted as a patron in extending credit to his fishermen clients for canoe and gear repairs. Through the debt relationship created between these patrons and their clients, fish salesmen—as patrons—were often able to purchase the catch of fishermen for less than bargained prices by making partial payments and by continually deferring on the remaining balances. On the other hand, fishermen who found themselves in debt to particular salesmen were not in a position to demand full payment or to extricate themselves from the relationship without paying off their debts in full.

This system quickly came to an end with the formation of the KFA. Led in part by the first nylon net fishermen of the village, who are now retired from fishing and are successful shopkeepers, the fishermen instituted an auction system for wholesaling at a new centralized marketplace controlled by the KFA. Competition between fish salesmen bidding in the auction soon raised wholesale prices over those in the old system.

This organizational innovation brought about by the formation of the KFA resulted in a radical change in the structure of transactions between producer and buyer. Prior to this change, fish salesmen essentially stood outside of the local community and were not subject to its moral norms, with the result that fishermen had little or no control over the price of fish or over the conduct of sales. Now, with the change from the old system the roles of patron and client were reversed, inasmuch as the fish salesmen were no longer the sole arbiters of the rules governing transaction. However, this change in the structure of social and economic relationships made it imperative for the fishermen to support the cooperative in order to create for themselves an alternative source of credit. This was accomplished by charging the members of the cooperative a sales tax or "cess" on individual auction sales which developed into a substantial bank account after a few years.

In making the auction system work, and in maintaining the credit fund, it was obviously essential that fishermen support the KFA by selling exclusively through the cooperative's market. As one of the rules of the cooperative provided for expulsion of a member if he sold outside of the market, the threat of being cut off from the KFA's credit fund was one sanction which could be used with good effect to enforce conformity to the cooperative's rules. However, other appeals were invoked to enlist broad support of the cooperative by the village's fishermen. This was done by bringing the ideology of brotherhood and unity into play and identifying the general interests of the community with those of the KFA.

These appeals apparently fell on very receptive ears, as most of the fishermen in Kigombe subsequently became members. Not only were they receptive to sustaining the higher wholesale prices brought about by the market reforms, but their own desires for modern technology provided further incentive for joining the KFA. Nylon nets were already recognized as valuable pieces of modern technology several years before the cooperative's formation, and indeed, some of the KFA's own leaders were prosperous because of these nets. Due to the desire to acquire this modern but expensive gear, participation in the KFA by the village's fishermen was secured by extending credit to members. This need for credit was made all the more acute when sisal prices fell one year after the KFA was founded, depressing the regional economy and forcing many people in the region back into the rural labor force and into such occupations as fishing.

In a sense, the rules of conduct implicit in the ideology of brotherhood and unity that individual entrepreneurs were constrained to fulfill were those that the leaders of the KFA were trying to enforce on the membership. Inasmuch as the fish salesmen could not be constrained by community norms and values and the fishermen could, the reversal of the patron-client relationship between fish salesmen and fishermen and the appeal to the fishermen to remain united as brothers represented an attempt to bring the commercial transactions of the marketplace within the moral framework of the community. Thus, the KFA, by keeping a monopoly on the wholesale marketplace and by maintaining discipline among its members, became a patron able to circulate its own values in the marketplace by regulating the nature and rules of its transactions (see Paine, 1971: 15). As a practical matter, the KFA membership also took the precaution of choosing an auction master from the ranks of the fishermen and paid him an adequate salary. This assured that the moral and economic interests of the fishermen and their cooperative would be represented in the auction process. Furthermore, as a safeguard against the potential corruption of the auctioneer, the members were careful to choose one who was born in the village and thus a citizen of Kigombe in the fullest sense, and who was related as well as obligated by close kin ties to many of the KFA's members.

The members and elected leaders of the KFA metaphorically equate the interests and goals of the cooperative with those of the community. Moreover, practical attempts to implement some common goals through the use of the cooperative's resources for village development projects have been the subject of debate among the membership. At the time, however, none of these projects had been implemented. One plan, for example, called for the purchase of a milling machine to aid the women in grinding corn and rice. Another called for purchasing a vehicle to insure transportation to the city of Tanga market, in the eventuality that the cooperative might become involved in marketing its own produce. The vehicle also would be intended for use as a source of transportation for the village's inhabitants for attending intervillage religious festivals. Still another plan called for the purchase of a tractor for the plowing of larger areas of land for cultivation, especially for rice, the most laborious crop raised in Kigombe. All of these plans, based on the model of investment strategies used by individual entrepreneurs, were conceived in the interests of the community's general welfare, but also with the goal in mind of making profits for the cooperative. In other words, in this context it would seem that they conceived of the KFA as an entrepreneurial group using investment strategies parallel with those used by individual free-holder entrepreneurs. On these matters the KFA's rhetoric also parallels those of individual free-holder entrepreneurs toward the community. Members of the cooperative often refer to their relationship to each other as they would to their metaphorical relationship with other members of the community by saying that "We are one brotherhood" (*Sisi ni udugu moja tu*).

KIGOMBE AS AN "UJAMAA FISHING VILLAGE"

While Kigombe free-holder entrepreneurs and the KFA were successful in bringing about technological and organizational change in the village, the modern technology needed to transform the existing local organization of fisheries production clearly exceeded the individual and collective assets of the community. In forming the KFA, however, the fishermen were operating under no illusions about the high costs that would be involved in further modernizing the local fishing fleet. Nylon gill nets, the most modern fishing gear in use at the time of the cooperative's formation, were relatively expensive by local standards. Moreover, the fishermen already knew from previous experience that, relative to local methods of agricultural production, fixed capital costs in fisheries production generally were much higher, and that these costs would probably become still higher with inputs of more and newer technology. Therefore, as the fishermen were aware of the expense involved in fisheries modernization, a powerful collective incentive among fishermen in the formation of the cooperative derived from the hope that capital could be obtained from outside the community by the KFA qualifying for government development funds. [14]

Eventually, in 1970, the Kigombe fishermen's commitment to their cooperative was rewarded when the KFA, one of the most successful of Tanzania's fishing cooperatives, was largely responsible for Kigombe Village being chosen as one of the government's first *Ujamaa* [15] Fishing Villages. As an Ujamaa Fishing Village, Kigombe has received substantial inputs of new technology in the form of several mechanized fishing vessels, and probably will continue to receive new forms of technology as the government's development project unfolds. [16] In the short time the project has been in operation, fishing productivity and profits have increased dramatically. Implementation of the Ujamaa Fishing Village Program will undoubtedly bring about changes in the community, as it apparently already has in the structure and organization of the KFA itself. [17]

CONCLUSIONS

In the future, as in the past, modernization in Kigombe will not take place in a vacuum; rather, the process will include a larger whole, involving the local community and its inhabitants in the national political structure and economy. As Tanzania's national development programs begin to have an effect, many of the economic and social constraints that formerly kept most of the working males in villages like Kigombe in the rural sector of the economy as primary producers will either disappear or diminish in importance as holding factors. Regardless of the local success of programs like the Ujamaa Fishing Village, the degree to which Kigombe's young men will remain in the rural sector of the economy as fishermen and/or farmers no doubt will be determined in the future mainly by the opportunities that are available to them in the wider economy.

Historically, the reticence of Kigombe's inhabitants to move into other sectors of the economy has not been one based on strict adherence to a conservative set of religious beliefs and values. As we have tried to show, the community's system of values and beliefs, especially as reflected by the ideology of brotherhood and unity and its appeal to traditional authority, was used as one of several local resources by free-holder entrepreneurs and entrepreneurial groups to bring about innovation in the local economy. Indeed, we suspect that as a reflection of the community's system of values and beliefs, tradition within Kigombe has always referred to the present rather than to the past. In this sense it provides a moral framework within which the processes of social change are ideologically rationalized and transactionally regulated by the community's members.[18] Thus, within this meaning of tradition, we have argued that the social and economic responses of the inhabitants of Kigombe to the external regional economy have probably never been based on a backward-looking ideology. Instead ideology has been used, and indeed probably has been molded, to fit with contemporary political, economic, and social situations and to legitimate community and individual responses to changing conditions.

The extent to which the ideology of brotherhood and unity will remain effective in regulating entrepreneurial activities and legitimating a free-holder style of entrepreneurship in Kigombe as the economy develops remains to be seen. However, as the indigeneous ideology parallels the political ideology of the Tanzanian Government on many essential points, we suspect that Kigombe's Islamic-based tradition with its emphasis on village unity and brotherhood will remain a powerful force for legitimating change. It is probably no coincidence that shortly after Kigombe became an Ujamaa Fishing Village, the inhabitants of the community began building a new and much larger community mosque by the main road. There it will stand for all passersby to see as a symbol of Kigombe's piety and prosperity.

NOTES

[1]Our research in Tanzania, conducted in 1968 and 1969, was supported by a joint grant from the Foreign Area Pre-Doctoral Fellowship Program. While in Tanzania we carried out fieldwork as Research Associates of the Department of Sociology, University College, Dar es Salaam. In addition to our own field data included in this paper we have used some unpublished material on the Kigombe Sisal Estate, and for these data we are indebted to Dr. Adolfo C. Mascarenhas, Department of Geography, University of Dar es Salaam, and Mr. A. Brunner, Manager, Kigombe Sisal Estate, Amboni Estates, Ltd. We also would like to thank the many government civil servants and TANU party officials who were so helpful to us throughout our fieldwork. For an introduction to Tanzanian fisheries development problems, and for continuing assistance while in the field, we owe special thanks to Mr. John J. Kambona, Director of Fisheries; to Mr. John Wood, Regional Fisheries Officer; and to the fisheries staff in Tanga Region. At the local level our research was made possible by the enthusiastic support of the officers and general membership of the Kigombe Fisherman's Association and by the close cooperation of other residents of Kigombe. To all of our friends in Kigombe we owe a very special debt of gratitude.

Finally, we would like to thank T. O. Beidelman for reading the final draft of this manuscript. Any errors of fact or interpretation that might appear in this paper, however, are our own responsibility.

[2]For the definition of a dual economy, see Boeke (1942), and for further comments, see Furnivall (1944) and Dalton (1971:267-303).

[3]For a fuller anthropological discussion of entrepreneurship see Barth (1963) and Belshaw (1965).

[4]For different definitions, social and political, of the label *Swahili*, see Wijeyewardene (1959), Bienen (1970:45-46), and Eastman (1971).

[5]The general relationship between ideology, mobility, and authority, as well as variations in their relationship in different Swahili communities, are discussed for the same general cultural area by Middleton (1961).

[6]In our survey of Kigombe men over 20 years of age, who up to the time of interview had spent the greater part of their lives farming and following various occupations in the village, only 6 percent (4 out of 71) owned more than 100 coconut palms each. Moreover, none of the four men was under 40 years of age. This pattern is common elsewhere on the coast of the Tanga Region. North of the city of Tanga, a government scheme to improve the cultivation of coconuts attracted mainly smallholders having large numbers of mature coconut palms. The average age of the 1,452 participants was 43 years of age, and the number of older members in the scheme was quite large. Approximately 58 percent of the total membership came within the age

group of 30-50 years and another 25 percent of the membership was over 50 years of age (Groeneveld, 1968:237).

[7]We say "nearly" because there were two persons employed on the Kigombe Sisal Estate who were living in Kigombe Village but who were not interviewed in the survey. However, we were able to determine that the jobs they held on the estate were not unskilled field labor. While not all persons living in the village were interviewed in our social survey, we did account for all persons in the village's households, and including the two sisal estate workers not interviewed, we are certain that the number of Kigombe *wenyeji* currently working on the Kigombe Sisal Estate does not exceed ten individuals.

[8]Data on the total number of persons employed on the Kigombe Sisal Estate were obtained through the courtesy of Dr. Adolfo C. Mascarenhas, Department of Geography, University of Dar es Salaam, Tanzania. During our fieldwork we also received a very helpful introduction to the organization of Kigombe Sisal Estate from its Manager, Mr. A. Brunner.

[9]The pattern of rural-urban intercommunication on the coast that we describe is very similar to that reported for the Dar es Salaam area, south of Tanga Region, both for the colonial period (Leslie, 1963) and the contemporary situation (Swantz, (1968).

[10]The economic difficulties that Africans in East African cities faced during the colonial period is made vividly clear for the city of Dar es Salaam by Leslie (1963). Leslie's survey, which was concerned with investigating urban overcrowding and a severe housing shortage in Dar es Salaam that developed in the colonial post-World War II years, also underscores the importance of residential real estate as investments for Africans living in urban areas.

[11]A similar point is made by Bruner (1970) in discussing the role of kinship in an urban setting in Indonesia.

[12]Generally, this reflects the efforts of Swahili born in Kigombe to keep disputes among themselves within the moral boundaries of the community. Very rarely do cases involving disputes between Swahili *wenyeji* go as far as court action. The one dispute between Swahili *wenyeji* that did end up in the local primary court while we were there, for example, was considered scandalous by most people in the village because it had caused such rancor and could not be settled by traditional means.

[13]Given the domination of sisal growing by corporations before Independence, the Tanzanian Government's encouragement of smallholders to grow sisal is a double irony in that sisal prices dropped very drastically shortly thereafter. In Kigombe Village there were six smallholders involved in sisal growing; however, with the drop in prices, they soon quit cutting sisal and maintaining their fields, turning their energies instead to more profitable enterprises in which they previously were engaged.

[14]In other words, the fishermen themselves felt the need for a "transformational" approach to fisheries development that called for major inputs of government capital. For a general discussion of the limitations imposed on indigenous modernizatiorn efforts, or grass roots efforts "from below," without major outside sources of capital, see Geertz (1963:156-157; 1967).

[15]Ujamaa fishing villages are part of the Tanzanian Government's implementation of the Arusha Declaration, proclaimed in 1967. The Arusha Declaration called for an emphasis on rural development and the building of Ujamaa, or socialist-cooperative villages. After the Arusha Declaration, the concept of Ujamaa villages was developed further by Tanzania's President, Julius K. Nyerere, in his essay, *Ujamaa Vijijini* (*Socialism and Rural Development*). In that essay he called for the development of "economic and social communities where people live together and work together for the good of all" (Nyerere, 1968:348).

As part of the emphasis on *Ujamaa Vijijini*, a number of new Ujamaa villages have been started through government sponsored pilot programs. However, as part of the government's program for mobilizing broader support for Ujamaa villages (see Bienen, 1970:421-424), long established villages such as Kigombe have also been designated as Ujamaa villages for the development of local cooperative projects.

[16]The Tanzanian government's Agricultural Credit Agency (Nairne, 1965; Makame, 1965), with which the Kigombe Fishermen's Association is registered, extends loans to cooperatives for fisheries development. However, Kigombe's Ujamaa Fishing Village derives from the fisheries development scheme for Village Fishing Units outlined in Tanzania's Second Five Year Plan (United Republic of Tanzania, 1969:48).

[17]We are indebted to Mr. D. M. Masasi, Fisheries Officer, formerly assigned to the Kigombe Fisheries Project, for information on the changes brought about in Kigombe by the Ujamaa Fishing Village Program.

[18]For examples of the complex interplay between religious symbols and the processes of modernization in other Islamic societies, see Clifford Geertz, *Islam Observed* (1968), especially pp. 21, 59, and 69.

9

There have been a number of "common sense" generalizations in the social sciences about the effects of urbanization on rural peoples. These generalizations include such formulations as the Gemeinschaft-Gesellschaft of Ferdinand Tönnies and the folk-urban continuum of Robert Redfield. However, careful empirical studies of urbanization and common sense generalizations do not often coincide. In their study of urbanization in East Africa, Robbins and Thompson have come to the conclusion that modernizing peoples' willingness to forego immediate gratification and "save for a rainy day" does not depend directly on their exposure to city life, as our Western experience and our Protestant Ethic might lead us to believe.

Gratification Orientations and Individual Modernization in Buganda[1]

MICHAEL C. ROBBINS AND RICHARD W. THOMPSON

Michael C. Robbins is Associate Professor of Anthropology at the University of Missouri, Columbia, and holds a Ph.D. from the University of Minnesota.

A specialist in psychological anthropology, he has carried out extensive field research in East Africa, and has been a frequent contributor to anthropological publications. Richard W. Thompson received his Ph.D. from the University of Missouri and has done fieldwork in Mexico and in East Africa. His research interests focus on the psychological aspects of the urbanization and modernization processes. Professor Thompson is currently teaching anthropology at Lawrence University.

A growing number of studies of the modernization process in developing countries have been concerned with the causes and consequences of individual change. Most studies of "psychological modernization," "individual modernization," "psychological acculturation," "value change," etc., have produced a large amount of information which suggests that so-called "modern man" is somehow different from "traditional man" with respect to certain constellations of cognitive and personality attributes and behavioral dispositions. After an extensive review of several studies of individual modernization, Triandis (1972) has recently summarized these psychological constellations in the following terms:

> Modern man is apparently open to new experiences, relatively independent of parental authority, and concerned with time and planning and willing to defer gratification; he feels that man can be the master over nature and that he controls the reinforcements he receives from his environment; he believes in determinism and science, has a wide cosmopolitan perspective, and uses broad ingroups; he competes with standards of excellence and is optimistic about controlling his environment. Traditional man has narrow ingroups, looks at the world with suspicion, believes that good is limited, and that one obtains a share of it by chance or by pleasing the gods; he identifies with his parents and receives directions from them; he considers planning a waste of time and does not defer gratification; he feels at the mercy of obscure environmental forces and is prone to mysticism; he sees interpersonal relations as an end, rarely as a means to an end, and does not believe that he can control his environment but rather sees himself under the influence of external, mystical powers (1972:352-53).

While a large measure of effort has been devoted to describing and contrasting modern and traditional man in terms of these and other psychological and behavioral characteristics, considerable attention has also focused on the various influences which presumably *make men modern*—that is, contribute to the expression of these personality, cognitive, and behavioral profiles. Several studies have produced rather impressive arrays of correlations between various indicators of these outlooks, attitudes and dispositions and certain hypothetical determinants—schooling, urban residence experience, industrial work, military service, exposure to mass communications media (often associated with literacy) and a wide scale of extralocal social contacts acquired through travel and migration.[2]

One of the most salient "contrast-features" normally employed to differentiate modern man from traditional man is the apparently greater willingness and ability of the former to delay gratifications (or postpone immediate satisfactions and desires in order to obtain more substantial future rewards). The disposition to delay gratification has also been assumed to be linked to and be a logical function of modern man's greater feelings of efficacy, personal control, levels of aspiration and achievement motivation, and extended future time perspective (Graves, 1966:296-297; Graves, 1967:339; Rogers, 1969:35-6).

The tendency to delay gratification has not only been conceptualized as a core feature of the psychological constellation of modern man but has also been recognized as occupying a dominant position in the value system of Western society (cf. Dundes, 1969) and is ostensible in several activities as indicated by Graves:

> Many of our most valued activities (planning ahead, hard work, saving, education, pre-marital chastity and post-marital fidelity, sobriety, concern with child-rearing, etc.) have their major reward not at the moment they are engaged in, but at some future time (1966:296).

Furthermore, an individual's willingness and ability to delay gratification is considered to be highly adaptive for a successful adjustment to urban-industrial society and a functional desideratum of modern urban-industrial society itself:

> In terms of adequate urban-industrial adjustment, an important personality trait . . . is the tendency to delay gratification. . . . Such valued behavior is highly adaptive for successful functioning in an urban-

industrial society. Not only is immediate gratification behavior likely to be considered 'deviant' and therefore subject to social censure, but the very foundations of industrial society rest on delayed behavior (Graves, 1966:296-97).

In sharp contrast, the great bulk of research suggests that traditional, rural man is typified by an immediate rather than a deferred gratification style. Everett Rogers, for example, in a comprehensive description of a hypothesized "subculture of peasantry," (which draws heavily on central elements often used to depict cultures of poverty), emphasizes that immediate gratification is a major component of peasant "subculture" and is functionally interrelated with a syndrome which includes low aspirations, fatalism, and low achievement motivation. He asserts that,

> For whatever reason, deferred gratification is not characteristic of peasants. In Aesop's terms, subsistence farmers behave more like the grasshopper than the ant. This lack of deferred gratification tends to perpetuate their position as hungry grasshoppers rather than as well-provisioned ants (1969:35).

Several studies have contributed to the image of traditional-rural peasants as "impulses-gratifiers." One common observation is that traditional-rural peasants usually opt for spending rather than saving or investing their resources. Foster, for example, in speaking of Mexican peasants in Tzintzuntzan observes, "When people have money they spend it; when they have nothing they hope to borrow" (1967:115). Hendry notes that in a Vietnamese village he studied, "thrift is not particularly valued as a virtue among these people, and fewer of them make conscious efforts to save for particular goals" (1964:182). Freilich, in contrasting the cultural practices of East Indian and Negro peasants in Trinidad, observes that Negroes spend more money on food, clothing and "fetes" (a situation consisting of people, talk, rum, music, dance, and sexual play) and less on housing, education, and religious matters:

> In short, Indians spent more money on capital items which would affect their future (housing, education, religion), while Negroes spent more money on non-capital items which were fairly quickly consumed

and which related to a present rather than a future time orientation (Freilich, 1963:31).

Several investigators of rural peasant communities have remarked on the large portion of resources that is dissipated on weddings, festivals, funerals, and religious ceremonies. In a survey of the values of several Southern Italian villagers (n=545), Langworthy reports that, "62.7 percent of the Abruzzesi believe that one should spend a lot of money for weddings, feasts, and first communions" (1968:215-16). Fals-Borda (1955), in his study of peasants in the Colombian Andes, records that twenty percent of his respondents' expenditures went for drinks and tobacco, rising to forty percent during fiestas, with forty percent left for food, twenty percent for clothing and ten percent for farm inputs. And Sol Tax reports that for the Guatemalan peasant:

> The alcoholic intoxicant's budget is far greater than the housing budget and the amount of money spent on liquor is about a fourth of that spent on clothing. It is more than that for any item of food excepting corn and meat, and it is almost as much as is spent on all tools and household utensils and supplies (1963:177).

Ausubel, in a comparison of the personality traits and values of Maori and Europeans in New Zealand, notes that:

> Maori culture places less emphasis than Pakeha (European) culture on personality traits important for implementing achievement goals. . . .
> The Maori is less willing than the Pakeha to practice initiative, foresight, self-denial and self-discipline, to persevere in the face of adversity or to defer immediate, hedonistic gratification. in favor of remote vocational goals (1965:69).

Ausubel also mentions that rural Maori display these traits to a greater extent than urban acculturated Maori.

A few studies suggest that the immediate gratification pattern is evident in other areas. Banfield (1958:98) notes that Italian peasants will not use the ballot for their long run interests in their voting behavior if it interferes with obtaining short run material advantages, and Phillips, in his study of the

Thai village Bang Chan, observes that peasants are rarely concerned with much more than the short run advantages of interpersonal relationships:

> They readily permit personal impulse, diversion and unforeseen circumstance to take precedence over commitments they may have undertaken in the face-to-face encounter. They often pay little attention to the rights, obligations and responsibilities which are supposed to form the substance of enduring relationships (1967:347).

Numerous scholars have recognized that peoples' gratification orientations are intimately related to modernization and economic development, and there has been a corresponding concern with those factors which perpetuate and change them. Development programs, for example, often depend on both the ability and willingness of people to postpone immediate pleasures in order to seek more substantial future rewards, to spend long years being educated before the fruits of education are realized, to save and invest capital rather than spend it to satisfy immediate desires, and to accept innovations, such as soil conservation technology and family planning, which offer no immediate empirical proof of their effectiveness or future value and require the renunciation of immediate needs and wants. Peshkin and Cohen clearly articulate deferred gratification to both a future orientation and modern economic values and development:

> We suggest that plans for the future which include saving or any other means that delay a person's immediate gain so that an investment will increase in value, involve a modernizing economic value. Examples of this value are the farmer's 'saving his soil' through crop rotation or banking the proceeds from his cash crops. Future orientation does not grow readily when the demands of the present are so insistent that they absorb all available labor and capital, but to some extent, economic modernization is dependent upon increased future orientation on the part of ordinary individuals and groups (1967:12).

Similar observations have been made concerning the relationship of deferred gratification to upward social mobility (Rogers, 1969:35-36), business successes and failures (Isaac, 1971:294), the ability to complete educational and vocational training programs (Peil, 1970:148), the adoption of agricultural innovations (Rogers, 1969:377), and higher levels of economic output, capital accumulation, levels of living and material welfare (Mellor, 1969; Firth and Yamey, 1963).

A number of studies suggest that immediate gratification orientations are both a reaction and adaptation to the exigencies of poverty and constricted socioeconomic opportunities, and are a by-product of persistent cultural traditions which emphasize and rationalize the past or present rather than the future. Concomitantly, it has been suggested that as traditional-rural populations begin to acquire more wealth and access to expanding economic opportunities (e.g., urban-industrial employment, wage-earning incomes, and commercial farming) and exposure to value systems and cultural traditions which emphasize postponement and the future (e.g., through education, exposure to mass communications media), their gratification dispositions will become more deferred. Rogers observes in noting Chu's findings that Taiwanese banana growers exhibited little deferred gratification until they attained a minimum living standard, that:

> The deferred-gratification pattern may well be a way of life that only those with more-than-adequate resources can afford to follow. If deferring means going hungry now, one can hardly expect peasants to put much aside for the future (1969:35).

We are, of course, reminded of Foster's (1965, 1967) observations of the static economies, limited socioeconomic mobility systems, and forced redistributive mechanisms which characterize closed peasant communities. According to Foster, these conditions work against economic progress and capital accumulation and produce low achievement and aspiration levels and an "Image of a Limited Good."

> Capital accumulation, which might be stimulated if costly ritual could be simplified, is just what the villager wants to prevent, since he sees it as a community threat rather than a precondition to economic development. . . . The Anglo-Saxon virtues of hard work and thrift seen as leading to economic success are meaningless in peasant society. Horatio Alger not only is not praiseworthy, but he emerges as a positive fool, a clod who not knowing the score labors blindly against hopeless conditions (Foster, 1965:307-08).

Foster further suggests that progressive economic values can best be promoted through changing the economic rules of the game and expanding economic opportunities. "Local entrepreneurs arise in response to the increasing opportunities of expanding national economies, and emulative urges, with the city as the model, appear among these people [sic]" (1965:310). Foster therefore assigns a clear priority to expanding the social and economic universe of traditional-rural peasants in order to foster both economic values and growth. This perspective can be contrasted with that of other scholars (e.g., McClelland, 1961; Banfield, 1958; Freilich, 1963) who perceive peasant inprovidence more as a consequence of lack of initiative, low achievement motivation, and economic irrationality reinforced and perpetuated by persistent conservative value systems which do not encourage or rationalize planning for and striving toward more substantial future rewards.

Recently, Turner (1971) has found positive relationships between economic development and futuristic value orientations. In an investigation of four economically diverse communities in the southern United States (which were assumed to represent distinct stages in the process of economic development), he found, with regard to future time orientation, that individuals in modern bureaucratic and industrial communities have significantly more futuristic responses than individuals in subsistence and traditional farming communities. Turner feels that it is only during the latter stages of economic development that a future orientation becomes necessary: ". . . since incomes in modern systems are considerably above that necessary for subsistence, actors can be oriented beyond the immediate present. In less modern economic systems, structural conditions are not conducive to a value of futurism" (1971:135).

In a similar vein, Rosen (1971) has shown from a study of five communities in Brazil chosen to represent points along a rural-urban-industrial continuum that industrialization, with its diversity of occupations and openness of opportunity structure, is positively related to both social mobility and an achievement syndrome containing several value components reflecting deferred gratification and future orientation. Rosen's research suggests that both the nature of the socioeconomic system *and* an individual's achievement motives must be considered together and that the effects of both are additive.

Several other studies have been concerned with either the conjoint or separate effects on gratification orientations of exposure and access to greater wealth, socioeconomic opportunity, and modern (often Western) value systems which stress postponement, renunciation and future concerns. From his research in Jamaica and three African societies, Doob has offered a modicum of evidence in support of his hypothesis that, "People changing centrally from old to new ways are likely to become more tolerant of delay in the attainment of goals" (1960:88). He observes that,

> More of the highly than of the poorly educated Africans and Jamaicans feel favorably disposed towards planning for the future. . . . They prefer money for investment or prefer a large sum in the future instead of a smaller one immediately. . . . Fewer of the better-educated Jamaicans think of money as something to spend or find it impossible to anticipate events in their country. In comparison with less well-educated adults, fewer of the Luo and Ganda youth in European schools disapprove of planning . . . and in one Ganda school taught by Africans, disapproval of planning runs significantly higher, particularly in the lower grades (1960:89).

Dolores Gold, in research concerned with the psychological acculturation of Indians in Saskatchewan, Canada, found that:

> The urban, acculturated Indians were more similar to the White subjects in showing a predominantly deferred gratification pattern than to the reserve, unacculturated Indian subjects who followed a predominantly immediate gratification pattern. . . . Doob's hypothesis regarding the acceptance of a deferred gratification pattern in complex societies and the acceptance of a more immediate gratification pattern in simple societies is upheld by these results (1967:182-83).

Gold also suggests that the better socioeconomic conditions found among her urban Indian samples were also related to their more deferred gratification tendencies.

In a study of Ugandan school children, Wober and Musoke-Mutanda (1971) found that children from higher socioeconomically placed families attending boarding schools display greater patience in waiting for more substantial future rewards than children from lower class families and day schools. They found this difference to be most pronounced among boys. One of their interpretations of this finding is that sons in upper-class families are brought up in a neo-colonial Victorian model of ideal manhood which emphasizes delayed gratification. Moreover, boarders may learn to delay the expectation of their rewards because of the closed and highly regimented society they live in, which stresses an accurate awareness of time. Furthermore, boarding schools normally have greater numbers of expatriate teachers who have contributed to a climate of opinion which values preference for delayed gratifications and patience over outcomes. Indeed, there is some empirical evidence from social learning experiments that suggests that gratification orientations can be modified through exposure to and imitation of "live" and "symbolic" models. Bandura and Mischel (1965), for instance, were able to alter the delay of self-reward in fourth and fifth grade children by exposure to adult models who displayed the opposite delay orientations.

Finally, in a study of psychological acculturation in a tri-ethnic community, Graves (1967) found that American Indians and Mexican-Americans displayed less future time perspective than a comparable sample of Anglos. He suggests that as these populations experience greater exposure and access to, and identification with, the dominant White middle-class culture through education, acculturation and occupational opportunities, they tend to display more future time perspective, which Graves has also related to "the deferred gratification pattern of behavior distinguishing the Anglo group" (1967:339).

CRITICISMS AND NEW DIRECTIONS

Although many of these observations of the gratification tendencies of traditional-rural and modern-urban populations and the factors which presumably contribute to both their persistence and change have received some empirical support, the evidence is by no means unequivocal, and a growing measure of criticism has been accumulating (cf. Harris, 1971; Castillo, 1969). Among the numerous problems plaguing much of this research, three conceptual inadequacies stand out: (1) The frequent use of hidden reference standards and invidious comparisons; (2) The inconsistent, inadequate, and often biased manner in which the criterion "gratification orientations" has been measured; and (3) The inattention to important intervening variables and equally plausible alternative interpretations.

In many of these studies, reference is often made to the peasants' improvident use of his resources for alcohol, tobacco, festivities, and ceremonies and his devaluation of thrift and foresight. Yet a comparison group is often not specified. When comparisons are offered, they are usually invidious. For example, the observed behavior and expenditures of certain populations (e.g., for luxuries, leisure-time activities, etc.) are often compared with the ideal standards and values of postponement among other populations (in particular, the Western middle-classes). It would seem far more equitable to compare the real behaviors and actual expenditure patterns of both groups. For example, the American "fly-now-pay-later" consumption style, the use of credit cards, and the laxity of premarital sex behavior among American teenagers suggest that much of the actual behavior of the white middle-classes may, in fact, be quite similar to that reported for peasants (cf. Castillo, 1969).

A second related problem concerns the many deficiencies in the way gratification orientations have been measured. In many studies reference is made to the actual behavior of populations with regard to their expenditure patterns, possessions, and activities. In other studies, ideal values are assessed through attitude surveys, responses to hypothetical situations (e.g., "What would you do if you had a hundred dollars?") and hypothetical choice-tasks where a respondent is asked to decide whether he would rather have an item of a smaller amount now or a similar item in a larger quantity later. What is often neglected in many of these hypothetical choice situations or aspiration-listing tasks is a person's present possessions and his values regarding the choices. For example, an individual may be asked, "would you rather have a bicycle now (supposedly an indication of immediate gratification) or an automobile next year (supposedly an indication of deferred gratification)?" Yet his present possession of an automobile might influence his choice; why not opt for a bicycle now if you already have a car? In addition, choices may reflect the overall desirability of the items rather than dispositions to wait to acquire them. Some choice-items, for example, may be sex-specific and proscribed or devalued by the opposite sex, yet these choices ("new shirt now or suit of clothes in a year", or "tennis shoes now or leather shoes in a year") are used to indicate the gratification orientations of both. Furthermore, as in the above examples, the choices may be between qualitatively different things rather than between the same things in different quantities at different times. Many of these difficulties could be surmounted and the criticisms avoided if more contextual qualitative data were available, so that the "definition of the situation" could be more clearly assessed. Spiro (1966), in his study of Buddhism and economic action in Burma, shows how certain attitudes and behaviors which appear on the surface to be improvident, irrational, and reflective of immediate gratification tendencies turn out on closer analysis and from the perspective of the actors themselves to be economically rational future-oriented behaviors. He describes, for example, how lavish spending on religious feasts and displays, monks, monasteries, and pagodas is instigated by a desire for the acquisition of merit and reward in the *remote future* of rebirth. Immediate consumption is economically rational in a situation where the accumulation of private wealth is subject to the threat of government confiscation, where political security is at a premium, and where low interest rates and rising inflation do not produce more substantial future rewards. As Spiro points out:

. . . if he hoards or saves, the Burman does not merely *defer* whichever gratifications his small income allows him to enjoy in the present for questionable albeit greater gratifications in the future; given the meagerness of the returns and the great risks they entail, he will most likely also *forfeit* all gratifications, future as well as present" (1966:1166).

A third problem centers on the failure to consider other variables that may intervene between factors presumed to promote a disposition to defer gratification (e.g., wealth, economic opportunities, exposure to modern value systems) and which may attenuate their effects. It is often argued, for example, that one of the necessary conditions for promoting deferred gratification and capital accumulation is exposure and access to expanding economic opportunites normally associated with urban-industrial employment, commercialization, and wage earning incomes. It could be argued just as plausibly that subsisting in urban-industrial commercial areas with their corresponding periods of unemployment and inflation provides less security and economic predictability, higher risks, and consequently more uncertainty, present time orientation, and a tendency not to delay gratification due to lower perceived probabilities of obtaining future rewards. William Rodgers (1967) compared the gratification orientations of individuals from three communities in the out-island Bahamas representing points along a continuum of relative exposure to economic development. He found that individuals in the most exposed community who were most dependent on wage earning incomes displayed more immediate gratification than those individuals practicing subsistence farming and fishing in unexposed communities. He interpreted this as a response to an unpredictable economic environment controlled by outside capital.

In addition, there is some support for the assumption that exposure to modern value systems and the rewards of a modern way of life may undermine saving, capital accumulation, and a disposition to delay gratification by stimulating consumption. That is, knowledge of new goods and services, enhanced by advertising media and urban residence, may create rising frustrations and temptations. In a study of the consumption patterns of newly urbanized Africans in Zaire, Baeck (1961) describes how the confrontation with the tremendous range of goods and services which modern society offers and the fact that the consumption patterns of Europeans have tended to capture the imagination of many Africans are major determinants of their conspicuous consumption. Wallman (1972) has also shown that Basuto migrants to the industrial cities of South Africa rapidly acquire a taste for urban goods to conform to the value of being *smarti* (corruption of "smart"). Although many goods of the city are more satisfying, they are also more prestigious, and upon return "A considerable part of the most meager household budget is spent on this value" (Wallman, 1972:256). Mellor (1969), Firth and Yamey (1963), Barber (1967), and McLoughlin (1970) have all alluded to a "frustration-gap" which may result from exposure to desirable new lifestyles without a corresponding means of obtaining them. Mellor (1969) describes the dilemma of enhancing the salience of attractive commodities this way:

> A strong drive toward improved material well-being might in itself discourage saving and investment as the farmer makes an effort to maximize his current level of consumption. On the other hand, more attractive consumer goods may encourage the farmer to reduce consumption now, so that a greater increase can occur later. With more attractive consumer goods, he may aspire to reach a higher income level and be willing to wait to achieve it through investment . . . Given two farmers with the same values and introducing more attractive consumption goods to them, one might increase consumption and decrease saving while the other acts conversely" (1969:215).

In a general critique of several studies of gratification orientation, Marvin Harris has also observed that

"The general propensity to consume is constantly heightened by the immense persuasive resources of mass media advertising" (1971: 496).

In a previous study in rural Buganda, Pollnac and Robbins (1972) found a nonlinear relationship between futuristic consumption aspirations and a variety of measures of modernization. They suggest that as modernization increases, deferred gratification also increases but eventually levels off and decreases. They concluded that after a person reaches a certain level of economic success (often going along with modernization) he will no longer have reason to defer. He has achieved the level he has been deferring for and can now enjoy life with a more immediate style of gratification. They also recognize that it is often the more modernized individuals who experience greater exposure to more consumer items. Mischel and Ebbesen (1970) and Mischel, Ebbesen, and Zeiss (1972) have demonstrated in several social-psychological experiments with children designed to measure gratification dispositions that when the rewards are present and individuals are attending to these rewards, it is more difficult to wait to obtain them. That is, the salience of the rewards for which people must wait creates conditions of frustrative "non-reward" and reduces dispositions to defer.

Therefore, in sum, it could be alternatively proposed that greater exposure and access to and a heightened awareness of modern urban lifestyles and standards may induce considerable frustrative "non-reward" and coupled with feelings of socioeconomic insecurity, may promote less rather than more of a tendency to delay gratification.

POPULATION AND SCOPE OF PRESENT RESEARCH

Our research was undertaken in an effort to resolve some of the ambiguities surrounding the sociocultural determinants of gratification orientations and to rectify some of the conceptual problems noted in previous research. More specifically, the objectives were (1) to develop a series of appropriate multiple-measures of gratification dispositions in order to provide the convergent validity necessary to measure gratification orientations cross-culturally; and (2) to determine how certain socioenvironmental and psychocultural aspects of the modernization process relate to the nature and magnitude of differences in gratification orientations.

●*Population*

Our Study was conducted among the Baganda, the most numerous and socioeconomically diverse population in Uganda. They are the predominant inhabitants of the rural and urban areas surrounding the northern and western shores of Lake Victoria. Numbering over one million persons, they comprise about one fifth of Uganda's population. Formerly, Buganda was the largest, most centralized, and well organized of the several surrounding Interlacustrine Bantu kingdoms. Since the beginning of contact with the outside, Buganda has displayed considerable military, political, and cultural success in extending its spheres of influence (cf. Beattie, 1971; Kiwanuka, 1971). The temporal and regional dimensions of the development of Buganda's polity, economy, society, and culture have been thoroughly documented through the last 100 years, making it one of the most "ethnographically well known" areas in all of Africa.[3]

Most Baganda are rural peasant cultivators of a wide variety of food staples and cash crops. The most important of these are plantains, sweet potatoes, cassava, coffee, tea, and cotton. The physical environment provides a secure subsistence with relatively low labor output and supports a large, dense, permanently settled population. Crops bear food the year around, and there is little need for storage. Since most subsistence agriculture, and to a lesser extent commercial farming, is mainly in the hands of women and porters (*Abapakasi*) from other areas, men, as in the past, are relatively free to engage in trade and fishing. Today they also pursue wage earning occupations in towns and cities. Formerly, they also used their extra time fulfilling political, military, and social obligations for the king (*Kabaka*) and were expected to spend a large amount of time at his palaces.

There is a strong patricentric focus to Kiganda[4] society, expressed in male authority, patrilineal clans, and rules of inheritance and succession. Polygyny, though formerly the ideal and prerogative of wealthy and successful men, is now uncommon. Marriage has always been unstable and is so today. Education and urban residence and employment have been especially important in providing avenues for women to achieve economic independence and escape the drudgery of rural agricultural work, and there is a growing reluctance among women to subordinate themselves in marriage. The social system has always encouraged spatial and social mobility, and status is based on achievement. Considerable upward and downward social mobility is and has been common, and a dyadic conception of superordination and subordination is a central cultural theme. Prestige, influence, and precedence are positively related to ostensible manifestations of wealth, estates, cattle, consumer goods, women, and retainers (cf. Fallers, 1959, 1964; Perlman, 1970).

Kiganda culture is notably ambiguous with regard to gratification orientations. A similar number of institutions, myths, stories, songs, proverbs, and sayings support and reflect strategies of both immediate and deferred gratification.

Since the beginning of Arab contact in the 1840s and European contact in the 1870s and 1880s, the Baganda have displayed a policy of adventurous modernization, receptivity to innovation, keen acquisitiveness, and the ability to take advantage of new economic opportunities. Their absorption of new technology, education, religion, trade goods, and commercial activities has allowed them to achieve one of the most advantaged positions in East Africa.

It is most interesting, however, that while avidly desiring to secure the advantages of the outside world, they have also tenaciously maintained their political and territorial integrity and endeavored to preserve their own cultural tradition and identity (*obuwangwa*). This policy of dualism has long intrigued scholars, perplexed administrators, frustrated Ugandan nationalists, and irritated other Africans, who often describe the Baganda as ethnocentric, arrogant, and disdainful (cf. Fallers, 1961; Low, 1971a, 1971b). As Richards surmises:

> In fact it would be difficult to find a more striking instance of an ethnic group in an African state so relatively advanced in the political, educational, and economic fields and which could most aptly be described as an advanced enclave. The Baganda were the pivotal tribe in Uganda (1969:46).

Their political policy has always been concerned with enhancing their cultural "destiny," and threats to their polity (and especially kingship) are perceived as a threat to their sociocultural integrity. Therefore, while education and "civilization" are desirable, "foreignization" is repugnant, and their unwillingness to submerge their preeminence has been reflected in their opposition to East African federation and economic competition by Asian traders, and in their extreme reluctance to participate in a non-Baganda dominated Uganda. All of this has culminated in the turbulent political crises of the last twenty years, including the destruction of the Buganda kingdom by former President Milton Obote in 1966 and the exile and eventual death of the last *Kabaka* of Buganda. Until the time of the Second Independence and the 1971 takeover by the current President, General Idi Amin, the Baganda suffered extremely harsh military, political, and economic reprisals. Many were killed or imprisoned and their positions and possessions confiscated. Since then there has been a resurgence of Kiganda culture, a partial revivification of traditional institutions, and a restoration of social and economic order.

In sum, although Buganda has been highly favored economically, administratively, and educationally, its recent history has been quite unsettled, paralleling the troubled course of Uganda itself.

Our research was carried out in three areas of Buganda selected to represent "points" along a rural-intermediate-urban continuum. Each is described below.

●*Rural Area*

The rural area consists of a parish (*muluka*) comprising four villages located forty miles southwest of Kampala (the major urban center) down the Masaka road. The area covers twelve square miles and includes approximately 1,500 persons. The settlement pattern is dispersed and there are no electric, water, medical, or telephone services available in the area. The single unimproved six mile road leading into the community from the Masaka road is maintained by the government.

With the exception of clothing, salt, metal roofing, tools, and cooking utensils (and occasionally beds), practically all necessities can be produced locally. Inexpensive aluminum saucepans and tea kettles have largely replaced traditional pottery cookware, and manufactured plates, cups, and glasses are now in common use. Clothing and shoes are the most expensive items not produced in the village. Very few men other than store owners, teachers, and chiefs wear Western style tailored clothing. Most wear the traditional *kanzu*, a long loosely fitting white gown. Among women the

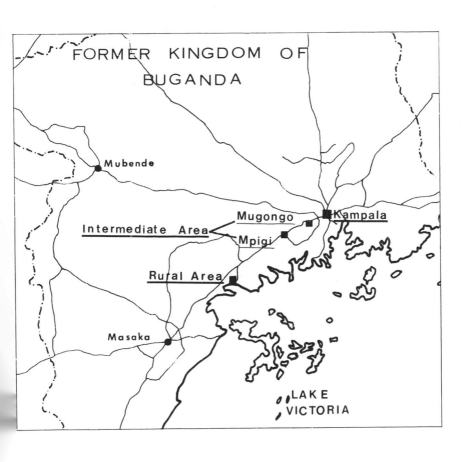

Map 1. Location of Three Major Research Areas in
Uganda

Buganda Woman Farmer at Home in Rural Area
Photo by Michael Robbins and Richard Thompson

Victorian style *busuuti* is the prevailing form of dress, although a few younger women and school teachers wear Western style skirts and blouses when visiting the city.

Most material artifacts associated with fishing are also local products, although nylon gill nets, lines, and metal hooks are purchased in local shops and nearby trade centers. Only one boat in the area is powered by a gasoline engine. One informant indicated that most fishermen would like to own engines but that the slight increase in catch would not pay for the initial and continuing costs.

Agricultural activity in the community is mainly for subsistence but provides some opportunities for earning cash income. Some subsistence crops, like groundnuts, maize, and fruits, are occasionally sold to supplement cash incomes. The bulk of a farmer's cash income comes from marketing coffee and cotton. Fishing is also an important source of income for several men. Fishermen's wages range from 30 to 80 shillings per month (seven shillings equal one U.S. dollar) and informants indicate there are frequent wage disputes between boat owners and hired fishermen. Since fishing is frequently supplemented by other part-time agricultural activities, fishermen are considered to be extremely secure in terms of cash income and subsistence needs. One informant summed this up by saying, "Fishing, they [fishermen] will never give it up, it brings too much money and too many lovely things. Those fishermen can eat well and have money too."

There is a relatively low level of commercialization in the area. Shopkeeping, carpentry, bicycle repairing, tailoring, and teaching are the major activities. Today there are six one-room retail shops in the parish, four of which operate on a part-time basis. Items sold include sugar, rice, flour, tea, soap, salt, razor blades, patent medicines, kerosene, metal cooking utensils and tools. Each shop is owned and operated by a single individual and his family. A partial reason for the low level of commerce in the parish is that the population is self-sufficient and uses little cash for necessities. As one villager put it, "you get everything peacefully and freely in the village."

Public taxi transportation to and from Kampala is available twice daily. The round trip fare is twenty-four shillings. Along with passengers, taxis carry mail, messages, and packages. A significant portion of the rural population makes monthly visits to Kampala and gains first-hand knowledge of urban conditions. The radio is the major source of regional and national information in the parish. Forty-nine percent of our sample survey

Buganda Men Dancing, Drinking, and Entertaining in
Rural Area

Photo by Michael Robbins and Richard Thompson

population (described below) owns a radio and most individuals have at least some access to someone's radio. Other forms of mass media (e.g., magazines, newspapers, and television) are not regularly available.[5] For many children, schooling represents another important source of information about life beyond the parish. A primary school in the area employs teachers from other areas of Buganda, several of whom have lived in Kampala. There is also a Protestant and a Catholic church. Opportunities for recreation and entertainment in the parish are restricted to drinking parties, traditional forms of music, dancing, games (particularly the board game *omweso*), sports (e.g., soccer, wrestling), church attendance, and visiting friends and relatives.

There is little apparent economic differentiation, and significant interpersonal relationships tend to be based on kinship. Villages are composed primarily of patrilineal clansmen and their wives. Each village in the parish tends to be dominated by a single clan and several large areas are referred to as clan land (*butaka*).

The rural parish is perceived as a desirable place by most inhabitants. Of our sample, eighty-four percent indicated they preferred to live in the village rather than a larger town or city. The major advantages of rural life mentioned are the low cost of living and subsistence security. Informants are quick to point out that "everything you get in the city you have to pay for." The village is also preferred because it is "peaceful," in contrast to the city where, "any trouble they come and beat you," and "there are too many thieves," whereas in the village "you can get get what you want peacefully without fighting." Finally, the village is seen as providing strong social supports from kinsmen and friends. "In the village they drink beer and invite their friends, and they are happy together like brothers because the village makes us friends."

Yet several negative perceptions of rural life are apparent. First, cash is a scarce commodity. As one person said, "no one has money in the village, there is nowhere to get it." Second, those with some exposure to urban life complain about the lack of attractive consumer goods and educational facilities. Third, physical hardships are often associated with rural life. One person said, "those in the city don't suffer from digging as we do in the village." Women in particular lament the physical strain of rural life. Finally, informants indicate that life in the parish is dull and there is no entertainment. A man who had been to school in the urban area commented, "there are no entertainments in the village, only this local beer, no beautiful houses, no cinemas or jukeboxes or even any excitements."

●*The Intermediate Area*

The intermediate area consists of two communities which lie seven (population ca. 1,000) and twenty (population ca. 2,500) miles southwest of Kampala along the same road which goes on to and beyond the rural area. One is a trade center and rapidly growing district headquarters. The settlement patterns vary from rural to near-urban conditions. Electricity, telephone, and medical services are available in the area. The population structure is more heterogeneous than in the rural area. In addition to the Baganda majority, there are Asian shop owners and Luo, Bachiga, Banyaruanda, Banyankole, Batoro, and Acholi workers.

Although a variety of subsistence crops are produced, the area is not self-sufficient. A trend toward conspicuous consumption is apparent, and many of the clothing styles, houses, and household furnishings emulate urban and Western standards. Carpets, lounge chairs, couches, and beds manufactured in Kampala and elsewhere are found in place of more traditional locally produced furnishings. Men's dress styles conform to Western fashions more than in the rural area. Tailored shirts, long trousers, and leather shoes are common, although a large portion of the men wear the *kanzu* at least part of the time. The *busuuti* remains the predominant form of women's dress. However, many women employed as secretaries, barmaids, and waitresses wear blouses, miniskirts, slacks, and nylons.

Agriculture is important but not the primary occupation. Shopkeeping, government employment, skilled and unskilled wage labor, and a variety of service occupations provide cash income for most men in the area. Commercialization is reflected in the following list of business licenses issued during 1971 in one of the communities: thirty retail shops, three restaurants, six butcher shops, nine milk sellers, two petrol stations, six "native-beer" bars, two "first-class" beer bars, and over 300 "native-beer" brewing licenses. A survey of sixty-two privately owned commercial establishments in the area indicated that 246 wage earners were employed. Two hundred and thirteen employees were listed in government and medical occupations. In addition, several men and women commute daily to jobs in Kampala.

Public transportation to Kampala is always available during daylight hours. Commuters owning motorcars frequently assist their friends and

Trade Center Market Scene in Intermediate Area
Photo by Michael Robbins and Richard Thompson

relatives and not infrequently charge others. Educational facilities in the area include nine primary schools and two secondary schools. Modern and traditional drinking (native beer bars and European-style bars), dancing, music (Kiganda music and jukeboxes), games, and sports (soccer, netball, card games) are available, although there are no night clubs or cinemas. In one area there is one Protestant and two Catholic churches; in the other area there is one Protestant church.

Interpersonal relations are increasingly based on economic considerations. Friendships are made and discarded quickly and relationships between the sexes are more impermanent than in the rural area.

Many respondents expressed ambiguous attitudes towards life in the intermediate area and only 33 percent of the sample indicated a distinct preference for their present (as opposed to rural or urban) residence. Conversations with many informants yielded several favorable views such as the following: "You know, here we can enjoy many lovely things without having worries as in the city;" "I enjoy all the good things in Kampala every day, but still live cheaply;" "There were too many people and bad people in Kampala; here, as you see, I don't have to worry about my wife and children." These statements seem to indicate that the intermediate area is recognized as combining many of the advantages of both the rural and urban areas and manifesting only a few of the disadvantages of either.

●*The Urban Area*

Kampala-Mengo, with a population of 331,889, is the commercial and geographical hub of Buganda. The city boasts numerous high rise tourist hotels, banks, electric traffic signals, a major general hospital, a modern university, large markets, the national theater and museum, and a nearby international airport at Entebbe. Kampala is the capital of Uganda and houses a large portion of the government's administrative apparatus. Until recently, the residential sector immediately adjacent to downtown Kampala has been dominated by Asians and Europeans. The African population is distributed among housing estates, low income temporary settlements, and middle to upper class residential areas on the city's periphery. Our urban sample included respondents from a centrally located temporary settlement and a more peripheral middle-income residential area. In 1970, 18 percent of all officially enumerated wage earners in Uganda lived in Kampala. These include those working in construction (13,492), manufacturing (10,510), educational and medical services (10,439), government (7,853), wholesale and retail trade (8,313), and transportation and communication (6,001). The national government is the largest single employer, and its additional role as regulator of the economy makes political stability a major concern of urban dwellers. A large portion of the urban population is permanently or temporarily unemployed at any time, and of these women are the most numerous. Kampala's population is almost entirely dependent upon rural agricultural production for its daily subsistence needs. Food is the major expense, and government surveys of unskilled workers in 1957 and 1964 indicate that over 50 percent of household resources in Kampala were allocated for food. Since few migrants to Kampala own houses, rent is the second largest expenditure for most urban dwellers. Most unskilled and semi-skilled workers live in small one room flats which they rent at 40 to 90 shillings per month. Most Baganda consider expenditures for food and rent the most burdensome aspect of urban life. As one young migrant to Kampala noted:

In Kampala everything you need you buy it with money, food for one. Also one in Kampala has no house, he must rent a room 80 shillings, what a waste of money, imagine, where does he get the money? Sometimes you fail to get the money and you are sent away.

Clothes are also a large budget item in Kampala. Both men and women strive to look *smarti* and *omulembe* (or up-to-date) by emulating Western European and Central and West African dress styles. Young working girls and university students are especially eager to adopt modern fashions and they display a considerable appetite for shoes, dresses, raincoats, handbags, and wigs. Remittances to relatives in rural areas represent still another drain on the income of most urban residents. In addition, small children are often left in the care of relatives in rural areas, and parents are obliged to provide something for their support.

The high cost of living in the city is further aggravated by a high rate of inflation. The overall cost of living rose 29 percent between 1966 and 1971. The price increase in necessities has been even greater; for example, food and clothing increased 47 percent and 64 percent respectively. One informant

Mid-day Street Scene in Downtown Urban Area
Photo by Michael Robbins and Richard Thompson

affected by inflation asserted that, "the price of sugar is too high now. You can even pay 200 shillings for the same shirt that cost 150 shillings last year. Where will I get money even to eat and wear clothes—steal it?"

Entertainment (e.g., nightclubs, bars, cinemas, sports events, and celebrations) is a major attraction of Kampala and yet another major expense incurred by individuals in the city. Social relations in the city are both casual and uncertain. Status is reflected in material life styles and expenditures, in particular houses, cars, clothes, and the ability to entertain.

The pace of life is rapid and people are conscious of time and concerned with punctuality. This prompts informants to complain that they do not have time to plan their activities or budgets. Additionally, they complain about thieves and the erosion of traditional standards and values in the city.

The more positive aspects of urban life include economic opportunities and access to a variety of goods and services, especially rapid transportation. Several informants placed particular emphasis on the speed with which aspirations can be gratified:

Uses in being in the city are that every work gives you money, men carrying goods on barrows get money, also road sweepers, also cheap clothes, and if you need electricity you can get it quickly, and taxis you don't wait for so long, you can get money and watch football matches and everything you want you can get quickly, even if you want to keep money in the bank you are quick, even if you are a beggar, food you can get quickly because you can beg money.

In sum, although the city provides a variety of attractions and opportunities, these advantages are to a large extent offset by monetization and the cost of living. Gerald Mukasa, in the popular Luganda song recording, "Let Me Go Back" ("Kaneddireyo")[6], vividly contrasts urban and rural subsistence.

Gerald, let me go back to Masaka/
Because I found out that things are too expensive in Entebbe and Entebbe town is bad [not worth it]
An orange costs 20 cents and in Masaka, they sell three for 10 cents
You find a bunch of *mattoke* [cooking plantains] costing ten shillings, whereas, in Masaka, you buy it for two shillings/

You find small fish costing three shillings, whereas, in Masaka, they buy it for twenty cents/

Greens cost two shillings, whereas, in Masaka, you get them free/

One yellow banana costs ten cents, whereas, in Masaka, they rot in the plantation [no one eats them]/

Gerald let me go back to Masaka, because I found out that Entebbe town is too expensive/

Entebbe is a town for big people (*banene*), because they earn a lot of money/

You find a small house of two [cubic] feet. You pay a rent of thirty shillings per month/

Gerald let me go back to Masaka/

I didn't come to work for house and food/

To know that things are so expensive, all the money you work for goes for house and food/

If you make a mistake and befriend a woman, she asks for two kilos of meat every day/

I don't deceive. She asks for two kilos of meat every day/

If you make a mistake and take her to a bar where they sell European beer/

She wants to drink it while eating a piece of chicken/

Many people have run away from Entebbe because the food is scarce/

I don't deceive/

The food is scarce/

To know that things are very expensive/

The money you work for goes for house and food/

You find less than ten tomatoes. The seller will say, "Two shillings."/

Small pineapple without juice; the seller will say, "Three shillings."/

I don't deceive. He will say, "Three shillings."/

If you long to eat chicken/

The cock will cost thirty shillings/

A fried egg costs three shillings/

This way [Masaka] small bread costs ten cents/

At the Entebbe airport, it costs two shillings/

I don't deceive. It costs two shillings/

You find a small, two inch bottle of traditional beer [*Omwenge O'muganda*] costs thirty cents. They call them *"bufukunya"*/

A cluster [*kiwagu*] of mattoke costs two shillings/

Whereas, in Masaka, you can get a whole bunch [*enkota*] for one shilling/
I don't deceive. A bunch at one shilling/
Gerald, let me go back to Masaka, because I found out that things in
   Entebbe are very expensive/
Gerald, let me go back to Masaka, so that my parents may see me/
If you long to eat chicken, a cock will cost thirty shillings/
Fried egg costs three shillings/
This way [Masaka], a small loaf of bread costs ten cents, but in Entebbe
   Airport, it costs two shillings/
I don't deceive. It costs two shillings/
Gerald, let me go back to Masaka/
I didn't come to work for house and food.

In addition to the obvious differences revealed in these brief descriptions,
the rural, urban, and intermediate areas can also be differentiated with
regard to a variety of quantitative comparisons. Some of these appear in
Table 1. These data indicate quite clearly that starting in the rural area and
progressing along a continuum through the intermediate to the urban area,
one finds increasing amounts of formal education, income, and wealth, a
younger population, ownership of more tangible consumer goods (e.g.,
radios, automobiles, televisions, wrist watches), more knowledge of consumer items, and more exposure to mass media.

●*Propositions*

Our foregoing description of previous research, its problems, and the
nature of the population and research areas provides the basis for advancing
two alternative propositions:

(1) That Baganda living in the urban area, through their greater exposure
and access to modern values, life styles, socioeconomic opportunities, and
rewards, will display *more* disposition to defer their gratifications than
Baganda living in the intermediate or rural areas whose exposure and access is
less. A corollary of this proposition is that individuals in the intermediate
area will display *more* disposition to defer than individuals in the rural area for
similar reasons. *or:* (2) That Baganda living in urban areas, despite their
greater exposure and access to modern values, life styles, socioeconomic
opportunities, and rewards, will display *less* disposition to defer their gratifications than Baganda in the other areas because of the attendant mitigating

Table 1.

Sample Population Comparisons

	Rural	Intermediate	Urban
% of Males	48	51	56
Mean Age	36.2	34.2	31.5
Mean Years of Schooling	3.7	5.2	5.8
Mean Annual Income in Shillings	1,056/-	1,909/-	2,805/-
% Owning Radio	49	57	66
% Owning Television	—	1	10
% Having Electricity	—	18	35
% Owning Wigs (females only)	—	4	18
% Owning Motorcars	2	8	10
% Owning Wristwatch	19	36	49
% Owning Bicycle	49	35	20
% Owning Kiganda Drum	21	23	13
% Having Galvanized Iron Roof	74	95	92
% Report Regular Cinema Attendance	26	29	44
% Report Regular Newspaper Reading	38	68	81
% Report Regular Television Watching	18	22	29
% Report Regular Radio Listening	85	90	91
% Report Ability to Read English	18	41	51
Mean Number of Consumer Items Heard of from a list of 8 Items	2.9	3.7	4.2
Mean Number of Consumer Items Heard of from a list of 10	2.3	4.3	5.2

effects of their greater perceived socioeconomic insecurity and subjection to conditions of temptation and frustrative "non-reward." A corollary of this proposition is that individuals in the intermediate area will display *less* disposition to defer than individuals in the rural areas for similar reasons.

METHODS

The quantitative data used here are derived from a social survey interview schedule administered in the Luganda language to a sample of 100 respondents in each of the rural, intermediate, and urban areas.[7] The interview, which lasted about two hours, was designed to elicit general demographic and socioeconomic information and data for assessing gratification orientations as well as their anticipated correlates.

●*Gratification Orientations*

In attempting to overcome the measurement deficiencies of other studies, major emphasis was placed on developing multiple-measures of gratification orientations. Gratification orientations were operationalized in terms of actual observed gratification behavior, hypothetical behavioral-choice tendencies, and a measure of gratification tendencies through projections in a story. The following measures were selected because each possessed "face-validity" (based on preliminary observations) and was "situation independent" and because together they possess convergent validity. When the interview was completed, the interviewer read the following instructions:

> You are now finished. You may take your payment of three shillings now, but if you are willing to wait until tomorrow to be paid, you will receive three shillings more, a total of six shillings. What is your choice?

Respondents choosing the larger deferred payment were scored (2), while those choosing the smaller immediate payment were scored (1).

Behavioral-choice-tendencies were assessed by the following six questions:

> (1) Which would you prefer, one egg today or three eggs tomorrow?
>
> (2) Which would you prefer, half a kilo of meat today or two kilos of meat next week?

(3) Which would you prefer, six shillings today or thirty shillings next month?

(4) Which would you prefer, a sweater today or a suit (male Ss) or dress (female Ss) in three months?

(5) Which would you prefer, a new chair today or new lounge furniture in one year?

(6) Which would you prefer, a round trip to Nairobi today or a round trip to Europe or the U.S.A. in five years?

Individuals selecting the greater future reward were scored (2), others (1). In constructing each question, care was taken to insure that choices would be made on the basis of quantitative rather than qualitative differences in the items and that items would be desirable regardless of whether or not the respondent presently owned the item (e.g., if an individual presently owned one egg, he would still be able to use more eggs).

In the projective measure, respondents were read the following hypothetical episode and asked to agree with the point of view expressed by one of the two protaganists.

Two farmers, Kirigwajjo and Zirimenya, who are friends and neighbors are having an argument. Both are old men and have lived in this village for a long time. Kirigwajjo says, 'We should not plant groundnuts in this field now, but wait until next season. Because if we do plant now, we will get only four *ddebes* (tins). If we let the land rest until next year, when we plant we will get eight *ddebes*. Let us not eat an egg and deny ourselves the chicken that would come from it' (Luganda Proverb). Zirimenya agrees, but says, 'That may be true, but it is better to get four *ddebes* now and enjoy what we have when we have it, than to have to wait for one year and enjoy twice as much. You never know what may happen while we wait for a whole year. I would rather have the little that will come soon than having to wait for the much which will take long in coming' (Luganda Proverb).

Agreement with Kirigwajjo, who opted to wait until next year to plant ground nuts, was scored (2) deferred, and agreement with Zirimenya, opting to plant immediately, was scored (1). This story was constructed in consultation with several rural and urban Baganda who wrote and selected from several stories. Numerous respondents made favorable remarks regarding the story and several requested copies, finding it one of the most interesting parts of the interview.

Measures of gratification orientations were intercorrelated, and the results presented in Table 2 indicate an acceptable level of interrelatedness with all but one correlation coefficient statistically significant beyond the .05 level. A principal-components analysis of the correlation matrix produced only one component with an eigenvalue over one, and the loadings indicate that each of the eight gratification variables is significantly involved in one dimension (see Table 2). Principal-component scores were calculated and each respondent was assigned a weighted gratification orientation score based on his responses to the eight measures. The interrelatedness and unidimensionality found among the eight measures of gratification orientations suggest considerable construct validity and provide the rationale for the use of the initial component as a gratification orientation index.[8] Several items, including age, education, residence, economic success, ability to read English, and degree of modernity, were correlated with this index (see Table 3). Each item and the rationale for its inclusion and scoring is described in footnote 9.

RESULTS

The results presented in Table 3 indicate that with the exception of "residence" none of the hypothesized correlates are significantly associated with gratification orientations. In addition, neither sex nor marital status are related. These results provide no support for our initial expectation that orientations to defer gratification are *positively* related to urban residence; instead, they support our second expectation that urban residents will be *less* disposed to defer gratifications.

The association of urban residence with less disposition to defer gratification is all the more impressive when we examine the distribution of deferred responses for each item separately across the three areas. These results, presented in Table 4, indicate that urban residents display the least propensity to defer each measure, followed by people in the intermediate and rural areas. Similarly, results of an analysis of variance of the gratification orientation index scores for the three residential groups indicate significantly lower deferred gratification scores among the urban sample. These survey results receive additional support from our other qualitative and quantitative data regarding gratification behavior in the different research areas.

Table 2.

Zero-Order Correlations Among Measures of Gratification Orientations

Variable:	1	2	3	4	5	6	7	8
1. Willing to wait until the next day for payment instead of taking payment immediately.	1.00							
2. Prefers 3 eggs tomorrow instead of one egg today.	.28	1.00						
3. Prefers 2 kilos of meat next week instead of ½ kilo today.	.29	.39	1.00					
4. Prefers 30 shillings next month instead of 6 shillings today.	.29	.47	.43	1.00				
5. Prefers a suit or dress in 3 months instead of a sweater today.	.35	.46	.40	.48	1.00			
6. Prefers new sitting room furniture in a year instead of a chair today.	.26	.37	.43	.49	.48	1.00		
7. Prefers a round trip overseas in 5 years instead of a trip to Nairobi today.	.29	.30	.38	.41	.34	.40	1.00	
8. Chooses deferred response in story.	.18	.10*	.15	.21	.27	.15	.16	1.00

Principal-Components Analysis:

	1	2	3	4	5	6	7	8
Principal-Component Loadings of Variables.	.54	.67	.69	.76	.75	.72	.64	.35

Eigenvalue = 3.40
% of Various = 42.45

*Not significant at .05 level.

Table 3.

Sociocultural Correlates of Gratification Orientation Index

Variable:	Index
Age	.099
Education	-.079
Income	-.090
Researcher's scale rating of respondent's wealth	.055
Interviewer's scale rating of respondent's wealth	.081
Respondent's subjective evaluation of his modernity	.026
Researcher's scale rating of respondent's modernity	-.058
Interviewer's scale rating of respondent's modernity	.058
Ownership of a modern material item (wristwatch)	-.111
Ownership of a traditional material item (Kiganda drum)	-.025
Reported ability to read English	-.065
Residence	-.217*

*$p < .01$

Table 4.
Distribution of Gratification Responses Across Three Areas

	Percentage		
	Rural	Intermediate	Urban
Willing to wait until the next day for payment instead of taking payment immediately.	49	34	27
Prefers 3 eggs tomorrow instead of one egg today.	49	40	37
Prefers 2 kilos of meat next week instead of ½ kilo today.	35	21	16
Prefers 30 shillings next month instead of six shillings today.	44	40	29
Prefers a suit or dress in 3 months instead of a sweater today.	44	41	31
Prefers new sitting room furniture in a year instead of a chair today.	38	35	24
Prefers a round trip overseas in 5 years instead of a trip to Nairobi today.	41	33	22
Chooses deferred response in story.	38	29	26
Mean Principal-Component Scores of Gratification Orientation Index[*]	.258	.002	-.254

[*] *Differences significant at .01 level using one-way analysis of variance.*

Perhaps the most obvious indication of differences in gratification behavior is the rate at which cash assets are converted into consumer goods and
services instead of being saved in the three areas. Urban informants are quick
to point to a sharp rise in spending for fashionable clothes, luxury food items,
transportation, and entertainment near the end of the month. This they
attribute to pay periods during the last week of the month. Our own
observations over several months in the urban area indicate that patronage of
nightclubs, bars, restaurants, taxis, and buses appears to increase significantly at the end of the month when people are paid. During the second and
third weeks of the month, nightclubs and bars are infrequently crowded, few
individuals purchase noon meals in downtown restaurants, and streets and
roads are crowded with pedestrians while buses and taxis operate well below
capacity. One informant commenting on the "end-of-the-month" syndrome
of spending in the city remarked:

> People who get a lot of money by salary, he may be with four or five
> hundred shillings in his pocket. He attempts to use it very uneconomi-
> cally. For example, he may have taken home one loaf of bread, but you
> find that he could take three full loaves of bread which could be just
> unnecessary, then he wouldn't buy any cheap, let's say bad, soap, he
> will always try to find the most expensive one. He cannot have time to
> budget and go on trying to save anything. He may go out to drink and
> then whoever he finds at the bar he says, 'I have booked the whole bar,'
> [i.e., bought drinks for everyone]. Another case, let's say, he may give
> the barmaid one hundred shillings, he never remembers the change,
> just walks out like this, he goes out and takes a private car [taxi] for
> maybe ten shillings and if he goes on doing such things he may find that
> he doesn't have a coin on him by the end of the month.

In the following statement, another urbanite reveals some of the rationale
behind end-of-the-month spending.

> At the end of the month you will have to pay debts and rents and so and
> so, and you find you hardly remain with any of your salary. Then you
> really feel disgusted and frustrated and you give up the whole idea of
> beginning to bank your money. You begin just using your money as
> you feel, for expensive shirts and cinemas and women to do what with.

You may just go out to the bar and drink most of the money. At the end of the month you find three or four days after you got your salary, that you're just as broke as you were before.

An Asian businessman in the urban area reported that his sales increased sharply during the last week of the month when people are paid. With regard to end-of-the-month spending, he mentioned, "People spend too much of their money when they're paid. They will pay any price, 90 shillings for something worth 40 shillings when they have money, but when they don't they won't buy it at any price."

Services provided by women in the urban area, especially prostitutes, barmaids and beersellers, are in great demand at the end of the month, and male informants indicate that it is difficult to "get women" then because they have access to cash through their husbands, lovers, or regular clients. However, by the middle of the month women have spent their money and are much more available. Along with "end-of-the-month" spending, and closely related to it, one finds more informal borrowing and credit accounts in the city. With money gone well before the next pay period, individuals are frequently pressed into borrowing from friends and seeking credit accounts at unfavorable interest rates. Complaints about monthly debts are common, leaving little to save, and just enough to "go to the bar and feast." One person suggested that if people were paid twice a month or even weekly, the need to borrow would be greatly reduced because people could budget more easily.

Expenditures for entertainment, bars, cinemas, and nightclubs increases markedly during the long national holidays (e.g., Christmas, New Year's and Independence celebrations). Relatives come to Kampala to observe festivities and urbanites must maintain and entertain them. Several informants complain that it is impossible to save money with so many holidays. Salary advances are made prior to the holidays to encourage spending.

Finally, weddings in the urban area are both extravagant and expensive. The husband and his family supply dresses for the bride and bridesmaids, cakes, invitations, flowers, church rentals, bands, bride payments (*mutwalo*), a bachelor's party (*kasiki*) before the wedding, and receptions afterwards. Most middle to upper income urbanites are heavily involved in a monthly to bimonthly round of attending and participating in weekend weddings and parties.

In the rural area cash is consumed more slowly and usually for more durable household goods (e.g., galvanized roofs) or other long-term investments. Opportunities for expenditures on entertainment other than at local beer parties are minimal in the rural area, and conspicuous consumption in terms of up-to-date clothing and furniture is frowned upon. One rural informant remarking on the use of money in the village observed:

> People in the village, make a sell of twenty or thirty sacks of coffee this year then he would like to bank the money. Then he thinks he made just a little and says 'what about if I made another part, you know, another acre or so and planted more cotton or coffee?' Then he will go out again and use the money, you know, to improve and enlighten his farm. So he goes out and hires a tractor and then digs up, pulls down the trees and all the weeds on the other two or three acres and then he goes on planting again. In this way he feels happier seeing his real money work rather than being wasted, you know, on booze and women and whatnot!

Rural people allocate a smaller amount of their resources on entertainment and luxury items than urban residents. Our survey revealed (see Table 5) that ruralities "go out for entertainment" less and spend less when they do than the respondents from the other areas. They also play the national lottery less, smoke fewer cigarettes, and drink less European style beer on the average than people from the intermediate and urban areas.

Anticipation of delayed rewards, associated with agricultural activities and long-term social relationships, is central to rural life. Farmers wait several months between cash crop harvests. Following harvests, coffee farmers have the option of marketing it immediately or delaying until their coffee is dry and thereby selling at a better price. Over a period of three weeks at the height of the coffee harvest, not one bag of green (undried) coffee was sold to the coffee cooperative in the rural area. In addition, reciprocity in social and economic relationships is often delayed over several weeks or months. For example, in ritualized drinking partner relationships (*abekinywi*), obligations to reciprocate with drinks may be carried for an indefinite period (cf. Robbins and Pollnac, 1969). Relationships between the sexes are also similar in this respect. In the urban area, both men and women appear to opt more for the relatively short-term sexual and economic satisfaction of casual

Table 5.
Reported Gratification Patterns

	Rural	Intermediate	Urban
Mean number of times per year plays the national lottery.	2.8	7.5	8.5
Mean number of times per month goes out to bars, nightclubs, cinemas or other entertainments.	3.2	4.9	6.2
Average usual amount spent on drinks, music, friends, food and other things when goes out (in shillings).	2.2	3.6	9.3
Mean number of cigarettes smoked per week.	8.1	9.5	18.0
Mean number of times drinks European-style beer per month.	0.9	2.0	4.7

relationships. Indeed urban people seem more impatient overall. Urbanites in our survey reported they would consider a friend late for an appointment after an average of fifty-three minutes, and respondents in the intermediate area seventy-six minutes, whereas in the rural area the average was eighty-six minutes.

National holidays and celebrations have much less influence on consumption patterns in the rural area. Traditional beer parties, visiting, weddings, and succession ceremonies, while frequently requiring considerable energy expenditures and large quantities of food and drink, for the most part require only small cash outlays.

DISCUSSION AND INTERPRETATION

In sum, both our quantitative and qualitative evidence consistently suggests it is the urban sector of the population which displays the least propensity to delay their gratifications, followed by the intermediate and rural areas. These findings offer little or no support for our initial proposition. Though it might be argued that for some unusual reason this urban sample has had less exposure and access to wealth, opportunity, and modern value systems, our evidence does not confirm this and in fact suggests quite the opposite. Urbanites have had more formal education than people in other areas, have more possessions and income, and have been more directly and indirectly exposed to modern values and life styles through both their residence in the commercial and industrial center and their exposure to mass communications media. Moreover, many have occupations which offer them opportunity for advancement. It is most contradictory, however, that these variables contribute little or nothing to any explanation of individual variation in the disposition to defer gratification. In fact, "place of residence" appears to be the only factor which offers any significant explanation of the variance in gratification orientations (cf. Table 3).

This suggests that there is something about "the situation" which is affecting individual gratification orientations, and that a more plausible interpretation of the results can be acquired from a closer inspection of the differential nature of the environmental context in which behavioral choices are made. This provides the rationale for examining the implications of our alternative proposition which calls attention to two components of the psychological "meaning" of an individual's environmental circumstances:

(1) The relative degree of socioeconomic insecurity he perceives; and (2) the relative degree of temptation and frustration he experiences. We contend that these features of the environment, as subjectively experienced, are most important in accounting for gratification orientations in Buganda.

Another suggestion, of course, is that the urban area selectively attracts and retains people less willing to defer their gratifications. The results reported here may be due to the urban migration of individuals seeking immediate satisfactions (while escaping the arduous, more slowly rewarding life of the village). We certainly believe this explanation merits consideration and that for some, urban migration *is* an expression of immediate gratification in itself. Unfortunately we do not at present possess the necessary data to adequately evaluate this interpretation. In any case, we would probably have to discount any claim that this offers a total explanation of our results. Nevertheless, it does underscore the need for longitudinal data of a "before and after" nature in future studies. Moreover, an interpretation along these lines would provide no solace for our initial proposition, according to which migrants should become more disposed to defer *after* acquiring exposure and access to modern values and rewards in the city. With respect to our second proposition, to which we will now turn, a "selective-migration" interpretation is in no way contradictory. For accordingly, the subjectively experienced "urban situation" should in this case, if anything, aggravate pre-potent dispositions to seek immediate gratifications.

● *Perceived Socioeconomic Insecurity*

It is apparent that the Baganda have been subject to a variety of economic, political, and social uncertainties in the last ten or so years since independence. First, the anti-Baganda political campaigns of the former Obote regime and the subsequent military oppression had a number of pernicious economic and personal consequences for Baganda. This was especially true for those living in the urban areas of Kampala-Mengo and Entebbe, due both to their geographic proximity and overrepresentation in government-affiliated economic positions. The exile of the *Kabaka* and the dismantling of their traditional regional government were perceived by most Baganda (even those without strong loyalist allegiances) as a direct threat to their cultural identity and personal security. From 1966 to 1971 especially, many Baganda saw their land, wealth, and possessions confiscated. Those in government affiliated and controlled occupations were threatened with unemployment. In short, a larger portion of the economic and job insecurity of urban Baganda emanated from internal political instability.

Second, the Ugandan economy itself has been subject to periods of sharp economic recession, subsequent unemployment, and a rising cost of living. Those in the urban areas and those most heavily involved in the highly monetized economy have been most seriously affected. The unpredictable nature of the economy and relatively low rate of return on investments and financial securities has served to discourage the propensity to invest in saving institutions and other long-term capital-producing ventures. To this should be added the rising rate of government taxation on assets.

These macrostructural political and economic conditions have been recognized by the Baganda and have been of considerable significance in both their daily lives and their decisions concerning the future. One clear manifestation of this is the number of popular "topical" Luganda song recordings which extoll the suffering and reactions by the Baganda to their persecution, detention, confiscations, and the economic gyrations occurring during the Obote regime. Many of these are obvious by their titles, for example: *Twali Bakufa"* (We Are Going To Die), *"Waliwo Entisa"* (There Was Terror), and *"Balaba Taliwo"* (They Looked But He Was Not There—meaning the *Kabaka*). A particularly poignant example is *"Serukama Mayute"* (The Traitor) performed by Cristopher Sebadduka:

Since I was born, I've never seen a deceiver like Obote/
He is first among all deceivers/
Obote started in 1962. At that time, he deceived Baganda too much/
He made an alliance with Baganda, and he won the election/
After defeating Ben (Kiwanuka Democratic Peoples Party candidate), he
    visited Mutesa *(Kabaka)* in his palace to thank him/
He was one of those who elected Mutesa, first president of the indepen-
    dent Uganda/
But he was deceiving/
When he started to deceive, he declared the alliance dissolved/
In 1966, he bullied Mutesa. He doesn't fear. He attacked Mutesa in his
    palace/
But Mutesa was courageous/
He showed bravery like a man/
He first fought and then ran away, but he was neither killed nor captured/

He made world history/
Obote was sorry he did not kill Mutesa. He put himself in power which he
    captured for himself/
"I am the full President of Uganda." "I am the commander-in-chief of the
    army"/
"I have all the power"/
"I can't be prosecuted"/
Then he started detaining [or imprisoning people without a trial]/
He hunted people with guns like buffalos/
The traitor!/
The taxi fares went up, but the common man suffered/
The farmers' crop values went down/
But the price of commodities went up/
He deceived people like the devil does/
"I have saved people from poverty"/ (Obote said)
But he was a traitor number one/
He took all the good things for himself/
Taking them to his home county [*Akokolo* in Lango],
The common man could not profit from his labors/
Then his comrades were praising him, even dancing/
He wanted people to work at forced labor for seven years without pay/
Leaving their families behind/
The workers had to drink their sweat/
When he mocked us his boys were thankful/
Forgive them. Let me tell you, I was there on the 25th of January, 1971/
God unloaded our burden. What you call big, God calls small/
Let us be thankful for all the good things he has done [Amin]/
God worked through him and we succeeded/
In 1962, we did not get independence/
When Obote was overthrown recently, we got our independence/
We thank Idi Amin. You led the army. Thank you/
We thank our brothers down [army] and up [air force]/
You did a good job for God and our country/
You saved us from the devil and his boys/
Spies had surrounded the whole country/
Thank you/

You saved us from the traitor/
Furthermore, Obote bullied us too much/
He married a Muganda woman/
Obote was an unkind devil/
He reigned by murdering people/
He killed people like locusts/
He even buried people alive in their graves/
God was angry because he saw him/
Now, our friend Obote, you thought you couldn't be prosecuted. We
    reported to God in heaven, and now he has judged/
The traitor was betrayed/
He wept four calabashes full of tears/
Who knew he would also look for accommodations. Let him look for a
    refuge like his friends had to/

Another especially good example of the fears and realities of confiscation is
expressed in the song *"Zinsanze"* (I Am Sorrowful) sung by Kawalya:

I'm sorrowful, my friends. I'm unhappy. I'm nothing/
I don't even have money to buy tobacco/
I am very poor/
The Mercedes-Benzes that I used to move about in were confiscated/
Even the storied [two story] houses were demolished/
The suits I was wearing were stolen/
I'm extremely poor/
I'm sorrowful, my friends. I'm unhappy/
My beautiful wife ran away/
She couldn't stand eating berries and flour millet/
I'm sorrowful, my friends. I'm unhappy/
The plot I had—I mortgaged it/
The plot I had bought—I mortgaged it/
I have no money to pay taxes and the plot I had bought—I mortgaged it/
I'm sorrowful, my friends. I'm unhappy. My beautiful wife ran away/
She couldn't stand eating merely berries and millet flour.

Finally, Hadija Namale encourages people to adopt a strategy of immediate gratification, because of the uncertainties of death, in her song of advice (*Nnyimba Za'kubu-ulirira*), "Death Comes Secretly" (*Ekyama Ky'okufa*):

> Let me enjoy/
> Let me also be proud, because I don't know when I shall die/
> When you have something to eat or to drink, drink it because you won't know when you will die/
> Teen-agers, even myself, I don't know when I will die/
> Many people die in accidents on the road/
> If they knew, they would say, "We don't want to go."/
> Let me enjoy/
> Let me be proud, because I don't know when I shall die. If you are eating or drinking, drink it because you won't know when you will die/
> Young people, even me, I won't know when I shall die/
> Many people die of accidents on the road. If they knew, they would say they don't want to go. Oh, my God! I am sorry, my Mother, My Father/
> Repent because I am tired of death/
> You can see death offers no promise.

Although these circumstances have affected people living in the rural and outlying areas of Buganda and have curtailed their opportunities, they have not suffered the same measure of economic and subsistence insecurity. Their self-sustaining subsistence economy was not as radically affected, and many perceived the tumultuousness of the period as a series of events occuring "in the city" or "at the palace." Most rural people felt relatively secure, and several urban Baganda returned to their rural natal areas during the periods of the worst upheaval.

Another factor inhibiting urbanites from accumulating standing capital for future investment is the constant pressure to remit portions of earned income and possessions to relatives and friends. In addition, there are greater real and imagined dangers of loss to thieves. Many informants explained that their most rational recourse was to rapidly consume resources and acquire commodities not easily begged, borrowed, or stolen. One Muganda, whom we knew to be always seeking advances on his comparatively high salary, explained it this way:

I want to get all my money straightaway, so I can get furniture. They can't steal furniture. Maybe they can come and take your clothes, maybe your radio and other small things, but a bed and mattress, they can't take. Even if you get a big radiogram, they won't take it. It is mainly relatives who borrow money. But once you tell them, 'I've spent all my money buying such and such,' then they won't bother you. When anyone suspects that you've got money, that they see you're not wasting it on drinking or loving women, then they come crying, and you can't watch your relatives crying when you don't give her money.

Another person noted that certain investments and visible assets encourage people to seek remittances, and added that they are more easily taxed. "Let me say you've got a lot and you build there some buildings, buildings to bring in money. When they see them they say, you've got money. If your land has nothing, they can't bother you."

A major problem of the urban dweller is also his insecure social status and continual need for status definition and affirmation. The heterogeneous, impersonal, and anonymous nature of the urban environment makes it necessary to "prove who you are." This makes it incumbent on the city person to display the symbols of success and position. Others must be shown that one is educated (*muyigirize*), successful, and a high and important person (*munene*). This is not only essential for establishing and maintaining valuable social relationships and attracting members of the opposite sex, but also for seeking and retaining jobs. In other words, ambiguities surrounding social status in the urban area require an individual to consume a large portion of his income in a conspicuous manner, acquire clothes, automobiles, homes, and furnishings and entertain lavishly, for these all figure into his social evaluation. The urban dweller, then, experiences a dilemma in "being a success." As one person explained:

We all have to save something, but for us to just start work we have so many expenses. Like me, say a boy of my age. When your friend comes to visit you and he finds you with a set of chairs, the good ones which he likes, and a good radio to give him music, and a very good bed so he can sleep well; they think you are a good person. They will talk to their friends. And to get jobs it is important that you have a nice place. If you don't have these things and then they talk to their friends they will say 'That man drinks too much, wastes his money like anything. He hasn't got a set of chairs at his home.' And people want to know, 'How does that man and his house look like? How does his room look like? Is it nice? Where does he put his money?' They want to know what type you are by the way you use your money. Let me say some can come and once they find you have a very good room they can trust you and everything.

Another informant also mentioned that it was wise to acquire commodities like home furnishings "because then one's home looks very well and it gives a good impression and then keeps up his name." The inability of urbanites to save money was explained this way by another person:

Well, some of the major problems that give rise to this failure of keeping money are pleasures mostly. But besides this, the point of desiring for high things, things which in most cases are very expensive. And you know, wanting to look much higher than you are.

A Kampala resident, in contrasting his situation with the village observed that, "people out here are not like people in the village where you can go to your neighbor and say, 'well, my friend, I don't have anything for supper today. What can I do?' "

The problem of attracting and maintaining women in the city also requires large expenditures for men, especially if they desire the company of "high" and decent girls, an important symbol of success (e.g., nurses, schoolteachers, secondary school girls, and university co-eds). As a 23-year-old man pointed out:

Women want money. They want to be with rich men. They will ask for expensive things to test you. I think women are the richest people because they get everything and they don't have to pay anything and they get some cash. For man, everything he gets he must take it from his pockets. But not for a woman. She receives some cash to hide in her pocket. A woman always needs more money. She may start thinking. 'This man has got money.' Then she has to try and see if he can afford to spend it on her. After going with you some time she can tell you, 'You don't have enough money.' And then sometimes for young men like ourselves just to attract a girl you have to buy nice things for her. Once she comes to your place she may suspect you've got money even though you don't have so much. But she suspects you've got much money and she thinks that maybe next month, next time she would get more money. Once she sees that no increment has been done, so she goes to get other people. That is why rich men get everything.

On the same theme, a woman also stated that:

Some of the things I think bring about wasting money in the city are excessive drunkenness, maintenance of women outside the family, and then other pleasures—let's say parties, films, going out to marriage feasts and all this sort of stuff is what I talk of as pleasures. Many of these young bachelors waste a lot of money trying to support and entertain women who are hard on them. You know, somebody may be by the best bar and then going home with her and trying to give the impression that maybe he has a lot of money. In this sense, he will find himself in a lot of trouble, borrowing from time to time, losing a lot of money, buying wigs, buying shoes, buying all sorts of things. And then they will find that they can hardly maintain themselves and those women outside. Then they find they get into debt. They begin borrowing money and all this sort of junk develops around them.

The need to indicate one's success and ability to afford a high style of life extends into the need to be present "where the action (and information) is," i.e., local hotels, bars, restaurants, and nightclubs, and to entertain and attend parties, weddings, and other gatherings. These immediate pleasures, however, often result in long-term gains. One astute Muganda observer, describing the future economic advantages of drinking, noted that:

There are so many opportunities of meeting people who are in high positions when you go out drinking. There somebody unemployed may fall onto somebody who may give him a job. People have found people who give them wives. That way they got married and then solved some of their problems.

While the urban situation which requires conspicuous consumption and continuous status clarification, more or less the opposite is characteristic of resource allocation in rural areas. People in the rural villages often fear ostentatious displays of wealth, opulence, or success, for it is felt they may attract thieves, jealousy, and supernatural sanctions (e.g., *mayembe*). Furthermore, one's economic position and social relationships do not require enunciation. Social identity is established and reinforced through daily face-to-face contacts with limited numbers of people to whom one is related and already well known.

In contrast, then, to the rural dweller, the urbanite is subject to several political, economic, and social uncertainties which he can resolve only by increasing his level of immediate consumption and which are inimical to his confidence in the future. One interesting indication of this is that 65 percent of the rural sample and 64 percent of the intermediate sample felt that "hard work can change the way things will turn out in the future," whereas only 50 percent of the urban respondents agreed.

●*Exposure and Frustrative Non-Reward*

Our observations and data additionally demonstrate that people in the city are much more directly and indirectly exposed to new and changing commodities, services, and lifestyles and are more externally stimulated to consume their resources than people in the other areas (see Table 1). They directly confront wealthy elites, tourists, shops, store windows, markets, and numerous outlets for entertainment (e.g., cinema, sporting events, night clubs and bars). More indirect but equally strong is their high exposure to mass media advertising (e.g., cinema, radio, newspaper, television and signs). In addition, the government makes efforts to increase consumption by exorting people to be patriotic by purchasing lottery tickets and products from the Uganda Trading Corporation. There are also the many public holidays when people are paid in advance. Large sums of money are also available at monthly pay periods. Continuous exposure to these temptations and the need as well as the desire to always buy and spend is accentuated by the pace of urban life and the time consciousness of the urban population. All of these factors working in concert make waiting for future rewards seem longer and more frustrating. This is apparent to many Baganda; one lucid account of the reaction to so much exposure and "reward salience" was offered by a lifelong resident of Kampala:

Most people fail to keep or bank their money because of pleasures and failure to have categorizations, or what you call budgets. They never get advice from anywhere, and in the end, they find that they just waste most of the money they get. While as their salaries in most cases are an average of 300 shillings, at a house rent of at least 50 shillings, they remain with 250 shillings to last the rest of the month, and without this budget control, and with looking on all these pleasures, dressings, going to films, going to parties, going to the theatre and all these things, going to the bar especially, wastes a lot of money and they have no time to sit down and think of how to try and save and they just find that they go on in life just like that.

Another person, referring to the temptation to spend and the wisdom of investing in household commodities, succinctly stated, "it is good (to use one's money that way) *because when you have money, whatever you want is what you buy!*" (italics added) In contrasting the impact of exposure levels in the rural and urban areas, a villager reported:

If a person is in town, he can learn things of different sorts of civilization. As in the village, if you don't know something, it is difficult to learn it. You find that if you stay in town, you can see people coming from other countries, whereas in the village you only hear about such people. And when you have never been into town, the day you go, you just gape.

In addition to a higher level of awareness of desirable goods and services in the city, there is also a stronger desire to be "up-to-date." This exerts a profound influence on people in Kampala; as one individual mentioned:

Whatever comes, you do. Especially things that concern money. You hear of a good movie, you go out. You hear of good music going to be played somewhere, you go out. You hear of a big full adventure with your friends, you just, you know, follow as long as the money is around.

Even more to the point is the following excerpt of an extended interview with another informant from Kampala:

All the time a man wants to improve his life. He wants to change, you know, clothes from time to time so that he looks 'changing.' Taking an example of radios. Such a man would, if he had a radio of six cells, in two or three months he would like a radio that uses twelve volt or so batteries so that he would feel a bit more on the standard. And in that sense a lot of money is wasted. He wants to buy expensive radiograms, big ones, and these days you can hardly get one below, let's say 1000 or 2000 shillings. Then comes the feeding of the radiogram. He has to buy records and records, you know, go on changing from time to time. Better records are being produced from day to day. And after that he will get fed up with the music and he would like to buy a TV. Then the TV's are also expensive and they take a lot of power plus a lot of music and in that sense you lose a lot of money.

Considered together, these data suggest that at least two components of the environment—perceived socioeconomic security and awareness of rewards, differentially experienced in each of the three areas along the continuum—are at the source of the explanation of our results. Given his present circumstances, the urbanite is less prone to defer his immediate gratifications in order to obtain more substantial future rewards than his counterpart in the other areas, because for him: (1) the future rewards for which he must wait are more salient and tempting, making the waiting period more frustrating and difficult; and (2) the perceived probability of obtaining, retaining, securing, and profiting from future rewards is less.

In short, it is not only difficult but also irrational for the urbanite in Buganda today to adopt a "deferred gratification strategy".

CONCLUSION

Our interpretations are obviously tentative, pending further research designed to investigate more specifically the many ramifications of these complex interrelations. However, we would contend that at the very least, our second proposition merits greater acceptance than the first.

One of the pressing needs, of course, in any further work will be to examine gratification patterns in a wider variety of choice situations. Most of the research by ourselves and others has concentrated on economic behavior while many other decision areas have been largely ignored (e.g., kinship, family, cross-sex behavior, child rearing, politics and religion). More comprehensive data also needs to be collected on the occasions where choices are made in each environmental context (rural, intermediate, and urban), and in many other decision areas. This will be essential in any further examination of the *post hoc* interpretations of the results we have put forward so far. Not all urbanites are immediate "goal gratifiers," nor, for that matter, are all rural people inclined to delay. We would also anticipate that the same individual may be both an immediate or deferred, "gratifier" depending on the situation. More intensive longitudinal data from smaller samples of individuals selected to represent various socioeconomic and cultural dimensions of the society should be collected on a more or less "day-to-day" basis, so as to observe the specific attributes of occasions which promote different gratification orientations in decisionmaking.

This preliminary study of the manner in which "the situational context" relates to gratification orientations has further convinced us that a regional, multicommunity research strategy is crucial to an understanding of the full scope of the modernization process as it occurs in any given area (cf. Pelto, 1972 and Pelto and Poggie in this volume). Not only may a single community inadequately reflect the entire range of transformations taking place, but important variables may appear in different combinations and assume different relations of magnitude and direction, as communities variously experience and respond to modernizing influences.

We feel our results have certain implications for research aimed at economic development and modernization. First, we believe that those who have been convinced by the persuasive arguments concerning the "hypodermic effect" of stimulating economic progress by increasing economic access and opportunity would do well to consider the value of concomitantly monitoring the manner in which these new opportunities and advantages are perceived by members of the local population. While these may be necessary ingredients for economic development and modernization, by themselves they are probably insufficient unless they are also accompanied by a sense of security and expectation that productive inputs will result in profitable future rewards.

Second, we would caution those who advocate heightening the awareness of new commodities and lifestyles to encourage capital accumulation and saving, so that these endeavors may have the opposite of the intended effect. Our results would suggest that increasing the exposure, availability, and salience of rewards may erode dispositions to wait, save, and invest to obtain them. Unless the instrumental means for obtaining new goods and services are readily provided and conditions of economic predictability and security prevail, accentuating the awareness of rewards may induce a situation of frustrative "non-reward" and ultimately reduce a disposition to wait and work for them.

Finally, we feel that many of the inherent problems and criticisms of research concerned with individual modernization could also be avoided if greater concern were devoted to investigating the situational and environmental conditions in which the modernization process is occurring. Most studies have probably focused too narrowly on the psychological and behavioral dispositions of "the people" themselves. We feel this could be redressed by paying more attention to what is "external and affecting" these populations. Many "development project" failures in the fields of education, agriculture, medicine, and commerce and industry have been attributed to the conservative mental and cultural habits of target populations. Many of these failures may in fact be due to the nature of the situation in which development is occurring, the nature of the innovations themselves, and the agents charged with the responsibility of implementing them. Educational problems, for example, might as easily be blamed on teachers as students, and agricultural agents may be as culpable as conservative peasant farmers for agriculture blunders. Magubane, for example, has sharply criticized several studies in Africa for neglecting external situational factors:

> I do not deny here that individual interpretations of African behavior are important. But I maintain that the first facts to be established are the physical organization and position of the individuals. Once these are established, we may surmise the consequences of the structural situation and how it affects behavioral patterns (1971:428).

The need to add to our knowledge with information regarding "independent variables" has been pointed out with specific regard to education by Triandis et al (1972:66):

> . . . we have not made enough progress in our description of the independent variables—ecology, environments, etc.—that determine the phenomena of interest. For example, one finds repeatedly the

statement that the respondent's level of education is a major determinate of his responses to perceptual, cognitive, or attitudinal tasks. Yet in most cases there is no further analysis of the meaning of the educational variable. What exactly mediates between education and the other pehnomena? Is it literacy, participation in institutional environments, manipulation of symbols, conformity to a life style requiring attention to time, getting rewarded for what people do rather than for who you are, being able to communicate with people you do not see and to receive communications from the outside world, or some other variable that mediates between education and cognitive development?

It is also our feeling that collecting more information on the conditions in which modernization is occurring with particular attention to the specific attributes of situations, as subjectively perceived and experienced by individuals, may help alleviate other conceptual inadequacies in individual modernization research. For example, many studies devoted to differentiating modern man from traditional man suggest that modern behavior and attitude patterns replace traditional patterns, and that modernization itself is a unilinear additive process. In so doing, they fail to account for the widely recognized fact that it is often the same individual who participates in both modern and traditional institutions and who on different occasions may express and manifest either modern or traditional attitudes and behavior. Many of these apparent inconsistencies, plus the frequently observed disjunctions between material, behavioral, and ideational modernity, might be more adequately explained if more information were available about the specific nature of the circumstances in which these phenomena occur.

NOTES

[1] This investigation was supported by PHS Research Grant No. MH 20210-01, for which we are grateful. We would also like to thank the Makerere Institute of Social Research, Makerere University, Kampala, Uganda for their hospitality, kind cooperation, and assistance during our tenure there as Research Associates. We would also like to express our gratitude to Richard Pollnac, John Bukenya, John Wamala,

Gerald Kibirige, and Michael Wojcicki for their assistance in the planning, collection, and analysis of the data and preparation of the manuscript.

[2]The reader is here referred to Doob (1960, 1967), Inkeles (1969), Smith and Inkeles (1966), Rogers (1969), Schnaiberg (1970, 1971), Armer and Schnaiberg (1972), Bendix (1967), and Gusfield (1967) for examples of several of the studies and criticisms.

[3]The reader is referred to Roscoe (1911) and Fallers (1960) for extensive summaries, and to Kiwanuka (1971) and Low (1971a, 1971b) for historical syntheses. Gutkind and Southall (1957) and Parkin (1969) provide recent material on urban life in Kampala. A concise overall summary of the Baganda can be found in Southwold (1965).

[4]In the Bantu languages nouns are qualified by prefix changes. Thus Kiganda refers to the "way of life" of the people, the Baganda (singular Muganda). Their language is Luganda and their territory is Buganda.

[5]Robbins and Kilbride (1972) present a summary of the role of these and other small-scale items in a rural parish forty miles away.

[6]In this and all subsequent Luganda folk songs translations into English are by the authors and their assistants.

[7]The interview schedule was translated and back-translated several times by Baganda research assistants. After pretesting ($N=52$) in both rural and urban areas, the instrument was modified slightly and administered to simple random samples in the rural and intermediate areas. Multistage cluster sampling techniques were employed in the urban area in an effort to include the full range of socioeconomic diversity.

[8]A detailed description of principal-components analysis employed here is available in Rummel (1970, pp. 112-3). Gratification orientation scores were obtained by multiplying each respondent's score on a variable by that variable's weighting (e.g., principal-component score coefficient) in the principal-component and summing these products for each respondent. Higher gratification orientation scores indicate greater orientation to defer gratification.

[9]*Level of Formal Education*: Education was scored as the number of years of reported schooling. Inclusion of this item was based on the expectation that the educational experience leads to contact with and acquisition of modern value systems and attitudes which have been shown to be related to both deferred gratification (e.g., Doob, 1960) and economic opportunity (e.g., Graves, 1967).

Age: Respondent's age was scored in years. Inclusion was based on the expectation that younger people would be more likely to manifest deferred gratification, both because they would be more subject to modern influences and have more to look forward to (cf. Rodgers, 1967; Pollnac and Robbins, 1972).

Residence: Rural, intermediate, and urban residents were scored 1, 2, and 3, respectively. As in the case of education, urban residence provides individuals with greater economic opportunities and increased exposure to modern goods and value systems.

Economic Success: Three measures of economic success were employed. Income was measured by the amount of money reported received from all sources that year. Independent scale ratings of each respondent's overall wealth from (1) very poor to (7) very wealthy were also judgmentally made by an experienced Muganda interviewer and the supervising researcher. These were highly intercorrelated (.82). Economic success has been both positively and negatively related to deferred gratification in other studies.

Ability to Read English: Ability to read English was measured by reported capability and scored (2) able, (1) unable. Ability to read English in Uganda provides individuals with greater exposure to modern value systems through books and mass media, and opens the door to increased economic opportunities. It was expected that ability to read English would to some extent be positively related to gratification orientations.

Modernity-Traditionalism: Several measures of modernity were employed. First, respondents' subjective self-impressions of their modernity were assessed by answers to the question, "Do you consider yourself to be a traditional person (scored 1), a modern person (scored 3), or someone in between (scored 2). Independent scale ratings of each respondent's level of modernity from (1) very traditional to (7) very modern were also made by the interviewer and supervising researcher. These were also highly interrelated (.78). Material modernity and traditionalism were operationalized by ownership of a wristwatch (modern item) and/or a Kiganda drum (traditional item). Each material item was scored as (2) present and (1) absent. Several previous studies suggest that some or all of these measures of modernity should be associated with gratification orientations.

10

There has been a long tradition of ideological antipathy between anthropologists and Christian missionaries. While anthropologists have frequently acknowledged logistic and other types of field support from missionaries, their philosophical position is most often basically opposed to the objectives of missionaries. Probably for this reason, we have learned relatively little about missionaries and their impact on tribal and peasant societies. In this paper Thomas Correll shows how differing Christian missionary activities have affected the language and social organization of two widely separated Eskimo communities. It is clear from Correll's study that the "anthropology of Christianization" is a complex topic that deserves much more attention, particularly as it pertains to the ideological side of modernization.

Language, Christianity, and Change in Two Eskimo Communities[1]

THOMAS C. CORRELL

Thomas C. Correll received his Ph.D. from the University of Minnesota. His extensive fieldwork among Eskimo peoples has focused on the study of language and culture. He is presently preparing a grammar of the Inupik Eskimo language of central Canada, as well as a contribution on Eskimo dialects for the forthcoming Handbook of North American Indians.

If we are to understand the impact of Western ideas on traditional societies, more attention must be given to the role played by specific agents of change and to the manner in which unfamiliar ideas are synthesized with the familiar in those societies. Among the Eskimos, for instance, the shaping of responses to new concepts has in most cases been mediated if not engineered by Christian missionaries. It is not merely a question of what new information has effected traditional systems in the form of technological innovations and an inventory of material culture. The crucial inquiry must be: "how does an Eskimo, for example, come to understand new interpretations of reality and what is the effect of exposure to new paradigms of knowledge"? In other words, studies of modernization and change are perhaps best viewed as statements describing underlying shifts in epistemology. Societies that are altered significantly through the adoption of a more modern technology on the one hand or by Western models for decisionmaking on the other may be viewed as systems in which more or less radical change has occurred with respect to their theory of knowledge. The impact of Christian missionaries on the Eskimo culture has involved such fundamental change in every case with which I am familiar. This paper may be seen, therefore, as an attempt to develop an anthropology of Christianization among the Eskimos and an effort to characterize the basic change in epistemic processes that seems to have occurred in them.

CULTURE AS KNOWLEDGE

It is useful to view culture as knowledge (Roberts, 1964; Paine, 1969). More accurately, any culture is an extremely complex semiotic system represented in the minds of all those persons who contribute to, share in, and interact with respect to that system. In this view, culture is information shared and exchanged by humans in groups. A specific culture is a contrastive information regime, a particular system of knowledge that characterizes a given human group. Goldschmidt has recently adorned this approach to the study of culture with the following statement:

Anthropology has taught us that the world is differently defined in different places. It is not only that people have different customs; it is not only that people believe in different gods and expect different post-mortem fates. It is, rather, that the worlds of different peoples have different shapes. The very metaphysical presuppositions differ: space does not conform to Euclidean geometry, time does not form a continuous unidirectional flow, causation does not conform to Aristotelian logic, man is not differentiated from non-man or life from death, as in our world. We know something of the shape of these other worlds from the logic of native languages and from myths and ceremonies; as recorded by anthropologists (Castenada, 1968:vii).

Paine has captured the essence of the approach in his comment, ". . . Knowledge is an inert capital fund in a culture which, when subjected to certain manipulations, flows as information through the realtionships between members of the culture" (Paine, 1969:29). How and what a people knows and believes becomes the basis for their unique ethnicity.

There are a number of means for maintaining boundaries between societies. None is more powerful than speech, however. The minimum relationship that can be shown to exist between language and thought is that the former is some kind of index of the latter; speech is the best available scan of the total information repertoire of a culture (Roberts, 1964). The possibility of discovering and understanding aspects of the articulate knowledge of peoples different from ourselves provides a basis for viable ethnography and, hence, of anthropology itself.

Yet even more powerful relationships between language, thought, and culture appear to exist. Newman (1913), for instance, suggests that a capacity for *illation* is at the heart of human distinctiveness. Beyond specific acts of speech, a deep illative competence controls what man thinks and says. When confronted by reality, humans make inferences concerning the nature of its organization and its meaning for persons. The illative sense is only known to us through the variety of symbolic statements that are made by members of cultures. It is increasingly clear that though all men share this capacity, the systems of knowledge that result from differing assumptions and inferences concerning nature constitute radically unique epistemologies.

Polanyi (1958, 1966) elaborates this human faculty still further and posits a notion of *tacit knowledge* as fundamental to human experience. Even though the particulars of a given situation may be specifiable through speech, "the relationship of the particulars jointly forming a whole may be ineffable . . . " (Polanyi, 1958:88). The tacit dimension of human knowledge is not aside from the articulate but an extension of it in a manner that the discrete describable parts of a whole compose that whole but do not comprehend it. That comprehension is often tacit knowledge and significantly affects the set of heuristic expectations and experiences that any individual or group may possess. That peculiar corporate essence that sociologists frequently term "ethnicity" may well be an expression of a tacit dimension of human knowledge and of a penchant for certain illative directions over others.

The study of modernization has focused on aspects of change related to technological advance or on the characteristics of societies undergoing political reformation. Western impact on traditional groups has frequently been described in these and other similar terms of reference. What is attempted in this article is not therefore a typical contribution to studies of modernization! A process more fundamental to the question of the influence of Western ideas on traditional societies is in focus—the shift in epistemic paradigms that inevitably seems to parallel that influence. As a result, language (speech) data will be selected at the expense of others and the history of Christianization will be reviewed in the belief that the church has been the primary aegis of change among the Eskimos.

VOICES FROM THE INSIDE

One of the most interesting conflicts in contemporary anthropology arises from the increasing number of books by *native* authors, voices from the inside. These intruders into the *visually*-oriented profession of anthropology are always writing about how things smell, taste, feel, sound; toes gripping roots along a slippery bank; peppery food burning the rectum; . . . 'he became aware of gentle heat playing on his right cheek, and a fine smoke teasing his nostrils; while on the left he heard an odd gurgling sound . . .' One sensory image after another.

Anthropologists, most of whom are 19th century in outlook, don't know what to do with such data; they can't fit them into their visual models; they don't know how to translate odors or sounds into sequences that lead somewhere, because these data just won't fall in line. So they put them into a new category: Native Autobiographical Reports (Carpenter, 1966:59).

The quotation above comes from a fascinating article by Edmund Carpenter titled "If Wittgenstein Had Been An Eskimo." Though Wittgenstein and others have believed that persons cannot perceive two images simultaneously, Carpenter doubts that we have good reason to believe that Eskimos do not. An Eskimo "composite mask," thought by the Western anthropologist to be an "assemblage of parts with the *soul* added as an eye" (1966:54), may have been viewed by the Eskimo as an "organic whole." One of the aspects of modern man is that he is literate. Literacy, according to Carpenter, ". . . is achieved at the price of muted sensory awareness (except sight) and shattered sensory orchestration" (1966:59). Carpenter believes that an Eskimo may possess a significantly different view of himself and his surroundings when compared with Western man. That view is evinced through his ability to grasp significantly different gestalts than do other men.

I shall never forget an early experience I enjoyed with Atausilik, an old Paatlirmiuk "Caribou Eskimo." We were hunting geese together in the autumn of 1954 in the delta marshes of the Maguse river mouth. It was a warm day and no geese were flying, so we spoke of many things. In the distance he saw a *sik sik* (ground squirrel). We sat quietly and observed. Atausilik said that he believed that he could learn the behavior of the *sik sik* well enough to imitate it and even to speak its "language." I was intrigued and encouraged him to continue by being still. As I listened, I became increasingly confused. I do not believe it was merely that I did not completely understand his speech. Rather, seemingly at random, he passed back and forth between his description of the *sik sik* behavior and his beliefs about the role of *sik sik* in the mythic past. He confounded me by "confusing" the immediate and the real with the distant and symbolic. He seemed to pass over that boundary—so real to me—with utter disdain. It simply did not exist for him!

The current emphasis on "the native point of view" in anthropology is healthful. Bookstores maintain whole sections of autobiographical and biographical works concerning the American Indians. For the most part, unfortunately, these works are descriptive of the traditional or contact period in American history. Few of them treat the facts of modernization, but from these sources our awareness of other cognitive worlds has grown.

The rise of *ethnosemantics* in anthropology has provided some base for appreciating change "from the native point of view." Castenada's (1968) recent treatise on the Yaqui appears to be shaking a number of sacred trees in anthropology. Jean Brigg's (1970) brilliant investigation of Utkusiksalirmiut emotionality is a dramatically good example of the kind of study I believe we need concerning the effects of Western ideas on traditional societies. In fact, what is needed is an ethnography of modernization. According to Kroeber, ethnography:

> . . . does not find its documents; it makes them, by direct experience of living or by interview, question and record . . . The ethnographer tends to envisage his problems or objectives holistically; and he prefers to acquire his data by holistic contact, person to person, face to face, by word of mouth plus his own observation (Kroeber, 1957:193-4).

Such a view of ethnography is one that suggests it is necessary to consider the indigenous explanations of a culture as viable theories of that culture. Moreover, data are obtained through intimate human interaction—"face to face, by word of mouth." One must learn the "language." The ethnographer in this view shares basic ends and means with the phenomenologist:

> In the face-to-face situation the conscious life of my fellow man becomes accessible to me by a maximum of vivid indicators. Since he is confronting me in person, the range of symptoms by which I apprehend his consciousness includes much more than what he is communicating to me purposefully. I observe his movements, gestures, and facial expressions. I hear the intonation and the rhythm of his utterances. (Shutz, 1962, II:29).

This paper is an attempt to use language as a means for observing and understanding the impact of Western ideas on the Eskimos. By isolating certain historical and contemporary aspects of linguistic change, speech use, and attitudes toward the language, I hope to point out the direction and effect of modernization in two Eskimo villages. The two communities have different histories, represent two variations on a single cultural-ecological

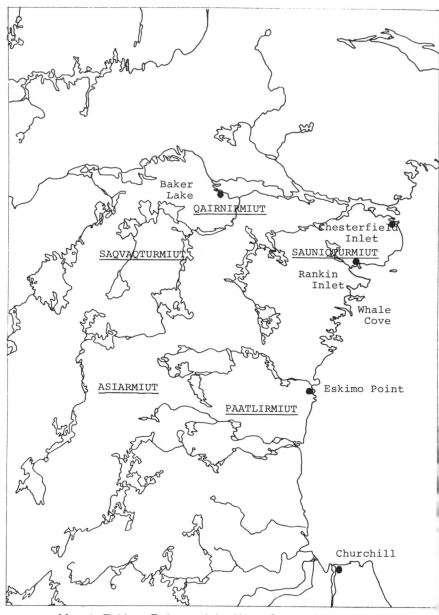

Map 1. Eskimo Point and the West Coast of Hudson's Bay

theme, and are passing through markedly similar stages, but they show some opposing tendencies which are noteworthy. The "feel" of change is different in the two communities; the question is, why? Since 1968 I have cooperated with my former colleague Dr. Ernest S. Burch, Jr. of the University of Manitoba in a long-range study of two Eskimo populations, the Caribou Eskimos of the southern District of Keewatin in ' Canada and the Eskimos of Northwest Alaska.[2] Our purpose has been to understand continuities and changes in the societies in these areas. This paper compares materials I collected in 1968 and 1970 in two villages, Unalakleet, Alaska and Eskimo Point, District of Keewatin, Canada.

The two villages represent very different habitats and economies. The traditional peoples of Eskimo Point on the Southern Barrens combined caribou hunting with seal hunting, fishing, bird hunting, and, more recently, trapping. In western Alaska, the people of Unalakleet were mainly salmon fishermen, but they, too, formerly hunted caribou, seal, and beluga whales and added commercial fishing, trapping, and herding to their repertoire since the contact period.

ESKIMO POINT AND THE SOUTHERN BARREN

Eskimo Point is located about two hundred miles north of Churchill, Manitoba on the west coast of Hudson's Bay (see Map 1). The village had a population of some 500 people in 1970. It is a relatively new settlement, dating from 1923 when the Hudson's Bay Company built its first store near the point. The Roman Catholic Church appeared on the scene by 1924 and the Anglican Mission in 1926. It was not until 1934 that a Royal Canadian Mounted Police detachment was established at Eskimo Point. When I first encountered the village in 1953 these were the only "modern" institutions. There were only about 25 permanent residents at the village while the bulk of the people were still living inland in seasonal camps. The missionaries and the police travelled inland to the people, and the Eskimos made occasional trips to Eskimo Point to trade at the Hudson's Bay Company.

In the past decade, several additional agencies have appeared on the scene at Eskimo Point. In 1970, besides the abovementioned representatives of Euro-Canadian culture, there were a federal day school, an adult education center, a nursing station, an office of the Department of Indian Affairs and Northern Resources (DIANR), an arts and crafts shop, and an Alliance

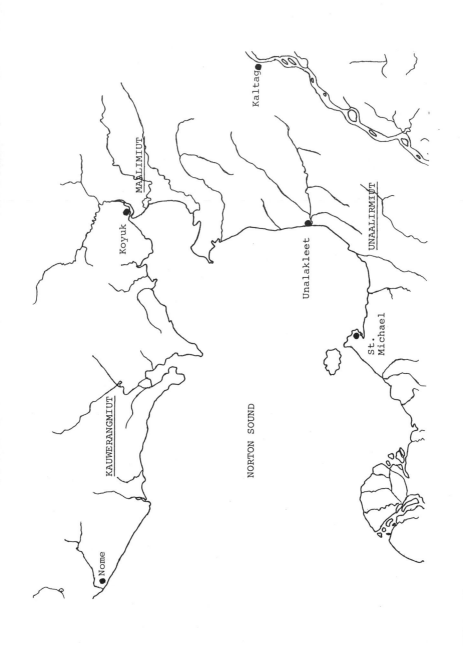

MAALIMIUT

KAUWERANGMIUT

UNAALIRMIUT

Kaltag

Koyuk

Unalakleet

St.
Michael

NORTON SOUND

Nome

(Protestant) mission. In addition, electric power, water delivery, sewage pick-up, telephones, a curling rink, roads, snow toboggans, and a landing strip are recent material evidence of the growth of modernity.

UNALAKLEET AND NORTON SOUND

Unalakleet is located at the mouth of the river of the same name at approximately the easternmost extension of Norton Sound (see Map 2). It was a village of about 480 people in 1968. Unalakleet has been a village site for as many years as any of the local people can recall; based on descriptions of the village by Zagoskin (1847) and Whymper (1869), we have a picture of the early viability of the settlement (despite the setback of a smallpox epidemic in 1936).[3] Unalakleet served as an important center of traditional exchange between neighboring Eskimo groups, between Eskimos and both inland Athapaskans and Siberian peoples, and between village inhabitants and representatives of the Russian-America Company.

These Company representatives had settled in Unalakleet by 1840. They carried with them not only European trade items and concepts but the elements of Russian Orthodox Christianity. After the sale of the territory to the United States in 1867 came Axel Karlsen of The Evangelical Covenant Mission of America. By the late 1880s he had instituted religious services and established a school, a foundling home, and services for the aged. Unalakleet became a center of Covenant Church activity in Alaska. The following decades brought Sheldon Jackson's reindeer experiment, the gold rushes to Nome, the Bureau of Indian Affairs, the Alaska Commercial Company, the Federal Communications Commission, a fish processing plant, a native cooperative store, Alaska Airlines, and finally the DEW line installations. Today the Ungalaglingmiut—"the people of Unalakleet"—are no strangers to electric power, running water, flush toilets, outboard motors, air travel, vehicles of many kinds, movies, a mayor and council, and the influences of radio station KICY in Nome. There has indeed been an impact of Western ideas! Figure 1 compares the villages of Eskimo Point and Unalakleet for respective dates at which similar outside influences were introduced in each village.

DEMES AND DIALECTS

Both Unalakleet and Eskimo Point are comprised of a number of groups

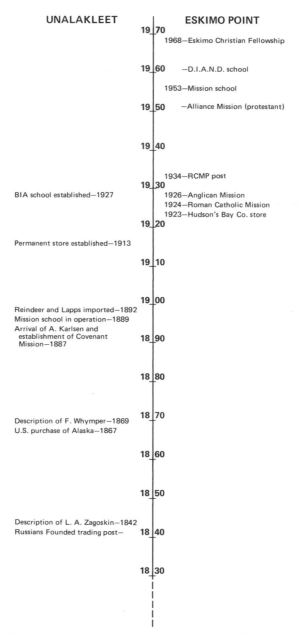

Figure 1. Outside Influences in Eskimo Point and Unalakleet, by Year

UNALAKLEET | ESKIMO POINT

19 70

1968—Eskimo Christian Fellowship

19 60

—D.I.A.N.D. school

1953—Mission school

19 50

—Alliance Mission (protestant)

19 40

1934—RCMP post

19 30

BIA school established—1927

1926—Anglican Mission
1924—Roman Catholic Mission
1923—Hudson's Bay Co. store

19 20

Permanent store established—1913

19 10

19 00

Reindeer and Lapps imported—1892
Mission school in operation—1889
Arrival of A. Karlsen and
  establishment of Covenant
  Mission—1887

18 90

18 80

18 70

Description of F. Whymper—1869
U.S. purchase of Alaska—1867

18 60

18 50

Description of L. A. Zagoskin—1842
Russians Founded trading post—

18 40

18 30

which were traditionally distinguished from each other on the basis of speech. At Unalakleet there are Unaalirmiut, Kauwerangmiut and Maalimiut and a few representatives of still other groups. At Eskimo Point, Paatlirmiut, Hauniqturmiut, Harvaqturmiut, Asiarmiut, and Qairnirmiut predominate. To this day adults identify one another on the basis of membership in these localized groups which I am calling *demes*.

Each deme is differentiated by the following general attributes:

(1) Distinctive characteristics of sound and lexicon in their speech.

(2) Identification with a general territory, and, specifically, named locales.

(3) A high degree of endogamy.

(4) A settlement pattern of population clusters between which a high density of communication existed.

Since all of these criteria involve language variables, it is difficult if not impossible to identify deme members if one does not know the language well. When a number of representatives from sundry demes come together,[4] an Eskimo need not ask another for his membership—he can *hear* it. For example, when speaking of "dogs" at Eskimo Point, a Paatlirmiuk will refer to *qipmiq*, an Asiarmiuk to *qi'miq*, a Hauniqturmiuk to *qingmiq* and so on. The same variations occur at Unalakleet. Highly regular phonological distinctives are maintained by contiguous demes; the underlying grammatical unity remains undisturbed while surface features of morphophonemic patterns and lexical selection vary. When I landed at Unalakleet in 1968, I wanted to introduce myself in Eskimo. I walked up to the first person nearby, an Alaska Airlines attendant, and inquired in Eskimo where I might find the mayor. He laughed and responded in English, saying that I must be some kind of "Canadamiuk." At least he knew my dialect was from the east! He had no real trouble understanding my dialect and even made a guess as to my place of origin.

Eskimos know well the myriad place names associated with their own general locale. They use them frequently to describe travels, tell stories, and, I believe, to mentally "dwell" in their own world even when they are not physically in it. The use of the terms makes the referents theirs. Furthermore, one can determine the limits of a deme's territory by the fact that an Eskimo will not use the names for another group's locale except in very special ways. For example, he will refer to another's deme by adding the suffix *-guuq* which means "it is said that" or "I hear that . . ."

To establish the fact that a deme member considers all other members to be specially related to himself or herself, one may turn for evidence to the use of personal names, to the extension of closeness through kin terms, and to preferential patterns of marriage. All those who call themselves by the same deme appellation are considered to be *ila*, "family" or "relatives," as opposed to *tuujuq*, non-relatables, "aliens" or "strangers."

The last criterion defining demes, that each be comprised of lesser aggregates demonstrating relatively high intensities of communication, is a means for elaborating and understanding intervillage polity. In Alaska, the "kashim" or men's house became the locus of local and intergroup formal and informal contact. Messenger feasts, for example, became the means for keeping in touch with surrounding peoples. In Canada, intergroup activity was institutionalized much less, but the *qatgi* iglu was a recognized center for entertaining guests from nearby and distant groups. It was there that *unipqaat* (stories) were regularly exchanged and the *irinaliut* (songs) were sung.

Today, the old demes are still recognized by adults at both Unalakleet and Eskimo Point even though the traditional distribution of populations has been radically altered. However, in both villages adolescents and children who speak English as well as or better than Eskimo, refer to themselves more frequently as either *Ungalaklingmiut* or *Arviarmiut*, "the people of Unalakleet" or "the people of Eskimo Point" (*Arviaq*) respectively. This usage reflects a growing sense of membership in the village rather than the traditional deme. Whereas in 1953 any Eskimos on the Southern Barrens would have identified themselves as members of one or another of the traditional demes, today they more frequently specify that they are from a particular village.

THE CHURCH AND THE ESKIMO LANGUAGE

The Christian missionaries were among the earliest Western influences at both Unalakleet and Eskimo Point. Historically our earliest insights into the nature and quality of the language of the Eskimos come to us almost without fail from churchmen. It is from people like Egede (1745) for Greenland, Turquetil (1926) for Canada, and Jetté (1908) for Alaska that we have learned about the meaning and use of their languages. In both villages under study, relatively long periods of time elapsed before acculturative agencies other than the church, the trader, and the police were represented. The reconstruction of the early periods of modernization (as well as the more recent periods) requires that the researcher attend to the *anthropology of Christianization*. An Eskimologist friend of mine disagrees with me and tells me I should simply ignore the church in my study of Eskimos. I do not see how that is possible; beside the fact that almost every person in Unalakleet and Eskimo Point has his or her name on one of the church roles, almost every change that has occurred in those villages until recently was either initiated or supported in some way by church representatives. Hence the road to an understanding of what Eskimo societies are about today or were about in the traditional past requires a study of the history of conversions and an ethnography of missionization.

UNALAKLEET

Axel Karlsen in the 1880s brought a form of evangelical Protestantism to Unalakleet hard on the heels of the withdrawal of the Russians. Karlsen had earlier worked in Caucasia and had been imprisoned there for his activities as a preacher. He originally came from Sweden, however, and upon his release he accepted another assignment under the auspices of the Swedish Evangelical Mission Church of America to go to the aboriginals of the newly acquired and little-known Alaska. He first set foot in Unalakleet on July 12, 1887 after a year spent in the United States learning English. He already spoke Swedish and Russian, a fact that undoubtedly had something to do with his selection for this post, and he had knowledge of still other languages. He first preached in Russian and later in English with the aid of an interpreter. Only after several years did he learn Eskimo well enough to preach in that language, and then only in a mixture of English and Eskimo. A number of missionaries have followed since his death in 1910.

Karlsen was instrumental in setting in motion practices which resulted in the deployment of some fifteen Eskimo "pastors" in the area from Nome to Bethel from the turn of the century to the present (see Map 3). He and his successors were also responsible for setting up a children's home, a center for old people, and a school. They sponsored the first medical services in the area; the mission boat frequently brought medical relief to Unalakleet and

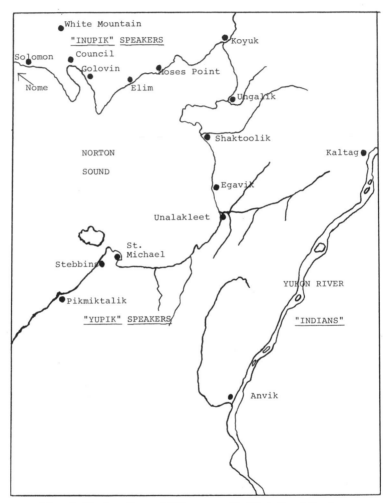

Map 3. Norton Sound Villages with Christian Missions

Reuben and Kathryn Panipchuk
of Unalakleet.

"Malemiut" Speakers.

Photo by Thomas Correll

Shafter Toshaavik of Unalakleet.

"Unaalirmiut" Speaker.

Photo by Thomas Correll

nearby villages. Thus the original impact of Western ideas on the village was definitely mediated by the Christian church.

Interestingly, Karlsen never became fluent in the Eskimo dialects of the region. In fact, language learning has not been a distinctive attribute of the Covenant Mission's activity, nor was anything like an authentic Eskimo Christian literature developed. Songs and hymns were translated and memorized, but the literacy of Eskimo peoples in their own language was never a great concern of the mission.

Another early influence for change in the Norton Sound region was the introduction of reindeer and herding under the leadership of Reverend Sheldon Jackson. The experiment was important for many reasons, not the least of which was the fact that Norwegian Lapps were brought to Unalakleet and elsewhere to train the Eskimos as herdsmen.

Finally, there was the gold rush. One might expect that in the race for "mammon" one would find a clear alternative in the church, but alas! The Covenant missionaries abandoned their posts and joined the mobs in their quest for wealth. Even to this day some Eskimos at Unalakleet are bitter with the memories of the period. Subsequent to the involvement of the missionaries in the search for gold, a series of litigations was instituted involving the Covenant Mission, certain of the missionaries, and some Eskimos. The law suits are described in Carlson's *An Alaskan Gold Mine: The Story of Number 9 Above* (1951). Since that period the Christian church in Unalakleet has not enjoyed the same success as in other areas.

ESKIMO POINT

Earliest contacts with the Eskimos in the Hudson Bay region were divided between the Hudson's Bay Company (and earlier, the Northwest Company) and the church. Father Turquetil's early contacts and those of Hearne (1795) are fairly well known. As early as 1869, however, a lesser known contact was made with the Caribou Eskimos by Father Alphonce Gaste, an Oblate missionary (1960). He set out from the Chipewyan Indians of the Reindeer Lake region of northern Manitoba to contact the Eskimos of the Southern Barrens. However, it was not until the 1920s that regular contact was established with the people at Eskimo Point. Contrary to the situation at Unalakleet, the Anglican and Roman Catholic missionaries became quite versatile in Eskimo dialects, translated the Christian scriptures and other catechistic materials, and introduced a syllabic system which adapted the Eskimo language to writing. The formal teaching of English was only introduced in 1950. The church has been one of the primary protagonists of the maintenance of the Eskimo language in the central Arctic.

All the earliest modernizing influences at Eskimo Point, saving those in the economic sphere, were also first introduced or mediated by the church. The first snow toboggans, radios, films, schools, medical services, and postal service were located at one or another of the missions.

Today, all the individuals in Eskimo Point belong to a church. In addition to the Roman Catholic and the Anglican missions, there are now two new denominations, the Alliance Church and the Eskimo Christian Fellowship. The Eskimo Christian denomination is an indigenous development organized within the past few years by Anglican "dropouts." The defrocked Anglican minister Armand Tagoonah of Baker Lake, an Eskimo, is its leader. The group meets in the members' homes and is strongly in favor of preserving ethnic and linguistic heritage.

COMPARISON

Two contrasting attitudes were displayed by the church at Unalakleet and Eskimo Point. At Unalakleet, little effort was made by whites to master the

The Church-School at Maguse River, N.W.T., 1955.
(Near Eskimo Point.)

Photo by Thomas Correll

Paatlirmiut Speakers Learning to Read in 1954.

Photo by Thomas Correll

Eskimo language; English was encouraged instead as the language of religious expression and everyday interaction with whites. There was little support for literacy and development of a literature in the Eskimo language. Instead, a program to install Eskimo church leaders who were bilingual was established, and a secondary education program was developed. The program was highly successful prior to the gold rush period (1880 to 1910) in Alaska but only moderately effective after that.

The more recent history of contact at Eskimo Point is likewise a record of Christianization and change. Catholic and Protestant missionaries alike have become relatively fluent speakers of Eskimo. Religious services are conducted in Eskimo, and a few native leaders were trained; one has even emerged as a leader of a new sect. A program of literacy for Eskimos was introduced using a syllabic alphabet, and a Christian literature resulted.

Whatever our understanding of traditional Eskimo attitudes toward their language before contact, as anthropologists we must view the Eskimo language against the backdrop of the churches' policies and practices relating to language. Although some contemporary Eskimos may be withdrawing their allegiance to the Christian model for life, it is clear that most Eskimos since contact have been profoundly influenced by Christian values. Inasmuch as the churches in the two communities had different policies regarding the Eskimo language, differential effects may be anticipated. Furthermore, because Christianity embraces a philosophy of language, implicitly or explicitly, one must expect it to have an effect on changing Eskimo concepts of language and ethnicity.

The arrival of the Russians and later the Americans served to rearrange all of the traditional trading, subsistence, and residence patterns in west Alaska. Traditionally, the demes described above were almost constantly in a state of feud often resulting in warfare (Burch, 1972). Seward Peninsula and the southwest coast of Alaska were also the loci of conflict between Eskimo groups and between Eskimos and Indians (Nelson, 1899:327). The redistribution of population following European contact was accompanied by hatred and many killings due to the "mixing" of traditionally antagonistic demes. The earliest descriptions of the presence of Maalimiut and Kauwerangmiut peoples with Unaalirmiut at Unalakleet point out that they were isolated from one another in these camps and constantly on guard against any insidious actions of one against the other. Feelings were especially intense because the traditional boundary between "Yupik" speaking

Eskimos (represented in this case by the Unaalirmiut) and "Inupik" speakers (Maalimiut and Kauwerangmiut) occurred in the Norton Bay region of Norton Sound. I have records of feuds between representatives of those two major linguistic groups that endured over several generations. The coming of the church defused this volatile situation. The churches appeared and took root in villages up and down the coast. In so doing they bridged the conflict-ridden "Yupid"-"Inupik" boundary and partly healed traditional enmities. Itinerant preachers, first white and later Eskimo, traversed the circuit between the missions, using English on most occasions. By using English they were removing the "hostility loading" which Eskimos associated with speakers of dialects other than their own. Furthermore, the intense feelings of loyalty to one's dialect group that would have led to possible rejection of "new ideas" associated with other demes were minimized.

By contrast, intergroup animosities in the less abundant habitat of the central arctic certainly existed but did not rise to the same level of feud and warfare as in the more densely settled Alaska coast. The demes on the Southern Barrens were in such regular contact, the populations so small, and the differences (including linguistic ones) so slight that it was not as difficult to master all the dialects. Tensions between groups were frequently alleviated by story telling and joking which included verbal puns, innuendo, and the lampooning of speech idiosyncrasies of neighboring groups.

THE CHURCH AND LINGUISTIC ACCULTURATION

With Bible in hand and liturgy in mind, the first missionaries impressed the Eskimos with such concepts as The Word of God ("a communicating spirit"), The Holy Scriptures ("taboo-like stories that leave a mark") and good language ("helping words") (Burch, 1971). None of these notions were really alien to Eskimos; what was unique was that they were written. That non-human beings could speak was not new. The idea that some words were more useful than others was also one of their native concepts. There was also a body of knowledge comparable to the scriptures, institutionalized in the "unipqaat", the stories and accounts entrusted to those who knew and owned them. However, to *write* was new.

At Eskimo Point the missionaries moved at once to introduce writing. As early as 1885, Reverend E. J. Peck, an Anglican clergyman in northern Quebec, adapted the Cree syllabary for use with the Eskimos (see Figure 2). The Anglicans were more successful at proselytizing than the Catholics during the early years in Quebec and on Baffin Island. A translation of the Bible, prayer books, and hymnals appeared soon thereafter. The Catholic Church soon developed a modified version of these same syllabics and began their own literature program.

Literacy programs were initated at all mission centers. At first only those who had become leaders in the church learned the new script, but before long all the members of some communities could use the syllabics. When I first arrived at Eskimo Point in 1953, most adults could use some simplified version of the syllabics and were convinced that the system was Eskimo in origin. That feeling is so complete today that one cannot speak to some Eskimos in this area of a preliterate society. Their attachment to the script is so complete that they discredit all arguments against its use.

The syllabics are also indelibly associated with the church in the eastern and central regions of the Arctic. Until quite recently, the *only* literature in syllabics consisted of church documents. This has had an effect on the nonreligious use of syllabic writing. Central Eskimos have become inveterate letter writers in recent years. The penchant for letter writing was enhanced by the fact that during the 1950s a great number of them were taken away to tuberculosis sanatoriums for extended periods of time. A constant stream of personal letters went back and forth from village to hospital. These informal letters, however, display certain formal aspects of religious language and biblical form. One sees this, for example, in the word *taimaingmat* which translates approximately as "therefore" in Quebec and Baffin Island and is *not* found in the spoken vernacular at Eskimo Point. Yet it is used in letter writing by these same people as a grammatical pivot for changing subjects on the model of its use in the Bible.

The newly emerging indigenous Eskimo Christian Fellowship Church, under the leadership of Tagoonah, has stipulated the use of syllabics as the "official" Eskimo language in the face of recent government efforts to teach all children English and to present Eskimo in Roman characters. Tagoonah has interpreted these efforts as evidence of a government conspiracy to kill the Eskimo language. Concurrently, the future of the Eskimo language as a viable medium at Eskimo Point is attached to the notion that syllabics must

Syllabarium

	a		*e*		*o*		*u*		
	ᐁ		ᐃ		ᐅ		ᐊ		
								FINALS	
pā	ᐯ	*pe*	ᐱ	*po*	ᐳ	*pu*	ᐸ	*p*	ᑉ
tā	ᑌ	*te*	ᑎ	*to*	ᑐ	*tu*	ᑕ	*t*	ᑦ
kā	ᑫ	*ke*	ᑭ	*ko*	ᑯ	*ku*	ᑲ	*k*	ᒃ
gā	ᒉ	*ge*	ᒋ	*go*	ᒍ	*gu*	ᒐ	*g*	ᒡ
mā	ᒣ	*me*	ᒥ	*mo*	ᒧ	*mu*	ᒪ	*m*	ᒻ
nā	ᓀ	*ne*	ᓂ	*no*	ᓄ	*nu*	ᓇ	*n*	ᓐ
sā	ᓭ	*se*	ᓯ	*so*	ᓱ	*su*	ᓴ	*s*	ᔅ
lā	ᓓ	*le*	ᓕ	*lo*	ᓗ	*lu*	ᓚ	*l*	ᓪ
yā	ᔦ	*ye*	ᔨ	*yo*	ᔪ	*yu*	ᔭ		
vā	ᕓ	*ve*	ᕕ	*vo*	ᕗ	*vu*	ᕙ	*v*	ᕝ
rā	ᕃ	*re*	ᕆ	*ro*	ᕈ	*ru*	ᕋ	*r*	ᕐ

REMARKS. 1. ADDITIONAL VOWEL SOUNDS.

The sign ° placed over the syllabics in second column is used to express the vowel *i*, as in the word *thine;* e.g. *i* ᐃ̊, *pi* ᐱ̊, *ti* ᑎ̊, etc. A dot placed

SOURCE: Peck et al., 1950.

Figure 2. A Central Eskimo Syllabary

over the characters in the third column lengthens the vowel sound to *oo*, as *oo* in the word *good;* e.g. *oo* ▷, *poo* ⟩, *too* ⟩, etc. Dotted characters in the fourth division are sounded as *a* in the word *far;* e.g. *a* ◁, *pa* ⟨, *ra* Ċ, etc.

2. DOUBLE CONSONANTS.

The nasal sound (almost expressed by our letters *ng*) is formed by the character ˙⟩, while the guttural sound *rk* (almost *ark*) is expressed by the two small final characters ᶜ ᵇ.

EXERCISES.

Single Characters.

ς, △, ?, ▷, ◁, ∀, <, ᐊ, >, ᐅ, ᔨ, ≼, ᔑ, σ,
ᒉ, ᖴ, ᒍ, ᖀ, ᔑ, U, ᐧ, ∩, ᐸ,), ᐪ, ᑕ, ᔾ, ᖳ, ᒪ, P,
Γ, ᑐ, ⅃, ᑲ, L, ᒡ, ᐡ, Γ, ᒥ, ᒐ, ᔲ, ᑭ, ᒣ, ∇, ᑐ, ᒉ,
L, ∩, P, ᐪ, Γ, ᒥ, Å, Λ, ᐃ, ᗷ, ᒥ, Γ, ᔗ, ᒉ, ᒧ,
ᐱ, ᐱ, ᐱ, ᐅ, >,), ᑰ, ⅃, ᐅ, ᒉ, ᔑ, ᐪ, ᐅ, ?, ◁,
⟨, Ċ, ᑲ, L, ᐅ, ᔨ, ᑕ, ᔭ, ≼, ς.

survive, and the distance between these Eskimos and those whites who cannot or will not learn syllabics is currently increasing.[5]

No effective literacy programs were ever instituted at Unalakleet, nor were translations of the Bible produced there. Dependence over the years has been on English and the practice of preaching via interpretation. Today, the church services at Unalakleet are almost entirely in English; only a short period is allocated during each service for testimonies, greetings, and singing in Eskimo. Shortly after the turn of the century it seems that a similar emphasis on scripture, liturgy, and "word of God" inveyed the Eskimos in western Alaska with sufficient interest in literacy to attempt a writing system on their own. Some Eskimos felt the need to develop their own script if the missionaries were not going to provide one. The result was a picture writing system of a rather simple sort (see Figure 3). Words and phrases were symbolized in such a way as to aid the user in remembering the form of a favorite passage of the Bible or a hymn. Although the system never attained wide use, many of the older people still have well-worn, highly valued copies of hand-inscribed texts.

There are no longer any Eskimos at Unalakleet who do not speak English. It is clear that some older adults have only limited competence in the language, but they do use it. English is not only the language of worship but also of everyday life. The bulk of communication in either the Northern Commercial Company or the Native Cooperative stores is done in English. However, I have noted a greater use of Eskimo dialects in the Co-op. Transactions at the post office, fish plant, and airlines offices are carried on exclusively in English. Of course, English is the medium of intercourse in the schools, mission, the Bureau of Indian Affairs, and at the DEW Line site a few miles away.[6] The use of Eskimo is determined by situation and partly by age.

In the Canadian Arctic, at Eskimo Point, everyday exchange is still in Eskimo. The language of faith (in the church), fortune (in the Hudson's Bay store), and fun (in the curling rink), is Eskimo. It is only in the area of politics and administration that English has made significant inroads to date. The settlement manager is an English-speaking white. He deals with individuals and groups within the community by means of an interpreter, a pattern common in central Arctic communities. For the lack of policy regarding Eskimo and other indigenous languages, the Canadian govern-

THE TEN COMMANDMENTS

Thou (man points to another) **shalt have no other gods** ('God is a cross beneath a rainbow'; check mark makes it negative) **before** (last symbol, 'the front end of a boat') **me** (oval enclosing dot, 'in this world', 'in the mind' or 'me'. Phrase 'Agayutiqago' means roughly 'God in mind'; therefore symbol for me follows symbol for God).

Thou shalt not make ('making parka, or image', negative check mark) **any graven image** (parallel lines mean 'a likeness') **and bow thyself to them.** (a man bowing; negative check mark).

Thou shalt not take (hand shown 'in strong taking hold') **the name** ('In Eskimo, when coming down stairway, same word as name') **of thy God in vain** ('a dishpan but the check mark means 'take it away', so it is an empty vessel, or 'in vain.').

Remember (first two letters of 'itkagaluwu' or remember) **the sabbath** (sitting figure is resting) **day** (nest in tree, a word that sounds similar to 'day' in Eskimo) **to keep it** (first letters of 'kaunayilago' or 'keep it') **holy** (arbitrary symbol. 'This was my mother's own symbol').

Honour ('Just a symbol') **thy father** (man) **and thy mother** (woman wearing parka with hood).

Thou shalt not kill (post-European grave. Also the symbol for death).

Thou shalt not commit adultery ('This is a symbol for life, only in a rough way').

Thou shalt not steal (box indicates treasure; negative check mark 'take it away, makes it not').

Thou shalt not bear false witness (mouth speaking) **against thy neighbour** (a non-native dwelling, the kind in which almost every Alaskan Eskimo lives today).

Thou shalt not covet anything that is ('sic' reminder for the Eskimo phrase 'siknatiyuminaichin') **thy neighbour's** (a house, with negative check mark).

Figure 3. Western Alaskan Eskimo Picture-Writing

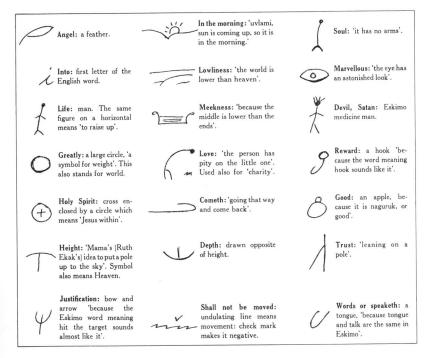

Angel: a feather.

In the morning: 'uvlami, sun is coming up, so it is in the morning.'

Soul: 'it has no arms'.

Into: first letter of the English word.

Lowliness: 'the world is lower than heaven'.

Marvellous: 'the eye has an astonished look'.

Life: man. The same figure on a horizontal means 'to raise up'.

Meekness: 'because the middle is lower than the ends'.

Devil, Satan: Eskimo medicine man.

Greatly: a large circle, 'a symbol for weight'. This also stands for world.

Love: 'the person has pity on the little one'. Used also for 'charity'.

Reward: a hook 'because the word meaning hook sounds like it'.

Holy Spirit: cross enclosed by a circle which means 'Jesus within'.

Cometh: 'going that way and come back'.

Good: an apple, because it is naguruk, or good'.

Height: 'Mama's [Ruth Ekak's] idea to put a pole up to the sky'. Symbol also means Heaven.

Depth: drawn opposite of height.

Trust: 'leaning on a pole'.

Justification: bow and arrow 'because the Eskimo word meaning hit the target sounds almost like it'.

Shall not be moved: undulating line means movement: check mark makes it negative.

Words or speaketh: a tongue, 'because tongue and talk are the same in Eskimo'.

SOURCE: Dorothy Jean Ray, "The Bible in Picture Writing," *The Beaver* (Autumn 1971): 20-24.

ment contrives to educate Eskimos almost solely in English.[7] Some teachers, on the other hand, are introducing Eskimo into the classroom, but these individual efforts seem too little and too late to actually revive the native language.

PRE-CHRISTIAN LINGUISTIC ACCULTURATION

In order to understand somewhat more fully the Eskimo attitudes toward the concepts of language, it seems necessary to at least illustrate what the pre-contact (American and Canadian) linguistic situation was like. I have already mentioned that each Eskimo deme was characterized by peculiar linguistic features. They comprised speech communities that linguists think of as "dialects." The Eskimo inhabitants at Unalakleet spoke at least two other dialects besides their own. For all of them, it meant spanning not only a "dialect" gap but a "language" level shift, inasmuch as Unaalirmiut people spoke the "Yupik" language while the Kauwerangmiut and Unaalimiut dialects were the westernmost varieties of "Inupik." Simple examples of the levels of difference are given below.

Gloss	Unaaliq (Yupik)	Maalimiut (Inupik)	Kauweraq (Inupik)
seashore	tsnaq	sinaa	sinaq
four	tstamat	sitamat	sitamat
man	yuk	inuk	inuk
Indian	ingkalik	itqilik	itqiliq

Most early residents of Unalakleet and the general Norton Sound region experienced enough contact with each other so as to be able to automatically recognize and imitate different dialects. There are many examples of discourse wherein an adult Eskimo *automatically* shifts to the dialect (and even voice quality) of the speaker of another variety when that speech plays a prominent role in the conversation. Occasionally, even today, an older Eskimo man will walk from house to house passing the time of day and efficiently shift dialects as he goes.

Even more surprising to me, however, was the fact that Eskimos in that region had a rather open attitude to the languages of other ethnic groups. For too long we have been told that Eskimos hate Indians and vice versa; never the twain did meet! I went to Unalakleet expecting this to be the case and, to be sure, my first inquiries regarding Eskimo-Indian relations were met with essentially negative responses. The more I pressed the point with the older people, however, the bits and pieces of information slipeed out to indicate that Eskimos not only killed Indians but traded with them, occasionally married them, and even *talked* with them. In fact it appears that western Alaska was a veritable multilingual paradise in the pre-contact period. As early as 1847, Zagoskin pointed to the fact that at least two villages were located on the Unalakleet River between Unalakleet and Kaltag on the Yukon river. Kaltag was a Koyukon (Athapaskan-speaking) village. Zagoskin indicates that the two intermediate villages were inhabited by a mixed Indian-Eskimo population (Zagoskin, 1847). One of those villages was on the Chiroskey River, some twenty miles upstream from Unalakleet and the other, Ulukuk, was nearer to Kaltag. The Eskimos called the former Iktigalik and the latter Uluksaq. The inhabitants of those settlements were middlemen in an active trade between the coast and the interior. Jette stated:

> The people alluded to . . . were the Ttamasrotana, living on the overland portage between Kaltag and Unalakleet, on the confines of the Eskimos and T'ena territories; these presented a mixture of Tina and Eskimo blood, and formed a small group of mixed breed, the offspring mainly of T'ena women that had been taken by the Eskimos after those had killed their husbands in war. (Loyens, 1966:19).

Another situation of this type of ethnic mixture existed further down the Yukon River at Anvik. Anvik was on another portage from the interior to the coast situated on the Yukon River near the Eskimo-Indian "boundary." Reverend J. W. Chapman, an Episcopal missionary who came north with Axel Karlsen, responded to an inquiry from the anthropologist Franz Boas with the following letter:

> It is not surprising that skulls of the Eskimo type are found here. Living in such proximity to each other, the two races frequently intermarry, and the traces of the mixture are quite noticeable to one who has lived among them for some time, though not nearly so much so as on the Kuskokwim, where for some two hundred or more miles above the point of contact between the two races the women of the coast greatly predominate as wives, and retain their own language and teach it to

their children, so that even among the Ingiliks the Eskimo language is perhaps more commonly used than their own tongue, which is a dialect so closely resembling that of the people of Anvik, Koserefsky and the lower Chageluk Villages, that I can understand it more readily than I can the dialect of the upper Chageluk, only 50 miles from here (Chapman, 1904).

At Kaltag I found a Koyukon man who spoke some Eskimo and sang songs he procured in trade from Eskimos of King Island and the Stebbins area while he attended a "potlatch" at Unalakleet. When he was still a youth, his father was regularly invited to ceremonies at Unalakleet. Ungalaklingmiut also came to Kaltag. There are a number of Athapaskan loan words in the Eskimo dialects spoken at Unalakleet, and although none claim to be able to speak an Indian language today, the natives remember that their deceased relatives could. Some claim that in "the old days" most Eskimos could speak at least a "trade jargon" of the Siberians who came to trade with them. If we can accept Valene Smith's reconstruction of pre-contact Old World-New World inter-relations across the Bering Strait involving Seward Peninsula Eskimos, some forms of communication must certainly have developed (Smith, 1968).

At Eskimo Point one becomes quickly aware of the relatively more simple character of cultural life. Populations were smaller, interregional contacts less frequent and more peaceful, and the linguistic differences between demes less substantial. Nevertheless, to the south were the Chipewyan, also Athapaskan-speaking Indians, beyond the treeline. Again, the literature indicates a bitter enmity existed between Indians and Eskimos, and, of course, we do have accounts of actual conflicts. However, at least one group (the Asiarmiut) of Eskimos on the Southern Barrens experienced limited contact with the Chipewyans. The Asiarmiut, though were relatively few in number, traded, exchanged women, and communicated with the "caribou-eater" Chipewyans.

In conclusion, Eskimos at both Unalakleet and Eskimo Point have lived in linguistically complex worlds. The pre-contact Unalakleet peoples were involved in local multilingual experiences so far as their own dialects were concerned. Some also spoke Koyukon or Inagalik Athapaskan varieties as well as speaking or otherwise communicating with Siberians. Since contact they have continued to have multilingual history including Russian and

English, with some influence from Swedish and Lappish Norwegian. Fewer forms of bilingualism have prevailed at Eskimo Point.

It is also interesting that the relatively more complex linguistic environment has emerged in Alaska in spite of the more monolithic patterns of unilingual English usage. Eskimo Point seems destined to retain its Eskimo-English linguistic duality. I see no other explanation for this than that the influence of the missionaries, with their differing views of man, language, and society, have brought about alternative results.

THE ESKIMO LANGUAGE: UQAUTSIIT

There are many misconceptions today concerning the nature of Eskimo life and culture. Many authorities have written books about their experiences among the Eskimo which contain distortions about their language and way of life. The following quotation illustrates one kind of confusion concerning Eskimo language and thought:

> It is interesting to note that the Eskimo language lacks words for general or abstract ideas. Missionaries had a hard time finding the Eskimo equivalent for God. The mysterious force that played so great a part in Eskimo fate was called 'Sila.' Sila was a mightly spirit with many meanings: it meant the universe, or wisdom, or the weather, snow, rain, the fury of the sea, all forces of nature. As far as I could determine in talking to the older people, Sila meant a greater force in the beyond (Fejes, 1966:105).

Surely there is a contradiction in this passage, for "Sila" is an explicit example of an abstraction!

We can be thankful for recent studies like that of Jean Briggs (1970). It is the most accurate work on the Eskimos to date, giving. the reader an understanding of the "insides" of the culture. Briggs' careful search for the social and psychological contexts of Eskimo terms for emotionality results in the exposure of a vast panoply of concepts appropriate to the needs of Utkusiksalingmiut culture.

In their apparent haste to make the point that Eskimos, being traditional peoples, do not have the same moral hang-ups that "modern" people do, some authors have concluded that Eskimos do not have concepts of morality and immorality. For example, in one of the Bampton lectures given at Columbia University, G. B. Chilsom stated that:

> I think there is no doubt that this idea of sin creates much havoc in our relationships with other cultures, and that we should begin to think far more clearly and more extensively than we have in the past about it. We must remember that it is only in some cultures that sin exists. For instance, the Eskimos didn't have this concept until quite recently. Now they have; they caught it from us (1957:55).

Whatever the merit of his point about the need to view the concept of "sin" as a hindrance to intercultural communication might be, Chisholm nevertheless misrepresents Eskimo culture. Eskimos have long had a well elaborated set of concepts about sin and they have "words" for those concepts in their lánguage.

As is well known, the Eskimo's language is one in which suffixation is the sole morphological process. One begins with a small piece of language, a root, and systematically adds suffixes of various kinds in order to develop the concept desired. The final product is a word which is in turn employed in larger syntactic contexts comprising what I call the external syntax. There are basically three types of suffixes and three types of roots: free, or noun-like; bound, or verb-like; and ambivalent, or those which fit neither or both categories. Hence, as a word is constructed it may be thought of several times over as being a noun, then a verb, then a noun again, then a verb again, and so on. In translation, single Eskimo words may, as a result, require an entire English sentence. A number of examples can be drawn from the Eskimo words for "language" or "to speak," both of which interestingly derive from the word "tongue":

> *uqaq*—tongue
> *uqaqpuq*—he/she speaks
> *uqausiq*—word, or in the plural, language (*uqautsiit*)

One may go further in order to embrace related concepts.

> *uqalimaaqpuq*—he/she reads

uqaanikpuq—he/she is silent
uqarut—telephone; tape recorder
uqaluktuaq—narrative; legend
uqaqti—interpreter; spokesman

A lexical universe is described by the Eskimos in this way, integrated by its common referent or root, the tongue. It is also apparent that the Eskimos can incorporate items like the phonograph or new cultural experiences like reading with no real difficulty.

In a changing society undergoing the process that we identify as modernization, there are crucial questions to be answered concerning linguistic change. For example, how important is the group's understanding of the concept of language? More directly, does a society's patterns for interaction cross-cut a set of rules for speech situations which specify the conditions for talking? What happens when the rules get changed? Or, more significantly perhaps, how does one change the rules? Given the reality of change, the salient questions are: What effect have Western ideas had on the Eskimo's explanation of what language is all about? What has been the result of the continuing influence of missionaries in Unalakleet and Eskimo Point upon Eskimo perceptions of *uqautsiit*, his own language? These questions represent the kinds of inquiries currently being made by many sociolinguists dealing with what Hymes and others have called the "ethnography of communication."

An example of the dynamic nature of Eskimo conceptions of language is seen in their concepts of "word" and "language"—uqausiq and uqautssit respectively—which refer essentially to *the acts of speaking* rather than to a compilation of lexical items. The suffix from which these concepts are formed (*-usiq*) might be translated "way," "manner," or "habit", each of which refers to action rather than state. Notice this action orientation in the following uses of that suffix:

> *innusiq*—life, or life style
> *unipqausiq*—narration, story, lengthy conversation
> *pisugusiq*—manner of walking
> *iklarusiq*—way of laughing

My research in the use and perception of language leads me to conclude that here are four general functions or purposes for language from the Eskimo point of view. First, language is for *identification*. Simply by hearing a person speak, one is able to determine who that person is and to what group he belongs. One names things so that he can identify them. Note Briggs' description of this aspect:

> In the course of many years of moving up and down the river, from campsite to campsite, from one fishing place to another, the countryside . . . had become to its inhabitants as grooved with association as a familiar face. . . . They pointed out and *named* correctly all the major rivers, lakes, inlets and islands. (1970:34).

Second, language is for the *extension of closeness*. In ways rather well known to social anthropologists, Eskimos extend essentially familial relations to other unrelated persons. Third, language is for *possessing or belonging*. Whether one is contemplating persons, animals, other beings, things, places, or ideas, one affirms his control over them and his relations with them by matter-of-factly speaking to and about them. Finally, language is for *transaction*. To speak is to will! To talk is to "create." To utter a wish or a command is to evoke response or obedience in man and things.

Of the many anthropological and other published sources that have provided hints and clues regarding this topic, Jenness' study of the Copper Eskimos has been one of the more salient. Notice the implicit functions in the following quotations:

> . . . to *will* that the fish should enter the creek. . . . cherish good thoughts of him and his family so . . . they would come to no harm.
> ... seemed to think that if you told the weather to clear up or a wind to spring up or anything at all to happen your appeal would very probably take effect.
> . . . the very expression of one's thought, the mere utterance of a wish in some dim and obscure manner worked for its fulfillment.
> Dogs . . . have the status of servant children, as it were, and are *named*, like real children, after the dead relatives of their owners (Jenness 1922).

FROM KASHIM TO CHURCH

One thing that stands out in the ethnography of Eskimo communication is that there are places to talk, and that the talk that is done in each particular place may be unique. Eskimos can be and frequently are silent. Most of us who work among the Eskimo in the north country experience considerable uneasiness when, in a visiting situation, an Eskimo sits for seemingly endless periods of time without saying anything. Surely, I think, he is upset, or embarrassed, or is waiting for me to say something, or wishes to go home, or something! But no, he just sits there, slowly drinking his tea, remaining silent. There *is* a language of silence, of course (Samarin, 1965), and Eskimos frequently use it when they visit (*uplaluktuq* or *pulaaqtuq*). It is clear to me now that just being present is adequate for much of what visiting is all about. It is the same at Eskimo Point or Unalakleet. Visiting places, frequently the home, have their own communicative rubrics, one of which is silence!

There are of course other places to talk, such as the store, the nursing station, the kitchen table, and the bed. Certainly it is not merely on the *dramatis personae* and the time. Women, for example, while picking berries in the autumn, seem to undergo an annual life change while they anticipate, plan, and then enter into the seasonal episode. I am convinced that it is not merely the general absence of mosquitos at that time of year or the delightful fragrance of the land or the bittersweet flavor of salmon berries that they enjoy so thoroughly, though all of these are certainly involved. It seems more likely that there is a mutual renewal engendered by the opportunity to be a woman among women for a time and to satiate the desire to gossip (*sanquukliqtuut*) about any and all subjects. As Jenness extrapolates:

There is a good deal of backbiting and scandal-mongering, especially among the women, who will sit and talk scandal for hours. (1922:235).

One of the loci for that genre of communication is the berrypicking scene, wherever that might be. It seems more important today than it might have been in the past due mainly to the anathema pronounced upon gossip by the church. One is beyond the sight of the spire for a time while picking berries and *sanguukliqutaluk*!

The church building itself is another important locus for ongoing verbal interaction at both Unalakleet and Eskimo Point. Both formal (preaching, singing, praying, testifying) and informal (greeting, planning, informing) communications occur there. Nearly all people in the village are members of one or another of the churches. Services are frequent, sometimes several times a week. Sunday services and associated happenings are important enough to many so that they will leave a good hunting situation to return for church. Everyone is conscious of who was present in church, or of who walks by the house on the way to the "other" church. I have been told by the villagers that there are no longer any "unbelievers" (*nallujut*), only backsliders (*naalatsiangitut*), "those who do not obey."

But did the church constitute a *new* locus? Apparently not! Karlsen and Marsh were equally vociferous in their condemnation of what they judged to be the "evils" in the old culture. They specially singled out the shamans (*angatquut*) and their centers of activity, the "Kashims" or "men's houses." These are referred to as *qasgi* at Unalakleet, and as the *qatgi*, "dance igloos," on the Southern Barrens. The kashims began to be neglected at Unalakleet shortly after the turn of the century and the dance igloos were seldom if ever used in Eskimo Point following the establishment of the churches.

The fact that these centers served purposes other than conjuring in the traditional and contact societies was unfortunately not taken into consideration by the missionaries. The ethnological literature from either area holds many illustrations of social concepts that were dramatized in these places (Nelson, 1899; Lantis, 1947; Dall, 1870; Edmonds, 1966; Hawkes, 1913 and 1914; Spencer, 1959; Birket-Smith, 1927; and van den Steenhoven, 1958). A partial transference of kashim functions to the church occurred. Some of the traditional concepts associated with these structures were adopted, some were abandoned, and all were changed. My first clue that this was the case at Unalakleet came in a discussion with Stephan Katchatag. We were talking in English. He indicated in answer to my questions about the old days, that the "potlatches" (a term the people of Unalakleet have learned from the anthropologists) used to be a lot like the missionary conferences. By potlatches he was referring to *pualuq qatituq*—ceremonial gatherings in the kashim on special occasions like the Messenger Feasts. By conferences he meant the annual gatherings of the Covenant Mission when missionaries, native workers, and other adherents gathered at one or another village and used the church for business and religious meetings. When Stephan and I then switched to speaking in Eskimo, he used a lot of terms in reference to behavior at the church conferences which I had heard earlier in reference to the old kashims. On the other hand, at Eskimo Point, while helping

Unaanuk to read and translate his Bible, I had similarly found terms which applied to both the Christian worship rubrics and the traditional Eskimo dance-house practices. Thus it would appear that many of the functions of the kashims have been imputed to the church.

By referring to the indigenous speech rubrics, I shall attempt to document this shift in one locus of communication—the abandonment of the kashim and the substitution of the church. The following five points seem most applicable to this replacement process:

(1.) A preacher or missionary is called an *ajuqiqtuiji*. The term comes from a cultural practice that was focused in the kashim. The root "ajuq" refers to those things that are difficult, impossible, or inescapable for a person. Ajuqiqtuiji names the person whose function it is to remove those impediments (sins). *Ajuqiqtuijuq* was a regular aspect of the ceremonial life in the kashim of every village. In situations where a village temporarily or permanently had two or more groups of persons representing different demes, there was a corresponding number of kashims. Ajuqiqtuijuq was required to keep matters in balance, or balanced motion (*angalaniq*). That state, or the attempt to achieve it, was dramatized by dancing (*angalatuq*), which included turning around (*mumiq-*), shaking the body (*uamit-*), and another form of motion (*aularuq*). During the dramatization, which controls things (*angalataraa*), the person or persons who were out of sorts were treated by a shaman (*angatquaqtaujut*).

The missionaries were ready, given their theologies, to adopt the role of the "impediment remover" (ajuqiqtuiji), while rejecting the social prescriptions for the role of curer and the dramatization of catharsis and renewal. Those other aspects of the traditional "burden removal" ritual (ajuqiqtuijuq) are redistributed to the modern patterns of Saturday night dancing, on the one hand and to the "old leaders and advisors" (*angajuqqat*) on the village council on the other. What was formerly a unitary experience or concept is, in modernity, fragmented.

(2) Hymn writing and singing are integral parts of the modern church life of Christian Eskimos. The hymns are almost without exception translations rather than creations, but such "new" hymns are constantly being produced and learned. There are a number of terms for singing in the language that reflect the old practices in the kashim. The word most commonly used for song or hymn today is *inngiut*; its derivation *inngiuqtuq* means "to sing." Actually, however, inngiuqtuq implied singing or talking *together*, in un-

ison. This concept was appropriate to the form of the Christian service and the term was readily employed.

However, songs (inngiut) were only one part of the chanting practiced during the kashim ceremonies. A person did not originate his own songs, he used (atuqpaa) them, and in this context a song is known as an atuun. Songs or choral pieces, after all, are messages between communicants. One uses the words to accomplish certain ends. The words do not "belong" to the user; they are merely employed or borrowed, as it were, because they are efficacious for a certain need. The leader, the angatquq, directed the congregation in the kashim to an appropriate atuun; they sang it (inngiuqtut) and danced. Each song had its voice or sound (irinaq). In this regard, when one sings he makes the sound, iriniqpuq, while he awaits or longs for the desired effect, irnivuq. Apparently the kashim songs got quite loud (irialaaqtuq—a term now reserved for the screeching cry of an infant child). Again, the church divided the constellation of concepts that were once a whole. They accepted inngiut (songs), but have rejected atuun (song that a person is "using") and irinaliut (voice); the former implied power in words, while the latter frequently referred to the voice of the appropriate spirit.

(3) Whereas prayer is a separate lexical category in the Western tradition, it was a part of the previously described concepts in the traditional Eskimo cultural experience. There is not really a separate rubric; what was considered to be prayer was the command or creative genius of a word or song. The churchmen turned to another verb, tuksiarniq, "to ask." This verb is one that is essentially unrelated to the whole kashim pattern.

(4) Kashims were the traditional counterparts of libraries, radio stations, and the country store; they were information centers. Those who had news reported it at the kashim. Those who were aware of solutions to problems in the village were expected to share them in the kashim. Those who knew special parts of the local history or of a distant tradition were provided a forum there. Those who spoke regularly in this latter fashion were known as storytellers or announcers (unipqaaqtit). A narrative (unipqaaqtuaq) might take days to complete and would be carried on in serial form. The fact that it was a unit was signalled by the use of the suffix "-tuaq."

Many such accounts were more like confessions (quliaqtuaq). Some people might doubt (qulaqpuq) the veracity of a story, but there was generally someone who "put a roof on it" (qulivaa), attesting to its truthfulness. The church has accepted the latter concept under the notion of confession, but no place has been made for the stories that transmit the information that is their culture (*unipqaaqtuat*). The Bible has supplanted the old narratives as the preacher has displaced the old *angatquq*.

(5) The less formal speech genres that were located primarily in the kashims included greeting and welcoming (*paaqtuqtuq*), making plans (*sivuniqsuq*), and gossiping (*sanguukiqtuq*). The latter has a specific biblical injunction forbidding it. Planning—for hunting, travelling, or anything at all—used to be accomplished in the leisurely context of the men's house. I have several accounts of plans for killing someone from another deme being made in the kashim. However, the future was unknown and terrified a person (*sivurarinaqpaa*). One needs to have an atuun as he makes plans to secure himself in his planning. Therefore, only certain kinds of planning could now be done in the church. The church has, however, become the place for greeting and welcoming (*tuujurmiut*) strangers. In the traditional past, strangers were welcomed into the kashim and put up there. The *paaq* is the entry porch of an *iklu*. The kashim was the place for welcoming and "understanding" visitors (*paaqaaqtipaa*). At Unalakleet and at Eskimo Point, this old practice is still maintained at the Covenant Mission and the other churches.

The kashim was formerly the locus of patterns of behavior which were conceived by the Eskimos to be holistically interrelated. A structure which provided for an integration of a good deal of the traditional Eskimo ethnicity could be found in the kashim. In trying to elicit information about the kashims from my Eskimo informants, I was impressed with the fact that they did not find it an easy thing to discuss. It seemed, in fact, to represent a *tacit dimension* in their thinking, an ineffable domain which they nonetheless perceived and used for a number of purposes.

To become a Christian involved the early converts in a realignment of their awareness of the constituent behaviors that were associated with the kashim. Thereafter, participation in kashim activities was curtailed if not prohibited. The old kashim practices were supplanted by a synthesis of old and new ideas in the church. Some of the old particular behaviors were anathemized; others were adopted by the missionaries. The result was that the whole that was jointly formed by the new set of particulars was something quite different from the kashim.

CONCLUSIONS

While studies of modernization have continued to emphasize the effects of technological change, new forms of government, new medical programs, and so on, very few have dealt with the problem in the terms of reference of epistemological change. To consider the impact of Western ideas on traditional societies as a shift in a knowledge base, anthropologists must involve themselves in the ethnography of native epistemic paradigms and Christianization. In the case of the latter, it is probably true that we are as myth-bound as we once were concerning animal behavior. Granted the world wide nature of Christianization and its close association with the rise of modernity in many cases, the phenomena of proselytization and religious conversion deserve a great deal more research than they have received.

Whether attended by religious conversion or not, changes in traditional societies that are moving along a modernization continuum involve members in dramatic alterations of their basis for knowing and believing. One manner in which this kind of change can be monitored is through consideration of changes in the structures and uses of languages over time. Language provides the best of all possible scans of the fund of knowledge available to any culture.

The differential results of Christianization in Alaska and Central Canada are the product of two interrelated processes. On the one hand there is the difference in language policies of the various mission groups and on the other hand there are the pre-contact differences in population size and density, subsistence base, and degree of local interdeme communication. In Alaska the input consisted of an emphasis upon English as the medium of both sacred and secular communication, and while this served to unite feuding groups it did not erase the linguistic diversity which accompanied the traditional cultural and environmental diversity of the highly varied and productive ecological setting of the Bering Strait region. The situation was just the opposite among the native people of Central Canada. The emphasis of Christian missionaries was on the accommodation of Christian teachings and scriptures to the native language. However, the less rich ecological setting of the Southern Barrens was responsible for pre-contact linguistic and cultural homogeneity, as well as small, less antagonistic populations.

It would seem that Eskimo Point is destined to retain its Eskimo-English linguistic duality mainly because of missionary emphasis on the native language. In this duality, Eskimo is used in the domains of "faith, fortune and fun" while English is used mostly in government. At Unalakleet, on the other hand, English has become the dominant code of communication in most situations. It began in the religious domain and spread to other areas of the culture. The initial use of English as a *lingua franca* was due to the great linguistic plurality of the native setting which proved too formidable for the missionaries to master, and was too emotionally charged for cross-deme acceptance.

NOTES

[1]This paper was originally prepared for the Symposium on the Impact of Western Ideas on Traditional Societies which was held at the University of Rhode Island, May 1971. The author wishes to acknowledge contributions made by Ernest S. Burch Jr., Kenneth P. Gowdy, Donald Larson, John Poggie, Robert Lynch, and Miss Pamela Farr to the final form of the paper.

[2]Support from the Canada Council and the Northern Studies Committee of the University of Manitoba for field studies in Alaska in 1968 and in the District of Keewatin in 1970 is gratefully acknowledged.

[3]The population of Unalakleet was quite large by Eskimo standards when the people were contacted by Europeans for the first time. The 1836 smallpox epidemic reduced the population to thirteen individuals. Since that time, the population has grown fitfully.

[4]Most modern villages contain representatives of several demes. In the traditional period, the "potlatches," messenger feasts, and trading fairs were examples of cosmopolitan gatherings. They also occurred on the southern barrens but on a much less intensive scale.

[5]My own situation in both Unalakleet and Eskimo Point was greatly enhanced by the fact that I could speak and write the language. It simultaneously alienated whites and facilitated the building of relationships with the Eskimos.

[6]The DEW site has recently been closed.

[7]An interesting exception to this practice is the Eskimo Language School at Rankin Inlet, N.W.T., administered by M. Mallon.

11

It is quite clear that some of the effects of modernization have been contrary to the needs and goals of peoples in different parts of the world. This is due in part to the fact that we have not developed the social concern nor the holistic perspective to accurately assess the consequences of various types of innovations, and in part because local communities usually lack the power to ameliorate the negative consequences of change once they become obvious. Norman Chance argues that the consequences of the operation of an essentially American educational system among native Alaskan peoples have been primarily negative, in that there is a very poor correspondence between this system and the type that would best fulfill local needs and aspirations.

Modernization and Educational Reform in Native Alaska

NORMAN A. CHANCE

Norman A. Chance is Professor of Anthropology at the University of Connecticut. Professor Chance received his Ph.D from Cornell University and has done extensive

*field research among Alaskan Eskimos as well as among Indians in Sub-Arctic
Canada. His major concerns have been with the study of development, both in its
social and psychological aspects. Professor Chance headed the McGill University
program in the anthropology of development, and is currently engaged in planning
programs for social and cultural change.*

The process of modernization is frequently perceived as an external and
largely uncontrollable force (e.g., the acquisition of industrial technology by
non-Western populations). By implication, the task of anthropologists and
allied social scientists is to study people's response and mode of adaptation to
this external force. I strongly question this unidirectional conceptualization
of the modernization process. Instead, I prefer to speak of societies which are
modernizing as those, past or present, which are engaged in transforming
action designed to emphasize the creative humanizing qualities in man's
social development. Given this broad definition which I will elaborate more
fully later on, it can be suggested that some minority and Third World
societies are more actively modernizing than many industrialized Western
ones.

This latter approach also assists in demythologizing the "theology" of
modernization which has as its major tenants the importance of changing
attitudes, values, techniques, cultural practices, and other internal psychological and social attributes which constrain the individual or group from
becoming more "modernized." Not only does this new "theology" frequently disregard historical relationships of the economic and political
power of nonindustrial nations vis-à-vis other more technically developed
ones, but it also has little or nothing to say for the future. A concept which
telescopes a long historical past into the phrase "traditional" and poses the
future as a neverending present would appear to have a rather limited
potential in any critically oriented social science.

Keeping these introductory remarks in mind, I would like first to focus
particular attention on one small aspect of the modernizing process, educational reform, and relate it to one small minority population, the Eskimos,
Indians, and Aleuts of Alaska. Second, I will raise what I consider to be some
of the more fundamental questions about the whole process of educational
reform as it relates both to northern minorities and modern society, and will
conclude with a series of recommendations.

AN EVALUATION OF ALASKA NATIVE EDUCATION

In the spring of 1970 my wife and I undertook a brief study of existing education programs for Alaska's natives.[1] The overall conclusion of that study was that unless existing educational programs for Alaska natives are dramatically improved and expanded in the near future, the economic, social, and psychological costs to the native people, the state, and appropriate federal agencies will assume major proportions by the end of this decade. Even with recent advancements, the present undereducation of the large majority of Alaska's Indians, Eskimos, and Aleuts, one fifth of the total state population, is appalling by any statewide or national criteria.

Equally important was the conclusion that the undertaking of a significant educational effort now will show major benefits in the same time span. However, if substantial improvements are not made for another five to ten years, the present interlocking pattern of poor education, a high dropout rate, and socioeconomic incompetence among the young native population will have become sufficiently calcified as to largely insure their exclusion from any real participation in Alaska's economic, social, and political development. A dramatically improved educational system is not in itself a sufficient condition for effective native participation, but it is a necessary and very vital one.

Where do the problems lie? Native education in Alaska today is under attack on two fronts. Existing facilities are insufficient to keep up with the expanding population, and the quality of existing programs is inadequate to deal with mounting economic, social, and political pressures.

Due to greatly improved comprehensive health services and increased birth rate, the median age of the Alaska native population is 16.8 years.[2] In 1969, of the approximately 16,000 native elementary students, over 11,000 were located in predominantly rural native communities. Overcrowding is endemic in many of these communities. At Barrow, for example, recently constructed buildings designed to expand the secondary school program have had to be used for primary level students.

Secondary school facilities are even more limited. Of the seventy-seven village schools operated by the state, only six offer work beyond the eighth grade. Of the seventy-three Federal Bureau of Indian Affairs (BIA) operated village schools, only four offer ninth grade courses and only two offer tenth grade courses. High school education for most rural youth must be obtained away from home. Although a number of new regional high schools are in the planning stage, none are yet under actual construction. Of the 4,600 natives attending secondary school in 1969 (total population 55,000), over 1,000 were sent outside the state for their education, primarily to Chemawa, Oregon and Chilocco, Oklahoma. Given increasing pressures on these two high schools to accept Indian children from the northwest and midwest regions of the United States, the number of Alaskan natives attending them was drastically reduced this past fall. Many were placed in the already overcrowded Boarding Home Programs and borough high schools in Fairbanks and Anchorage. Considering the mounting interest of native students attending high school and the lack of adequate facilities, present prospects for minimally adequate secondary education appear gloomy indeed.

As to improving the quality of existing schools, personnel at the senior levels of BIA and State operated school systems have become increasingly interested in supporting new teacher preparation programs and introducing bicultural and bilingual materials into the predominantly native schools. However, an important counterforce to this approach is the continuing influence of Social Darwinian views found among whites and some natives throughout Alaska, including many older teachers and school administrators. Belief in the supremacy of white middle-class values and institutions sets the stage for either outright rejection of Eskimos, Indians, and Aleuts or at least the necessity of making them become "white."

Institutionally, this view is reflected in the success-failure orientation of the schools which are perceived as important in that they provide a ladder where the "most fit" gain access to the white world. Where middle-class uniformity rather than cultural plurality has been the desired end product of the school system, so-called "unsuccessful" students are left with strong feelings of inferiority and ambivalence about the outside world.

Teachers who operate on this premise not only insist on the use of English for all communication, but emphasize grammar and proper usage more than expressive language development. In Nome, many native children spend two years in the first grade learning these "basic skills." When teaching is seen as the major instrument of education, the remedy for poor scholarship usually is larger doses of the same prescription. Eventually, the child accepts the underlying message that schools are infallible and that the child and his culture are inferior. Lack of any significant native community involvement in most rural Alaska school programs severely limits the perception of alternative views.[3]

Rather than elaborate on these well-known problems of Alaska native education, a more important question to ask is: what steps are presently being undertaken to help alleviate the problems? A surprisingly large number of studies have recently focused on this broad question.[4] Most have been sponsored by federal or state agencies and organizations. A few have actively involved Alaska natives in their deliberations and recommendations; almost none have been generated solely by native organizations or individuals. All emphasize the need for increased facilities, upgrading educational programs, and more funding. Taking into account the sponsorship of the studies, there is a strong tendency to de-emphasize or completely disregard the underlying powerlessness of the Alaska natives to actively become involved in those areas of educational decisionmaking in which they are interested and concerned.[5]

With relatively few exceptions, the efforts of federal and state educational agencies to effectively incorporate local and regional native populations in decisionmaking has been largely a failure. Reasons for this condition are varied. They include questioning of the native's ability to make good judgments, simplistic ethnocentric views regarding assimilation, problems of a centralized educational bureaucracy attempting to bring change to small rural villages, conscious and unconscious feelings of racism, and the threat of diffused decisionmaking to the professional status of administrators and teachers.

This failure is also attributed to the lack of motivation of Alaska natives in promoting their own ideas for educational change and improvement. In explanation, a well-known Barrow Eskimo leader stated, "Many Eskimos think of themselves as quite capable in dealing with whites in community affairs. But when it comes to school matters such as curriculum changes, teacher recruitment, or financial problems, they feel very inadequate." Feelings of psychological and social impotence become even more pronounced as rural schools are increasingly bureaucratized.

Even when active participation is sought, effective consensus is often hampered by important native differences in educational outlook and perceived purposes. Cultural variations between Eskimo, Indian, and Aleut, the impact of historically diverse acculturational experiences in the various regions of Alaska, and the strikingly different attitudes about the nature and purpose of education found between generational groups bring varying perspectives to bear on similar educational problems. State and federal policy makers, operating in a centralized bureaucracy and only minimally influenced by recommendations of native advisory boards, find it very difficult to take adequate account of these important cultural, regional, and generational differences in their comprehensive planning.[6]

Cognizant of the increased concern over the magnitude and complexity of the native education issue, the Governor of Alaska convened a Commission on Cross-Cultural Education in the fall of 1969. Composed of representatives of federal, state, university and native groups, the Commission set as its major goal: "To encourage improvements in the quality of education for Alaska learners of all ages as this education operates in cross-cultural settings." Drawings on other reports and existing knowledge of the Commission members, a Statement of Preliminary Findings and Recommendations was submitted to the Governor in February 1970.

In seeking means to achieve its long-range goal, the Commission proposed to: (1) identify the educational problem areas, priorities, and seek solutions; (2) serve as a clearing house for program proposals related to the goals of the Commission; (3) assume the duties of the Governor's former Rural Education Commission in coordination with the State and BIA to review the present "Overall Education Plan for Rural Alaska"; (4) provide a forum through which Alaska natives may express their ideas and concerns; and (5) stimulate and sponsor studies related to action programs. In each instance, the importance of direct involvement of Alaska natives was emphasized.

Of the recent efforts aimed at improvising programs for Alaska native education, this Commission seemingly has considerable potential for generating needed change. The composition of the Commission represented the major parties concerned, research and evaluation studies of average to high quality were drawn upon, fairly sound general recommendations were made, and a permanent coordinating agency was proposed to assist in further defining and implementing them. Unfortunately it appears that the Commission's preliminary report will be its only one and that a continuing committee will not be approved.

Although it is possible that the content of the report will generate more concern and action in the future than has thus far been the case, existing information does not suggest that this will be so. Nor can the University of Alaska, itself a state institution, serve as a major political catalyst in promoting the type of changes needed.

The one remaining representative group, the Alaska natives, are not presently able to mount a strong campaign to influence legislative support for the continuation of the Commission or the implementation of its findings. Most existing leaders are already overcommitted in dealing with land claims and related issues and funding is unavailable to assist in the training and preparation of other potential native leaders to assume such responsibilities.

If the educational problems of Alaska natives are as serious as the evidence suggests, three alternative courses of action appear possible. The first is to continue present stop-gap measures in the hope that future legislators will become more supportive of creative educational innovation and fiscal increase. The second is to encourage the immediate development of demonstration schools or districts, a proposal that already has at least the partial backing of several senior officials of the BIA, the State Department of Education, and Alaska University personnel. The third alternative is to offer much greater assistance to the group most involved but least informed, with the expectation that they can play a far greater role in bringing about needed change than heretofore envisioned.

The first option will be followed if no additional effort is expended. The second option is quite feasible, although its chances of success and degree of impact will be considerably heightened if it is incorporated as part of the third alternative. What is most needed, I feel, is a considerable input of new knowledge and organizational skill not presently available to the large majority of Alaska natives.

To summarize, evaluation of educational programs for Alaska natives suggests the following conclusions:

(1) Present programs are in need of major qualitative and quantitative improvement.

(2) Unless considerable pressure is applied, proportionately little interest or support for these improvements may be expected from the federal or state operated agencies in the next few years.

(3) Alaska University personnel and allied educational specialists cannot by themselves generate the type of pressure needed, although they can

contribute significantly in developing comprehensive planning, teacher preparation, curricula revision, and related issues.

(4) Most Alaska natives do not as yet have the knowledge, organizational skills, or political power to adequately influence reform or encourage financial support for this reform.

(5) Coalitions of representative groups, organized and controlled by a federal or state department or agency, have not developed the capability of generating needed planning and funding of quality education for Alaska natives.

When one traces the large number of reports, recommendations and commission findings dealing with Alaska native education from 1884 to the present, the conclusion becomes inescapable that unless dramatic restructuring of educational institutions takes place (along with other institutional changes), the Alaska native will be assured a permanent classification as one of the major oppressed minorities in America.[7]

DEMYTHOLOGIZING EDUCATIONAL PROCESS

When one steps back and looks deeply at the philosophical and theoretical underpinnings of our educational efforts, whether they be undertaken in Alaska or elsewhere, one realizes that the issues are not only economic, social and political. At the heart of the matter are divergent images of man.

Is the underlying purpose of education to assist man to serve the institutions he has created? Or is it to assist man to revise or create new institutions to serve him? Put most simply, is man dependent or autonomous? The answer, of course, is both. Recognizing the importance of cultural influences, I think most would agree, nevertheless, that man is not simply willing to be. The history of human development suggests that man desires to be more than what he is now and, furthermore, that he has the capability of transforming his existing world in a direction that he deems important. In the words of the Brazilian educator Paulo Friere, "He can undertake to change what he has already determined."[8] He does this by means of his *praxis*, i.e., by a combination of reflective thought and action, a testing of theory through practice, which is what true learning is all about. However, this praxis promotes a kind of backlash. The knowledge gained through theory and practice eventually becomes patterned such that it turns back on man and "overdetermines" him. It conditions him and defines his cognitive meanings and actions—what many anthropologists refer to as culture.

Formal education, as an important aspect of socialization, tends to reinforce this "overdetermination." Yet education does have an inherent ambivalence. Along with the passing on of existing knowledge (a kind of static praxis strongly emphasized in primary and secondary education), there is the search for new knowledge. The former process tends to overdetermine; the latter brings out in an individual that which is least determined.

If we look at education from this perspective, we can see that it is never neutral. It is either conditioning or deconditioning, adaptive or transformative; it promotes pacification or liberation. Psychological learning theorists have provided us with considerable insight into the conditioning and deconditioning process. A set of qualities unique to man is his capability of knowing what conditions him, his ability to reflect on what he knows, and his ability to perceive his perceptions. Only given these attributes can he engage in the deconditioning process of first asking questions about his conditioning and secondly questioning the conditions themselves. As an anthropologist, I would call this latter process an act of "cultural subversion" of the overdetermining qualities inherent in human socialization.

At this point the educator faces a crucial question. Essentially, he has two options; he can choose either an "adaptive" or a "critical" pedagogical approach. The former is associated with what Friere calls the "banking method" of education, the latter with a "problem" approach. In the banking method, the student is the depository and the teacher is the depositor. The more students store up deposits of knowledge, the less likely they are to develop critical skills. The more students adapt to existing "reality," the less likely they are to engage in transforming those features of society they feel are in need of change.

The problem approach, in contrast, challenges students from the beginning to look critically at the "reality" which they are studying. Again this involves a combination of theory and practice, reflection, and action.[9]

How does one develop this critical approach to education? One begins by looking critically at one's own life situation. One stands back and looks at one's self in relation to the external world and asks: "Am I an *object* of someone else's history or life pattern? Or, am I a *subject* of my own history, a self-determining person?"

If a person's self-perception is largely one in which he sees himself as an object, he should ask the further question: "How much is this due to internal psychological factors, and how much to the perceived external social reality?" If one does not look critically at the external social reality yet considers himself an object of someone else, that person is bound to focus critically on his own internal qualities.

Initially, then, the process of deepening one's self-perception and social awareness can be undertaken by reflecting upon this dichotomy of self as object and self as subject and the external social realities with which they intertwine.

However, reflection, by itself, is not enough. Effective learning only comes about through the combined process of reflection and action—action which brings about a reaction from others, which in turn stimulates further reflection. Taking this perspective and applying it to the issue of formal education, one rapidly comes to the conclusion that most education in the United States places far greater emphasis on the "banking method" than on the critical problem approach.

While I would criticize this educational philosophy in general, its application to American minority populations like the Alaska native is particularly devastating since it encourages them to adapt to a social world which for the most part is oppressive and dehumanizing. Of course, it also dehumanizes us! Our grade schools, secondary schools, colleges and universities continually condition us to live at peace with an uneasy conscience. They teach us to stay clear of ethics, trust, or dissent. As Jonathan Kozol recently stated, "they teach us to think *about*, not *into*, our social reality." This was certainly my experience during the first ten years of research with the Alaska Eskimo. I largely disregarded the fact that the Alaska natives are a highly oppressed racial and cultural minority. Among other statistics, they have one of the highest mortality rates and lowest economic standard of living of any minority group in the United States. Alaska's natives are clearly on the periphery of society, but like most minority populations they are not on the periphery by choice. They are kept there through various kinds of discrimination including economic exploitation and racism.[10]

In another sense, these people are not really "marginal" to the broader society because they are dependent on it. They are alienated from the benefits of that society. This poses a very fundamental question: "can highly alienated racially distinct people overcome their dependency by involving themselves in the very structure responsible for the dependency?"

Implicit in this question are two hypotheses and recommendations for action: (1) Alienated people are marginal to society. The educator must therefore "assist" them to enter the society. This is in many respects an "empty consciousness" theory in which the alienated population are not perceived as having a cultural history. (2) Alienated people are exploited within the society. They and the educator must heighten their awareness of this exploitation, i.e., demythologize their social reality, and take action to reduce the exploitation.

In the first instance, alienated people are perceived as objects to be integrated into the society. In the second, they develop their own sense of history and their own role as "culturemakers."[11]

As we have seen, most educational efforts in Alaska promote what Friere calls a "culture of silence", in that the native northerner learns how others make history but is not allowed to develop a sense of his own history. As a result, the Alaska native becomes dependent and therefore silent. As the Barrow Eskimo leader said, "on school matters. . . . we feel very inadequate". This frustration was echoed by a Bethel Eskimo proposing that culture history classes be held after school, "since the teachers would not approve of such a plan being part of the curriculum." A new social and political awareness is beginning to emerge among Alaska's native population, but it is rare within the context of existing educational institutions.

We can see, therefore, that the issues of educational reform for Alaska's natives are not simply those of increased facilities or improved quality of existing programs. Equally important is the question of how the native people are to increase their level of social awareness such that they perceive themselves as "culturemakers," capable of engaging in transforming action toward new and more humanizing social institutions.

Three levels of consciousness appear to be involved. The first is characterized by a "culture of silence" in which the native northerner is seen as an object by others. He has no consciousness of self except in a dependent relationship to those in a more dominant economic, social, and political position. Recognizing this dependence tests the limits of his "self-other" perception. The concept of himself as subject, as culturemaker, as a maker of his own history, is lacking. At this level he remains silent even in the face of extreme economic hardship or social conflict.[12]

In the second or transitional level of consciousness, man becomes aware of the dichotomy between himself as object and subject. He not only realizes that he is alienated from the dominant sector of society and as such is largely powerless, but that this alienation has deep societal roots. Reflecting on this new consciousness, he then begins to take action to remove the alienation. This action commonly promotes a backlash or reaction which then increases his understanding of the contradiction between the ideal reality he has been taught and the social reality he meets in practice. This is the crucial point at which he attempts to demystify the social world he previously accepted.

At the third transforming level of consciousness, man not only denounces dehumanizing social institutions and cultural practices but undertakes to formulate new humanizing institutions and values. Again, the role of the educator working in conjunction with rather than over the student is of major importance in stimulating learning geared to transforming action.

Thousands of Eskimos, Indians, and Aleuts in rural and urban Alaskan settings are still trapped in an overwhelming culture of silence. However, as was mentioned earlier, a second level of consciousness is rapidly emerging among most young native leaders in schools, government positions, and in native organizations such as the Alaska Federation of Natives. Significantly, some of these young people are making the decision to leave their jobs in government, industry, and allied occupations and return to their own communities where they can assume positions as local leaders.

The third level of consciousness, one which serves as a catalyst for transforming society in a more humanizing direction, is also beginning to appear among Alaska natives, although it is rare as yet. Examples of these new transforming activities include plans to establish new communitywide corporations where all village members are able to participate in the given enterprise, e.g., frozen fish plants and efforts to exert greater community control over schools at the primary and eventually secondary level. Similar kinds of efforts are now being discussed in conjunction with the new Land Claims Bill and the dissemination of funds provided by it.

An interesting parallel emerges as we turn from Alaska to our own society. Many middle-class Americans, and particularly the young, are attempting to move from a transitional to a transforming level of awareness and resultant action. The increasing polarization in our society stemming from this second level heightens the contradictions between the "old" and "new" culture. The so-called old culture emphasizes property rights over personal rights and social justice, competition over cooperation, efficiency over participation, means over ends, secrecy over openness, social forms over personal expression, striving over gratification, and loyalty over honesty. The new culture emphasizes just the reverse. Not only are we in a transition stage, but if we accept the findings of social educational researchers who suggest that each entering freshman college class is more critical than the previous one, increased numbers of college and university students may well engage in transforming praxis in the future. As stated previously, the role of education in this context is a crucial factor influencing this step.[13]

TRANSFORMING NATIVE EDUCATION

Significant educational transformation must be undertaken with active native participation in all program planning and implementation at the local, regional, and state levels. Furthermore, this participation should include an understanding of educational programming and administration in a cross-cultural setting; a minimal familiarity with curricula planning, teacher preparation and recruitment, and financial accountability; and sufficient organizational capability to carry responsibility for local school board control, to work with members of other communities in developing regional programs and high schools, and to gain access to state and federal funding sources necessary for adequate implementation.

Although some effort has been made to enhance native participation in decisionmaking, practically none has been directed toward increasing knowledge and organizational competence.[14] Increased participation without knowledge encourages indecision, often followed by inaction or failure. However, increased knowledge without participation encourages action leading to a demand for greater involvement. What is needed, I feel, is to first establish an Alaska Native Educational Committee designed to: (1) promote greater awareness of educational issues among the native population: (2) provide them with greater knowledge and organizational skills to take effective action at local, regional, and statewide levels; and (3) to assist them in their efforts to improve and expand local and regional school programs.

This idea has been proposed by several native leaders, many of whom feel that such a coordinating committee, organized under the aegis of the Alaska Federation of Natives (AFN), is a necessary first step in developing greater awareness and knowledge of educational issues among the native population.

Affiliation with AFN would provide a broad organizational base and regional linkages vital to the goals of the committee. The selection of members would be determined by the AFN Board with the understanding that continuing consultant assistance would be provided by appropriate federal, state, university, and/or private agencies and individuals.

The coordinating committee would serve several important functions. First, it would draw on existing knowledge within and outside the state and make this information available to regional and local native groups. Second, it could undertake to establish Regional Education Committees with at least one fulltime paid staff member. Depending on available funds, initial effort could be focused on one or more regions of Alaska. The regional committee staff members and available assistants or resource people would have the crucial functions of disseminating information from the coordinating committee to the rural villages in the region, generating greater interest in local educational issues, and feeding back to the state level committee ideas and recommendations emerging from the rural areas.[15]

An essential procedure for the successful organization of the coordinating committee is the careful selection of a small group of highly qualified and articulate native leaders who are knowledgeable about federal and state bureaucratic structures, economic and cultural attributes of rural Alaska, and ongoing programs in cross-cultural education. This is a difficult recruitment task but it can be accomplished.

Furthermore, the Committee should be chosen so as to insure a certain consensus of approach to the problems at issue. A committee facing numerous externally induced conflicts, whether they be between races, cultures, classes, or political groups, must have a widely shared perception of the educational future of the Alaska native and how diverse groups can move toward that future while at the same time, being sensitive to regional differences in approach.

Regional level staff members need not be as knowledgeable of governmental bureaucratic organization nor as articulate as the state coordinating committee members, but they must have an understanding of educational programs and be able to communicate effectively with rural villagers.[16] In many respects, the success of the overall effort rests on their ability to generate sufficient interest in educational issues to insure "grass roots" involvement of the local populations, the results of which can percolate back up to the regional and state level. Greater encouragement and reinforcement for this effort could come about through regional conferences sponsored by native groups.

A second effort is needed to establish regional conferences organized by native groups designed to elicit ideas and develop guidelines for establishing community and regionally controlled schools, demonstration projects, curricular planning, and related topics.

A major purpose of these conferences would be to provide an opportunity for individuals and groups earlier engaged in village level "grass roots" discussions to express and share their ideas with others in order to develop a regional coalition of natives able to undertake more unified comprehensive planning. For this reason, the conferences should be quite open and unstructured, similar in format to the original Alaska-wide native conference from which the AFN emerged. Conference organizers could also invite native representatives from other regions of Alaska, e.g., Barrow, to share their experiences. Given appropriate funding, experienced and innovative Indian educators from outside the state should be invited to contribute as well. There is little question that any unified recommendations stemming from a regional conference would carry considerable weight with government policymakers and funding agencies responsible for native education.

Another important feature of these conferences would be their tendency to promote among the regional population a greater organizational capacity to deal with common educational problems rather than rely on an external decisionmaking authority.

While it would be possibe to disregard the earlier proposal and immediately organize regional native conferences, this would have the serious defect of encouraging participation without adequate knowledge of the issues.

The same argument can also be applied to the immediate establishment of demonstration schools. It is true, of course, that these schools have a built-in propensity for success. Special funds not commonly available to school districts are usually provided. Unusually qualified teachers and administrators are more likely to participate. Every possible effort is made to plan for all eventualities and reduce errors in judgment. However, unless the native people themselves are involved in the plan, design, and implementation of the school it will be perceived as one more example of an externally imposed educational system, and one more opportunity to involve the community will have been lost. But again, effective participation involves learning appropriate skills—skills not presently found in many areas of rural Alaska. For this reason, I feel a "grass roots" effort enabling local and regional native populations to become more familiar with alternative school programs is an important prerequisite to the establishment of demonstration schools.

Third, I would recommend the establishment of a joint Native Association-University Research Study Team designed to explore ways of decentralizing statewide administration so as to maximize local and regional participation and control of educational and related community programs.

Increasing knowledge and organizational skills of Alaska's Eskimos, Indians, and Aleuts will not automatically bring about maximum local participation and community control. This effort must be coordinated with a restructuring of existing centralized decisionmaking in favor of greater local and regional autonomy in planning for educational change. Natives and non-natives alike commonly discuss educational problems in terms of regions—the Southeast, the North Slope, Bristol Bay, Central Alaska. Regional planning allows individuals and groups with similar historical experience and cultural background to work together more effectively. Regional native associations and representatives of local advisory boards can meet regularly to define and rank priorities, gather and share information, tackle problems of curricula and teacher preparation, call upon outside consultants, and relate their plans and problems to the appropriate government departments, the state legislature, and the universities.

The division into local regions for planning and implementation also helps to eliminate the sense of isolation and inferiority many villagers feel, facilitates training and recruiting, and gives government departments as well as natives a framework for the interrelation of villages and regions. At present, a continuing frustration exists over the authoritarian relationship of the federal-state system in its dealings with communities and schools. Proposals come down for community approval, but there is little attempt to involve the members in overall formulation of the plan. The BIA-state plan for a new high school at Barrow provides a good example. A completed plan was presented to the Barrow Advisory School Board for its approval. In an unusual affirmation of their own legitimacy, the Board rejected the proposal on the basis that it would provide Barrow teenagers with an inferior education and recommended another in its place.

The whole question of decentralization of state responsibilities and services is obviously a political issue of considerable magnitude and complexity. It is for this for this reason that a team of University and native association personnel should tackle the problem together. Fortunately, the Alaska constitution, unlike those of many other states, does stress the importance of maximum local self-government through the concept of "home rule." Taking into acount fairly distinct socioeconomic and geographical units, it would be possible to establish unorganized boroughs in native dominated regions of Alaska which would serve as state administrative and planning regions. Native cultural differences in political orientation and educational outlook could be given full expression by means of the Home Rule concept. As Morehouse and Fischer (1970) point out in their report, Home Rule status enables a self-governing body ". . . to change its electoral, administrative, and legislative organization in any way it sees fit, within the limits of its constitutional authority to 'exercise all legislative powers not prohibited by law or charter.' "[17] A Home Rule borough would thus be free, for example, to combine assemblies and school boards or to choose other administrative forms than those usually followed.

To suggest that community control is the ideal answer to present native educational problems is, of course, an oversimplification. The power structure of native villages can be dominated by negative forms of factionalism. Local leaders who control the economic power base may be able to exert considerable veto power over decisions of school board members where these decisions are perceived as a threat to their livelihood or affluence. Or, the forcefulness of a few white community leaders may negate native proposals for new school programs.

Finally, it should be noted that considerable educational autonomy in decisionmaking is now possible in any native community that chooses to become a third class borough.[18] A proposed new state law removes formal teacher certification requirements for such a borough. In communities with no viable tax base, the state will provide up to 98 percent of the cost for each $20,000 "instructional unit" (ten to eleven pupils in rural areas). However, these funds do not include financing for personnel training and curriculum development. If Alaskan natives can develop greater competence in organizing their communities and additional funds can be found to assist in establishing creative school programs, the third class borough can well provide an important political vehicle for effective educational self-determination in Alaska's rural areas.

A fourth and final proposal would encourage reordering of funding priorities to give greater weight to the training of native teachers, administrators, researchers, educational specialists, and assistants cognizant of the importance of culturally sensitive curricula materials, dormitory aides, teacher aides, first language teachers, boarding home coordinators, and other personnel categories in which native Alaskans may be placed.

Bureaucratic emphasis on formal certification closes many doors to natives who might become interested in an educational career. Those few natives who have gained the credentials and can assume school positions also represent the new native elite and are frequently offered more challenging and interesting positions elsewhere. Neither the federal, state, or university departments and agencies are giving sufficient attention to establishing training programs whereby natives can become more involved in teaching and related occupations. One positive effort in this direction is the Office of Education Career Opportunities Program combined with the Teacher Corps program. The project includes thirty teacher aides, thirty teacher corpsmen, and ten team leaders. Another is the Title VII bilingual education program introduced in Bethel area schools by the BIA and state operated schools in conjunction with the University of Alaska. However, these hardly begin to fill the need.

No in-depth changes are likely to come about in Alaskan education unless there is a commitment of money, energy, and time by state and federal agencies to make self-determination their policy. The process will necessitate retooling and retraining. Retooling will be reflected in curricula (including that used in predominantly- or all-white schools), school classrooms, and boarding facilities. Training and retraining can be done through University of Alaska and Alaska Methodist University where courses and seminars can be offered for natives, teachers, and administrators to inform them as fully as possible about new educational ideas and relationships. Each of these groups can work cooperatively to evolve the best programs. The institution of First Language Teachers in a bilingual and bicultural elementary program is a good example of the kinds of efforts that need to be made. The Alaska Rural School Project provides a model of preparation that teachers need for new positions in Alaska. It would be valuable to have all teachers come together after each year of teaching to compare and evaluate their experiences on a regional or statewide basis. The proposed new University of Alaska Center for Northern Education will hopefully take important responsibility in promoting these and other creative and innovative efforts.

Finally, it should be pointed out that the term "cross-cultural" now in use in Alaska is largely associated with placing more culturally specific bilingual and bicultural material into the native schools so that pupils can develop greater knowledge of their own background. Seldom does the term imply greater knowledge of other native Alaskan cultures. Yet this broader understanding is extremely important if Eskimos, Indians, and Aleuts are to work together to forge new and effective regional and statewide native associations, economic and social development corporations, and other programs aimed at assisting them in strengthening their role in modern Alaska. Appreciation of cultural diversity should be fostered in the primary and secondary schools for both native and white students.

However, along with this appreciation must be developed a critical pedagogical approach that asks questions which address themselves to fundamental problems of our time in order to help create an image of man which is adequate to the conditions in which we live.

A truly modernizing Alaska is one in which native and non-native Alaskans engage together in social transformation designed to denounce technological and social changes that dehumanize in favor of a more balanced approach to social development that "announces" the creative humanizing qualities presently submerged in a culture of silence.

NOTES

[1] Nancy Chance was a co-investigator in Alaska and in the write-up phase of the study, of which this chapter is a summary.

[2] All statistics in this section of the article are drawn from the preliminary findings of the Governor's Commission on Cross-Cultural Education, 1970.

[3] When visiting a small village outside of Bethel, a meeting with the community leaders elicited the comment that they would like to have their children learn more of Eskimo history and culture. However, they felt this would have to be done outside of school hours since the teachers would not approve of such a plan as part of the

curriculum. The teachers, husband and wife, have lived in the village for over ten years.

[4]See general bibliography.

[5]The most significant exception to this pattern is found in the U.S. Senate Special Subcommittee on Indian Education summary report, 1969, pp. 24-27.

[6]An Indian leader from Anchorage, in speaking about the advisory board system, said, "At most, advisory boards have the power to accept or reject, never to determine policy or engage in planning." The Barrow advisory school board provides at least one partial exception to this statement.

[7]The first Organic Act of 1884 stated: "Education to be provided for the natives of Alaska should fit them for the social and industrial life of the white population of the United States and promote their not-too-distant assimilation."

[8]Many of the ideas and concepts in this section of the paper have been drawn from the stimulating work of Paulo Friere, particularly his book *Pedagogy of the Oppressed*, New York: Herter and Herter, 1970.

[9]This in turn requires a solution to the teacher-student conflict, such that members of both groups become teachers *and* students. Authority or status must be replaced by trust as a dominant factor in the relationship, for without trust there is no effective communication and without communication there is no true education.

[10]Otherwise, it is important to remember that while marginal, they are still *inside* the society—a part of it. Otherwise, they would be perceived as a more severe threat, as radical blacks and Puerto Ricans are so perceived by many today.

[11]Herein lies a crucial contribution of the new cultural anthropologist—to assist minority populations in developing a greater awareness of their own capability as culturemakers.

[12]Or, he turns his conflict and resulting aggression inward. The rate of teenage suicide in the large town of Barrow is extremely high.

[13]The issue here is not whether middle class college students are going to enter a highly individualized "Consciousness III" as envisioned in Charles Reich's recent book, *The Greening of America* (1970); it is whether students and their teachers are going to join with a far more oppressed population in undertaking to transform society. Seeking a type of Consciousness III without developing a broader economic and political awareness leading to action is simply self-seeking individualism. At the same time, politicalization without developing a sense of humanity is manipulation. The goal must be to combine the political and human dimension into one, and the place to begin is by looking critically at the social reality which we presently perceive.

[14]An excellent analysis of reasons for failure of a community controlled native school board in the Aleutians is contained in a recent report by Jones and Kleinfeld.

[15]An example of the latter function would be the dissemination of a report on the

successful involvement of the Barrow Advisory School Board in determining teacher selection and their recent effort at comprehensive educational planning.

[16]If this plan is put into effect, native college students could be used as regional field assistants in the summer. Following a period of training at a university, they could be placed in a district of several villages and supervised by the regional staff member and university staff. This experience could also influence the student to become more interested in a career in education.

[17]The report, *The State and the Local Governmental System* (1970) gives an excellent coverage of the issues raised above.

[18]A third class borough is essentially a minimum political unit enabling communities to establish independent school boards. Bristol Bay is one such borough.

Rethinking Modernization: Concluding Comments

In the time since our conference on modernization we have had a chance to look over the revised papers and review the often heated discussion and debate that took place after the formal papers were read. In this concluding section we will attempt to sort out some of the main lines of thought that emerged during the symposium and discuss ideas in relation to contemporary events—the accelerating processes of modernization around the world. Naturally, in a summary chapter of this sort we cannot exhaustively review the symposium and the papers, but some highlights and important generalizations need to be examined.

A main concern that emerged over and over again during the symposium, especially during the discussions, was the problem we raised in the introductory chapter: "What is modernization?" As already indicated in our introduction, "modernization" means many things to many different people, but we need to give an overall view of what modernization looks like to anthropologists focusing on that topic in the early 1970s. A main theme expressed by a number of discussants in a variety of ways is the idea that modernization is a process of world-wide transformation involving a great complexity of different outcomes, and a complexity of "stages" in a shift from some forms of social and cultural institutions to others. It was further agreed that in the past modernization has generally been defined and discussed in overly simple terms.

In our introduction we have spoken of modernization as the second "phase" of the Industrial Revolution, and we have suggested that the current problems and patterns of modernization around the globe can and should be looked at as representing further movement in general cultural evolution. If we look at human cultural evolution as having passed from a hunting and gathering stage to the growth of food production systems and the subsequent growth of cities and greater social complexity with the Industrial Revolution, then we realize this evolutionary process is continuing today and modernization is a part of it.

In looking at modernization as a worldwide process we are not at all suggesting that every nation or every individual community will "develop" through a series of "stages" to reach some similar modern outcome. In fact our generalizations in the symposium were in quite the opposite direction, emphasizing the varieties of outcomes in different contexts. This perspective is much like that of general biological evolution in which it is generally assumed that processes of evolution will produce different kinds of organisms depending on specific details of local environments. Thus our discussion here is an attempt to get into the salient details of some of these complex processes without trying to offer yet another abstract definition of the concept. Several of the participants in the symposium quite justifiably expressed caution concerning the indiscriminate use of the concept of stages in talking about modernization, and their remarks underscore the importance of focusing clearly on the *complexities* of modernization processes. For example, Charles Leslie noted during the discussion period that:

> . . . the term [modernization] is a polytypical term, it refers to a number of different kinds of things, and in just ordinary language we know what we're talking about when we talk about modernization and we shift meaning constantly as we talk. One way of talking about it is in terms of historical stages . . . the modern period of world history . . . has taken a peculiar turn, particularly since the Second World War, but that modern period begins back in the Renaissance. The other sort of thing is to go to those general perceptual notions—"urbanization," "secularization," "perfectionalization," "rationalization". . . .

Margaret Mead added another aspect to this point:

> . . . the non-stage way of doing it . . . it's seeing we're all here at once . . . that when a New Guinea native stepped out of the Stone Age he stepped out to hold a transistor radio, and that we have simultaneously put on the whole planet one series of technological and institutional

activities that are being emulated or aspired to all round the world. Now that is the exact opposite of stages.

In connection with the bewildering complexity in the overall process of modernization (partly a reflection of the acceleration of modernization processes), various members of our symposium emphasized the importance of changing our ways of thinking about these processes themselves. Margaret Mead spoke of the need for a change from "unilinear thinking" to conceptualization and theory in nonlinear terms:

> . . . this process which we have so often conceptualized as one group of people doing something to another, as Christians converting pagans, literate people teaching illiterate people, and so forth . . . [which contrasts with a view of modernization as] a continual transactional effect, or feedback effect, from the consequences of any particular attempt at modernization to the next response . . . [and] you send a change agent in who's used to one reservation, and knows how to manage that group of Paiutes or something, and he goes to another place and they behave differently, and his behavior then is altered; and he goes to still a different place and his behavior will be altered in another say. . . .

Our emphasis on the complexity of processes was emphasized when Margaret Mead noted that ". . . modernization ought to be looked at on a world-wide basis and we ought to look as hard at the *overdeveloped* countries as we do the less developed countries." This emphasis on the world system as the frame of reference for looking at modernization fits with the Club of Rome's approach in their important book on *The Limits to Growth* (Meadows et al., 1972). In this book Meadows and her associates discuss the several main variables in the world system of natural resources, population growth, growth of environmental pollution, industrialization, and other factors which in their view set the limits to the future of growth trends around the world.

At several points throughout our symposium it was noted that some version of an ecological approach offered the best possibilities for an anthropological discussion of modernization. Only a systematic study in which social systems, economic processes, environmental features, and the inputs and outputs from larger systems are considered can make sense of the complex of processes and developments within particular localities. Along with this ecological approach to modernization, the anthropologists in this symposium felt that research efforts in terms of at least a regional focus often make better sense of the complexities of social change than can a focus on single communities conceptualized as entities unto themselves.

The overly simplified thinking of earlier decades among anthropologists and others has at times led to a view that goals could be achieved in the forms that they were proposed, and a general optimism of modernization prevailed:

> At the time of World War II we simply assumed that we were going to fix the world, and Russia had one theory of how to fix it and we had another, but everybody was going to fix it; there wasn't anybody anywhere that wasn't going to fix it somehow, and with short term goals . . . over purposive, over specialized, too short restrictive goals. . . . One of the things that we are moving towards now is the recognition that when we think about modernization we pay attention to the processes instead of setting up those little arbitrary goals, like how many houses with tin roofs or how many children in elementary schools or what the GNP is going to be (Margaret Mead).

Another aspect of the nonlinear thinking that was emphasized during the symposium was rejection of modernization as simply a replacement of traditional traits and institutions with new models, new factory goods, and new ways of doing things diffused from the developed nations:

> Modernization does not mean simply wiping out of traditional practices . . . there can be all kinds of reasons why "traditional practices" are maintained, sometimes intensified, sometimes revived from obscurity . . . the use of Hebrew in Israel today is what I consider to be an example of modernization, though they are referring back to a language that was not spoken widely in everyday discourse until very recent times (Pertti Pelto).

Thus, some of the processes of modernization such as nationalism and the development of renewed identifications with particular cultural groups for revolutionary or evolutionary purposes, may involve complex mixes of "traditional" and nontraditional institutions and cultural elements. Perhaps one of the best examples of this use of long standing and traditional cultural institutions is in Charles Leslie's paper on medical practices in Asia, in which we note that the "traditional" Ayurvedic medical practices now take on new institutional and cultural significance within modernizing India. Correspondingly, acupuncture and related medical practices are part of modernization in China. Since these papers were written and our symposium was concluded, the "ancient art" of acupuncture has in fact become part of modernization (at least in some people's eyes) in North America as well.

A NOTE OF PESSIMISM

Throughout our symposium it was mentioned that earlier views of modernization have assumed not only that "progress" toward modern lifeways in different parts of the world was a fairly straightforward linear process, but also that the potentials for further growth and development are relatively inexhaustable for the nations of the world; the future is wide open. Instead of this widespread optimism of an earlier time, there is now a growing realization that resources on the planet Earth are limited even for the most affluent nations. This somewhat more realistic or pessimistic note was injected into our discussions in part by Richard N. Adams in his analysis of the directions of growth among developed nations versus the developing nations. In a further pessimistic vein, he noted the likelihood that the processes of growth and development are made extremely difficult for the developing nations by the political and economic control over world resources exercised by the more affluent parts of the world. This realization of the unequal competition for world resources and the sobering fact of the finiteness of world resources were repeatedly discussed in the symposium. Events since that time have underscored the importance of these ideas. Adams' view of the discrepancy in growth potentials between the richer and the poorer nations has been seconded by the Club of Rome study mentioned above, in which the authors note that:

> Most of the world's industrial growth . . . is actually taking place in the already industrialized countries, where the rate of population growth is comparatively low. [These figures] *demonstrate that the process of economic*

growth, as is occurring today, is inexorably widening the absolute gap between the rich and the poor nations of the world. (Meadows and Meadows, 1972:43-44)

Adams' proposed solution for the problem of the widening gap between the rich and poor nations of the world was the deceleration of industrial growth in the most fortunate nations. He admitted that this solution is not likely to be adopted by the United States, Germany, Japan, and other leading industrialized nations. For a parallel to this note of pessimism we can refer again to the Club of Rome's projections concerning the outcomes of diminishing world resources. They also suggest that the world's industrial leaders are not likely to voluntarily act to curb the industrial competition that is rapidly devouring the remaining supplies of petroleum, natural gas, and other critical nonrenewable resources:

> [Richard Adams] stated at the end of his paper that the only solution that he could see, given his definition of the world situation, was deceleration in the advanced countries. And a great many others of us have come to this conclusion too, that what we have to do is develop a new style, in these over-consuming countries, because only by a new style can we set a style for the world that is obtainable in terms of the present goals of dignity . . . for the new nations (Margaret Mead).

THE IMAGE OF LIMITED GOOD

In somewhat earlier perspectives on modernization, the resistance or opposition of peasant peoples or other non-Western populations to development, economic modernization, and other outside influences has sometimes been explained as the product of a supposed cognitive view of "limited good" held by "the natives." This view of "limited good" has been seen by both development agents and anthropologists as some kind of "deficiency" in the local population's thinking—if only they realized, as we do, the endless potential for economic expansion, then they could profit and prosper as other populations have (it has been thought). Thus in the earlier view the "image of limited good" was contrasted with the supposedly more rational view of "unlimited development." We see now that the wheel has turned. Only in most recent times have the futurists and others in the developed nations come to recognize the possibilities that the goods are, after all, limited. *The Limits to Growth* has been widely cited by many people of different disciplines as the clearest and starkest exposition of this new realism. We face the realization, then, that peasants' views of "limited good" have not been so unrational after all. Furthermore, the supposed rationality of modern man in viewing economic development as unlimited must be seen as rational only in short-run selfish perspective, and is unreasonable and reckless, in fact, from the view of the future and the welfare of coming generations.

Throughout our discussion of "rationality" and related ideas it was noted repeatedly that the assessment of reasonableness and intelligent and adaptive "self interest" is a very difficult assessment to make when we view the institutions and behaviors of nonWestern peoples. Typically, modernization studies and development efforts have been flavored with an extreme and pervasive ethnocentrism in which Western European standards of rationality and reason have been invoked to judge the thinking and behavior of people in other cultural contexts. Only now, as we face the growing realization of the shortsightedness of Western "rational man's" view of limitless growth potential, do we see how far such ethnocentrism has been from the mark. Western man is not a totally rational being in his economic and social behavior, even in his own environment and cultural setting. Consequently, it is impossible for him to validly ascribe rationality or nonrationality to the thinking and behavior of others when he himself is culture bound. Frank Cancian's essay has shown quite convincingly that there is a mixture of both economic and noneconomic motives in practically all "economic" decisions. The true nature of day-to-day decisionmaking in individual nonmodern communities must be seen as a complex interplay of diverse motives. Economic decisions are not made simply to maximize economic advantage, but are often made out of consideration for a variety of cultural and social contingencies to which people are subject in varying degrees.

The particular way people behave and the institutions they create must be understood in terms of a number of local conditions—environmental, technological, sociological and ideological. In short, behavior is only understandable in terms of the total ecological context in which it occurs. In "pre-ecology" times, anthropologists frequently attacked ethnocentrism by claiming a total "cultural relativism" of the values and hence the aims of people's behavior. According to that line of argument, those other people (e.g., villagers in peasant regions) did not *want* to maximize economic values, and did not desire material possessions. This argument always seemed somewhat weak and unconvincing to non-anthropologists, development agents, and others. The analysis from the ecological perspective we are discussing here suggests that peoples around the world seek to maximize economic values in relation to other needs and wants, so their motivations are not "incomprehensible" to Western man but the sensibleness of their economic and social decisions requires a very careful analysis of their ecological contexts.

The case of the sacred cows of India is an excellent example of how Western ethnocentrism can be involved in misinterpreting the functions of a cultural complex. It has been alleged by many Indians themselves (e.g., Kuriyan, 1969, Shah, 1967, and Rao, cited in Whyte 1968) that there are numbers of "useless" cattle in the country. This interpretation of the functions of the cattle of India has been challenged by Harris (1966) and more recently in a detailed study by Odend'hal (1972). Many have assumed for quite some time that the "surplus" of sacred cattle in India was the result of noneconomic "religious" values and resulted in the waste of large quantities of potential animal protein. Yet when subject to careful systematic analysis, and with an understanding of the total use of the cattle, it is clear that the energy potential of these cattle is *not* "lost" to the population. Farmers make use of milk, dung as fuel and fertilizer, and bullocks for traction, and will slaughter an occasional animal for the hide and consume the meat in times of extreme need. The Indian method of using cattle is simply a different manner of tapping this energy source than the way Western man utilizes it; it is not a waste of energy. One could just as easily consider the Hindu prohibition on slaughtering cattle as a cultural sanction which regulates the utilization of this valuable renewable energy resource (cf. Rappaport, 1967).

Thus it is not surprising that people in low energy societies often do things based on different premises than do people in high energy societies, yet ultimately the patterning of their behavior and thinking is understandable in terms of the realities of the local situation.

In the Landberg and Weaver paper in this volume we see the kind of complexity groups of peasants must deal with in their adaptations to the local environment. Faced with a number of constraints (social, ideological, and economic), these East African peasants adopt a strategy of diversification of economic interests. Their adaptive responses involve very sophisticated means of providing for a fairly secure livelihood. For instance, the religious and ideological constraints involving Islamic beliefs in brotherhood place limitations on the activities of local entrepreneurs. Along with these constraints is the need for innovation and entrepreneurial activity for coping with the increasing complexities brought about through government economic development programs. Faced with these conflicting demands, the Kigombe people use a complicated mixture of traditionalism with elements of "modern" and innovative behavior that results in a maximizing of economic gain while minimizing social and other costs. Given this environmental context and adaptive strategy, going to work for the plantation would not make good sense.

Thus we have come a long way from the position which naive observers might take in assessing this case of modernization. It is not useful to ask the question: "Why don't these people work on the plantation which offers them a ready source of cash income?" To some observers, this situation in coastal East Africa might be explained in terms of "traditional peasant conservatism." Superficially it has the appearance of an irrational reluctance of traditional people to "mov into amodern economic setin." On the other hand, some observers might cite the "traditional cultural values" that the people hold, considering them prime factors in explaining their reluctance to move out of the "traditional economic sphere." Factors like kinship obligations and other traditionally important values have often been cited as contraints which maintain traditionalism among peasants. However, as we have seen, the Kigombe, like many other peasants, have complex ways of economizing and maximizing their resources that are highly pragmatic given the kinds of foreseeable returns in their social and physical environmental setting.

Through the example of the sacred cow of India and the case of economic behavior in Kigombe, East Africa in this section, we have emphasized how through the utilization of the ecological systems perspective, the behavior and thinking of people in low energy societies can be understood as rational and adaptive in nature. It would appear that this perspective is highly useful for overcoming the kind of ethnocentric traps which observers of non-Western peoples can fall into. Thus the ecological systems approach appears to be one way of moving away from the ethnocentrism of earlier approaches to the study of modernization.

MODERNIZATION AS DELOCALIZATION

In a number of papers in our formal session and in the informal discussions afterwards, there appeared a pervasive theme which we have labeled "delocalization." The concept of delocalization involves a number of different processes in connection with modernization, all of which have to do with the rapid increases in articulation of local communities to regional, national, and international systems. The delocalization processes that we noted in a number of different instances are not simply the arrival of the white man into a village, or the inflow of a few outside trade goods, or other diffusion of traits from one group to another. Rather, delocalization involves real shifts in interdependencies and points of decisionmaking, often with the result that more and more decisions affecting life in a particular location are made somewhere else in distant capitals or trading centers.

In the case of the North Alaskan Eskimo who are selling mineral rights to oil companies in the United States in return for cash, we see an example in which food supplies which had formerly been based on extraction from the local environments become more and more dependent on importation from food producers in other parts of the world. The result is that many Eskimos are now dependent on the transportation systems (and supplies of cash) which keep those imported food supplies flowing to them.

In a great many peasant and tribal communities around the world, modern machinery including motor vehicles, outboard motors, and other complicated equipment has changed the ways of living and brought about a dependence on imported supplies of fossil fuels and other energy sources. Pelto (1973) has recently described the ways in which importation of a single motorized item—the snowmobile—has resulted in profound changes in life ways among the reindeer herding peoples in Lapland and Eskimos in the far North American Arctic. In these instances of delocalization the dependence on outside energy sources frequently produces extensive changes in social networks, which inevitably relate to political changes as well.

Looking at some of the ramifications of delocalization in the domains of politics and economics, we see the importance of these processes as a central feature of modernization. One of the primary conditions resulting from modernization is *the loss of autonomy* on the part of *local* villages, towns, and other communities. Whereas subsistence farming and herding were primarily individual and kin affairs in the past, today they come increasingly under the sway of economic middlemen who transport goods and influence in and out of local communities, carrying the products of local communities to the wider market and at the same time exerting control over the local producers. At the same time, the increase in the number of occupations needed to manage the diversification of agricultural production and the dispersal of newly imported manufactured goods, increases local dependence on regional and national market systems. Local producers turn from their subsistence food crops to cash crops, thus placing themselves under the influence of the fluctuating regional, national, and worldwide impersonal market systems.

Delocalization in the economic sphere is generally a chain of complex events which results when food, energy sources, and services which had formerly been provided within the local setting are transformed into market exchange commodities, with the bulk of them originating from sources outside the local region. The case of Nopalcingo discussed by Pelto and Poggie illustrates how this process works. As the valley of Nopalcingo received inputs from the national government and beyond that from the United Nations to develop its agricultural resources, most of the farmers in the region were dependent on middlemen already operating in the area for marketing portions of their farm production. While productivity has increased with the input of hybrid seeds, flood control, commercial fertilizers, and other new technology, the prices paid to most peasant producers have remained relatively fixed (at a low level) as they are controlled by the middlemen who have been the main beneficiaries from this instance of economic development and delocalization.

Correll's discussion of the Canadian and Alaskan Arctic, while dealing with religious missionizing, may be seen as a different sort of delocalization in the hinterlands. In this case European missionaries came to Eskimo villages to convert the people; at the same time they became political and economic entrepreneurs linking the village to the wider social and economic systems of North America. Thus, religious and social decisions that formerly had been the concerns of local people became interwoven with the cultural intentions and political motives of international Christian organizations and related institutions. This delocalization of religious decisionmaking, coupled with increased specialization of production and marketing, has inevitably created a need for backup services in the form of health, education, and welfare programs replacing localized kinship and friendship networks that formerly performed these same functions at a local level.

Thus one of the important outgrowths of delocalization in many cases is the intensification of communications networks which enhance the effectiveness of commercial operations, political control, and industrialization and at the same time may provide local populations with better chances of influencing decisionmaking processes through the information which can be relayed and processed. This is especially evident in the case of a Northern Paiute community described by Robert Lynch, in which new political forms emerged, as the information processing structure of relationships between BIA and local Indian communities has changed. Additional channels of communication which have increased the flow of goods and services to and from Indian populations have at the same time increased flows of information and put the Bureau of Indian Affairs and its agents in very different political situations than had been generally the case throughout the nearly one hundred years of Indian-BIA relations. Indians now can get resources and information through alternate routes which did not exist in earlier periods. For example, there is now a statewide Indian organization which is part of the increased Indian role in governmental programs such as VISTA and Community Action. All of these programs are seen by Indians as resources over which they seek some control for economic benefits. Information spreading through Indian organizations and other sources provides local leaders among the Paiute, as elsewhere, with alternative interpretations of outside information as well as alternate proposals to counter the BIA policy. As Lynch points out, the result from this increased communication and delocalization is a structuring of policy and programs in ways that turn out to be different from what the BIA and other governmental agencies had originally planned and intended.

Similar outcomes resulting from the heightened communication effects and delocalization are visible in many other parts of the world as well. The Alaskan Eskimo groups that Norman Chance was referring to are also much more able now than in the past to receive sufficient information for formulating alternative plans and programs—sometimes with the anthropologist himself as a major link in this heightened communications system. Some applied anthropologists, in fact, now define themselves as taking major roles as information collectors and processors for local populations as clients. Stephen Schensul (1973) and his research associates in a Chicago area have not only carried out research for a Chicano community but have written research grant applications and engaged in other information processing activities for the people who in an earlier research style would have simply been the passive objects of study. This function of anthropologists as information carriers is not, of course, new in this decade, but the increase of this type of activity reflects the increased ethical concerns of our discipline (cf. Weaver, 1973).

In the concluding discussions of our symposium a number of points were made about the general idea of delocalization, including the following statement by Pertti Pelto:

. . . delocalization of technology means that most of the technology of a particular community comes from somewhere else; they didn't make it there; they didn't create it there; and delocalization of social influence or social power in [Richard] Adams' terms means people in local communities become very greatly hooked into the national systems and international systems of influence. . . .

Some of the implications of the delocalization process were commented on by Margaret Mead when she noted that:

. . . we include in the idea of modernization the diffusion over the whole world of these sequences that have taken a very long time in particular places and are now made available to everybody in the world, so that everybody, everywhere, has a transistorized radio available. Now this is something that you suddenly have right around the world—a coincidence of access, not of good access, you can't get a good radio, but you can get the same popular song on it, everywhere in the world. This worldwide access to an existing set of technologies and an existing set of proved institutions like health . . . everywhere in the world they are going to have some kind of a clinic, it may be quite an odd clinic, but everyplace where they don't do something about health the people are going to complain. But I think we have to include the peculiarities of this period in history when the whole world has been explored and every people on this planet are known now, and are the responsibility of somebody who ought to see that they get a baby clinic, or to do something else about them. This is a new situation in the world, and we are talking about this period, while looking for an understanding of process. . . .

In our discussion about the definition of modernization John Poggie noted that:

> Modernization can also be conceptualized on a world-wide basis as the degree to which an extra-local articulation is involved, and when you're talking about planetory adaptation, you're talking about the end product of modernization—this is the future, what is going to happen—unless of course we wipe ourselves out.

Turning from the examples that came up during our symposium to other recent events and research in anthropology and elsewhere, we might note the reporting by Colin Turnbull on the Ik people in Uganda as an extreme example of what can happen under conditions of delocalization, in this case political delocalization. As Turnbull (1972) has reported in his book *The Mountain People*, the Ik were successfully adapting to a principally hunting and gathering subsistence and way of life in northeastern Uganda until the central government decided that their area should be converted into a preserve and the people relocated to the unpromising and fruitless hillsides and mountains. These people now have an existence that appears to be so marginal that they may not survive, according to Turnbull. At the same time, their wretched existence is patrolled by the police and other official-dom of the Ugandan government.

Many people would object to our reference to the Ik as an example of modernization. However, as Adams argues persuasively, the process of modernization, at least as we see it at this time, inevitably seems to result in the creation of a great amount of wastage and despoilation of resources—the production of garbage and pollution as well as the spoilation and marginalization of human populations in such cases as inner city ghettos, plantation labor forces, and "reservationized" Indian peoples. The Ik described by Colin Turnbull are simply an extreme example of this marginalizing process that we must accept as a very frequent consequence if not an inevitable result of delocalization.

MODERNIZATION AND THE INDIVIDUAL

Discussions of the abstract and complex process of "modernization," "delocalization," "technological development" and so on very frequently take on a style that appears as though institutions and historical stages have a life of their own, independent of individual actors. In our symposium discussion, however, we frequently referred to the fact that individuals with personalities are the actors, the decisionmakers, and the carriers of goods, political influence, and other elements of these generalized processes. Our focus on the role of individuals and their characteristics in the processes of modernization was well put by Margaret Mead when she commented that ". . . it's the anthropologist's business to interject people into the picture, and show that the people are part of the environment, both in what they do to it and what they suffer from it."

The concern with individuals and their characteristics took two different forms in our symposium. On the one hand, we discussed the decisionmaking adaptive qualities of persons in East Africa, the North American Arctic and elsewhere as rational behavior in given environments. Thus, a general view of the symposium would fit in well with Edward Sapir's dictum (1917): "It is always the individual that really thinks and acts and dreams and revolts." On the other hand, our discussion of the place of the individual in modernization focused on the psychological characteristics and psychological changes that may or may not accompany different degrees and types of modernization. The Robbins and Thompson paper focussed on the concept of "deferred gratification," especially as it varied in relation to the urban migration of Baganda peoples. Robbins and Thompson also explored the subjective view of the Baganda themselves concerning the meaning of urbanization and modernization. In their review of relevant literature on psychological aspects of modernization they add further notes to our earlier statements concerning complexity of the modernization process. As in other aspects of earlier studies, the psychological concomitants of modernization have probably been greatly oversimplified in earlier research. It may be that the impression of a linear change of psychological characteristics from "traditional" to "modern," as depicted in the studies of Lerner, Inkeles, Kahl, and others, is more a reflection of the simplicity of research design than the simplicity of modernization. Furthermore, while our discussions focused on the impor- tance of psychological variables in relation to these processes of social and cultural change, it was pointed out in several contexts that these psychologi- cal or personality characteristics can seldom be regarded as the "causes" of social change patterns or of "resistance to modernization" or other observed processes. Rather, psychological variables do appear to co-vary with processes of social change at least under some circumstances. However, the directions of change in psychological characteristics in relation to particular patterns of modernization require much more exploration than has been carried out thus far. In this volume we have seen that economic and technoenvironmental influences and other external factors frequently have a powerful impact on people's behavior and ideas; at the same time individual decisionmaking and adaptive strategies provide important force in shaping the directions of change.

The participants in the symposium were in full agreement that the psychological dimension is an important one. Robbins and Thompson's discovery that the middle class, the most "modernized" people in Uganda, showed the *least* deferment of gratification in their behavioral patterns contrasts sharply with assumptions that have been made until now about psychological features of economic development. It has been part of the assumptions surrounding the North American "Protestant ethic" that deferred gratification is an essential element for progress and modernization, as frequently cited in social science literature. Modern industrial people are therefore presumed to have a "delayed gratification" orientation in order to produce the savings and capital accumulation that operate the machine of economic growth. The argument goes on to assume that as people in the Third World modernize, they become exposed to the thinking of "modern man" and acquire a "delayed gratification" orientation. Robbins and Thompson show that real events do not follow this logical projection, at least not for the Baganda in Uganda.

It appears that there are as many complex processes at work in the psychological domain as in the other more institutionalized aspects of modernization. Individuals at various points in their personal life histories of modernization may go through a "series" of gratification orientations as they become more and more a part of a cash-based, consumer-oriented urban society. This is just one of the different individual psychological processes that may be importantly related to the broader systems of social change.

As suggested in our symposium, other domains of potential importance for this analysis could include color perceptions, aesthetic appreciation, and cognitive styles. There are also important questions to be answered about the psychological characteristics of successful entrepreneurs, political innovators, and other social middlemen.

MODERNIZATION AND ANTHROPOLOGICAL ETHICS

Those anthropologists who began to struggle with the study of modernization after World War II found themselves with an additional task, the often painful assessment of ethical questions in relation to planned social change. As anthropological sophistication has developed regarding the study of modernization, so have the views of anthropologists concerning ethical questions and the ethics of the field worker himself changed over the years. Some of Margaret Mead's remarks on these matters were especially pertinent:

Twenty years ago when the Society for Applied Anthropology first worked out a code of ethics the thing we were struggling with then was how you could have a code of ethics that would make allowance for the very young anthropologist with almost no experience, and a new situation, and at the same time the very experienced anthropologist . . . because you can't have an absolute code; in medicine you can say you mustn't kill the patient, and you could work that through any degree of experience and say that young surgeons must not operate up to a certain point, or must have an older surgeon there. But with the complexity of responsibility for the orders of change that we are discussing here, it is very difficult to set up any kind of ethics.

The individual who consciously participates in change—and I think we have to add to this anybody who does a piece of research and formulates it—is consciously participating in change by making it available, and has to take responsibility for all foreseeable effects. Now if you're inexperienced you can't foresee much, and your capacity to foresee goes up with wider experience.

Pertti Pelto added that there are:

. . . ethical issues in our choice of research, in our publication of research, in our doing research, and . . . imbedded at all points in this is the structure of value judgments and the ethical decisions we are all concerned with. . . . There has been recently in some circles of anthropology the claim made that the theoretical researcher who is simply trying to describe what's going on out there is being unethical and immoral because he doesn't get involved and "do something" about it. [On the other hand] the problems that we are talking about are so very complex that we are, if we make ethical judgements or value judgements, saying well, I think this is what should be done, then one must take the responsibility for the possible consequences. He may be wrong. It's possible that a plan is going to be a fiasco, or bring about all kinds of unforeseen bad things, and it seems to me one thing that comes out of our whole discussion is we're pretty much all in the same boat, we have on the shoulders of each and all of us the same ethical burdens whether we have injected these formally into our programatic statements or whether we are doing descriptive research out here and trying to use "clean" methodological modes of getting the data.

The heightened concern among anthropologists about ethical issues and social responsibility was also expressed by Margaret Mead:

It's a more participatory position of our anthropological knowledge in world-wide process that is far more than anthropological, and that is what's happening here, that we haven't been as parochial as we've often been, and that we haven't been as political as people often are at present, and as blindly partisan in terms of local issues, and that this is an approach to anthropological participation, in the re-evaluation of the whole process of purposive change that's been inaugurated by governments, and by large foundations and missions and what not, especially since World War II.

Mead went on to point out further that the anthropologist's involvement and values concerning international development often stem from his own cultural environment and from the people he has studied:

I think also the break in Rick Adams' paper which is so striking is that half the time he's talking from the point of view of the area he studied . . . from the standpoint of South America; and the other half the time he's talking as an American who believes you can do something about it . . . Everybody here has these two positions, that is, to the extent that we're Americans we have one kind of expectation of possibility and to the extent that we have studied Eskimos or South Sea Islanders or

Africans or South Americans our vision of what can happen is shaped by the areas in which we have worked.

There are two principal types of ethical concerns which appear in the papers in this volume. One concern is that reflected in Richard Adams' paper and the comments about it and in Margaret Mead's paper. Both these papers were concerned with the macrolevel ethical questions of modernization. What is happening to the world as a whole as modernization occurs? What are the industrialized nations of the world doing as they grow economically at the expense of the secondary and marginal nations of the world? Margaret Mead was concerned with such questions as the rationality and consequences of technological transfers in different parts of the world, and the role of industrialized nations as "trend setters" for the rest of the world. All of us were also concerned about the "rising tide of expectations" that accompanies technoeconomic change around the world. The fact was also frequently stressed that higher and higher levels of energy consumption in the industrialized nations will place greater and greater burdens on the world environment until it becomes untenable.

Following from Margaret Mead's and Richard Adams' papers there was a discussion of measures that might lead to more equitable distribution of the world's resources. Thus at a number of points throughout the symposium the participating anthropologists, all of us, were making frank value judgments about equity and welfare of the world's populations.

The other area of ethical concern seen in the papers is well represented by Norman Chance's paper. He is concerned with a local level problem of modernization, the cultural "fit" of an educational system among the Alaskan Eskimos. The perspective here is quite different from that taken by Mead and Adams, who recommended changes in the primary developed nations to effect more manageable modes of modernization. Chance was suggesting modifications at the "client" level of the modernization process. He is concerned with the individuals in their communities and the development of consciousness and self-direction to overcome the "culture of silence" that has often developed in connection with colonial dependency relationships.

Having made a series of value judgments and ethical commitments, Chance argues that the educational system of the Alaskan native should be tailored more directly to their localized needs and values. Thus the educational structure that has been imposed from the outside should be structured in ways that are not alien to established Eskimo tradition. This kind of tailoring of a local education system could only be accomplished if either the outside educational decisionmakers recognize the need or the local population becomes politically active and able to control its own educational programs. This example points to the processes of political awareness and control of decisionmaking that are included in the ethical judgments anthropologists must be prepared to make.

POWER AND SOCIAL STRATIFICATION IN MODERNIZATION

As anthropologists have become more sensitive about ethical matters and more directly involved with the fates of populations undergoing rapid modernization, the theoretical orientation of anthropology has manifested a greatly increased awareness of social stratification and political power differentials as significant factors affecting modernization. Whereas in past decades modernization was often seen as simply a diffusion of cultural features or technological items from one group to another (primarily from Europe and North America to peasants and tribal peoples), in more recent times anthropological literature has shown overt awareness of patterns of exploitation and colonialism that very frequently accompany these processes. The problems of great inequalities of economic power and resources are focused on especially in Adams' paper, in which he points out that the rich nations are getting richer and the poorer nations are falling farther behind. Furthermore, on a different scale, Pelto and Poggie noted in their examination of modernization in Mexico that technological inputs generally have significant consequences for local patterns of social stratification.

The general topic of power differentials and the importance of these pervasive inequalities was referred to in a number of different ways throughout the symposium. Gretel Pelto emphasized during our discussion that our new conceptualization of modernization involves:

> . . . a new kind of evolutionism . . . a focus on social stratification, and on power relationships emerges again and again in our discussions, and there is a new vocabulary, a new set of concepts that are emerging.

The suggestions by Norman Chance concerning the development of a "community-oriented" educational system for Alaskan natives through the development of their own political and social influence and consciousness illustrates one type of solution suggested for ameliorating the pervasiveness of power differentials. No one in the symposium felt that access to scarce economic resources and political power could be equalized entirely through the development of consciousness and political organization among local groups, but it was recognized that one of the forces that can have influence on power relationships is the arousal of political activism in local communities. This may in fact be one of the further distinctive characteristics of this phase of worldwide modernization; unlike the previous relative helplessness of the "recipient populations" in the face of European colonization and economic exploitation, many areas have developed strong nationalistic and revolutionary movements to offset the onesided power relationships and economic stratification of the past.

Overall, however, our discussion remained fairly pessimistic with regard to the possibilities of significant change at the macrolevel. The vast differences in economic and political resources that separate the affluent portion of the world from the rest will continue to be a significant factor in Phase II of the Industrial Revolution. Our view of the likelihood for any change from the present degree of competition among the more affluent powers over the dwindling scarce resources of the world was equally pessimistic. Underlying these concerns with social inequalities and limited resources is that other significant major factor, population increase. The differences between the affluent populations and the rest of the world lie, in fact, to a considerable degree in their differing population growth rates. While the rate of industrial growth—using up more and more of the world's resources—is very high in the developed nations, the developing nations have continued for the most part to have very low rates of acquisition of scarce resources, energy resources, and other aspects of industrialism. However, their populations have continued to increase at a rate much higher than the world average. This is part of the increase in "marginalization" of populations referred to by Adams.

RETHINKING MODERNIZATION: ANTHROPOLOGICAL PERSPECTIVES FOR THE 1970S

The results of this two day symposium can hardly be regarded as having produced a definitive position paper on theory and methods of the discipline; but we felt that we had treated some very important aspects of modernization, and that a perspective had emerged that differed significantly from the lines of research in modernization of earlier anthropology. In our rethinking of modernization we were somewhat surprised to find that the general orientation of an evolutionist perspective, coupled with the general ecological orientation, made most sense of the variety of materials reviewed in our several papers. Not everyone in the symposium was a full-blown evolutionist before or after, but most of our thinking was carried forward in terms of a series of evolutionist assumptions. Not the least of these assumptions was a general acceptance of an economic and "neo-materialist" interpretation of social processes, though not to the exclusion of the causal force of many nonmaterial factors including ideologies, religious movements, and individual personal psychological attributes. In fact, the ecological frame of reference adopted by many of the participants in our discussion favored in most cases an eclectic "systems interpretation" in terms of which no one set of factors, whether material or "ideal-mental", could account for all the complexities of modernization processes. The evolutionist perspective, as we noted in the introductory chapter to this book, involves ideas of general evolution and the specific effects of adaptation to particular environments, the latter concern calls for the analysis of the adaptional strategies of individuals and local groups. In analyzing these materials we have found that in many respects this perspective is much like that of biological evolution. As in biological evolution, outcomes of particular concatenations of change in local circumstance can have a variety of outcomes, depending on the raw materials (the cultural and social system of a particular community) and the array of environmental forces acting on a particular local group through time. Some local communities that "look alike" may end up with quite different outcomes during the processes of modernization, and communities that appear very different in culture and social institutions may converge sharply and surprisingly when environment constraints act on them in similar ways.

Our emphasis on the idea of delocalization in the earlier discussion is intended to force researchers to face squarely the issue of the broader regional, national, and international systems to which local populations are articulated. Thus one of the differences between localized adaptation in the animal world as compared to human populations is the fact that the active environment of a local human group now extends very broadly, far beyond the physical boundaries that we might encounter in a community study. The wider environment impinges directly on local adapting communities —through the television set, tax forms that arrive through the mail, and the shipments of gasoline that fail to arrive at the local filling station. This feature is in fact one of the striking differences between human and infrahuman populations—the degree to which the adaptive arena can be expanded and delocalized. Many of the modernizing communities that anthropologists have studied are in fact highly dependent on outside resources of cash, goods, and food for maintaining their way of life. The present mode of living among North Alaskan Eskimos, villages in the Nopalcingo valley, and many other parts of the world cannot be maintained solely through local resources; they are supported through "transfer payments" from the wider systems to which they articulate.

Almost all of the cases of modernization that made up the focus of our discussion in the symposium involved some kind of major international economic and social transactions. In fact, practically all problems of modernization, because of the extreme delocalization and worldwide articulation that has now developed, involve complex interdependencies in different sectors of economic market systems, as well as interactions among different political institutions among nation-states.

Some of the pessimistic tone of our discussion in the symposium reflected the feelings among many of us that the problems involved in this phase of modernization are indeed acute. They are international in scope, yet the decisionmakers who must try to deal with these international problems do not have an international scope of political jurisdiction. The problems are worldwide, but decisionmaking is still nationalistic and localized. Up to this point the world somehow has managed to get along with the glaringly evident defects of nationalistic competition, but it may be that the solution of many of the problems we reviewed in the symposium will require the development of international decisionmaking bodies so that political power and structure will be more congruent with the scope of this stage of cultural evolution. The development of such a worldwide political structure might signal the beginning of the next stage of cultural evolution, the "limits to growth phase," as a culmination to the Industrial Revolution. Let us hope that our knowledge of the first two phases of the Industrial Revolution will in some way enable us to insure the well being of future generations.

Bibliography

Abernathy, V. "Against 'Modernization,' " *Newsletter of the American Anthropological Association* (1971), 12(10):8.

Adams, R. N. *The Second Sowing*. San Francisco: Chandler Publishing Co., 1967.

————. *Crucifixion By Power: Essays in the National Social Structure of Guatemala, 1944-1966*. Austin: University of Texas Press, 1970.

Adams, W. *Reports on the State of Education in Bengal (1835 and 1838)*. Anathnath Basu, ed., Calcutta: University of Calcutta Press. 1941, 436-37.

Alaska Department of Education. *Source Book on Alaska*. Juneau, 1970.

Alaska Federation of Natives. "Proposal for Support of the Alaska Federation of Natives Program to Develop the Ability of Eskimos, Indians and Aleuts to Participate Constructively and Live Rewardingly in Alaska," Anchorage, 1967.

Alaska Rural School Project. "Interim Report", 1966.

Alaska State Commission for Human Rights. *Study of William E. Beltz School, Nome, Alaska*. Anchorage, 1969.

Anderson, R., and B. Anderson. *Vanishing Village*. Seattle: University of Washington Press, 1964.

Armer, M. and A. Schnaiberg. "Measuring Individual Modernity: A Near Myth," *American Sociological Review* (1972), 37: 301-16.

Arnold, R. D. "Characteristics of the Economy of Village Alaska and Prospects for Change," paper given at 20th Alaska Science Conference, College, 1969.

Aronoff, J. *Psychological Needs in Cultural Systems*. Princeton: Van Nostrand Co., 1967.

Ausubel, D. *Maori Youth: A Psychoethnological Study of Cultural Deprivation*. New York: Holt, Rinehart and Winston, 1965.

Baeck, L. "An Expenditure Study of Congolese *Evolués* of Leopoldville, Belgian Congo," in *Social Change in Modern Africa*, A. Southall, ed. London: Oxford University Press, 1961.

Bandura, A., and W. Mischel. "Modification of Self-Imposed Delay of Reward Through Exposure to Live and Symbolic Models," *Journal of Personality and Social Psychology* (1965), 2: 698-705.

377

Banfield, E. *The Moral Basis of a Backward Society*. New York: Free Press, 1958.

Barber, W. J. "Urbanization and Economic Growth: The Cases of Two White Settler Territories," in *The City in Modern Africa*, H. Miner, ed. New York: Praeger Publishers, 1967.

Barth, F. "Ecological Relationships of Ethnic Groups in Swat, Pakistan," *American Anthropologist* (1956), 58: 1079-1089.

————. "Introduction," in *The Role of the Entrepreneur in Social Change in Northern Norway*, F. Barth, ed. Bergen: Universitetsforlaget, 1963, pp. 5-18.

Basham, A. L. "The Practice of Medicine in Ancient and Medieval India," in *Toward the Comparative Study of Asian Medical Systems*, C. Leslie, ed. Berkeley: University of California Press, forthcoming.

Beattie, J. *The Nyoro State*. Oxford: Clarendon Press, 1971.

Behrman, J. R. *Supply Response in Underdeveloped Agriculture: A Case Study of Four Major Annual Crops in Thailand, 1937-1963*. Amsterdam: North-Holland Publishing Co., 1968.

Belshaw, C. S. "The Cultural Milieu of the Entrepreneur," in *Explorations in Enterprise*, H.G.J. Aitken, ed. Cambridge: Harvard University Press, 1965, pp. 139-162.

————. "Anthropology" (Disciplinary Contributions to Development Studies), *International Social Science Journal* (1972). 24(1): 80-94.

Bendix, R. "Tradition and Modernity Reconsidered," *Comparative Studies in Society and History* (1967), 9: 292-346.

Bennett, J. W. *The Hutterian Brethren*. Stanford: Stanford University Press, 1968.

————. *Northern Plainsmen: Adaptive Strategy and Agrarian Life*. Chicago: Aldine, 1969.

Bernard, H. R. and P. J. Pelto, eds. *Technology and Social Change*. New York: Macmillan Co., 1972.

Bienen, H. *Tanzania: Party Transformation and Economic Development* (Expanded edition.) Princeton: Princeton University Press, 1970.

Birket-Smith, K. *The Caribou Eskimos: Material and Social Life and their Cultural Position* (Descriptive Part I and Analytical Part II, Report of the Fifth Thule Expedition 1921-24, Vol. 5), Copenhagen: gyldendalske boghandel, Nordisk Forlag, 1929.

Boeke, J. H. *The Structure of Netherlands Indian Economy*. New York: Institute of Pacific Relations, 1942.

————. *Economics and Economic Policy of Dual Societies as Exemplified by Indonesia*. New York: Institute of Pacific Relations, 1953.

Bonilla, F. "Beyond Survival: Porque seguiremos siendo Puertoriqueños," M.S., 1971.

Bowers, J. Z. *Medical Education in Japan*. New York: Harper and Row, 1965.

————, ed. *Medical Schools for the Modern World*. Baltimore: Johns Hopkins University Press, 1970.

Briggs, J. *Never in Anger: Portrait of An Eskimo Family*. Cambridge: Harvard University Press, 1970.

Brothwell, D., and A. T. Sandison, eds. *Diseases in Antiquity*. Springfield, Illinois: Charles C. Thomas, 1967.

Bruner, E. M. "Medan; The Role of Kinship in an Indonesian City," in *Peasants in Cities*, W. Mangin, ed. Boston: Houghton Mifflin, 1970, pp. 122-134.

Burch, E. S., Jr. "The Nonempirical Environment of the Arctic Alaskan Eskimos," *Southwestern Journal of Anthropology* (1971), 27: 148-165.

————. "The Caribou/Wild Reindeer as a Human Resource," *American Antiquity* (1972), 37:339-368.

Burling, R. "Maximization Theories and the Study of Economic Anthropology," *American Anthropologist* (1962), 64:802-821.

Campbell, D. T. "Variation and Selective Retention in Socio-cultural Evolution," in *Social Change in Developing Areas*, H. R. Barringer, et. al., eds. Cambridge: Schenkman, 1965, pp. 19-49.

Campbell, J. *Culture as a Variable in Directed Agricultural Change in East Africa*, Ph.D. dissertation, Columbia University, 1971.

Cancian, F. *Economics and Prestige in a Mayan Community*. Stanford: Stanford University Press, 1965.

————. "Maximization as Norm, Strategy and Theory: a Comment on Programmatic Statements in Economic Anthropology," *American Anthropologist* (1966), 68:465-470.

————. *Change and Uncertainty in a Peasant Economy*. Stanford: Stanford University Press, 1972.

Caplan, A. P. *Non-Unilineal Kinship on Mafia Island, Tanzania*, Ph.D. dissertation, University of London, 1968.

Cardoso de Oliveira, R., et al. *Mito e linguagen social*. Rio de Janeiro: Tempo Brasileiro, 1970.

Carlson, L. *An Alaskan Gold Mine, The Story of No. 9 Above*. Evanston: Northwestern University Press, 1951.

Carpenter, E. "If Wittgenstein Had Been An Eskimo," *Varsity Graduate*, University of Toronto Press, Spring, 1966.

Carson, R. *Silent Spring*. Boston: Houghton Mifflin, 1962.

Castaneda, C. *The Teachings of Don Juan: A Yaqui Way of Knowledge*. New York: Ballantine, 1968.

Castillo, C. "A Critical View of a Subculture of Peasantry," in *Subsistence Agriculture and Economic Development*, C. Wharton, ed. Chicago: Aldine, 1969.

Chagnon, N. *Yanomamö: The Fierce People*. New York: Holt, Rinehart and Winston, 1968.

Chapman, J. W. Letter to Dr. Franz Boas at American Museum of Natural History, New York City, February 1, 1904, m.s.

Childe, V. G. *What Happened in History*. (Revised edition.) Baltimore: Penguin Books, 1954.

Chilsholm, B. *Prescription for Survival*. New York: Columbia University, 1957.

Cochrane, G. *Development Anthropology*. New York: Oxford University Press, 1971.

Cockburn. T. A. "Infectious Diseases in Ancient Populations," *Current Anthropology* (1971), 12: 45-62.

Coleman, J. S. "Modernization: Political Aspects," *Encyclopedia of The Social Sciences* (1968), 10:395-402.

Commoner, B. "The Hidden Cost of Economic Growth," *CBNS Notes* (1971), 4:3. (Center for the Biology of Natural Systems). St. Louis: Washington University.

Conference on Alaska Native Secondary Education. Transcript of Proceedings, Sitka, Alaska, December 19 and 20, 1968.

Conference on Cross-Cultural Education in the North. Background Papers, Montreal, August 1969.

Correll, T. *The Ungalaglingmiut: A Study in Language and Society*, Ph.D. dissertation, University of Minnesota, 1972.

Cristaller, W. *Die Zentralen Orte in Süddeutschland*, jena, 1933; (Translated by C. Bastion.) Bureau of Population and Urban Research, University of Virginia, 1954.

Croizier, R. C. *Traditional Medicine in Modern China: Science, Nationalism, and the Tensions of Cultural Change*. Cambridge: Harvard University Press, 1968.

Dall, W. H. *Alaska and Its Resources*. Boston: Norwood Press, 1870.

Dalton, G. "Economic Development and Social Change," in *Economic Anthropology and Development, Essays on Tribal and Peasant Economies*, G. Dalton, ed. New York: Basic Books, 1971, pp. 269-303.

Davenport, W. *A Comparative Study of Two Jamaican Fishing Villages*, Ph.D. dissertation, Yale University, 1956.

Derksen, R. *Civics for Tanzania*. Nairobi: Oxford University Press, 1969.

DeWalt, B., R. Bee, and P. Pelto. "The People of Temascalcingo: A Regional Study of Modernization," (Preliminary Report, Department of Anthropology). Storrs: University of Connecticut, 1973.

Division of Statewide Services. "Proposal and Preliminary Plan for Development of a Cultural and Educational Center for Alaskan Native and Other Students," (Report submitted to the Bureau of Indian Affairs). College: University of Alaska, September, 1969.

Doob, L. *Becoming More Civilized.* New Haven: Yale University Press, 1960.

―――. "Scales for Assaying Psychological Modernization in Africa," *The Public Opinion Quarterly* (1967), 31:414-421.

Dubos, R. *Man Adapting.* New Haven: Yale University Press, 1965.

Dundes, A. "Thinking Ahead: A Folkloristic Reflection of the Future Orientation in American World View," *Anthropological Quarterly* (1969), 42:53-72.

Eastman, C. M. "Who Are the Waswahili?" *Africa* (1971), 41:228-236.

Economist Intelligence Unit, Ltd., The. "Wholesale and Retail Trade in Tanganyika," in *Readings on Economic Development and Administration in Tanzania,* H. E. Smith, ed. (Institute of Public Administration, University College, Dar es Salaam, Tanzania, Study No. 4). London: Oxford University Press, 1966, pp. 253-268.

Edel, M. "Innovative Supply: A Weak Point in Economic Development Theory," *Social Science Information* (1970), 9:9-40.

Edmonds, H. M. W. *The Eskimo of St. Michael and Vicinity,* D. J. Ray, ed., College: University of Alaska, 1966.

Egede, H. *A Description of Greenland.* London: Printed for C. Hitch, 1745.

Eisenstadt, S. N. *Modernization: Protest and Change.* Englewood Cliffs, New Jersey: Prentice-Hall, 1966.

Erasmus, C. *Man Takes Control: Cultural Development and American Aid.* Minneapolis: University of Minnesota Press, 1961.

―――. "Culture Change in Northwest Mexico," in *Contemporary Change in Traditional Societies,* J. Steward, ed. Urbana: University of Illinois Press, 1967, Vol. 3.

Fallers, L. "Despotism, Status Culture and Social Mobility in an African Kingdom," *Comparative Studies in Society and History* (1959), 2:11-32.

―――. "Ideology and Culture in Uganda Nationalism," *American Anthropologist* (1961), 63:677-86.

―――, ed. *The King's Men.* London: Oxford University Press, 1964.

Fallers, M. *The Eastern Lacustrine Bantu.* London: International African Institute, 1960.

Fals-Borda, O. *Peasant Society in the Colombian Andes: A Sociological Study of Saucio.* Gainesville, Florida: University of Florida Press, 1955.

Faron, L. "A History of Agricultural Production and Local Organization in the Chancay Valley, Peru," in *Contemporary Change in Traditional Societies,* J. Steward, ed. Urbana: University of Illinois Press, 1967, Vol. 3.

Federal Field Committee for Development Planning in Alaska. *Alaska Natives and the Land,* Washington: U.S. Government Printing Office, 1968.

Fejes, C. *People of the Noatak*. New York: Alfred A. Knopf, 1966.

Filliozat, J. *The Classical Doctrine of Indian Medicine*. Delhi: Munshi Manoharlal, 1964.

Firth, R., and B. Yamey. *Capital, Savings and Credit in Peasant Societies*. Chicago: Aldine, 1963.

Fonaroff, L. S. "Navajo Attitudes and the Indian Reorganization Act: A New Document," *Plateau* (1962), 34:97-100.

Foster, G. "Peasant Society and the Image of Limited Good," *American Anthropologist* (1965), 67:293-315.

————. *Tzintzuntzan: Mexican Peasants in a Changing World*. Boston: Little, Brown, 1967.

————. "Comments on an Article by Huizer," *Human Organization* (1970), 29:303-322.

Freilich, M. "The Natural Experiment, Ecology and Culture," *Southwestern Journal of Anthropology* (1963), 19:21-39.

Friere, P. *Pedagogy of the Oppressed*. New York: Herter and Herter, 1970.

Furnivall, J. S. *Netherlands India, A Study of Plural Economy*. New York: Macmillan, 1944.

Galanter, M. "The Modernization of Law," in *Modernization*, M. Weiner, ed. New York: Basic Books, 1966.

Gaste, A. "Father Gaste Meets the Inland Eskimo," *Eskimo* (1960), 57:3-15.

Geertz, C. *Peddlers and Princes*. Chicago: University of Chicago Press, 1963.

————. "Social Change and Economic Modernization in Two Indonesian Towns: A Case in Point," in *Tribal and Peasant Economies*, G. Dalton, ed. Garden City: Natural History Press, 1967, pp. 366-394.

————. *Islam Observed*. Chicago: University of Chicago Press, 1968.

Gerschenkorn, A. *Economic Backwardness in Historical Perspective*. Cambridge: Harvard University Press, 1962.

Ghai, D. P. "An Economic Survey," in *Portrait of a Minority, Asians in East Africa*, D. P. Ghai, ed. Nairobi: Oxford University Press, 1965, pp. 91-111.

Gladwin, T. "Modernization and Anthropology," *Newsletter of the American Anthropological Association* (1971), 12(8):9-10.

Gold, D. "Psychological Changes Associated with Acculturation of Saskatchewan Indians," *The Journal of Social Psychology* (1967), 71:177-184.

Goldschmidt, W., et al. "Theory and Strategy in the Study of Cultural Adaptability," *American Anthropologist* (1965), 67:402-408.

Governor's Commission on Cross-Cultural Education. *Time for Change in the Education of Alaska Natives*, February 1970.

Graves, T. "Alternative Models for the Study of Urban Migration," *Human Organization*. (1966), 25:295-99.

————. "Psychological Acculturation in a Tri-Ethnic Community," *Southwestern Journal of Anthropology* (1967), 23:337-350.

————. "Behavioral Anthropology and the Poverty of Culture," paper presented at the annual meeting of the Society for Applied Anthropology, Miami, 1971.

Groeneveld, S. "Traditional Farming and Coconut-Cattle Schemes in the Tanga Region," in *Smallholder Farming and Smallholder Development in Tanzania*, H. Ruthenberg, ed. (IFO-Institut für Wirtschaftsforschung, München, Afrika-Studien 24). Munich: Weltforum Verlag, 1968, pp. 220-248.

Guerra, F. "Discussion," in *Medicine and Culture*, F.N.L. Poynter ed. (New Series, No. 15), London: Wellcome Institute of the History of Medicine, 1969.

Gulliver, P. H. *Alien Africans in the Tanga Region.* (M.S., Cory Collection, University Library.) University of Dar es Salaam, Tanzania, 1956.

Gusfield, J. "Tradition and Modernity: Misplaced Polarities in the Study of Social Change," *American Journal of Sociology* (1967), 72:351-362.

Gutkind, P., and A. Southall. *Townsmen in the Making.* Kampala, Uganda: East African Institute of Social Research, 1957.

Hagen, E. *On The Theory of Social Change: How Economic Growth Begins.* Homewood, Illinois: Dorsey Press, 1962.

Hah, C-D., and J. Schneider. "A Critique of Current Studies on Political Development and Modernization," *Social Research* (1968), 35:130-158.

Hameed, A. A. *Physician-Authors of Greco-Arab Medicine in India.* New Delhi: Institute of History of Medicine and Medical Research, no date.

Harris, M. "The Cultural Ecology of India's Sacred Cattle," *Current Anthropology* 1966, 7:51-66.

———— *Culture, Man and Nature: An Introduction to General Anthropology.* New York: Crowell, 1971.

Hartenberger, W., and L. Kayes. *Planning Proposal for Designing a Community Oriented Change Process Model*, Portland, 1969.

Hawkes, E. W. *The "Inviting-In" Feast of the Alaskan Eskimo.* (Canada . . . Geological Survey, Memoir 45,3, Anthropological Series.) Ottawa: Government Printing Bureau, 1913.

————. *The Dance Festivals of the Alaskan Eskimo.* (University Museum Anthropological Publications 6, 2.), Philadelphia: University of Pennsylvania, 1914.

Hearne, S. *A Journey from Prince of Wales' Port in Hudson's Bay, to the Northern Ocean . . . in the Years 1769, 1770, 1771, 1772.* London: 1795.

Heilbroner, R. "The Multinational Corporation and the Nation-State," *New York Review of Books* (1971): 16,2.

Hendry, J. *The Small World of Khanh Haw*. Chicago: Aldine, 1964.

Hippler, A. E. *Barrow and Kotzebue: An Exploratory Comparison of Acculturation and Education in Two Large Northwestern Alaska Villages*. Minneapolis: University of Minnesota, 1969.

Honigmann, J., and I. Honigmann. *Eskimo Townsmen*, Ottawa: Canadian Research Center for Anthropology, 1965.

Iliffe, J. *Tanganyika Under German Rule, 1905-1912*. Nairobi: East African Publishing House, in association with Cambridge University Press, 1969.

Inkeles, A. "Making Men Modern: on the Causes and Consequences of Individual Change in Six Developing Countries," *American Journal of Sociology* (1969), 75:208-25.

Institute of Social, Economic and Government Research. *The Impact of Two Rural Alaska Development Programs*, College: University of Alaska, April 1970.

International Bank for Reconstruction and Development. *The Economic Development of Tanganyika*. Baltimore: Johns Hopkins University Press, 1961.

Isaac, B. "Business Failure in a Developing Town: Pendembu, Sierra Leone," *Human Organization* (1971), 30:288-294.

Iwanska, Alicia. *Purgatory and Utopia: A Mazahua Indian Village of Mexico*. Cambridge: Schenkman Publishing Co, 1971.

Jenness, D. "The Life of the Copper Eskimos." *Report of the Canadian Arctic Expedition 1913-1918,* Vol. 12 Ottawa, 1922.

Jette, J. "On Ten'a Folklore," *Journal of the Royal Anthropological Institute of Great Britain and Ireland*, London (1908-9), 38:298-367, 39:460-505.

Jones, D., and J. S. Kleinfeld. "Community Control of the Schools: An Aleut Case Study," College: University of Alaska, unpublished paper, 1970.

Jones, W. O. "Economic Man in Africa," *Stanford University Food Research Institute Studies* (1960), 1:107-134.

Jorgensen, J.G., et al. "Toward an Ethics for Anthropologists," *Current Anthropology* (1971), 12:321-356.

Kahl, J. A. "Some Social Concomitants of Industrialization and Urbanization," *Human Organization* (1959), 18,2:53-74.

Kaplan, D., and R. A. Manners. *Culture Theory*. Englewood Cliffs, New Jersey: Prentice-Hall, 1972.

Kiwanuka, S. *A History of Buganda: From the Foundation of the Kingdom to 1900*. New York: Africana Publishing Corp. 1971.

Kleinfeld, J. S., and D. M. Jones. "The Sources of Parental Ambivalence Toward Education in an Aleut Community," (Unpublished paper), College: University of Alaska, 1970.

Kroeber, A. L. *Ethnographic Interpretations 1-6*. University of California Publications in American Archaeology and Ethnology (1957), 47,2.

Kuhn, T. S. *The Structure of Scientific Revolutions*. (2nd edition.) Chicago: University of Chicago Press, 1970.

Kuriyan, G. *India, A General Survey*. New Delhi: National Book Trust, 1969.

Langworthy, R. "The Peasant World View in Italy and India," *Human Organization* (1968), 27:212-19.

Lantis, M. *Alaskan Eskimo Ceremonialism*. Seattle: University of Washington Press, 1947.

Lerner, D. *The Passing of Traditional Society*. New York: Free Press, 1964.

Leslie, C. *Now We Are Civilized*. Detroit: Wayne State University Press, 1960.

————. "Modern India's Ancient Medicine," *Trans-action*, June 1969: 46-55.

————, ed. *Anthropology of Folk Religion*. New York: Vintage Books, 1960.

————, ed. *Toward the Comparative Study of Asian Medical Systems*. Berkeley: University of California Press, forthcoming.

Leslie, J.A.K. *A Survey of Dar es Salaam*. London: Oxford University Press, 1963.

Low, D. *Buganda in Modern History*. Berkeley: University of California Press, 1971a.

————, ed. *The Mind of Buganda*. Berkeley: University of California Press, 1971b.

Loyens, W. J. *The Changing Culture of the Nulato Koyukon Indians*, Ph.D. dissertation, University of Wisconsin, 1966.

Lynch, R. N. "The Role of the B.I.A. on the Reservation: Patron or Client?" in *Native American Politics: Power Relationships in the Western Great Basin Today*, R. M. Houghton, ed. Reno: University of Nevada Press, 1973.

Magubane, B. "A Critical Look at Indices Used in the Study of Social Change in Colonial Africa," *Current Anthropology* (1971), 12:419-48.

Makame, V. S. "The Agricultural Credit Agency," in *Agricultural Development in Tanzania*, H. E. Smith, ed. (Institute of Public Administration, University College, Dar es Salaam, Tanzania, Study No. 2), London: Oxford University Press, 1965, pp. 70-77.

Mangat, J. S. *A History of the Asians in East Africa*. London: Oxford University Press, 1969.

Mascarenhas, A. C. *Resistance and Change in the Sisal Plantation System of Tanzania*, Ph.D. dissertation, University of California Los Angeles, 1970.

Mauss, M. *The Gift: Forms and Functions of Exchange in Archaic Socieites*. (Trans. I.

Cunnison). London: Cohen and West, 1954. (Originally published in French, 1925).

McClelland, D. *The Achieving Society*. Princeton: Van Nostrand, 1961.

McKeown, T. "Discussion," in *Medicine and Culture*, F.N.L. Poynter, ed. (New Series, No. 15). London: Wellcome Institute of the History of Medicine, 1969.

McLoughlin, P., ed. *African Food Production Systems*. Baltimore: Johns Hopkins University Press, 1970.

Mead, M. "The Role of Small South Sea Cultures in the Post-War World," *American Anthropologist* (1943), 45:193-196.

————. *New Lives for Old: Cultural Transformation—Manus, 1928-1953*. New York: Mentor, 1956.

————. "Patterns of Worldwide Cultural Change in the 1960s," *Social Problems of Development and Urbanization* (1963a), 8:1-15. (U.S. Papers Prepared for the U.N. Conference on the Application of Science and Technology for the Benefit of Less Developed Areas). Washington: U.S. Government Printing Office.

————. "Geneva: Helping the Less Developed Nations—Lessons from the U.N. Conference," *International Science and Technology* (1963b), 16:86-87.

————. "The Rights of Primitive People: Papua-New Guinea: A Crucial Instance," *Foreign Affairs* (1967), 45:304-308.

————, ed. *Cultural Patterns and Technical Change: A Manual Prepared by the World Federation for Mental Health* (Tensions and Technology Series). Paris: UNESCO, 1953.

————, and R. Modley. "Communication Among All People Everywhere," *Natural History* (1968), 77(7):56-63.

Meadows, D. H., et al. *The Limits to Growth*. New York: Universe Books, 1972.

Mellor, J. W. "The Subsistence Farmer in Traditional Economies," in *Subsistence Agriculture and Economic Development*, C. R. Wharton, Jr., ed. Chicago: Aldine, 1969.

Middleton, J. *Land Tenure in Zanzibar*. (Colonial Studies No. 33). London: Colonial Office, H.M.S.O., 1961.

Miller, F. C. *Old Villages and a New Town: Industrialization in Mexico*. Menlo Park, California: Cummings Publishing Co., 1973.

————, and P. J. Pelto, eds. "Social and Cultural Aspects of Modernization in Mexico." (Typescript, Department of Anthropology), Minneapolis: University of Minnesota, 1968.

Mischel, W., and E. Ebbesen. "Attention in Delay of Gratification," *Journal of Personality and Social Psychology* (1970), 16:329-37.

————, E. Ebbesen, and A. Zeiss. "Cognitive and Attentional Mechanisms in Delay of Gratification," *Journal of Personality and Social Psychology* (1972), 21:204-18.

Morehouse, T. A., and V. Fischer. *The State and the Local Governmental System*

(Institute of Social, Economic and Government Research), College: University of Alaska, March 1970.

Mundale, C. *Local Politics, Integration, and National Stability in Mexico*, Ph.D. dissertation, University of Minnesota, 1970.

Nairne, R. W. "Co-operatives and the Co-operative Bank," in *Agricultural Development in Tanzania*, H. E. Smith, ed. (Institute of Public Administration, University College, Dar es Salaam, Tanzania, Study No. 2), London: Oxford University Press, 1965, pp. 67-69.

Nash, M. *Machine Age Maya: The Industrialization of a Guatemalan Community*, Memoir 87 of the American Anthropological Association, 1958.

———. *The Golden Road to Modernity*. New York: John Wiley & Sons, 1965.

Needham, J. *Clerks and Craftsmen in China and the West*. Cambridge: Cambridge University Press, 1970.

———, and Lu Gwei-djen. "Chinese Medicine," in *Medicine and Culture*, F.N.L. Poynter, ed. (New Series, No. 15), London: Wellcome Institute of the History of Medicine, 1969.

Nelson, E. W. *The Eskimo About Bering Strait*, (U. S. Bureau of American Ethnology, 18th Annual Report 1896-97), Washington: U.S. Government Printing Office, 1899.

Newman, J. H. *An Essay in Aid of a Grammar of Assent*. (New edition 1947.) New York: Longmans, Green, 1913.

Nyerere, J. K. "Socialism and Rural Development," in *Freedom and Socialism/Uhuru na Ujamaa*. Dar es Salaam: Oxford University Press, 1968, pp. 337-366.

Odend'hal, S. "Energetics of Indian Cattle in Their Environment," *Human Ecology* (1972), 1:3-22.

O'Malley, C. D., ed. *The History of Medical Education* (UCLA Forum in Medical Sciences, No. 12). Berkeley: University of California Press, 1972.

Orvik, J. M. "Teacher Characteristics Applied to Forecasting Success in Rural School Teaching," 20th Alaska Science Conference, College, 1969.

Paine, R. "Entrepreneurial Activity Without its Profits," in *The Role of the Entrepreneur in Social Change in Northern Norway*, F. Barth, ed. Bergen: Universitetsforlaget, 1963, pp. 33-35.

———. "Informal Communication and Information Management." (Unpublished manuscript), 1969.

———. "A Theory of Patronage and Brokerage," in *Patrons and Brokers in the East Arctic*, R. Paine, ed. (Newfoundland Social and Economic Papers No. 2, Institute of Social and Economic Research, Memorial University of Newfoundland, St. John's), Toronto: University of Toronto Press, 1971, pp. 8-21.

Paredes, J. A. "Report of Pilot Study in Valle de Bravo, Mexico, 1970." (Unpublished manuscript).

Parkin, D. *Neighbors and Nationals in an African City Ward*. Berkeley: University of California Press, 1969.

Parsons, E. C. *Mitla, Town of Souls*. Chicago: University of Chicago Press, 1936.

Peck, E. J., et al. *Portions of the Book of Common Prayer . . . in Eskimo*. Toronto: Ryerson Press, 1950.

Peil, M. "The Apprenticeship System in Accra," *Africa* (1970), 40:137-50.

Pelto, P. J. "Research Strategies in the Study of Complex Societies: the 'Ciudad Industrial' Project," in *The Anthropology of Urban Environments*, T. Weaver and D. White, eds., Monograph 11, Society for Applied Anthropology, 1972.

————. *The Snowmobile Revolution: Technology and Social Change in the Arctic*. Menlo Park, California: Cummings Publishing Co., 1973.

————, et al. "Nonpalcingo: Rural Development in Mexico," Symposium presented at Northeastern Anthropological Conference, Albany, 1971.

Perlman, M. "The Traditional Systems of Stratification Among the Ganda and the Nyoro of Uganda," in *Social Stratification in Africa*, A. Tuden and L. Plotnicov, eds. New York: Free Press, 1970.

Peshkin, A., and R. Cohen. "The Values of Modernization," *Journal of Developing Areas* (1967), 2:7-21.

Phillips, H. "Social Contact Versus Social Promise in a Siamese Village," in *Peasant Society*, J. Potter, M. Diaz and G. Foster, eds. Boston: Little, Brown, 1967.

Poggie, J. J., Jr. *The Impact of Industrialization on a Mexican Intervillage Network*, Ph.d. dissertation, University of Minnesota, 1968.

————. "Ciudad Industrial: A New City in Rural Mexico," in *Technology and Social Change*, H. R. Bernard and P. J. Pelto, eds. New York: Macmillan, 1972.

————. "Toward Quality Control in Key Informant Data," *Human Organization* (1972), 31:23-30.

————. *Between Two Cultures*. Tucson: University of Arizona Press, 1973.

————, and F. C. Miller. "Contact, Change and Industrialization in a Network of Mexican Villages," *Human Organization* 28:190-198, 1969.

Polanyi, K. *The Great Transformation*. New York: Holt, Rinehart and Winston, 1944.

Polanyi, M. *Personal Knowledge: Towards a Post-Critical Philosophy*. Chicago: University of Chicago Press, 1958.

————. *The Tacit Dimension*. New York: Doubleday, 1966.

Policy Planning Statement of the Arctic Slope Region. "Setting Priority in Education," Point Barrow, 1970.

Pollnac, R., and M. Robbins. "Gratification Patterns and Modernization in Rural Buganda," *Human Organization* (1972), 31:63-72.

Pospisil, L. *Kapauku Papuans and Their Law*, Yale University Publications in Anthropology (1958): 54.

Pye, L. *Aspects of Political Development*. Boston: Little, Brown, 1966.

Rappaport, R. A. "Ritual Regulation of Environmental Relations Among a New Guinea People," *Ethnology* (1967), 6:17-30.

Ray, D. J. "The Bible in Picture Writing," *The Beaver* (Autumn 1971): 20-24.

Redfield, R. *The Folk Culture of Yucatan*. Chicago: University of Chicago Press, 1941.

————. *A Village That Chose Progress: Chan Kom Revisited*. Chicago: University of Chicago Press, 1950.

Reich, C. A. *The Greening of America*. New York: Bantam Books, 1970.

Ribeiro, D. *The Civilization Process*. Washington: Smithsonian Institution Press, 1968.

Richards, A. *The Multicultural States of East Africa*. Montreal: McGill-Queen's University Press, 1969.

Richardson, M. *San Pedro, Columbia: Small Town in a Developing Society*. New York: Holt, Rinehart and Winston, 1970.

Robbins, M., and R. Pollnac. "Drinking Patterns and Acculturation in Rural Buganda," *American Anthropologist* (1969), 71:276-84.

————, and P. Kilbride. "Microtechnology in Rural Buganda," *Technological Innovation and Social Change*, H. Bernard and P. Pelto, eds. New York: MacMillan, 1972.

————, A. V. Williams, P. Kilbride, and R. Pollnac. "Factor Analysis and Case Selection in Complex Societies: A Baganda Example," *Human Organization* (1969), 28:227-234.

Roberts, J. "The Self-Management of Cultures," in *Explorations in Cultural Anthropology*, W. Goodenough, ed. New York: McGraw-Hill, 1964, pp. 433-451.

Rodgers, W. "Changing Gratification Orientations: Some Findings From the Out-Island Bahamas," *Human Organization* (1967), 26:200-205.

Rogers, E. *Modernization Among Peasants: The Impact of Communication*. New York: Holt, Rinehart and Winston, 1969.

Roscoe, J. *The Baganda*. London: Kegan and Paul, 1911.

Rosen, B. "Industrialization, Personality and Social Mobility in Brazil," *Human Organization* (1971), 30:131-48.

Rostow, W. W. *The Stages of Economic Growth: A Non-Communist Manifesto*. Cambridge: Cambridge University Press, 1960.

Roszak, T. *The Making of a Counter Culture*. Garden City, New York: Doubleday, 1969.

Rubin, V. *Biennial Review of Anthropology 1961*, B. J. Siegel, ed. Stanford: Stanford University Press, 1962.

Rummel, R. *Applied Factor Analysis*. Evanston: Northwestern University Press, 1970.

Sahlins, M., and E. Service. *Evolution and Culture*. Ann Arbor: University of Michigan Press, 1960.

Samarin, W. "The Language of Silence,"*Practical Anthropology* (1965), 12(3):115-119.

Samuelson, P. A. *Economics*. New York: McGraw-Hill, 1970.

Sapir, E. "Do We Need a Superorganic?" *American Anthropologist* (1917), 19:441-447.

Schensul, S. L. "Action Research: The Applied Anthropologist in a Community Mental Health Program," in *Anthropology Beyond the University*, A. Redfield, ed. Athens: University of Georgia Press, 1973.

Schnaiberg, A. "Measuring Modernism: Theoretical and Empirical Explorations," *American Journal of Sociology* (1970), 76:399-425.

————. "The Modernizing Impact of Urbanization: A Causal Analysis," *Economic Development and Cultural Change* (1971), 20:80-104.

Schrodinger, E. *What is Life? and Other Scientific Essays*. Garden City, New York: Doubleday Anchor Books, 1956.

Schulte, P. "Suggestions for Programs in the Education of Alaskan Natives," (Typescript, Department of Anthropology), Storrs: University of Connecticut, May 1970.

Schultz, T. W. *Transforming Traditional Agriculture*. New Haven: Yale University Press, 1964.

Schutz, A. *Collected Papers*, Vols. I and II (M. Natanson, ed.) The Hague: Martinius Nijhoff, 1962.

Service, E. R. *Cultural Evolutionism: Theory in Practice*. New York: Holt, Rinehart and Winston, 1971.

Shah, A. B., ed. *Cow-Slaughter, Horns of a Dilemma*. Bombay: Halvani Publishing House, 1967.

Sharp, L. "Steel Axes for Stone Age Australians," in *Human Problems in Technological Change*, E. H. Spicer, ed. Russell Sage Foundation (1952): pp. 69-90.

Sherrington, C. *Man on His Nature*. Garden City, New York: Doubleday Anchor Books, 1955.

Simon, B. "Social Stratification in a Modern Mexican Community," paper presented at the annual meeting of the Central States Anthropological Society in Detroit, Michigan, 1968.

———. *Power, Privilege and Prestige in a Mexican Town*, Ph.D. dissertation, University of Minnesota, 1972.

Simpson, G. *The Meaning of Evolution*. New Haven: Yale University Press, 1949.

Small, H. K., D. W. Mills, and N. Koponen. *School Curriculum: A Follow-Up Study of Lathrop High School Graduates and Dropouts*. Fairbanks, 1968.

Smith, D., and A. Inkeles. "The OM Scale: A Comparative Socio-psychological Measure of Individual Modernity," *Sociometry* (1966), 29:353-77.

Smith, V. "Intercontinental Aboriginal Trade in the Bering Straits Area," MS, Chico, California, 1968.

Southwold, M. "The Ganda of Uganda," in *Peoples of Africa*, J. Gibbs, ed. New York: Holt, Rinehart and Winston, 1965.

Spencer, R. F. *The North Alaskan Eskimo: A Study in Ecology and Society*. (Bureau of American Ethnology, Bulletin 171), Washignton: U.S. Government Printing Office, 1959.

Spiro, M. "Buddhism and Economic Action in Burma," *American Anthropologist* (1966), 68:1163-73.

Steenhoven, G. van den. "Caribou Eskimo Legal Concepts." *International Congress of Americanists, 1956 Proceedings*, Copenhagen (1958), pp. 531-38.

Stern, T. *The Klamath Tribe: A People and Their Reservation*. Seattle: University of Washington Press, 1966.

Steward, J. H. *Basin-Plateau Aboriginal Sociopolitical Groups*. (Bureau of American Ethnology Bulletin 120). Washington: U.S. Government Printing Office, 1938.

———. *Theory of Culture Change*. Urbana: University of Illinois Press, 1955.

———. "The Foundations of Basin-Plateau Shoshonean Society," in *Languages and Cultures of Western North America*, E. H. Swanson, Jr., ed. Pocatello: Idaho State University Press, 1970, pp. 113-151.

Swantz, L. W. "Intercommunication Between the Urban and Rural Zaramo in the Dar es Salaam Area." (Conference Paper, Part C: Sociology, No. 473). Kampala: East African Institute of Social Research, 1968.

Tax, S., ed. *Anthropology Today*. Chicago: University of Chicago Press, 1962.

———, ed. *Penny Capitalism*. Chicago: University of Chicago Press, 1963.

Theobold, R. *Profit Potential in the Developing Countries*. New York: American Management Association, 1962.

Tipps, D. C. "Modernization Theory and the Comparative Study of Societies: A Critical Perspective," *Comparative Studies in Society and History* (1973), 15:199-226.

Topping, S., and A. Topping. "U.S. Biologists in China Tell of Scientific Gains," and "'Chinese Use Acupuncture Anesthetic in Heart Surgery," in *The New York Times*, June 24, 1971.

Triandis, H. *The Analysis of Subjective Culture*. New York: J. Wiley & Sons, 1972.

———, R. Malpass, and A. Davidson. "Cross-cultural Psychology," in *Biennial Review of Anthropology 1971*, B. J. Siegel, ed. Standord: Stanford University Press, 1972.

Turnbull, C. M. *The Mountain People*. New York: Simon and Schuster, 1972.

Turner, J. "Patterns of Value Change During Economic Development: an Empirical Study," *Human Organization* (1971), 30:126-36.

Turquetil, A. "Notes sur les Esquimaux de Baie Hudson. . . ." *Anthropos* (1926) 21:419-434.

United Republic of Tanzania. *Tanzania Second Five-Year Plan for Economic and Social Development*, (1st July, 1969-30 June, 1974, Volume II: Programmes), Dar es Salaam: Government Printer, 1969.

United States Senate Special Subcommittee on Indian Education. *Indian Education: A National Tragedy-A National Challenge*. Washington: U.S. Government Printing Office, 1969.

———. *Hearings, Part I*. Washington: U.S. Government Printing Office, 1969.

Utz, P. J. "Evolution Revisited," *Comparative Studies of Society and History* (1973), 15:227-240.

Vista Volunteers. "A Series of Events in Vista Alaska," a position paper written by Vista Volunteers, Past and Present, January 1970.

Vogt, E. *Zinacantan*. Cambridge: Harvard University Press, 1969.

Wallman, S. "Conditions of Non-Development: The Case of Lesotho," *Journal of Developing Areas* 1972:251-261.

Weaver, T., ed. *To See Ourselves: Anthropology and Modern Social Issues*. Glenview, Illinois: Scott, Foresman & Co., 1973.

Weiner, M. "Political Modernization and Evolutionary Theory," in *Social Change in Developing Areas*, H. R. Barringer, et al., eds. Cambridge: Schenkman, 1965, 102-111.

———. *Modernization*. New York: Basic Books, 1966.

Wharton, C. R., Jr., ed. *Subsistence Agriculture and Economic Development*. Chicago: Aldine, 1969.

White, L. *The Evolution of Culture*. New York: McGraw-Hill, 1959.

Whymper, F. *Travel and Adventure in the Territory of Alaska*. New York: Harper & Bros, 1869.

Whyte, R. O. *Land, Livestock and Human Nutrition in India*. New York: Praeger Publishing Co., 1968.

Wijeyewardene, G.E.T. "Administration and Politics in Two Swahili Communities." (*Conference Paper* No. 107). Kampala: East African Institute of Social Research, 1959.

Willard, R. Reports on Education Conference at Sitka, Alaska, 1968.

Winter, E. H., and T. O. Beidelman. "Tanganyika: A Study of an African Society at National and Local Levels," in *Contemporary Change in Traditional Societies*, Vol. I, J. H. Steward, ed. Urbana: University of Illinois Press, 1967, pp. 59-203.

Wise, T. A. *Commentary on the Hindu System of Medicine*. Calcutta: Baptist Mission Press, 1845.

Wober, M., and F. Musoke-Mutanda. "Candy Canes and Chronometry Among Ugandan Schoolchildren" (*Occasional Paper* No. 4, Department of Sociology), Kampala, Uganda: Makerere University, 1971.

Woods, C., and T. D. Graves. "The Process of Medical Change in a Highland Guatemalan Town," Los Angeles Studies Center, University of California, 1971.

Yoneyama, T. "Comparisons of Modernization in Two Japanese Villages," in *Contemporary Change in Traditional Societes*, Vol. 2, J. H. Steward, ed. Urbana: University of Illinois Press, 1967.

Yotopoulos, P. A. *Allocative Efficiency in Economic Development: A Cross Section Analysis of Epirus Farming*, (Research Monograph Series 18) Athens: Center of Planning and Economic Research, 1967.

Young, F. W. "Location and Reputation in a Mexican Intervillage Network," *Human Organization* (1964), 23:36-41.

Young, F. W., and R. C. Young. "Two Determinants of Community Reaction to Industrialization in Rural Mexico," *Economic Development and Culture Change* (1960), 8:257-264.

———. "Social Integration and Change in Twenty-four Mexican Villages," *Economic Development and Culture Change* (1960), 8:366-377.

———. "Key Informant Reliability in Rural Mexican Villages. *Human Organization* (1962), 20:141-148.

———. "Occupational Role Perceptions in Rural Mexico," *Rural Sociology* (1962), 27:42-52.

———. "Individual Commitment to Industrialization in Rural Mexico," *American Journal of Sociology* (1966), 31:373-383.

———. "Toward a Theory of Community Development," in *The Challenge of Development*, R. J. Ward, ed. Chicago: Aldine, 1967.

Zagoskin, L. A. *Description Based on Explorations on Foot of Parts of the Russian Territories in America by Lieutenant L. Zagoskin in 1842, 1843, and 1844.* Sanktpeterburg: Tip. Karla Kraiia, 1847.

Index

Abernathy, V., 7-8, 377
Aborigines, Australian, 63
Acculturation, 44, 51, 242-43
  linguistic, Eskimos and, 311-21
Acupuncture, 78, 357
Adams, Richard N., paper by, 37-68; 12, 18, 357-58, 365, 366, 370, 371, 377
Adams, W., 95, 377
Adaptation, 162-63, 188, 195, 198, 240, 360
Admiralty Islands, 22
Africa
  agriculture in, 33
  contrast between herdsmen and farmers in, 115-16
  economic modernization in Kigombe, Tanzania, 194-233
  gratification orientation in, 242, 246
  individual modernization in Buganda, 234-91
Agriculture, 31-32, 33
  subsistence, 143, 144, 147
  undeveloped, 143
  See also Monoagriculture
Aid, economic, 152
Alaska

modernization and educational reform in, 332-52
  pipeline project, 23-24
  See also Unalakleet, Alaska
Alaska Federation of Natives, 344-46
Alaska Methodist University, 349
Alaska University, 338, 349, 350
Aleuts, educational reform and, 333-50
Allopathy, 93
American Anthropological Association, 7
American Ethnological Society, 24
Anderson, B., 114, 377
Anderson, R., 114, 377
Anthropology
  modernization and, 4-14, 17-20, 369-72
  native point of view in, 295-97
Antiquity, 70, 73
Appalachia, 53
Arabic medical system, 76, 77, 89
Archer, E. James, ix
Armer, M., 290, 377
Aronoff, J., 115, 377
Aschenbrenner, Stanley, 192
Asian medical systems, modernization of, 86-108
Astrology, 72
Ausubel, D., 258, 377